Treasure
of the
Golden Grape

11th December 1641

A Chesil Beach Wreck

To Malcolm, Chesil Bench 9/1/2014 from Selwyn Williams

Selwyn Williams

Limited Edition

Deadman's Bay Publishing

2012

Treasure of the Golden Grape

First published 2012 by Deadman's Bay Publishing

ISBN 978-0-9573182-0-5

Typeset by Deadman's Bay Publishing

Printed in Great Britain by Henry Ling Limited, at the Dorset Press, Dorchester, DT1 1HD

Deadman's Bay

......at periods of a quarter of a minute, there arose a deep, hollow stroke like the single beat of a drum, the intervals being filled with a long-drawn rattling, as of bones between huge canine jaws. It came from the vast concave of Deadman's Bay, rising and falling against the pebble dyke.........

It was a presence--an imaginary shape or essence from the human multitude lying below: those who had gone down in vessels of war, East Indiamen, barges, brigs, and ships of the Armada...

***The Well-Beloved* (1897). Dorset author and poet Thomas Hardy describing the sound of the undertow of the sea in Lyme Bay upon the Chesil Beach.**

The Dead House is still at the back of the beach in Chesil Cove where all the bodies were taken when they were washed up.

Deadman's Bay with the "long-drawn rattling" of the undertow.

Contents

Contents 5

Acknowledgements

Archives/Museums
Buckland Abbey National Trust, Dorset Local History Centre,
Duke's Auctioneers Dorchester, National Archives,
Lawrences Auctioneers Crewkerne, National Maritime Museum,
National Maritime Museum Cornwall, National Portrait Gallery,
Penlee House Gallery & Museum, & Weymouth Museum.

Illustrations
Semi Vine for her wonderful paintings.
Photographic editing – David Brown, Joe Allen, Selwyn Williams.
David Carter for permission to use his coloured copy of the view of Wyke plus his help in the tidal research at the time.
Weymouth Museum, particular thanks to Barry and David.
Old friend Julie Kent for permission to use her photographs.
Eric Rickett's daughters for permission to use his illustrations of the Town Bridge and Hope.

Individuals
Andrew Fitzpatrick and Wessex Archaeology for artefact identification, Professor David Loades for his expert opinion regarding the ship's Major Flag, Dave Allan of PASTE for local historical advice. Maritime History friends Rodney and Linda Alcock, Ron Howse, Grahame Knott, David Carter and Ed Cumming. Debby Rose for research help and extra deciphering of Secretary Hand writing. Glynnis Rees-Jones for proof reading. Ian and Kevin Parry and now Sean Webb and Marcus Darler at O_3 for supplying diving suits etc. Special mention to Civil War Historian and "Crabchurch Conspiracy" authority Mark Vine for his extended and un-restricted help with the local Civil War history. Many thanks to the professional maritime historians for their interest, encouragement and willingness to answer my queries.

My Mother for her supply of local history books that first inspired my interest as a 7 year old in shipwrecks and Chesil Beach in particular, and her later interest in my research and writings about them and my wreck artefacts. She also drove me around before I was old enough to drive so I could go diving. My marine engineer father, who made my first diving cylinder backpack. All my diving buddies over the years but especially the late Les Kent who I dived with for 25 years, his partner Julie Kent who was on the beach with us, Tom Treloar and Jim Dunford, all five of us shared a dream that came true. Lynne Williams for putting up with being a summer diving widow.

Thanks to diving pioneers and Master divers, dive shop owners, and founders of the Weymouth Underwater Club, Ron and Joy Parry, (the Hans and Lottie Hass of Weymouth), who in 1966 inspired and taught me and many other locals to dive and literally opened up a whole new world of adventure to us. Karen & Steve Hall & Matthew Baldwin and staff at Quiddles Café at Chesil Cove, Portland where I read most of my research material while enjoying fabulous food and drink, their paella evenings and the Turneresque sunsets and constant vibrancy of the ever-changing Deadman's Bay. Ex diving buddy Bert Sheaf, and fishermen Derek Galpin and Ken Lynham for being old salts and sharing their local Portland knowledge. Another ex diving buddy and rigger Terry Weeks for the hangman's noose. My older brother Chris for having snorkel, flippers and goggles that I could borrow to take my first ventures under the sea at about the age of ten. Finally for being lucky enough to have been born overlooking Chesil Beach, which together with having a merchant seaman for a father ensured a love of the sea and that unique beach.

Dedicated to the real treasure in my life, my daughter Vivienne.

Foreword

As any diver will tell you, the first question you are asked is "do you dive on wrecks"? If so, this is followed swiftly by "have you ever found any treasure"? They have all heard of doubloons and pieces of eight yet very few would recognise them. We didn't.

Local Dorset author and poet Thomas Hardy named the waters bound by the 18 miles of Chesil Beach as Deadman's Bay for good reason. Dead men were indeed frequently washed ashore, sometimes from one of the 180 known shipwrecks that hit the beach but often from unknown and unseen shipwrecks that foundered during the night, for once caught in that bay with a SW gale blowing, there was usually only one fate that awaited any ship and those on board.

People associate shipwrecks with treasure, and together these conjure up visions of swashbuckling heroes, daring deeds, nefarious characters, romance and adventure. The wreck of the *Golden Grape* has all of these as the events of the wreck itself unfold to incorporate unforeseen consequences in the turbulent times that followed, where the gibbet awaited some of those involved in the wreck. Equally it was not possible to isolate the wreck from the piracy, smuggling and privateering that went on before the wreck and which involved the local gentry right up to the Queen herself.

The full story is based on the archive records of a contemporary High Court of the Admiralty Inquiry into the wreck and the salvage of this early 17th century Dutch ship, wrecked in December 1641 on the Chesil Beach opposite Wyke Regis in Dorset. As well as the surviving crew, over three hundred local inhabitants from the towns of Portland, Melcombe Regis and Weymouth and the surrounding villages, from Wyke, Chickerell, Fleet and Langton Herring to as far as Abbotsbury, gave evidence about the shipwreck. They detail what they had salvaged from the wreck and specify how they lived, their family, their home and their occupation and in doing so they mention another 200 like people in their sworn testimony.

The *Golden Grape* sailed first from Holland, half laden with goods, to Dover. There the crew loaded more trade goods and took on an English Captain and more crew for the longer voyage to Cadiz to exchange their cargo. At Cadiz they loaded barrels of raisins of the sun, jars of oil, sherry, tent and other wines. A fairly mundane cargo so far but it is then that they slipped surreptitiously into the bullion port of Sanlucar de Barremeda, a satellite port to Seville, the Spanish port and centre of trade for all the riches of gold and silver from South America.

Spain either couldn't supply all the necessary goods, or goods at the right price, to her colonies in the New World so they were smuggled into Spain and paid for in smuggled South American gold and silver by their merchants, well out of the gaze of officials in Seville.

In exchange for the rest of the *Golden Grape*'s outbound cargo, consisting of barrels of the highly valued spice, pepper, Spanish boats brought out two bags of red wool and forty three bolts of taffeta silk, two bags of silver plate, a bag containing five hundred pistoles, [Spanish 2 escudos gold coins later known as doubloons], another a mixture of pistoles and pieces of eight; an unspecified number of bags of pieces of eight, a peg of silver and a loaf of silver to be loaded on board the *Golden Grape*.

From there she sailed back intending to trade in France then to Dover, but half way up the Channel the *Golden Grape* encountered a fierce storm and was wrecked on the Chesil Beach where she sat a whole for 4 days while she and her goods were plundered. There is even a James Bond mentioned but it is a Walter Bond and his leader Fabian Hodder who feature in the wreck and in the events that follow.

* Conspiracy led them to their doom
All rotting in the late winter gloom
Hodder has flown the nest
The Bridport Dagger awaits the rest
They'll all be dancing very soon
Yes all to the hangman's tune.

Piracy, Smuggling,
Slavery, Shipwreck, Treasure,
Civil War, Conspiracy, Hanging.

An extraordinary story of maritime folk.

* Lyrics written by Mark Vine, taken from the superb "The Crabchurch Conspiracy" album by The Dolmen, lyrics and story by Mark Vine, music by Taloch aka Tony Jameson, (Josh Elliott, Jez Lee).

Chronology

1348 The Black Death enters England through the port of Melcombe Regis.

1377 French raiders raze Melcombe Regis to the ground.

1386 French raiders destroy Weymouth houses and ships.

1492 Columbus discovers the New World.

1545 The Discovery of a Mountain of Silver at Potosi in the Vice Royalty of Peru in South America – the New World.

1577-1580 Drake circumnavigates the World and captures a Spanish Treasure ship.

1581 United Provinces of Holland, Zeeland, Utrecht, Guelderland, Overijssel, Groningen and Friesland break away from Spanish rule.

1587 Drake attacks Cadiz.

1588 Spanish Armada defeated

1600 English East India Company formed.

1602 Dutch East India Company formed.

1603 Plague in London.

1603 Queen Elizabeth dies and James VI of Scotland becomes James I of England

1604 Peace between England and Spain.

1604 Barbary Pirates step up attacks on English shipping and coastal villages.

1606 Union Flag flown by all ships of the Kingdom.

1609 Truce between the Dutch and Spain.

1621 End of Truce between the Dutch and Spain.

1624 England declares War against Spain.

1625 Plague in London.

1625 Fear of invasion by Spain. Weymouth reinforces the Blockhouse and Nothe Forts with stone.

1626 Further threats of invasion by Spain mean more cannons and powder supplied to the defences of Weymouth.

1627 England at War with France.

1630 England at Peace with Spain.

1641 Dutch take Malacca from the Portuguese and so control the spice route.

1641 Wreck of the Golden Grape on Chesil Beach.

1642 English Civil War between Royalists and Parliamentarians.

1645 Crabchurch Conspiracy. Royalists take and lose Weymouth.

1649 Charles I executed.

1658 Oliver Cromwell dies.

1660 Restoration of the Monarchy, Charles II restored to the throne.

Julian to the Gregorian calendar

In 1752 Britain finally switched from the Julian to the Gregorian calendar, which had been used in Catholic countries since 1582. The adjustment meant that eleven days were lost in September to bring the country into line with Europe and the start of the year changed from March 25th to January 1st. A vestige of this is that the financial year that had always started on Lady Day on 25th March now starts on 6th April each year. The Dutch used Gregorian while England used the Julian.

I have used any date up to Lady Day, (e.g. as 1648/9) to show the date between January 1st and 24th March as 1648 in Julian and 1649 in Gregorian. I have not adjusted dates for the 10 days the Gregorian calendar was then ahead of the Julian calendar. Dates given by the crew of the *Golden Grape* in Amsterdam will use the Gregorian calendar while dates when in England will be from the Julian calendar.

List of Illustrations

Unless otherwise stated all illustrations are from author's collection

Front cover - painting of Dutch fluyt in heavy seas- Semi Vine

Rear cover - plate, bar, doubloons, pieces of eight – © *Peter Scott*

Colour plates (pages 129 - 160)

Black & White

Page

Glossary

Types of Vessel

Bark or barque - a 3 masted ship with fore and aft sail on the mizzen (aft) mast.

Brazilman – a ship trading with Brazil

Corvette – lightly armed warship, smaller than a frigate

Fleming – a Flemish ship

Fluit or fluyt – a three masted square-rigged Dutch built trading vessel

Flyboat - vlieboot, small Dutch 70 to 200 tons ship ideal for pirates

Frigate – fast lightly armed warship

Galleass – a ship with both sails and oars

Galley – a ship propelled by oars

Hoy – small sloop rigged coastal ship

Lerret – double ended clinker built boat once predominant off Chesil Beach

Patasse or patache – a Spanish 2 masted vessel, a cross between a brig and a schooner.

Pinnace - a small fast galleon, squared rigged with either two or three masts.

Pirate – a person or ship that attacks any ship

Polacre or polacca - Mediterranean vessel with fore and aft sails on fore and mizzenmasts and square sails on mainmast

Privateer – a person or ship that attacks enemy ships under licence

West Indiaman – a ship trading with the West Indies

Ordnance

Cannon	Shot size in lbs	Length in feet	Weight in lbs	Ranking	Range in paces
Culverin	17	13	4500	1	2100
Demi-culverin	9 to 12	11	2200 to 3000	2	1800
Saker or sacre	5.25	9.5	1400 to 2500	3	1500
Minion	4	8	1200 to 1500	4	1400
Falcon	2.5 to 3	7	600 to 800	5	1200
Falconet	1.5	6	400 to 500	6	1000
Robinet	0.75	4 to 5.5	300		700
Base	0.5	3.5	200		560

Murderer - a swivel hand cannon usually mounted on the gunwale, used as an anti personnel weapon

Clothing

Venetians – knee length breeches originating in Venice popular in Tudor England

Chapter 1 Before the wreck

Piracy, Smuggling and Privateering

In the 1530s piracy and smuggling were rife in England, and East Dorset was one of three areas notorious for both, the other two locations being Falmouth and South Wales. Within Dorset, Lulworth Cove was particularly infamous, as both acts had been encouraged to flourish by Sir Richard Rogers of Bryanston, who had bought the nearby manors of East and West Lulworth.

The pirates were supplied with food and beer and even powder in return for wine and Rogers' tenants were inveigled into the conspiracy by having to hide the smuggled goods, or sometimes have the pirates lodge with them if it became too tempestuous for the pirates/smugglers to sail out of the Cove. It was Rogers' brother Francis who was more involved in the trade, often patrolling the nearby coast in his armed pinnace but he made the mistake of stealing the mails from a Guernsey ship that included letters from the Guernsey Governor to the Queen. Somehow Francis Rogers avoided going before the Privy Council but it wasn't long after that Lord Howard of Bindon and Vice Admiral for Dorset, decided to build a castle at Lulworth. Howard was nephew of Lord Admiral Howard of Effingham a staunch enemy of pirates and this soon put a stop to the Rogers brothers' activities on that part of the coast.

Howard's authority didn't extend into Purbeck, part of the separate liberty of Corfe Castle, which was under the auspices of Sir Christopher Hatton, Vice Admiral of Purbeck. In 1576 in "consideration of his good, true and faithful service", Queen Elizabeth had given Hatton Corfe Castle and the Lordship of Corfe, which also covered the Isle of Purbeck, and her gift was exempt from any jurisdiction of Admiral or Vice Admiral. (Hatton was also later to be made Vice Admiral of Dorset on Howard's death in 1582). He was in effect untouchable as the Vice Admiral of Purbeck.

Knighted in 1578, he was both her Vice-Chamberlain at court, and a firm favourite of Queen Elizabeth and in 1587 became her Lord Chancellor and was even said by Mary Queen of Scots to have been Elizabeth's lover. He certainly adored the Queen and remained celibate to demonstrate his total devotion to her. When the Queen forced the Bishops of Ely to grant Hatton a lease for Ely Place in Holborn, it became his London home and the garden was renamed Hatton Garden. The area was fittingly (considering Hatton profited from pirate booty) to become known as London's jewellery quarter and diamond centre. However he died there penniless having spent vast sums on building Holdenby House, a palatial Tudor house in Northamptonshire, to rival Hampton Court. It had two staterooms; one for him and one for the Queen should she ever visit him there but alas she didn't. Despite owing the Queen £42,000 (over £6.2 million in today's money) she still visited him on his deathbed, walking through the rose gardens to bring cordial broths to tempt his failing appetite, such was her affection for him. He died on the 20th November 1591 and was accorded a state funeral and had a magnificent monument to him at the high altar of the old St Pauls Cathedral. The old cathedral was destroyed in the great fire of London in 1666.

Holdenby House was later bought by James I and in February 1647 during the Civil War, the Scots brought Charles I there to be handed over to the Long Parliament and he remained imprisoned there until June.

The Queen was herself heavily involved with privateers such as Drake and Hawkins and benefited greatly from their voyages. Hatton was Drake's friend and sponsor on his circumnavigation voyage and it was Hatton and Walsingham who suggested that the Queen invested in and authorised Drake's Voyage. The return for investors was a staggering 4,700 per cent, with the Queen's share claimed to be £300,000 (over £53 million in today's money). When Drake was waiting to go through the Magellan Strait he decided to rename his ship from the *Pelican* to the *Golden Hind* in honour of Hatton, whose manorial arms were surmounted by a Golden Hind. Drake had a new figurehead of a hind made by the ship's carpenter, had Hatton's arms adorn the ship and had the stern decorated in Hatton's livery of red and yellow.

Though Hatton was an absentee landlord, his deputy, Francis Hawley dealt daily with the smugglers and pirates who ventured ashore in Studland Bay and was there to take first pick of the goods aboard, in return for turning a blind eye. There was a thriving trade and people came from near and far to either buy directly or exchange provisions such as beer, beef, bread, and powder for the eclectic mix of smuggled or pirated goods of wines, sugar, parrots, hawks, gold, ivory, silver, silks and satins. Pirates who had taken cargoes from local ships in Cornwell would sail to Studland to sell them where no questions were asked. Independent factors made a living buying prize ships captured by the pirates and selling them back at a substantial premium to their owners.

The pirates were so confident that there would be no interference from the authorities that they even allowed credit to regular customers. They came ashore dressed in their finery of silks and satins, outlawed to their class of person in the Tudor Sumptuary Law when only Earls and Knights and their like, could officially wear silks and taffeta. Hence why the silk, later salvaged from the wreck of the Golden Grape, followed tradition and found its way to the Mohun and Strangways manorial families.

The appointed customs officials could not live on the salaries paid to them by the Exchequer, who in turn did not have the funds to pay more. The temptation for the officials was to take part in the trade of piracy and smuggling, for it was indeed an all encompassing trade that involved every level of society from the common sailor, the local provisioner, to the Vice Admiral for that part of the coast, the local gentry, and right up to the court, the Queen. Even if pirates were caught, they were taken away and locked up in local gaols from whence the great majority inevitably escaped.

Corruption was commonplace and life was hard and liable to regular life threatening plagues such as that of 1603, which swept Weymouth and Melcombe Regis, and from devastating attacks from the French and the Spanish, as well as from pirates. "The bark whereof W. Langer is Master under God, having come from London, where the plague is, no goods shall be landed from her until thoroughly aired". Weymouth & Melcombe Regis Council minutes July 5, 1625. 38,000 out of a London population of 200,000 died from a plague in 1603 even more than the 17,000 who died in the plague of 1563/4. Life expectancy throughout Europe at this time was between 30 and 32 years mainly due to high infant mortality, plagues and hostilities.

The most infamous of the Studland pirates were Philip Boyte, Thomas Walton alias Purser, William Valentine alias Vaughan or Baugh, Stephen Heynes alias Carless, William Arnewood, alias Arnold, Clinton Atkinson alias Smith, Thomas Beavin and John Piers.

In the summer of 1579 some of the goods brought into Studland on one captured ship were 529 lbs of saffron, 20 tons of iron, 100 gammons of bacon, 300 yards of sackcloth, 24 Spanish blades, reales of plate and jewels, bustians, fustians (a cotton and flax cloth), grosgraynes (a coarse ribbed fabric), soap, and mackadoes (mockado – a silk linen fabric for doublets or farthingales).

In early 1580, London merchant Clinton Atkinson became a pirate by firstly serving as the purser on the *Prosperity* of Rye, master Thomas Hankin. It is thought that the two of them then turned it into a pirate ship. Off southern Spain and in consort with the 60 tons "*Samuel*" otherwise known as the "*Golden Hinde*", of Weymouth, which was captained by Philip Boyte of Portland,

Pirates attacking a merchant ship

they took a large Italian merchantman from Genoa loaded with cochineal, hides, lead, bell metal, pewter, indigo and sugar. Its cargo was worth about £1300 and Atkinson and Boyte shared the spoils and sold them at Topsham and at Weymouth. As a result both were apprehended in April of 1580 and Boyte found himself and his ship's master Walter Wren in the Marshalsea prison in London while Atkinson was held in Exeter gaol.

Clinton Atkinson featured in the State Domestic Papers of November 1580 when on the 13th Thomas Wilford, President of the Company of Spanish Merchants, says they were content that Atkinson "condemned for piracy, should be pardoned at her

Majesty's pleasure."

This is followed the next day by Admiralty Judge, Dr Lewes, to Walsyngham about "how far Clinton Atkinson was concerned in the piracy committed on a Spanish ship."

On the same day "information of the escape of Clinton Atkinson, the pirate, out of Exeter gaol, not without the consent or great negligence of the Mayor and gaoler, the Mayor having given him two very favourable testimonials."

Subsequently, "on the 24th, the Justices of Assize in Devon were directed to inquire into the particulars of Atkinson's escape from Exeter gaol."

Atkinson had indeed managed to bribe his way out of his predicament even though a Dartmouth merchant named Giles still sued him for a bill of £100.

While Atkinson was languishing in Exeter gaol, Boyte and Wren were both dealt with more speedily. Boyte and Wren pleaded a pirate's common excuse that they had heard that war with Spain had broken out but never the less they were sentenced to death for piracy and were publicly taken from the Marshalsea Prison, over London Bridge, and on past the Tower of London to Execution Dock at Wapping. The Admiralty only had jurisdiction at sea so they were hanged between high and low water.

The short rope used for hanging meant that rather than the fall breaking their neck they died slowly from asphyxiation. Because the legs of their bodies often twitched while they died it was called the Marshal's dance, from the Marshal at Marshalsea. Their bodies were left hanging until three tides had covered them and then they were taken down and buried or if they were somebody as infamous as Captain Kydd, tarred to preserve the body and then hanged in a metal cage, for two years at Tilbury in Kydd's case, to warn seaman of the consequences of piracy.

At St Botolphe Church, Aldgate, not far from Wapping, the burial register records the following: -

Walter Wren and Charles Wakam who were executed at Wapping and buried the eighth July 1580.

This is followed by: -

Phillipp Boyte for piracy on the seas was executed at Waping and in this church buryed 21 daye of July 1580

At Whitsun in May 1581 the *Golden Hinde* or *Samuel*, owned by Luca Guido alias Warde sank at Poole, possibly on Hook Sands or at least near Studland. A pinnace picked up the soul survivor, Thomas Smythe of London. The pinnace was a fast vessel like a small galleon and was used as a small warship or as a merchantman but was also favoured by pirates because of its speed. The master of this pinnace was George Byrde and on being pulled aboard her, Smythe recognised three choice pirates, namely Stephen Heynes their captain, John Peers, and Thomas Walton their purser (hence his alias Purser). While Smythe was aboard her they took a Spanish ship laden with woollen cloth and linen, whose cargo they sold at St Helens Point, Isle of Wight and Smythe received some cloth and a "jewel of gold with a pearl hanging".

On 10th June 1581 Heynes, Captain of a 40 tons ship overhauled and captured the *Esperance* of Dieppe homeward bound from Brazil with a cargo of 12 puncheons of pepper, 405 tons of brazil wood, 6,000 weight of cotton wool, 360 parrots and "54 munkyes, apes and other beastes". The ship was brought into Studland Bay where some of the cargo was sold on board ship. In August Heynes brought into Studland Bay a Newfoundlander, laden with 35,000 fish and 10 puncheons of train or whale oil. This was followed in October by a Glasgow owned prize with a cargo of 9 lasts of salmon, 26 lasts of herring and cloth and then in December he, with Anthony Stile and Nicholas Gisborne, boarded the *Anne* of Plymouth laden with orchall dye, (a lichen based purple dye) hops, raisins and general cargo and took her back to Studland.

The Dorset Natural History Antiquarian Society published an article in 1949 on the Pirates of Purbeck stating: - "In September 1581 in Swannidge [Swanage] Bay, he (John Piers) made prize of the *Anne* of Lulworth (master John Longe alias Cade), from Sherbrooke [Cherbourg], Normandy, to Weymouth, with a lading of 5,000 aundes of canvas and other goods." Is this the same Captain John Cade and staunch Royalist who figures later in the Civil War in Weymouth?

However retribution is swift, for still in 1581 John Piers from Padstow was arrested at Studland and after a hastily arranged trial at Corfe Castle, and under pressure from the Privy Council, he and most of his crew were sentenced to death for piracy and hanged overlooking Studland Bay presumably to deter the rest of his ilk. He was described as of a sickly pallor, a tall thin man of about 30 years age with long black hair to his shoulders, and a wispy beard. His mother was said to be a witch. The bodies of the pirates were left hanging from the gallows on the beach, to swing to and fro as the tide came in and out. Three tides was normal to comply with Admiralty Court edicts but as soon as that March night came on, fellow pirates Clinton Atkinson and John Newman rowed ashore to pull the gallows down and take the body of Piers out to sea.

This is probably the same Newman mentioned in a memo to the Mayor of Weymouth in 1582, stating, "that J. Newman, kinsman of Hugh Randall, has become a pirate and has had to pece of ordenance [two cannons] out of Weymouth, either from J Brocke or H. Randall." It goes on to mention "the pirates cut down the gallows at Studland."

At about the same time, Clinton Atkinson even had the effrontery to sue James Covenaunte, part owner of the ship *Prosperity* alias *Phoenix*, in the High Court of the Admiralty for 200 pounds. At Studland in November 1581 he claimed to have a commission from the King of Portugal to attack Spanish ships. Pirates, who were recruiting a fighting crew, often used this ruse to assuage sailors that what they were doing was lawful and not piracy but in this case it was true.

In 1580 King Henry of Portugal died without direct descendants and the three grandchildren of Manuel I; Infanta Catarina, Duchess of Braganza; Antonio, Prior of Crato; and Philip II King of Spain; each claimed the vacant throne. Antonio was proclaimed King of Portugal by many of the cities and towns but the majority of the Council of Governors of Portugal declared Philip the King. Philip's 40,000 troops invaded and overwhelmed Dom Antonio's largely mercenary army at the Battle of Alcantara. Queen Elizabeth was dismayed at the Union of two such powerful maritime empires. Elizabeth, fearing it would be seen as an act of war against Spain, prevented Dom Antonio seeking refuge in England, (he went to France instead). However on Walsingham's advice, she allowed Antonio to issue Letters of Marque to English privateers to fight for him against the Spanish.

Clinton Atkinson sailing in the *Prosperity* was one of eleven ships attacking Spanish shipping under letters of marque from Dom Antonio, Pretender to the throne of Portugal in 1581/2. The anti Spanish action was encouraged by Walsingham, but Atkinson is described as a pirate in the *Prosperity*, others mentioned are Thomas Walton (Purser) in his ship *Diamond*, the *Archangel* from London, Thomas Beavyn in the *Greyhound*, the *White Bear* of Chichester, owned by John Young and captained by the pirate John Storye and the *Antonio*, a Plymouth based ship. Interestingly Atkinson's fellow Studland Bay pirates Walton and Beavyn are not described as such.

Both Atkinson and Purser were almost as well known as Drake and Hawkins who also sailed on behalf of Dom Antonio and they certainly dressed in the same flamboyant way. Though the latter were seen as privateers, the former were classed as pirates. As with Arnewood, who was later saved from being hanged supposedly because of his higher birth, Hawkins was well connected and could trace his ancestry to both Norman and French royalty as well as Anglo Saxon and Scottish kings, and Drake of course was second cousin to Hawkins. Atkinson and Purser were so infamous that several songs, plays and books were later based on their lives.

However Atkinson's past caught up with him in March 1582 when he was imprisoned in the Marshalsea for his former debt to Dartmouth merchant Robert Giles. Atkinson produced sureties totalling £100 from John Spencer and Andrew Payne, and he was released on the understanding that he appeared at Exeter. He didn't and they supposedly lost their money though it's more probable that it was once more a case of a prisoner buying himself out of gaol.

In 1581 Thomas Walton alias Purser from Northwich, Cheshire bought the ship *Little Diamond* intending to take the King of Portugal's commission but soon turned to outright piracy instead. His first prize was a ship called the *Hirundine*, which he took in Mounts Bay and then sold her £100 cargo of linen cloth at Studland but while anchored afterwards, pirates Vaughan and Ilande drove him out of the bay by firing on him.

On 26 December 1581 when prowling off Portland, Walton finally captured a Flemish flyboat, laden with bastards, sacks and wines, after a long struggle to board her. (Bastards meant second-rate wine whereas sack was first-rate wine). In Studland Bay he exchanged some of the wines with a Portuguese captain for 3 barrels of powder, matches and biskett [biscuit].

Pirates did not always get succour from the local inhabitants as Walton (Purser) found out, for the Weymouth & Melcombe Regis Council minutes of 10 Feb 1582 state: -

"T. Purser a notorious pirate has infested the coast and assaulted English and French ships near Weymouth. He took one of Rochell and tried to take another. The Townsmen came to the rescue, slew seven men and wounded others, and forced Purser to retire. He threatened the town and ships there with spoile and fyer. The council therefore fall in with the townsmen's application for help towards making a small bullwarke on the shore, and procuring guns and shot. Neighbouring inhabitants are urged to contribute."

The same February Walton captured a vessel off Handfast Point but was content just to remove her guns and 200 coins and let her sail on. In the April he took a French bark with wines and sold her back for £50.

It was in June 1582 that Atkinson and one Thomas Parson, (who could have been Walton as he was a known associate) while sailing in a French bark off Cherbourg took the 36 tons *Gift of God* of Treport, laden with 37 tons of cognac wine. She was swiftly sailed back to Studland where they sold the cargo and eventually ran the *Gift of God* ashore near Broncksey [Brownsea] Castle.

A letter from King James VI of Scotland to Queen Elizabeth complained about the treatment of the crew of the similarly named *Grace of God*, of Dundee, taken off Dungeness in July 1582 by Captains Clinton of London, Hencock of Harwich and Edmerston of Poole. Apparently the crew were tortured to make them confess to any extra money being on board. The common pirate practice of wrapping knotted cord around their fingers and then setting it alight was used, and then ropes were tied around their heads and tightened, so that some lost thumbs and fingers and others their sight and hearing.

Again off Dungeness, Atkinson and Walton together with Stephen White used their three ships to take the *Mary* of Cork, and they sold her cargo of orchall (the purple lichen dye), hops, wool cards, candelabras and Flanders goods in the Isle of Purbeck.

In August, after another long fight of six hours, Walton with his captain James Pickett (or Piggott) and one William Ellis took the *Katarina*, a French vessel, of 160 tons, off Alderney. She was loaded with Newfoundland fish and "trayne, tonge and sowndes". Part of the cargo was sold back to the owners for £18 but Walton kept the larger vessel and renamed her *Great Diamond*, replacing his previous vessel *Little Diamond*.

On 13th August Walton (Purser) boarded the Danish ship *Angel Gabriell*, of 220 tons, which for some reason had anchored at Handfast, the western end of Studland Bay, the infamous pirate haunt. Purser removed 3,000 daalders from her, daalders being the Dutch equivalent coins to Spanish dollars or pieces of eight.

William Arnewood, described as a gentleman of Fordingbridge, later to be known as Captain Arnold, became a pirate in June 1582 when he visited Studland and bought a ship of war named the *Roebuck*, 70 tons, from Captain Powndes. The same Powndes had in May given Atkinson a small bark already fitted out and victualled, and ready for sea. In the August, off Cape La Hague, Arnewood took a Spanish bark, the *Pelican* bound from the Canaries to Antwerp with sugar and wine. Another prize, the *Muget* of Atvill, 80 tons, with Newfoundland fish swiftly followed suit into Studland Bay. French merchants came with an interpreter to buy back any goods not already sold. Five more ships were brought into Studland by Arnold between that August and February 1583, one of which, a Spanish ship, Purser sold back to the owners.

Yet another pirate appeared at Studland in August 1582, an experienced fighter named William Valentine alias Vaughan, alias Baugh. Originally from London he had fought with the Turks against the Italians. He seems to have been quickly taken into the brotherhood by Atkinson, Heynes and Walton for on 14th September, near to Portland, he in his ship and Heynes in his pig nosed 50 tons ship, attacked the *Salvator* of Danzig, 300 tons, Master, Gregory Neueman, bound from Lisbon with 100 tons of salt and spices. It must have been a fierce fight between the two smaller ships and the large merchantman for five of the crew of the *Salvator* were injured, the master badly, having been shot in the leg by a "peece of ordenance" and stabbed in the shoulder by a sword thrust.

They were all taken back to Studland and kept in the hold of Vaughan's ship for eight days while their goods were traded. Despite having handed over £35, Neueman, the injured Master, was tortured to divulge where any hidden money might be. Arms outstretched, he was held between two pirates while Heynes tied a knotted rope around his head and then used a short truncheon to tighten the rope until blood seeped from Neueman's head and the rope finally broke. Two more ropes broke before it was the turn of the cook and the purser for similar treatment, which only stopped when Heynes' own crew pleaded with him to desist.

Disappointed by a lack of further money and despite the awful state the Master must have been in, Heynes sent Neueman ashore to beg for a loan from the Vice Admiral's man to buy the ship back. Hatton's man, Hawley, was not home so Neueman was then sent off to Poole to try there but to no avail. The pirates removed what they could from the ship but instead of firing or sinking the ship as they had threatened they abandoned it and sent the rest of the *Salvator*'s crew to Poole. Hawley then demanded 20 nobles and 15 shillings from the owners to buy the abandoned ship back. Although Neueman didn't return to his ship from Poole, he must have survived for at least some time, as his statement was given at the subsequent High Court of the Admiralty inquiry on 5th December 1582, - tough times and tough men.

On 3rd October 1582 within the range of Sandown Castle near Deal, Heynes brazenly boarded the *Anne*, Master, Richard Buckley, and took part of her cargo of brimstone, wax, Manchester cottons and other goods before selling them in the Isle of Purbeck. Buckley later stated that Heynes boasted that he "had better friends in

Englande than eanye alderman or merchante of London had, naminge Sir Christopher Hatton" the Vice Admiral of Dorset.

At Christmas time, Atkinson brought a French ship with a cargo of salt into Studland, which he sold for £50 and gave half to John Uvedale and Thomas Aires, deputies to Hawley to keep them sweet. Atkinson then came in with a series of ships, a flyboat laden with deals, an Irish ship with orchall, silks, hops, and then a Scottish ship, the *Peter*, 60 tons of Dundee. Three men of war; a 55 tons flyboat commanded by Atkinson, Vaughan's ship and Purser's ship, had taken the Scottish prize off the Caskets, when it was homeward bound from Rochelle with a cargo of salt and wine worth 800 marks. The crew of twelve were put into a flyboat naked and without food or water.

French merchants from Rochelle complained about their ships being taken, one was the *Esperance* of Antwerp with a cargo worth 5,000 French crowns, another was the *Hope* of Rochelle with a general cargo and another, possibly the *Jane*, was taken on 13th June 1583 by Atkinson and Arnewood between Guernsey and the Caskets.

Since February 1583 Thomas Walton had been attacking English and French ships in Weymouth Road out of shot of the forts nearby.

In July the same year Walton brought in to Studland, two French barks laden with salt, which he had taken near Alderney. He gave one to Hawley and the other to Arnewood in exchange for a pinnace. In the meantime Vaughan had taken two ships, one off Yarmouth the other off Winterton in the June and sold the cargos of trunks full of clothes and books, which were mainly bibles, on the Isle of Wight and at Purbeck. He dispersed bibles to Cooke the parson for Swannidge, to Francis Hawley and to a minister of Purbeck.

There is no doubt that everyone in the vicinity of Studland from Bere Regis to Christchurch and the Isle of Wight and beyond, benefited from what was basically an entrepot, a port free of import duties, either in buying the goods offered by the pirates or by selling them provisions. Buyers and provisioners were ferried out to the anchored ships in small boats to view all the exotic goods displayed on board. Silks and every type of material and cloth one could imagine, wine, raisins, fruit, parrots, and monkeys. Local hostelries were full of these hard living, hard playing, extravagantly dressed, well armed mercenaries. Atkinson described one such establishment memorably. "William Mundaye of Studland his howse is the hell of the worlde, and he is the devil".

Even Weymouth was involved, for in January 1583/4 J. Hawke, Ric Bownell, H Huigens and W. Bonde are examined that on June 8 1583 they went on board the ship of T. Purser, Pirate, in Portland Roads to deliver a letter written in French and bring a response back from Purser. Neither Purser nor his crew could read French and declared that if he could take any ships in Weymouth Harbour he would set them on fire but was willing to sell the ship, presumably a French owned Prize, back for £100.

The band of pirates must have thought they were untouchable and even ventured inland to visit friends. When Atkinson lost his ship at Sandown Castle in November

1582 he stayed at John Fludde's house in Erith from the 6th until the 11th when having sat down with his wife and another woman for supper he was warned that constables would arrive imminently to arrest him so he left quickly out of the kitchen door.

Thomas Heywood in his 1639 book "A True Relation of the Lives and Deaths of Two most Famous English Pyrats, Purser and Clinton who lived in the Reigne of Queene Elizabeth" suggests that there was a bounty of £1,000 (£177,000-2011 value) on their heads. According to Heywood this was after the Queen had offered to pardon both Clinton and Purser and their crews if they gave up piracy, forfeited their ships and goods and served in the Navy instead. The two discussed the merits with their highest ranking crew members but they decided that a life where they risked their lives but were two "Princes of the Sea" with all their finery and wealth was to be preferred to a harsh and hazardous life in the Navy and the possibility that they would be hanged anyway.

The authorities were indeed closing in and between 1582 and 1583; Admiralty Judge Dr. Lewes examined more than one hundred people in the Marshalsea prison. The forty or more vessels captured and taken into Studland between the years 1581 to 1583 had caused consternation and claims by English and foreign ship owners for recompense in the High Court of Admiralty had highlighted Studland as the worst area for piracy. Hawley was summoned to explain what was going on. Hawley said that he had done his best to alleviate foreigners' sufferings by lending them money to buy their vessels back and that he was powerless against the band of pirates. He said that when he invited Purser to bargain the release of a French ship taken by him, Purser came to him with thirty men armed with harquebusses. He also claimed that the pirates were provisioned by ships from nearby ports coming to Studland Bay rather than being supplied by local inhabitants from the shore. Finally he pleaded for armed help to suppress the pirates.

While the pirates were at their most productive William Aboroughe, clerk to the navy and Benjamin Gunson were appointed in June 1583 to command the *Bark Talbot* and the *Unica*, their remit was to clear Studland of its pirates. News of their enterprise had somehow reached the pirates and they had dispersed. However the *Bark Talbot* caught up with Purser and Beavin on their way to Guernsey in a pinnace. During the ensuing fight the gunner and his mate were killed and Purser and Beavin surrendered. The same ship, between Christchurch and Alum Chine, then found Valentine, who made a run for Swannidge Bay, ran his vessel ashore and made off into the countryside but he was found at Robert Green's house in Woodhouse Farm near Studland.

The *Bark Talbot* then caught Atkinson on board a French prize called the *Jane* in Swannidge Bay and he was taken to Corfe Castle. Atkinson later claimed he had to pay £20 to ensure his trial took place in Purbeck, then £50 to get bail, which was not forthcoming, and finally £100 to be pardoned. William Ellis, captain of Purser's *Great Diamond* surrendered and Arnewood was captured with his French prize and taken to London. Altogether ten ships had been captured; seven pirate ships and three prizes.

Between 6th and 8th of August 40 pirates were questioned and most confessed but Atkinson, Purser, Beavin and Valentine would neither say with whom they traded nor who had supplied them and consequently they were sent to the Tower to be tortured. Atkinson and the others then gave fuller accounts of their history and Atkinson signed his with his usual flourish suggesting that he had not been tortured. (As well as the rack or the alternative of being crushed to death, the most common form of torture at the time was being hanged off the ground by manacles around the wrists and when the person fainted they would be supported back on wicker steps until they were revived then the process was repeated. One priest suffered this 9 times during one day. The swelling of the hands above the manacles and the strain would have left the hands in a state that would affect the normal signature.) The others did not sign theirs but unlike Atkinson they had not provided signatures beforehand that can be compared. Atkinson offered to pay £800 to recompense the merchants, the money coming from those who owed him money, but Lord Burley turned it down on the 15th August.

On the 10th August the Lords had already said "We intende to have a convenient number, for example, to be executed and the rest to passe under her Majesties mercie and pardon". Of the forty-three, ten were to be executed; fifteen were of the second grade and eighteen of the third. This was approved on the 22 August, four days before the trial was to start. Although most records for the sentences are missing Vaughan's was found. "Upon gallows situated in the public river of Thames between flood and ebb of the sea and water and in the jurisdiction of the Admiralty of England before the bank called Wapping, to be hanged until death".

Pirates Atkinson & Purser

On the 30th August 1583 nine were hanged for piracy at Wapping; "Thomas Walton alias Purser, Clinton Atkinson, William Ellis, William Valentine alias Baugh, Thomas Beavin, John Pollard, Edmund Copinger, Robert Woodman, and John Evans". The tenth, Arnewood the so-called gentleman, probably had enough influence to avoid even being tried. Atkinson and Walton (Purser) were certainly the most well known pirates and Ellis, Irland,

Valentine and Beavin their chief accomplices so they could have no reason to feel aggrieved by the verdict. However Pollard of Poole, a boatswain, and Copinger were no worse than others in Walton's crew and Woodman and Evans had only been with Arnewood for three weeks.

It was the usual practice for the crowd at the hanging of a pirate to be entertained by the sight of the pirate dressed in all his finery but Atkinson had already given away his "murrey velvet dublet with great gold buttons and his like coloured venetians layd with great gold lace" which he said he had bought from a Dorset gentleman for £5, the very same apparel he was wearing when he left Corfe Castle for the Tower.

However Purser did not disappoint, wearing his Venetian red taffeta, which he ripped apart and threw to his supporters in the crowd. Again they used the short drop method of hanging people so death usually came from asphyxiation rather than breaking the neck, and that could take 5 or 50 minutes depending if you had friends or had paid people beforehand to be "hangers on", to literally hang on your legs to speed the process up.

The burial registers of the nearby churches to Wapping for the day after bear testament to the swiftness of the execution and subsequent burial but confirm that Atkinson was indeed a merchant of London. They also show how young some of the pirates were.

St Botolph, Aldgate, burial register 1583.

Clinton Atkinson years/ 36/executed
Clinton Atkinson some tyme a housekeeper & dwelling in Grace Church Street & sold haberdashe ware was for piracy executed at Wapping & was buryed the last day of August 1583

William Valentine years/ 23/ executed
William Valentine bacheler borne in Tower Street was buryed the last day of August 1583

Edmund Coppinger years/ 44/ executed
Edmund Coppinger a sailler a maryed man was for piracy executed & buryed the last day of August 1583

St Mary, Whitechapel burial register 1583
Will Ellis 31 August 1583

The men of Purbeck felt betrayed as they had been willing to buy Atkinson's freedom and in their disgust they stormed Corfe Castle ripping the lead from the roof and ruining Christopher Hatton's lodge. Although Atkinson and the other pirates had implicated Hatton, Hawley and others, their connivance was never pursued and on

20th November 1591 Hatton died, followed by Hawley's death in 1594. Hawley had not only retained his office of deputy to the Vice Admiral of Purbeck but had also taken on the post of deputy to the Vice Admiral of Dorset, which covered Weymouth.

Most of those pirates arrested were set free because of the collusion of the coastal landowners and the local populace in the ingrained trade of smuggling and piracy. Also the threat of war against Spain meant that England would need good sailors and these sailors were certainly that. Many had started out as honest sailors but with the vagaries of war and trade embargos some routes were lost and that meant that many couldn't make a living and resorted to smuggling or open piracy. It is estimated that in the 16th Century 50% of the population of the country barely had enough clothes, food and shelter to survive and by the end of the 17th century things had barely improved, 30% were stated to be poor with 20% very poor.

In 1601 an act was brought in to appoint two overseers for each parish and they had the authority to raise a local tax to look after the old and the infirm, those who could no longer work, and also to find work for the poor who were able to work. The Protestation Returns of 1641 for the villages around Weymouth clearly show that two overseers were in place in all but the smallest communities.

Despite the testimony of the pirates, Francis Hawley was not punished however John Uvedale, Mayor of Corfe was and he appeared before Lord Burghley on the 8th September and was put under bond to appear before the Commissioners when they next met. Thomas Ayres was fined £40 but failed to pay and a warrant for his arrest was issued, which meant that while Hawley had got away with it, his two "deputies" or at least his two associates paid the price.

Several pirates were still about their trade for on the 20th September Hewson took the *Lizarte* of 50 tons bound from Rochelle to Caen with Gascoyne wines and she was duly brought into Studland. Hewson followed this on 1st October when he brought in the flyboat *Ostridge* of Stockholm bound from Amsterdam to Biscay laden with cheese, hides, Holland cloth and rye.

Meanwhile Arnewood was finally pardoned on 20 December and released from the Marshalsea but on 16th January 1584 a warrant for his arrest on charges of piracy was issued. He is mentioned as joining with pirates to take ships in May and June that year off the coast of Alderney and in July again with others he takes a hoy from Antwerp and is last heard of in December when he captures a prize off Lundy.

The port officials at Weymouth and Melcombe Regis heard that there were pirates once again operating out of West Lulworth and they provided and sent two ships on 17 June 1584, the *Archangel* and the *Saloman*, to apprehend them. Word had obviously reached the pirates and most had left leaving behind their prizes but Captain Beare and his crew fled ashore but were caught soon after and Beare at least, joined several other pirates in the Marshalsea to await their fate.

In August 1584 a letter is sent from Weymouth to Sir Francis Walsingham, spymaster and advisor to Queen Elizabeth, saying that a Weymouth bark had taken the pirate Sprage in Portland Roads and the Weymouth bark's pinnace had taken

Sprage's prize.

The execution of Clinton Purser and the others was largely down to political expediency, to show Philip of Spain that Elizabeth was doing something about the piratical attacks on his shipping and also to satisfy the powerful English Merchants who were worried about losing their profitable trade to Spain. The pirates had brought their own benefits of trade to England supplying goods and money that would have bypassed England otherwise and were part of the beginnings of England as a Maritime Country to eventually equal and surpass Spain, France and the Dutch.

Less than two years later Atkinson's and the other hanged pirates' undoubted skills as navigator, ship's Captain and leader of men would have served the country well. Luckily others like Sir Martin Frobisher who had been locked up in the Marshallsea after taking a French ship and was later accused in 1566 of fitting out a ship as a pirate became one of England's foremost Sea Dogs and captained the Queen's ship *Triumph* against the Spanish Armada.

Phoney and real war

While England feared its trade being dominated by Maritime Spain and the threat of invasion, Philip grew tired of England's support for the Protestant Dutch rebellion and of England's privateers freely attacking Spanish shipping so as a consequence on the 19th May 1585 King Philip of Spain issued a decree to seize English ships in Spanish ports, take their cargoes and incarcerate their crews. Luckily the *Primrose* of London managed to sail out of her Spanish port, with the Spanish arresting officer still aboard, and the alarm was raised in England. Merchants who had born the losses petitioned the Crown for compensation.

By 7th July the Lord Admiral was commanded to investigate the claims and subsequently provide letters of reprisal to the aggrieved merchants. This was the signal for those merchants to send out armed ships to venture forth for an allowed six months period to recompense their losses by capturing Spanish cargoes at sea, a position just short of outright war between the two countries. However the strict control of Letters of Reprisal soon lapsed and by the end of the summer a myriad of ships, some genuine reprisal ships, some where the letter of reprisal had been bought and ships then fitted out to attack Spanish shipping, and others just pirates who were now almost legitimate as long as they stuck to only attacking Spanish shipping.

Weymouth and Southampton were the foremost reprisal ports, fitting out armed ships and also specialising in the sale and dispersal of the prize cargoes and any captured ships. Promoters of reprisal voyages had to pay a £1000 bond for their letter of reprisal and follow the rules. Prize cargoes were to be valued and pay the Queen's customs duty plus a 10% levy to the Lord Admiral. After 1589 the Admiralty Court, who then oversaw reprisal letters, brought in new rules and failure to pay these charges meant the merchant promoter of the ship forfeited his bond of £1000, which soon rose to £3,000 within a couple of years.

Weymouth however claimed independent Admiralty jurisdiction and in April 1587 Deputy Vice Admiral Hawley of Dorset had told Weymouth to arrest Captain Laurence Prowse of the *Eleinor* and some of his men for piracy and send them to Corfe Castle. Earlier the Lord Admiral had complained that his man Middelton had been charged more than another when buying sugar from Captain Prowse's ship. Weymouth then wrote to the Lord Admiral and asked him to remind Hawley that Weymouth had ancient exemption from Admiralty jurisdiction.

Far from discouraging English Privateers attacking Spanish shipping, Philip's decree of 1585 had brought about an unofficial war between England and Spain meaning that both Spanish and Portuguese ships were legitimate English targets for privateers as well as Iberian ports as demonstrated by Drake's raid on Cadiz in 1587. The eventual consequence was the Spanish Armada of 1588 when Philip thought he could eliminate the English threat once and for all.

Against the Spanish fleet of 130 ships, Weymouth supplied six ships as part of the eventual 197 strong English Fleet: - the *Golden Rial* or *Ryall* of 120 tons with 50 men, owned by Thomas Middleton, the *Galleon* of Weymouth of 100 tons with 50 men, captained by Richard Miller, the *Bark Sutton* of 70 tons with 40 men, captained by Hugh Preston, the *Catherine* of 66 tons with 30 men, the *Heathen* of 60 tons with 30 men, and the *Expedition* 70 tons with 50 men, which also had 50 soldiers of Clifford's company on board.

As the fleets sailed up the Channel past Plymouth, the 958 tons Spanish ship *San Salvador*'s magazine exploded killing 200 of the 321 soldiers and 75 sailors on board. The Paymaster General together with heavy chests of Imperial Gold were taken off and the abandoned hulk was captured and brought into Weymouth where her much needed cannons, shot and powder were unloaded before eventually being sent to London.

On the 2nd August the battle off Portland took place lasting from morning until evening and despite fierce cannon fire all the Spanish ships survived. During the battle Sir Martin Frobisher is generally thought to have run out of sea room and had to anchor to prevent his six strong squadron from going ashore on Portland Bill.

Another view is that Frobisher set up an ambush to delay the Armada. Local fisherman Ken Lynham knows more than many about the currents around Portland Bill, its treacherous Race, (where conflicting tides meet to create turbulent seas) and the Shambles Bank, the long sandbank north east of Portland Bill. Ken helped prove the theory that Frobisher, in the 42 gun *Triumph*, had anchored in an eddy on a low spring tide just to the west of Pulpit Rock on the west side of Portland Bill. While Frobisher looked like he was in danger of running ashore the eddy kept him off it.

As planned he appeared to be an enticing target for Sidonia who sent Moncado's galleasses into attack. As Ken later showed, even in his fishing boat it was impossible to punch against the tide let alone for the galleasses to row from the West Shambles to Frobisher because of the currents of that particular low spring tide. Despite all the efforts of the rowers they could not get near enough to Frobisher to board him or use their cannons against him effectively. In return Frobisher used his longer-range English guns to decimate the rowers on board the four 40-gun galleasses. They eventually retreated having to use their sails to do so.

The English guns at distance were primarily anti personnel weapons, hence why none of the Spanish ships were sunk despite 500 shots hitting Sidonia's own flagship the *San Martin* that day. After all Drake, Hawkins, Raleigh, Frobisher, and Winter were basically privateers used to killing and overwhelming the enemy's crew but not destroying or sinking the prize in the process. They certainly did not want to get within range of the heavier but shorter-ranged Spanish guns or close enough to be boarded by the numerically superior Spanish soldiers. The Armada sailed on further up Channel passing Portland Roads, which was thought to be a possible landing point for the Spanish.

Weymouth Pirates and Privateers

What of the Weymouth, Melcombe and Portland sailors? Portlander Philip Boyte was hanged as a common pirate, and Studland pirate Purser had some of his men slain by the Weymouth sailors when he tried to capture the La Rochelle ship just outside the ports, and pirate Sprage had been captured by a Weymouth bark and its pinnace, however nefarious activities dated yet further back.

Henry Strangways, possibly born in 1530 and part of the well known Dorset family became a pirate in 1552 operating in the Irish Sea where like Frobisher, he was associated with fellow pirates, the Killigrews of Cornwall. They were all said to use Portland Castle to store their pillaged goods and certainly from about September 1556 until 29 May 1557 that was probably the case, as his brother George Strangways was the stand-in Captain of Portland Castle until John Leweston was reappointed.

In 1555 Henry Strangways is in the Tower of London, presumably as a pirate, but he manages to escape any punishment on that occasion. However he was arrested during 1559 with 80 of his men and condemned to death, though he again cheated the executioner and was set free.

The year had proved to be eventful for in August Lord Cecil writes "The Portugals that were robbed by Strangwish have brought letters from the King there requiring restitution, which is against all law and example." Strangwish is then accused in September of taking a Spanish ship. The Calendar of State Papers for Elizabeth says "His Orator, the Bishop of Aquila, will inform her how a Spanish merchant, Johannes de Bagnes, was plundered of his ship and stores by an English pirate, "Enrriex Tranguaz" [Henry Strangwish] of which restitution should be made. — Valladolid, 30 Sept. 1559. —*Signed*: Philippus [Philip II], - G. Perezius.

This is followed in January 1559/60 by "The pirate Estranguitz [Strangways], who has the command of a galley, has been informed by Captain Malbazart (a French prisoner of war in London, upon promise of deliverance) of the landing-places and harbours in Lower Normandy." Perhaps being a pirate ensured that he had good intelligence to trade with Cecil and others in Court and being a Gentleman by birth may have also helped to obtain his freedom.

It seems his piracy is fully confirmed and he is later imprisoned in December 1560 but then released on the promise of good conduct. He died in 1562 at Rouen and was posthumously given a full pardon by Queen Elizabeth. While imprisoned in 1554 his fellow prisoner Gerlach Flicke, an artist, painted a portrait of Strangways, so we have at last the face of a true Dorset born pirate.

Apart from piracy West Country ship-owners were foremost in warlike privateering with those from Bristol, Plymouth, Weymouth and Southampton the most prominent. The ships were reasonably armed and relied on the crew boarding targeted vessels brandishing a variety of personal weapons, knives, cutlasses, and pikes as well as using murderers and hand guns. So accomplished and widespread was the trade that some commodities originating from the Spanish New World were cheaper in England than they were in the West Indies or in Spain, and others, such as sugar, could only be bought in bulk from England.

Pirate Richard Gregory was a rich merchant, a deputy searcher for Weymouth and Melcombe Regis, and also deputy to Lord Howard of Bindon, the Vice Admiral for Dorset. No doubt the positions came because he was a prosperous merchant but no doubt they also helped him to become richer. In 1577 he had been convicted of victualling and aiding pirates, buying prizes and selling them back to the owners and had sponsored local pirate Bartholomew Belpitt of the *Golden Hind* to seek out ships. He had been Mayor in 1570 and then in 1588 became MP for Weymouth & Melcombe Regis despite his piratical associations, for this was the norm on the coast.

He had two houses near the chapel in Melcombe Regis and another house in Southampton. A Gascony wine merchant called Russell captained Gregory's own man o' war called the *Daniel*, which mounted 7 cast guns. Gregory would meet his pirate ship when it anchored in Portland Roads just outside the range of the guns of the twin castles of Portland and Sandesfort. There he would split the profits, gained from selling goods like jewels taken from prize ships, with his Captain and the crew. Then the ship sailed into Melcombe to unload its cargo into Gregory's cellars, where casks of Madeira sack stood next to exotic spices. While he entertained his Captain and crew overnight, his own men would brew beer and bake bread to provision his ship for a quick turnaround the next day. He had other ships, possibly named after relatives, the *Michael Gregory*, the *John Gregory* and the *George Gregory*, all of Weymouth.

On September 14 1586 Amyas Preston, Captain of the *Elenor* of Weymouth, found a ship between Bayonne and Viana in Spain with nobody on board except for one corpse, which they tossed over the side. Preston brought the ship, laden with fish into Weymouth, the ship being valued at £61. The cargo consisted of train oil valued at 8s per ton, wet fish at 16s per hundred, and dry fish at 9s per hundred. The four anchors were worth £16 and the two minions and four falcons another £16. After the Admiral's tenth had been taken Preston and Captain Ryman each had a third of the total value, while the other third was shared between the owners, victuallers and the crew.

Somerset born Preston was still privateering in the *Eleanor* of Weymouth in 1587 while his own vessel *Julian* of Lyme sailed to the Azores and shared a prize worth £25,000 with his own ship the *Delight* of Lyme, the *Swiftsure* of London and *Unicorn* of Barnstaple. Preston was to become Lieutenant on board Admiral Lord Howard's *Ark Royal* during the fight against the Spanish Armada in 1588 when he was seriously wounded off Calais.

One of Weymouth's most successful reprisal promoters and captains was Robert White who owned the *Catherine* or *Little Catherine*. She was a small 35 tons ship mounting four guns, two 3-pounder falcons and two 2-pounder falconets as well as four calivers (A matchlock shoulder gun). In 1590 she had been valued with all her equipment and guns at £90 and during that year she boarded 2 brazilmen (ships trading to Brazil usually with valuable return cargoes) with combined cargoes worth about £3,500 and this was followed the next year with another brazilman whose cargo was worth £2,850.

In 1592 White sold the *Catherine* to Peter Neville who continued the successful exploits taking a brazilman worth £4,239 and then in 1595 a West Indiaman loaded with a veritable treasure of Chinese silks, taffeta, pearls, emeralds, gold rings, 68 ½ ounces of gold chain, sapphires, and topazes amongst other precious stones, about £800 worth of reales of plate, as well as hides, sugar, blockwood, cassia fistula and cochineal and although the total value is unrecorded it must have surpassed £20,000.

Meanwhile White had bought the *Great Catherine* or *Catherine White* possibly named after his wife, as there is mention of a Robert White junior, a mariner of Melcombe and his wife Katherine in the 1580s. (Spelling was not consistent nor the ability to write one's name, at that time). A reprisal captain since 1587, White took further prizes, one in 1592, two in 95 and two in 98 worth £1,110 but after 95 the Captain is John White, perhaps his son, Robert by now being in his forties. Like other promoters/privateers he was successful enough to become Mayor of Weymouth in 1593/4.

In 1590 the *Riall* of Weymouth, 160 tons, jointly promoted by owner Sir Thomas Myddleton and Erasmus Harby and commanded by William Myddleton, took two prizes worth £25,000 in league with 5 other privateers, one being the *Bark Randall* of Weymouth, which was commanded by Harby's servant, Thomas Lowther, another one was one of William Waltham's ships, and the *Discharge* of London and the *Samaritan*. Both cargoes were spices such as pepper, cloves and mace together with sugar, brazilwood, ivory and precious stones.

Other Weymouth merchants heavily into reprisal privateering were Henry Rogers who owned the *Seadragon*, *Endeavour* and *Amity* (later *Tobacco Pipe*), John Reynolds who also had an interest in the *Amity* and was a promoter for the *Anne Huddy* in 1590 and *Diamond* in 1600, and Nicholas Jones, the Captain of Portland Castle, was a promoter for the *Amity* in 1591. Gentleman merchant John Randall, (son of Hugh Randall, who was accused of piracy in the 1570s and was a belligerent bailiff of Weymouth), was owner of the Weymouth ships *Bark Randall* and the *Grace* and joint owner with Sir Walter Raleigh of the Weymouth based *Hearts of Desire*. Raleigh also co promoted the *Bark Randall* together with Sir George Carey, Captain General of the Isle of Wight.

As well as the pre war destination of Cadiz, Weymouth ships, even as small as 35 tons, sailed to the Azores and the Caribbean to find prizes. The well-known Pitt family of Weymouth represented by William and Richard joined with John Bond and William Holman as promoters of the *Bark Bond*, 56 tons of Weymouth. In 1589, commanded by local man David Geyer, a brazilman was taken, its cargo of brazilwood, sugar and cotton wool worth £4,670 and then in 1590, captained by Edward Bond she took a leaguer (a French Catholic League ship) with a cargo of sugar, molasses and raisins from Malaga worth £660. The following year this time commanded by Roger Geyer she shared a prize with *Swallow,* and *Glebe* of London, worth £1500, consisting of sugar, hides, ginger, and ivory amongst other goods.

In 1592 the *Bark Bond* commanded by Nicholas Ayers brought back jewellery from the *Grace* of Dover, a ship carrying non-Spanish passengers who had already been the subject of a wrongful privateering seizure. The jewels were later returned. In 1595 the *Bark Bond* sailed to the West Indies with the *Scorpion* and the *Violet*, where they gathered prizes worth £1,500, a good return for John Bond and his London based merchant co-promoters.

The number of Weymouth ships used for privateering grew, for Bond had fitted out both the *Bark Bond* and *Jesus* as reprisal vessels prior to 1590 and the Pitts, Richard, William and Henry had likewise used the *Matthew* and *Lion* from the start of the war in 1585. In 1590, William Pitt joined Nicholas Jones the Captain of Portland Castle to co-promote similar ventures. John Pitt was part owner of the *Carouse* and in 93 owned the *Mayflower* and co-promoted the *Seraphim* in 1595 while Henry Pitt's own privateer, the *Greyhound* brought home a prize in 1597.

Several London and Southampton Merchants had interests in either owning or promoting the Weymouth ships and some Weymouth owners had other ships in Southampton but it was William Waltham, already owner and promoter of several Bristol ships, who had extensive Weymouth interests owning the *Jane Bonaventure* of 20 tons, the *Francis,* the *Prudence* and the *Pearl*. Over ten years from 1588, Waltham's ships registered at least 17 prize cargoes amounting to a minimum of £22,190. Waltham like other local privateers became Mayor of Weymouth in 1587.

1600s

Letters of Reprisal were usually specific against one country such as Spain. Letters of Marque however covered anywhere outside the jurisdiction of the monarch, i.e. "outside the marque" of their jurisdiction.

To obtain a Letter of Reprisal the applicant had to prove their loss, promise that all seizures would be brought to an English or later British port, and the ships and cargoes taken would not be sold until the court had agreed they were lawfully taken. Any customs duty had to be paid plus a tenth of the total value of ship and cargo was supposed to be paid to the Lord Admiral or his deputies. 1625-6 was a particularly busy period because of the war with Spain and an impending one with France and the Dorset deputies then were John Drake and his son Sir John. Of the residual value of the prize and cargo, 2/3 went to the owners or promoters of the voyage and 1/3 was distributed to the Captain and crew.

For the whole of Dorset in just 4 years there were 70 applications, three quarters were accounted for by Weymouth followed by Poole and just 3 or 4 for Lyme. Several of these involved not just one ship but had a smaller pinnace included. There are many instances of privateering ships from one port or from different English ports joining together to take and share a larger prize. Having a second ship would be an aid for attacking such prizes, the bigger ship using its longer-range guns to bombard the target while the pinnace harried and sought the best time to board it. Drake also used pinnaces to go close inshore to investigate creeks and to obtain supplies, which were then taken back to his larger ships off shore.

Pirates like Clinton Atkinson also favoured pinnaces because they were faster and more manoeuvrable due to having fore and aft rigged sails, not available at that time to larger ships that had square-rigged sails, so they could sail closer to the wind. Just as today when Somali pirates use small fast craft to board slow moving tankers etc, so a fast pinnace could get close to a slower lightly armed merchantman and use its anti personnel weapons of murderers, swivel guns, arquebuses, swords and pikes to persuade or overwhelm the targeted vessel's crew. The larger "mother" ship could then come up to take on board the cargo, and put aboard a prize crew from the extra men who had sailed with her.

According to John Masefield in his book "On the Spanish Main", when a likely prize had been identified, perhaps a deeply laden slow moving merchantman that didn't have too many guns, and was not built too high, pirates or privateers would follow her either rowing up in a ship's boat or by sail in a faster pinnace. Their steersman tried to keep in line astern and instantly reacted to any change of course, while the best musketeers were put in the bows so they could keep up a steady rain of fire on the ship's helmsman or on any gun ports that opened. If the ship was too high to expose the helmsman they approached under the stern before wedging the rudder in one position to disable the prey. Brandishing their knives and pistols, they then boarded her either over her quarter or by the after chains, the first man aboard being awarded something extra when the division of the loot was made later.

Likewise in David Cordingly's Buccaneer Explorers section in the book "Pirates" published by World Publications Inc. in 2007, pirate Basil Ringrose's journal confirms this. On St George's day in 1680 against Spanish crews of 228 in total, 68 buccaneers in five dugout canoes attacked three Spanish warships at Panama, their musketmen being adept at shooting the helmsman and any other crew they could see, before approaching the stern and then shooting away the braces to the sails, disabling the rudder. They boarded two of the Spanish ships in turn, the other ship retreating. They lost 18 men killed or wounded against over 100 Spanish killed.

If the prize ship was good it was either used by the pirates themselves or taken into a port and sold, often back to the owners. If it was of no value they would take the cargo and any ship's fittings or guns and either burn her or run her ashore. The crew and passengers were often stripped of their clothing as well as losing anything of value.

One reprisal detailed is in 1625 to merchant John Lockier of Weymouth & Melcombe Regis, to set forth the *Dragone* of Weymouth, burthen 80 tonnes, with Gyles Bonde as Captain and Francis Saunders as Master. She mounted 8 pieces of ordnance, with 40 men on board, and John Reeves captained her pinnace, the *Sealove* of Weymouth, both ships being victualled for 12 months.

Owner John Freke went one better and sought both Letters of Reprisal and a Commission to take Pirates on the coasts of Spain and Portugal for his ship the *Leopard* of 240 tons. She had been built in Weymouth by Nicholas Audney and was armed with 16 cast iron sacres, and 4 minions and commanded by Nicholas Strangways while the accompanying pinnace *Margaret* of 60 tons was commanded by the aforementioned Audney.

Not all Reprisal voyages were successful, the *Leopard* was sold two years later to Poole merchants and was later wrecked on the Irish coast and the *Willing Wind* was "sunk by enemies". In a report from Dartmouth dated 28 April 1626 it was stated that Sallee men-of-war [Barbary pirates] were in the Channel and in the previous ten days had taken a bark from Weymouth and one from Plymouth, both bound for Newfoundland.

Two Weymouth privateers, the *Harry and John* and the *Speedwell*, seem to have given up privateering and been exempted from the Press Gang in 1635 as they were being used to transport Portland stone for the rebuilding of St Pauls Cathedral.

In 1633 the deliciously named Antiochesten Phelps sues John Gardner, who was a merchant and controller of Customs at Poole and Weymouth, over the voyage of the *Content* of Weymouth. She had captured the *St Jago* of Lisbon, laden with sugar, Brazil tobacco and other cargo said to be worth in total £7,000 after the 10% Admiral's share had been paid. Phelps and others had fitted her out for £360 but it seems they wanted the fact that a sister ship, *Sarah*, had returned empty-handed to be taken into account when customs duties were levied.

A similar court suit involved the *Gift of God* of Weymouth, Edward Cuttance master, taking a Portuguese carvel valued at £7,900 while on a voyage to the Isle of Maye, followed by the capture of a French ship of £200 value. Weymouth shipowner and privateer Peter Sallenova captured a French ship called the *Dolphin* or more likely *Dauphin*, laden with [Newfoundland] Bank's fish and train oil and took another with a cargo of French wines.

A survey of shipping at Weymouth taken on the 11th March 1628 shows 176 sailors for the port of Weymouth with 111 for Melcombe Regis, representing almost a quarter of the total of Dorset sailors.

The list of 26 ships belonging to Weymouth and ranging between 25 and 100 tons, with 2 to 10 guns mounted, was: -

Name, tonnage, Guns, Owners, Age

AT SEA

Sara, 90 tons, 8 guns, (David Gyre & William Holmes), 7 years.

Pilgrim, 100 tons, 6 guns, (John Gallott & William Holmes,) 16 years.

Margaret, 60 tons, 6 guns, (Thomas Polhill & Nich. Cornew), 12 years.

Judith, 40 tons, 6 guns, (Jonas Dennis & Peter Salenesne), 16 years.

Eleanor, 30 tons, 4 guns, (Henry Waltham & William Charytie), 8 years.

Hopewell, 30 tons, 4 guns, (John Blackfood & William Collins), 20 years.

Peter, 50 tons, capable of 4 guns, (John Wall & Richard Wall), 20 years.

Fortune, 50 tons, 4 guns, (John Wall & Richard Wall,) 8 years.

Hopewell, 40 tons, 4 guns, (John James & John Blackford,) 10 years.

Desire, 30 tons, (William Davis & Elizabeth Drier), 10 years.

Content, 50 tons, 6 guns, (John Blackforde & Capt. Pettifitz), 8 years.

Hopewell, 40 tons, capable of 4 guns, (John Damon), 5 years.

Truelove, 60 tons, 7 guns, (Peter Salenesne & Henry Cuttance), 12 years.

AT HOME

Elizabeth, 90 tons, 5 guns, (William Waltham & Thomas Gyre), 30 years

Swift, 10 guns, (Henry Cuttance & Thomas Ledoze), 10 years.

Ark, 50 tons, 2 guns, capable of 2 more, (Thomas Ledoze & Henry Cuttance), 8 years

Samuel, 50 tons, capable of 4 guns, (Henry Russell. James James), 8 years

Phoenix, 35 tons, 4 guns (John Gardner & John Lockier), 10 years.

Shuttle, 40 tons, 4 guns, (Richard Wright & Henry Russell), 4 years.

Great Katherine, 80 tons, 8 guns, (Robert White & John Blackford), 20 years

Seahorse, 80 tons, 4 guns, capable of 4 more. (Henry Michell), 12 years.

Abigall, 100 tons, 10 guns, (Henry Michell), 20 years

Content, 40 tons, 5 guns, (Henry Russell & John Gardner), 10 years.

Hopewell, 25 tons, (John Gallott & Henry Cuttance), 9 years.

Caramouchy, 25 tons, 2 guns, (David Gyre), 10 years.

Fellowship, 40 tons, 3 guns and may bear 2 more, (Richard Berry), 20 years.

There is at least one ship larger than the *Swift* mentioned in a Trinity House Certificate of May 1626, which was issued for the *Leopard*, 240 tons, owner John Feake.

In the same 1628 survey Poole had 11 ships abroad, and 9 at home. Two ships were above 100 tons, namely the *Garland*, 150 tons, 14 guns and the *Dragon*, 150 tons, 12 guns. Wareham had no ships. Swanage had 1 ship of 35 tons. Lyme Regis had 18 ships the largest being *Bonaventure*, 80 tons, 9 guns, and *Mary*, 80 tons, 9 guns. Chideock, Charmouth and Bridport had no ships.

Letters of Marque were issued 40 times to Weymouth councillors during the period 1625 to 1630 with Gabriel Cornish's 30 tons ship the *Shuttle*, recording at least one prize. Other ships mentioned are the 120 tons *Gift of God* and the *Flower* of 40 tons both owned by Henry Cuttance.

There was no shortage of merchants, ships or crews for reprisal voyages. Certainly no merchant seaman would contemplate service in the Royal Navy for in the 1620s conditions were atrocious. The continual lack of payment of what little pay was due meant that men could not clothe themselves. One officer on the Vanguard implored "many of our men for want of clothes are so naked that, exposed to the weather in doing their duties, their toes and feet miserably rot and fall away piecemeal, being mortified with extreme cold. I beseech your Grace once more that some more clothes may be speedily sent down and also 500 hammacoes, [hammocks] for most lodge on the bare decks".

A naval seaman's pay had been ten shillings per 28 day month since 1585, far less than a merchant seaman could earn and even when in 1626 it was raised to 15 shillings per month it was still unlikely to match his civilian counterpart. In any case it has been calculated that for the war years 1625 to 1629 only between a third and a half of what was owed to naval seamen, was actually paid out. In 1629 two naval ships out of six that were anchored off the Downs, had neither food nor water on board and a third had drunk water for three days, implying a total lack of food. Seamen either mutinied or deserted throughout these years, many no doubt found their way into piracy or privateering.

The survey both confirms the size of Weymouth and Melcombe Regis as a port compared to the rest of Dorset and the numbers of guns mounted on the ships show they were capable of defending themselves and of taking other ships, ideal for their privateering reputation. The breech loading cannons and murderers together with any ship's equipment later salvaged from the wreck of the Golden Grape would find ready sales to the local shipowners.

The Spanish Armada in 1588 and the war with Spain put paid to open piracy for the time being, as former pirates could legally take Spanish ships as they now had the status of being privateers. Unfortunately, once the war with Spain finished coastal piracy returned despite the easing of trade between the two countries. But another greater concern to shipping was a consequence of that peace treaty.

Barbary Pirates, and Slavery

When James VI of Scotland became James I of England in 1603 he had immediately wanted to make peace with Spain, a country at war with the Ottoman Empire. By being the enemy of the Ottoman Empire's staunch enemy, Spain, English shipping had not been generally targeted by the Turks under the adage "mine enemy's enemy is my friend" but when Britain became friend or ally of the Turk's prime enemy, Britain too, became an enemy of the Turks.

Barbary pirates as they became known came from Morocco, Algiers, Tripoli and Tunisia. The latter three were part of the Ottoman Empire and hence why they were known as "Turks" though the term Barbary covered Arabs, Berbers, Moriscos and Ottoman soldiers.

Under the Algiers regency the governor there had a share of the profits from cargoes and captives taken by crews based in his territory. Christian shipping was targeted, French, and Danish amongst them and especially those they regarded as being at war with them such as Spain who had forced the Moors out of Spain in the late 15th Century.

Between the years 1600 to 1640 North African corsairs seized more than 800 English, Scottish, Welsh and Irish trading ships in the Mediterranean and Atlantic and a total of 12,000 men, women and children from Britain and Ireland were taken as captives and slaves between 1620 and 1640. The Barbary oar based galleys required fit slaves to man their oars but it was generally a short life because of the physical demands and the dangers in battle.

There were 115,000 tons of English shipping in 1620s but this had increased to 340,000 in the 1680s. Most British trading ships were small with limited crew and few or no cannon so seamen were the greatest victims and the poorest and consequently had the least chance of being ransomed, the average ransom price being £45. Captains and merchants stood a better chance of being ransomed, though it took a considerable time, up to a decade in the 1650s. Ransoming became such a big part of this piracy that in the 1630s Morocco had established an embassy in London to negotiate ransoms for English seamen.

Weymouth & Melcombe Regis Council minutes
June 24, 27 1618
Examination of W. Knott, Christmas Peeters and others about taking three men in a "Lirret" on board a barque in the Roads said to be bound for "Bristowe."

June 27, 1618. The boat's crew was bound over to appear at the Sessions

July 11, 1618. Examination of J. Bush and others about the above-mentioned barque.

He went with Christmas Peeters and the others in the boat from "Waymouth Key," and "did row her forth unto the Moldehead at "Waymouthe's north," and thence to the vessel in Portland Roads. They found on board Michael Taylor, J. Taylor, Anthony Knighte, T. Pitt, Samuell Vincent, J Roane and William Cropp, wch were of Sir Walter Rawleig his company in his late voyage," and three Frenchmen and a French boy "of Bryhocke in Brittaine." The vessel was laden with "Welshcoale," and was "taken away by them from the said ffrenchmen aboute the Lands End, where they did set on shoare other three ffrenchmen." Four of the crew, armed with two muskets and four swords, landed on Portland, killed three sheep and brought them on board. The barque then made sail and stood for Ste Adams and chased a vessel, but lost sight of her at night.

Next day the barque stood to the Westward, and chased another vessel of Lyme that came from " Murlez" [Morlaix], and would have taken her " yf their bareque's sayles had not splitt." The wind chopping round to the West, they went up Channel to "Sandwch Bay," [Swanage] where from a barque of Lyme they took a barrel of beer and four loaves. They then surprised a barque of Shoreham, and took from her only half a barrel of beer. After several unsuccessful chases they took with their boat a " Flemynge" of two hundred tons, laden with salt, and took out of her a hogshead of beer, a barrel of bread, a firkin of butter, and four cheeses, and " lett her goe." Next they took another Fleming, of one hundred and sixty tons, also laden with salt, "and thereupon did quit the said ffrench barque and three frenchmen and boye, giveing them victualls to serve their turne, and kepte the fflemyng and the Master and all the men on board with them." Meeting with a "Hoye" of London, laden with timber, they took passage in her for London, quitting the Flemish vessel, apparently without damage. Five of their number landed at Blackwall, and the other five at "Dickshoare," where they all supped "att, the signe of the Ostridge." They then separated; but on the next day, Sunday July 1st, two of them, Wynton and Wilbore, came to Bush at Limehouse, and asked him to tell Brian Gates to send them their clothes. And he says that the crew told him that they gave to the Weymouth boat's crew a barrel of flour, two " kettelles," two "coverledds," and two shillings "to thend they should procure them some good fellowes." The Weymouth boatmen, Matthew Knott, Christmas Peeters, Adam Cuttler and T. Ilkins were (on the above deposition being heard) re-examined and adhered to their first evidence, denying apparently all concern in procuring pirate recruits. Jas. Bush was bound over to appear at the next Sessions of Oyer and Terminer. - July 18, 1618

July 18 1618

For 4s they bought for the Master of the barque a quarter of mutton, a pound of butter, and four or five gallons of beer. For two trips to the vessel and their trouble in shopping they received in all 2s. "It appered unto Mr Mayor by all conjecturall likelyhoode" that the barque was a pirate vessel. The crew was reported to have stolen sheep on Portland.

In June 1620 £450 was demanded by the King from Weymouth & Melcombe Regis towards an expedition against the Turks i.e. the Moorish Pirates. The Mayor complained of the poverty of the town, pleading that the Turks had taken four ships and sunk one to the value of more than £2,000.

November 1623 "T. Mellin of Ligh, a Scotsman, more than a year ago shipped as mate on board the *Welkin*, of Dover, for Lisbon. Off Burleance she was taken by "Turks of Argier," at which place he was sold as a slave. About, eight weeks ago he was sent to sea in a Man-of-War, a " Pallacre" [Pollacre, a three masted Mediterranean ship] of about eighty tons, a crew of twenty-seven Turks, four Englishmen, himself, two Frenchmen, one " Portuguese " and three "Almeignes." About sixty leagues

West of Fromviana, " the shipp lyeinge ahull," the Christians rose on the Algerines, killed ten or twelve and put the rest in the hold then sailed for England. Three leagues from Portland a Dutch Man-of-War, the *White Bear*, of Amsterdam, Capt. Johnson, surprised them, brought them into Portland Roads, landed Mellin, the Englishmen, Frenchmen and Portuguese, and kept the ship and all in her. She carried five iron guns, "4 brasse bases with 8 chambers of brasse belonging thereto, six cables, etc". Base, was the smallest piece of Ordnance breech-loaders, where two chambers, belonging to each base, ensured quick firing.

Likewise on Aug. 16, 1624 the council was told of one local man's experiences of Barbary pirates. "J. Daniell, of Sutton Pointz, being on board the *Prudence*, of Weymouth and Melcombe Regis in Sept., 1621, was taken with the rest of the crew by the Turks of Algeer, at which place they were made slaves. Eight or nine weeks ago he, eight other Englishmen, one Frenchman and two "Easterlings" were sent to sea in an Algerine Man-of-War, commanded by " three Hollonders," with one hundred Turks and Moors. At sea "the company (of Europeans?) did raise a mutiny;" with success it seems, for "thereupon they putt into Salley." Here nearly all the Turks landed and the ship again sailed. About twenty-five leagues from Scilly a " flibotter [flyboat or fluyt] of Holland" met them and the captain with his crew boarded the Algerian ship, bringing all the " flibotter's " ammunition put the English, French and Easterlings on board the latter vessel and left them. They sailed to England, landing at Minehead. He reports ten Men-of-War ready, or making ready at Sallee, for the English coasts. The Algerine ship in which he first sailed was intended for the Severn, to catch ships coming from "Bristol fair" and she took one Bristol ship while he was on board. He says that the Moors show Dutch colours, and that "the Hollanders shall hail such ships as they meet and they will keep the Turks close until they have gotten the advantage of the ships." The end comment was "(Altogether this evidence seems to show that the Dutch were often leagued with the Moorish Pirates)".

Feb 22 and Mar. 22, April 26 and May 27 1633
The Town Clerk is to ride to Exeter to consult with the Mayor, etc., respecting a letter from his Worship about Pirates.
Mr. Bernard Mychell, now in London, is to act for the Corporation in petitioning for a "speedy course . . . against the Turks" (Moors), in accordance with "a treaty at Exon . . . the last of February,"

An appeal to the council on 15th Oct 1634.
40s for a "newe shute [suit] of appell [apparel] for H. Browne, late captive in Turkey (Morroco)"

July, Aug Sept 1636
Draft Petition to the Privy Council from the Mayor, etc., of Exeter. Although the Deputy Lieutenants, etc., of Devon have addressed the Council about the "Turkishe Pyrates," the Mayor, etc., are compelled also to petition because lately several ships have been taken near Dartmouth, three others from "St Malloes and Moreles" [St Malo and Morlaix] hardly escaping. Hereby merchants are "utterly disheartened,"

and seamen will not serve, fearing slavery under those Mahumitans". The Merchants of Exeter and the neighbouring ports have deputed Mr. J. Crewkerne to wait on the Council with their Petition. July (?) 1636.

"Instructions given to Mr. J. Crewkerne for sollicitation of ye Lords of ye Counsell." Fifteen "sayle of Turks" were off Plymouth coast, and five in the Severn. Five vessels of Dartmouth had been attacked, and three taken; also the *Rose Garden* of Topsham, and several fishing boats with forty men. The returning "Newfoundlandmen" will be in great danger. It is asked that guard ships, with seamen in command, may ride at the "Barr-foot of Sally" with "nimble ships" on the Devon and Irish coasts, and that privateers may be commissioned.

A letter from Mr. Adam Bennett, Mayor of Exeter, to the Mayor of Weymouth and Melcombe Regis. Supposing that Weymouth Merchants have lost ships through the Turks, and wish to have " the Channell cleared of those rogues," he asks the Mayor of Weymouth to join in sending, and paying, Mr. Crewkerne to go to the Council. July 23, 1636.

Draft Petition to the King from the Merchants and Ship-owners of Exeter, Plymouth, Barnstaple, Dartmouth, Weymouth, Melcombe, Lyme, etc. Besides the "Tunnis and Argere" pirates, those of " Salleye " by the " nimbleness of their shipps," and by the help of almost two thousand "Ynglish and Yrish captives," have done thousands of pounds worth of damage to the petitioners, and have almost, stopped commerce. The three hundred English ships due from Newfoundland in Sept. and Oct. will be in great peril. Some speedy help is asked for, etc., etc. At Tutbury, Aug. 15, 1636, His Majesty answered that the Earl of Northumberland had orders to remedy the evil. To this another Petition is sent in reply recalling attention to the first one and offering to suggest a remedy. A hearing was promised. (See below.) A Petition nearly like the first to the Right Hon. and Right Rev. the Lord Chancellor, and a similar one to the Council. It may be noted that the proposed guard ships for Sallee were to be of three hundred tons, and that it is again pressed that "seamen onlye maye be imployed" to command.

At last action was taken and a Royal expedition in 1637 to the Moroccan port of Sallee managed to free 340 English seamen after a 5 months blockade of the port. Although Sallee had been dealt with the Algerines were even more active. Because of a lack of numbers and the wrong types of ships, Charles' Royal fleet was unable to clear the pirates from either the Channel or the Irish Sea.

From 1616 until 1642 a total of between 350 and 400 ships had been taken, including between 6,500 to 7,000 seamen, by the Barbary pirates. Before 1642, less than a quarter of those captured by the corsairs returned home, and one in five died in slavery.

Barbary pirates regularly raided the South West coast and in 1625 they had even taken prizes in Plymouth Harbour and carried off over 1,000 seamen with them. It was calculated that £1 million of damage was done to English shipping. The coastal village of East Looe had 80 men taken in slavery in a raid in 1626 followed in 1636 by the loss of another 79 men.

For the decade starting 1631, 14 Cornish ships were carried off to Algiers, this out of a total of 84 Cornish owned ships during that time. The fear of being captured and enslaved restricted the local Channel fishing and trading fleets not to mention the returning ships from the Newfoundland fish trade, and most ships were taken within 30 miles of the shore.

One of the consequences of this "barbaric" trade was that Charles I levied ship money tax to pay for his navy, possibly adding to the disillusionment of the populace and the subsequent Civil War.

As well as renegade Dutch manning the pirate ships and even becoming Admirals in the Barbary Navy, there were also renegade English and German seamen who lent their expertise. They not only improved the standard of the pirate ships in being able to sail to the Channel coast but the English knew the trade routes and where best to capture ships, the villages where they could take prisoners or the coves and the inlets where they could be victualled without question. Again Studland was said to have supplied them and apparently the inhabitants of Poole at one time called Swanage people Turks, because of their swarthy appearance.

In November 1614 Hugo or Hugh Clerck, Captain of a 19 gun pirate ship mistook three well armed Dutch escort ships and pirate hunters for merchantmen and despite several hours of fierce fighting and failing to out sail his pursuers he finally had to surrender. Clerck and his crew were taken to Holland, where he was arraigned in Amsterdam on 24 January 1615.

The Dutch archives describe them as Barbary Corsairs and Hugh Clerck as a Gentleman, Captain, originally from Southampton. Of the 51 crew, 21 were from England including Richard Rider, a trumpeter/bugler from Plymouth and skipper's mate Nicholas Somer from Dorchester. Of the others, only 5 could be classed as "Turks", 3 from Morocco, 1 Algerian and 1 North African. There were 4 from Scotland, 3 French, 3 Norwegians, 3 from the United Provinces, 1 from the Southern Netherlands, 1 from Ireland and 11 of unknown origin.

The Barbary slave trade was over a longer period and of the same scale as the transatlantic slave trade and once Napolean had been defeated was only finally finished in August 1816, some two hundred years after its commencement, when Admiral Pellew, who had already persuaded the Deys of Tunis and Tripoli to desist their slave trade of Europeans, sailed with a mixed fleet of Royal Naval ships and British privateers.

They were joined at Gibralter by a Dutch frigate squadron and corvette and thence bombarded the fortressed harbour of Algiers. Despite sustaining their own large loss of life, the fleet won the day as the inhabitants of Algiers surrendered the next morning after suffering tremendous losses from the sustained bombardment. Over 1,000 Christian slaves together with the British Consul were freed and the ransom money was repaid.

At last the sentiments in James Thomson's 1740 poem, later set to music in 1745 rang true.

Rule Britannia!
Britannia rule the waves.
Britons never, never, never shall be slaves.

Fortifications

In 1586 the ongoing hostilities between Spain and England meant that there was a real threat of invasion looming over the south coast of England. This fear was exacerbated in the July when two Liverpool men, Nic Abraham and J. Lambert, were interviewed in front of the Mayor of Weymouth and Melcombe Regis. They said they had been prisoners for 12 months in Bilbao where they had heard there were "700 sailles of Shippes, Gallis, Galiasses, Pynnesses and Pattasses," and a force of two hundred and eighty thousand men, all of which were said to be bound for England. In August, a Portuguese seaman had heard of a Spanish build up of 60 to 80 ships in Lisbon to carry 40-50,000 men to England.

This naturally lead to concern for the defence of the twin towns and several petitions were sent from the Mayor in July and August, the first to Sir Christopher Hatton, a favourite of Queen Elizabeth and also Vice Admiral for Dorset, followed by two further petitions to the Privy Council and a fourth to Lord Burleigh, the Lord High Treasurer. All four letters pointed out that a great proportion of the anchorage of Portland Roads lay outside the range of the guns firing from the twin castles at Portland and Sandesfoot, both of which had been built by Henry VIII to defend and command the sea between Weymouth and Portland. It was claimed that foreign ships could easily stay outside this area in Portland Roads and there was nothing to stop them then attacking shipping sailing in and out of the ports and attacking the twin towns themselves.

The Mayor and other dignitaries, called for two forts or platforms with ordnance to be built at the mouth of the ports, asking for ten or twelve guns with ammunition and a contribution towards their cost saying that Weymouth and Melcombe Regis would maintain them once built. They also asked for a "fytte store of ordynance". The towns seem to have got some of what they begged for as two such defences, one on the Nothe called Queen Elizabeth Fort and a Blockhouse fort on the shore of Melcombe Regis facing out into Weymouth Bay are mentioned in that period. It has been suggested that they were originally earthworks with some guns mounted on them to guard the river mouth from both sides.

Having survived the Spanish Armada of 1588 it was again the threat of war with Spain in 1625 that once more raised the same fears with the authorities. The council decided to build up the walls of the Blockhouse Fort with stone and construct "a Purbeck stone platform to be made for the two guns on the North [Nothe] Oct. 6th 1625" thus corroborating the view that the previous structures had indeed been earthworks. The Blockhouse Fort is described as a fort 45ft square & built of stone and it was located on the sea front of Melcombe Regis at the end of a lane called Blockhouse Lane, which still exists.

In June 1626 such was the perceived threat that the King of Spain was planning an invasion that the Mayors of Poole and Weymouth were called upon by the Privy Council to provide 250 men for the Navy, a third of them to be musketeers, as well as providing two ships of twelve guns each, so that the war could be taken to Spain. The extent of this demand is shown in the shipping survey of 1628 detailing that there were 176 sailors for Weymouth port and 111 for Melcombe Regis, while the 1641 Protestation Returns show there are only a total of 482 Weymouth & Melcombe Regis men of all trades over the age of 18. The fleet was to sail from Portsmouth 31st July 1626.

Writing to Weymouth and Melcombe Regis on July 7th 1626, the Privy Council recognised the weakness of the port and ordered the justices to fortify the harbour and town and "they are to fire the beacons, warn the neighbours and also send word to Court" in the event of an attack. An estimate is recorded later in 1626 "for eight guns, six cwt. of powder, twenty cwt. of shot etc, also one platform for W. side, and one for M. R. side, in all £200". Melcombe Regis offered £20 towards the cost while the Weymouth proportion is unrecorded.

Simpson's Map of Waymouth & Melcombe Regis 1626

William Simpson's map entitled "True description of the Situation of Waymouth and Melcombe Regis 1626" shows the whole area from the tip of Portland to Weymouth as far north as Radipole and from the Chesil Beach in the west, eastward towards White Nothe.

It seems likely that Simpson was engaged to make a detailed chart of Weymouth and Melcombe Regis showing its improved defences of 1625 and 1626; the latter improvement called for by the Privy Council's letter dated 7th July 1626, because of the imminent threat of war with Spain.

Three ships lie at anchor in Weymouth Bay just outside the ports of Weymouth and Melcombe Regis and are depicted flying the Union Flag from their mainmasts. This Union flag was introduced in April 1606 to display the union of the two thrones after James I came to the joint throne of England, Wales and Scotland in 1603. The flag was first used at sea for both civil and royal ships from 1606 but in 1634 it was decided that only Royal ships could fly the Union flag.

They also fly the early English flag on their on their ensign staffs, consisting of the English red cross of St George on a white background in the canton, and one ship with seven red horizontal stripes on a white background for the remainder of the flag, while the other two ships have a greater number of red stripes in their versions. The later American "Stars and Stripes" flag started as a version of this red striped flag.

In Portland Roads there are another three ships at anchor. Two display a red ensign on their stern jack, this being a red cross on white background (in the canton) with the rest of the ensign red. This was the English red ensign flown by both naval and merchant ships in the 17th century. There are accounts showing payment by the navy for such flags made at Chatham in1621. Scottish ships would display the Scottish ensign with the cross of St Andrew in the canton. One of the ships is also flying the Union flag on the top of its mizzenmast and both have pennants flying from mast tops and at the end of their yardarms.

One of the ships seems to have a white streak across the red field of their red ensign similar to the wavy white motif known as a heraldic wavy pile or "stream blazant" emanating from the corner of the canton. This wavy pile was certainly used in the Civil War by the armies to denote that it was a flag of a Sergeant Major. The ranking of flags was one of full colour for the Colonel of the regiment; a Lieutenant Colonel would have a canton of St Georges Cross on that coloured flag, while the Major (Sergeant was later dropped) had the wavy pile from the canton. The only other known use of this "major" flag on ships is possibly in the flags of Sir Francis Drake and his Major's flag has a similar wavy pile. Altogether Drake has six flags from Colonel, Lieutenant Colonel, (Sergeant) Major, down to third Captain for six companies of men. Were these for use on his ships or to be used with his men when fighting on land? At the start of his circumnavigation voyage in 1577 he left with 164 men in 5 ships and picked up a prize to make six ships.

To confuse matters Basil Ringrose wrote a journal of his piratical activities and mentions in 1679 being one of 327 buccaneers armed with fuzee, pistol, and hanger, who attacked Santa Maria, an inland town on the Coast of Darien near Portbello. The men were divided into seven companies "and each company marched behind a coloured flag led by Captains John Coxon, Peter Harris (two companies each), Bartholomew Sharp, Richard Sawkins, and Edmund Cook."

Certainly in earlier Tudor times ships' ensigns reflected the ensigns and colours used by army regiments on land. I contacted Tudor expert Professor David Loades who said: "by 1626 it was normal to display flags indicating the presence on board of soldiers, and that seems to be what was being done in this case. These were often flown on separate staves, to make them detachable for use ashore. So the use of a Sergeant Major's ensign would have indicated that a contingent of troops was carried, although whether for use at sea or on land would depend on the context of the voyage".

Did Drake fly them from his ships or were they used on land or both? The Weymouth maritime example may suggest Drake and others used them on their ships. Not only would the background colours identify the ship as within their convoy, the individual motif would identify which ship it was. It's also interesting to note in the Weymouth chart that the Union flag is being flown on different masts for different ships perhaps mirroring Admiral, Vice Admiral and Rear Admiral positions?

The stream blazant is later seen on many (Sergeant) Major flags on both sides during the English Civil War and coincidently Sir Thomas Tyldesley's Regiment of

Foote, of the English Civil War Society flew the Major company's flag with stream blazant during a re-enactment at Lulworth Castle in 2007.

The third ship at anchor has a red black blue tricolour on its stern jack and her stern is being fired on as a ship with union flag on mizzenmast and red ensign on her stern jack sails past. Another is sailing across her bow and this ship also has a Union flag on her foremast and red ensign on its stern jack. A sixth ship with only a red ensign showing on her stern jack is sailing up to her before the southerly wind.

Shown sailing northward, just north of Church Ope Cove, off the east coast of Portland is yet another ship with a union flag on her mainmast and red ensign on her stern jack. At Portland Bill there is a ship displaying a red ensign on her stern jack rounding the Bill west to east and to the east of Weymouth is a ship sailing westward flying a blue flag from her mainmast. This could be a Royal Naval ship with an Admiral of the Blue's flag as it is being flown from the mainmast whereas a Vice or Rear Admiral of the Blue would fly his flag from one of the other appropriate masts. The lack of Fleur de Lys would seem to rule out it being a Frenchman.

To the south east of Portland Bill there is an engagement between a ship with Union flag on mainmast and also a red ensign flying on her stern jack and a ship with the Cross of Burgundy flown from her mainmast. The Cross of Burgundy is a feathered red diagonal cross on a white background and this flag was used by Spain as a naval ensign from 1506 until 1701 so this is a depiction of a Spanish ship engaged with a British ship.

Several of the union flags are crossed through with black as if a child has later coloured the map in and this may account for the tricolour being red **black** and blue on the ship being fired on in Portland Roads. Is it originally a red, white and blue horizontal tricolour with the white now crossed through with black, in which case it would denote a Dutch ship from the province of Holland?

The castles at Sandesfoot and Portland are shown firing as are two points at the Nothe Fort and there are three points firing from the Blockhouse Fort on the shore of Melcombe Regis.

The Battle of Portland in the first Anglo Dutch War did not occur until 1653 when Blake defeated the Dutch and the threat in the early 1600s was from the French, however both the Spanish and the Dutch were seen as other possible enemies at the time and it is probable that Simpson was sent to record the improved defences of the last two years and obviously depicts what will happen to any enemy be they French, Dutch or Spanish.

For good measure Simpson has included cartouches of two double-ended boats off Chesil Beach, which appear to be lerrets fishing using seine nets confirming their use at this time as mentioned in the local archive. He has even drawn the ubiquitous sea monster off Chesil Beach in West Bay.

Portland is very well detailed showing many track ways, which have become the roads of today and settlements at Chesil, Easton, Wide Street, Reforne, Weston and Southwell. Two stone piers are shown on the east coast of the island with a quarry above and two windmills between Easton and Weston. St Andrews Church is depicted with a tower and Church Ope Cove with the rocky shore before the landslip. As well as Portland Castle there is a signal station on high ground at the site of the Verne.

The narrows between the sandbanks at Smallmouth called "Passage" show Passage House and the rope ferry with boat, a settlement at Wyke with its prominent towered church and adjacent housing at Lanehouse and Belfield but the map shows how sparse the country was between the ferry and Weymouth, an advantage for the Royalists when they later attacked from Portland. The waters of the Fleet with the various coves run from south to north and the reddish grey bank of Chesil Beach bounds the western edge except for the two examples of a lerrets seine fishing off Fleet and off Passage House.

Settlements at Radipole (with the square towered church of St Anns), Chickerell and Fleet are shown and Weymouth has harbour side dwellings in a strip from Town Gate and Love Lane in the west, around the Ope and east along the harbour towards the Nothe with the Weymouth Chapel on the hill above the harbour. Across in Melcombe Regis the dwellings are more in a square area bounded by the sea and river. The bridge linking the towns has a curve to it. St Mary's Chapel is prominent as is the jetty and the Blockhouse Fort firing its guns. To the north of the town is a windmill with the expanse of the "Backwater" from Preston Beach to Radipole and back down to the wall across the Marsh.

The 1641 Populations of South Dorset villages.

An Act of Parliament in 1641 required all males aged 18 years and over to declare themselves members of the Protestant faith - those who refused were assumed to be Catholics. According to the Protestation returns of February 1641/2, the male over-18 population of the towns and villages in South Dorset was as follows: -

Abbotsbury	244
Melcombe Regis	207
Weymouth	175
Portland	147
Portesham	129
Preston & Sutton Poyntz	123
Upwey	103
Wyke Regis	89
Broadway	48
Chickerell	40
Langton Herring	38
Fleet	32
Radipole	31

Not a vast population even when adding females and under 18s, and certainly not militarily, as some of these males would be too old or infirm to fight, but the numbers give an idea of what size of military force was required to either take or pillage the towns and how easily they could be intimidated by a larger force into capitulating later without a fight.

The twin ports of Weymouth and Melcombe Regis had flourished since the Norman Conquest because of the resulting trade with France, and in particular, Normandy. In 1347 when Edward III called for ports to send ships to support the siege of Calais the combined ports of Weymouth and Melcombe Regis supplied 15 vessels and 264 men, third in the list behind Dartmouth and Plymouth but ahead of all other south west ports like Exmouth, Poole, Wareham and Lyme.

However in a short space of time both ports had declined. Both were later to suffer destruction from raids by the French but the main cause was the Black Death in 1348. It entered England via a ship from Italy coming into the port of Melcombe Regis. The subsequent death rate in the country as a whole was 2 out of every 5 inhabitants but in Melcombe and its surrounding area it was 3 out of every 4 in the first year. Not only did the population drop dramatically but also no ship would want to sail into these unhealthy ports. Even if they had, did the ports still have the manpower to unload them?

It's hardly a coincidence, after such a drop in population, that first the French in 1377 razed Melcombe to the ground, setting the houses and ships on fire while the men were in church in Radipole and then in 1386 it was Weymouth's turn to find its warehouses on fire and its vessels sunk with Portland stone blocks, while its men attended church at Wyke. In 1432 came an appeal from Melcombe, "To our soverayne Lord the King, plese it to your Royall Majestie that your port of Melcombe is suffering from scarste of people to resist your enemies." It wasn't until the 17th Century that trade built up again when there were 57 regular trading vessels coming into the ports in the early 1630s.

The size of Weymouth and Melcombe Regis can also be gauged from the following documents.

Rents of the burgages, tenements & lands in Waymouth taken the 18th Day of June 1617

In the East side of Hope	14 properties
In the West side of Hope	35 properties
South side of the High Street	68 properties
North side of the High Street	44 properties
North side of West Street	25 properties
South side of West Street	19 properties
In St Nicholas Street	22 properties
In Newberry	6 properties
In the south side of Francis Street	8 properties

Total of 241 properties

Rents of the burgages, tenements & lands in Melcombe Regis taken the 6th Day of August 1617

In the South part of St Edmund Street	10 properties
In the North part of St Edmund Street	14 properties
In the West Street	7 properties
In the West part of St Nicholas Street	12 properties
In the East part of St Nicholas Street	2 properties
In the West part of St Thomas Street	24 properties
In the East part of St Thomas Street	25 properties
In the West part of St Mary Street	30 properties
In the East part of St Mary Street	35 properties
In the West part of Maiden Street	4 properties
In the East part of Maiden Street	25 properties
In the East side of New Street	19 properties
In East Street	10 properties

Total of 217 properties

Simpson's map of 1626 shows the disbursement of each town's properties, a narrow built-up strip along the harbour side for Weymouth and a more square area for Melcombe Regis, confined by the sea and the river.

Dutch Trade with Spain

When trade with the New World started, the Spanish port used by ships to supply the goods to the new colonies and to receive the fleets bringing back the treasure was Seville, on the river Guadalquivir, some 40 miles inland from the coast. The advantage of Seville was it had a good and easily reached hinterland and was not exposed to enemy attack as was the somewhat open bay of Cadiz, which was set within high cliffs and thus neither had an easy access inland.

Any ships setting out for the New World from the alternative northern Spanish ports of Bilbao etc., would have had a far from easy voyage sailing down the coast to the Seville area in order to pick up the favourable trade winds to take them across to the New World, so Seville it was. The Casa de Contratación governed who supplied what goods to the New World and they decreed that there would be no export of gold or silver from Spain. The bullion coming back was to be invested in Spain only and only Spanish goods would be supplied to the colonies.

Because of the size of this trade and the fortunes in bullion coming into the city, Seville became one of the busiest and most populated cities in Europe. Agricultural produce from the fertile regions of Andalusia was favoured over other regions of Spain and there was a general migration of people from the north of Spain to the south. The banks of the River Guadalquivir from Seville down as far as Sanlucar de Barrameda at the mouth of the river were just one big port and over a time the region became denuded of trees as the timber had either been used for ship building, supplies for the maritime trade such as barrels or just used as fuel to keep the growing population warm in the winter.

Ships for the New World voyages were built in northern Spain as well as in Seville, and as the trade with the New World increased so did the need for bigger ships but these bigger ships when fully laden could not get over the sand bar at Sanlucar nor negotiate the silting-up river Guadalquivar to reach Seville. As a consequence ships would go to one of the three ports on the coast to be fully loaded or partially unloaded, however the bullion was still to be loaded and unloaded at Sanlucar de Barrameda.

In order to keep control of the trade the Casa de Contratación sent representatives down to the three coastal ports of Sanlucar de Barrameda, El Puerto de Santa Maria and Cadiz but the situation certainly made the possibility of smuggling goods in and out far easier for the merchants and boat owners than before.

In 1545 during the war against France, Robert Reneger a trader turned privateer of Southampton and said to be a forerunner of Francis Drake, seized a French ship as a prize and took her into a nearby Spanish port. He readily accepted that he would have to forego that part of the cargo that was Spanish but he soon realised that the Spanish were going to take his prize completely. As he sailed out of that Spanish port he determined to right the wrong and searched the nearby shipping lanes until he spied a Spanish ship homeward bound. He caught up with her and boarded her as a prize. She turned out to be the *San Salvador* from Hispaniola with a cargo of 124 chests of sugar, 140 hides and a large quantity of gold, in all the cargo was worth 7,243,075 marevedis (26,629 pieces of eight or about £7,000).

Reneger only wanted what was due to him to recompense for his French prize taken by the Spanish and was willing to give the Spanish Captain a receipt for that amount and leave the rest of the cargo untouched. The Spaniard hastened to say that it wasn't required and implored Reneger not to mention anything about the gold for it soon became apparent that the cargo of gold was smuggled gold, for which the Spanish crown's quinto (the one fifth tax) had not been paid.

Large scale smuggling of specie was later confirmed when Thomas Violet, an alderman and goldsmith of London, wrote in a report to Parliament in 1650 "It is well known to all merchants that trade from Spain that one third part of their gold and silver at least is never registered; which gold and silver is consigned to particular merchants for the avoiding of the King's duty before it comes within the bar at St. Lucar (and generally now is sent for Holland)."

Now that some of the smuggled bullion coming into Spain could be exported surreptitiously by way of buying goods from abroad, the trade with other suppliers built up. Spanish goods were either too expensive or they just couldn't supply what was needed and wanted by the colonies in the New World. As they had previously been part of the Spanish Empire the Dutch had strong, almost monopolistic, trade links with Spain and during the peace from 1609 to 1621 the Dutch supplied a lot of goods indirectly to the New World via Seville.

In 1641 even though they had been at war with Spain since 1621, (a war which was to last until 1647), and the Dutch Spanish inter-trade had diminished from the 400 to 500 ships a year, there was still a need for supplies to be taken into Spain. The Dutch circumvented their embargo by using Hamburg ships to carry the goods they used to bring from Northern Europe and from their almost monopoly of the Baltic trade taken from Denmark and Sweden. Now of course the English could trade with impunity to Seville because since 1606 they had been at peace with Spain.

Thus there would have been a surplus of Dutch shipping available because of the loss of the Spanish trade. At first the Golden Grape is said to be owned by Dutch Merchants then when it is sailed to Dover it is suggested that an English Merchant there has bought it. Either way it allowed the Golden Grape to be loaded with goods from Holland and Dover to ship to Cadiz. The Dutch still had the contacts with the Spanish merchants and had the goods from the Dutch East Indies that were wanted in Spain and the New World. Two hundred barrels of pepper bound for a merchant at Sanlucar de Barrameda were loaded on board the Golden Grape at Amsterdam.

By 1640 both England and Holland were great sea faring powers with growing overseas trade and colonies of their own so they had a ready supply of exotic goods that were wanted by the Spanish colonies, spices from the Dutch East Indies, ivory from Africa and India and they had the organisations and fabricators in place to supply the everyday goods required in the colonies at a substantially better price than the same Spanish sourced goods.

Almost all naval stores had to be imported from northern Europe by Spain and that was one reason why the Golden Grape was loading ships blocks at Dover, hewn from the forests of timber available in England and made in the very factories that supplied the English Navy.

English merchants had set up the East India Company in 1600. The United Provinces setting up the Dutch East India Company, which swiftly outstripped both the Portuguese and the English in the trade with Asia, followed this in 1602. The Chinese especially, only wanted one thing from the Europeans in return for Chinese goods and that was silver and in Asia the value ratio of silver to gold was 5 ounces of silver equal to 1 ounce of gold whereas in Europe it was 15 to 1, so the same silver coin bought 3 times as much in Asia as in Europe. The major source from which to get this much needed supply of silver was from Spain and this was how the Spanish piece of eight reales became the first worldwide currency, even though no silver or gold was officially allowed out of Spain.

The Dutch had tried to encroach into the New World's trade by force but Spain had managed to fight both them and the English off and keep their monopoly to their colonies in the New World. The Dutch found that legal trade with Spain sometimes brought better dividends than just force. They had started the first European bank in Amsterdam in 1609, and this accepted bills of exchange, cash and bullion deposits and it also transferred funds between its customers. The warring between Spain and England was finished when they signed the peace treaty of 1604 when England agreed not to support the Dutch rebels, to be more tolerant of English Catholics and to allow free passage to Spanish ships in the English Channel, the only point in England's favour was an easing of trade between England and Spain.

This was followed in 1609 with the end of war between Spain and the Dutch United Provinces and again Spain insisted on its unalienable right to its monopoly with the New World and both the Dutch and English had reluctantly agreed to this in both instances, however they insisted that this did not apply to lands unoccupied as yet by the Spanish.

In the depositions given by the crew of the Golden Grape about the voyage there is a great deal of detail about the Dutch Merchants, the ladings in Holland, then in England, the exchange of goods in Cadiz and what was sold to who and who loaded what cargo there for the return voyage. However as soon as the diversion along the coast from Cadiz into Sanlucar de Barrameda is mentioned the crew say what goods are loaded but when asked by whom they all say "but by whom I remembreth not". Hardly surprising as this part of the trade was undoubtedly that of the supply of smuggled goods and bullion in exchange for the smuggled pepper.

Under the Spanish Laws prohibiting the export of bullion and other trading laws, boatmen or ship owners caught smuggling were to lose their vessels. Merchants who claimed innocence of any smuggling of the highly valued goods concealed in loads of less valuable goods were to lose all the goods, as well as any animal carrying it. When smuggled goods were found, first the duty was taken then the rest of the value of the goods was divided, with a quarter going to the accuser, and another quarter to the royal officials, and finally one half to the royal treasury.

One of the factors for bringing an end to the war between Holland and Spain was the detrimental effect on trade between both countries. In not allowing a free trade between the European countries and themselves, Spain had instigated the decline of their empire. In the meantime both the Dutch and the English had started to supply goods directly to the Spanish colonies and had taken their chances of avoiding the Guarda de Costas (ships blockading the Caribbean ports) set up by Spain to deter such trade with foreigners. It would not be long before England set up a base in the Caribbean on the island of Jamaica to both trade with and attack Spanish colonies in the New World.

Chapter 2 The *Golden Grape*

Voyage of the *Golden Grape*

The merchant sailing ship *Golden Grape* was owned by at least four partners. All were Dutchmen in the United Province of Holland: Wesseilhen Norman, the brothers Derrick and Henrick Doomers, both merchants of Amsterdam, and Derrick Peters Redhoost of Pamarent [Purmerend, just north of Amsterdam].

There in Amsterdam on the fifteenth of March 1641 (Gregorian calendar for all dates given in the United Provinces, which were 10 days ahead of the Julian Calendar adhered to in England) Norman together with Cornelius Van Berkham the steersman of the *Golden Grape* began recruiting a crew for a forthcoming voyage to Cadiz. That day they took on Michael Hatherwick as bosun. During April the two of them signed Robert Coast as gunner, Norman giving Coast two months pay in advance. Later that month Redhoost and the other owners appointed John Smyth as bosun's mate, giving him one month's pay in hand. By the end of April they had a crew of sixteen and had begun loading the *Golden Grape* with cordage, two hundred barrels of pepper, barrels of nails, tallow and ship's rigging blocks.

On the fourth of May the *Golden Grape*, under the command of Cornelius Van Berkham, set sail from Texel (the Frisian Island outlet to the North Sea from Amsterdam) bound for Dover where she was to take on more cargo and also an experienced Master and new owner, John Holding, for the rest of the voyage to Cadiz and back. On reaching Dover, Van Berkham was confronted by the agents for the owners. The agents, two local merchants named Garratt Vanteen and Edward Peters, explained that Holding was not at home but they had managed to obtain the services of Thomas Redwood instead. According to Van Berkham, Vanteen and Peters then became the substitute owners of the *Golden Grape* but Redwood gave London merchant Robert Garland and Dover merchant Peters as the owners.

The term "not at home" probably meant that Holding had taken the Captaincy of another ship, for the *Golden Grape* remained at Dover for three weeks. During that time, David Hampson, another merchant of Dover, loaded aboard the *Golden Grape* more tallow, pepper, cordage, and blocks, together with some parcels of copper. Some of the crew who had sailed from Holland left the ship, but Redwood was able to recruit more men and actually increased the number of crew to twenty. Richard Rich, from Barnstable, went as gunner's mate, and George Allin and William Phillis as sailors. Phillis, a small man known to his comrades as 'Little Will', was servant to Henry Wallop of Dover but while the master was away the mistress had shipped him aboard the *Golden Grape*.

In mid June they set sail for Cadiz and after an uneventful voyage reached their destination where all the goods save the pepper were unloaded and delivered to Martin Laderoon De Gavarre. Spanish and Flemish merchants of that port then reloaded the ship. Amongst these, Martin Laderoon De Gavarre and Anthony Swaase together had a thousand and nineteen barrels of raisins and three hundred and ninety six jars of oil put aboard for consignment to a Monsieur Careiles and other merchants of Havre De Grace [Le Havre], in France. Albertus Martin shipped two hundred and thirty four barrels of raisins, consigned to Garratt Vanteen and Edward Peters of Dover. De Gavarre later put two bags of red wool aboard and a young merchant named Cornelius Williamson Heddah had twelve butts of sherry sack loaded. Eight of these were for a Merchant of Roane [Rouen] but four were for disposal by the master and the gunner. John Jacob Fabiansa, son of an Amsterdam merchant had four butts of sherry sack loaded aboard for his own and his father's account. Lastly the gunner Robert Coast had three pipes of tent, brought on board for him. Whilst at Cadiz, they took on John Pierce as a sailor.

The *Golden Grape* left Cadiz Roads and sailed back along the coast a short distance and anchored outside the bar of Sanlucar de Barrameda. Two boats were sent out to them and the pepper (the last of the cargo shipped aboard at Dover and in Holland) was transferred from the *Golden Grape* to these boats. However it is the goods that these boats brought out for loading aboard the *Golden Grape* that is of most interest. For as well as two bags of red wool and forty three skeins of taffeta; two bags of silver plate, a bag containing five hundred pistoles (doubloon coins) of gold, another a mixture of pistoles and pieces of eight (silver coins); an unspecified number of bags of pieces of eight, a peg of silver and a loaf of silver were all loaded aboard. Surprisingly, considering the details given regarding the rest of the cargo shipped at Cadiz, nobody could remember who loaded the bullion and to whom it was consigned. Had this money been smuggled into Spain from the bullion from the treasure fleets returning from the New World and was it now being used to buy foreign goods to send back out? For whatever reason, four un-named passengers, who were all Dutchmen, sailed aboard the *Golden Grape*. Were they the real Dutch owners?

From Sanlucar de Barrameda, the *Golden Grape* sailed for Havre de Grace but sailing up-Channel she encountered extremely foul weather, and sometime before noon on Saturday the eleventh of December 1641, she was driven ashore on the Chesil Beach near the village of Wyke. During the wreck seven men and boys were drowned and one other later died after being taken to Fleet House.

The *Golden Grape* must have been driven high enough up the beach for the crew, and later the local inhabitants, to be able to re-board her relatively safely for about four days. It is stated by witnesses that she was wrecked opposite Bridge at Wyke and today Little Bridge Farm still exists there, just west of Camp Road on the hill overlooking the Chesil Beach. However the original named Little Bridge Farm has moved to what was called Foxholes and the previous location is now called Lower Bridge. Bridge is an old place name as it is mentioned in the Doomsday Book stating that there were fishermen there.

If you had followed the track directly below these farmsteads to the Fleet there was also a crossing point, the shortest across the Fleet waters to Chesil Beach. The crossing point on this mainland shore was a sandy bay called Locket's Hole and was probably a natural depression in the slope of the bank rather than a steep cliff and it was where the Wyke fishermen kept their trows either tied down on the bank or tied to wooden poles driven into the bed of the Fleet. Trows were the local flat-bottomed boats designed to glide over the mudflats of the Fleet's waters and are still the best boats for use in the Fleet. Since the 1930s Locket's Hole has been buried under the Army Bridging Hard alongside the Fleet.

Although there is no bridge to be seen anywhere, the lane now called Bridge Lane, runs along the top of the hill, whereas to the south east, on the other track originally known as Red Lane but now called Camp Road, there is a deep ravine, which used to flood badly according to the local farmer and which now has a large diameter drainage pipe under the road to take the water away, though flooding in the nearby field still takes place. On the old map there is a stream marked running from the land south of Bridge Lane across Camp Road down to the Fleet at Green Lane or Pirates Lane. So the high ground (Bridge Lane) was a natural **land bridge** from Wyke to the shortest crossing point on the Fleet.

No fisherman would want to cross a swampy section in the bottom of a vale when they could walk on high draining ground down to the Fleet waters. The end of Camp Road has a steep cliff down to the waters so they would have had to traverse to the sandy bay of Locket's Hole after the swampy section in any case.

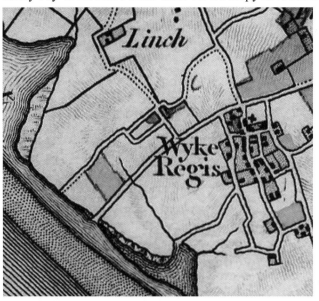

An extract from an original 1811 map confirms a stream in the ravine, starting halfway between Bridge Lane and Camp Road and then crossing what is now Camp Road and which carries on until it reaches the cove at the bottom of Pirates Lane or Green Lane. The map also shows the way the track (Bridge Lane) runs down from the present day Value warehouse site, diverts north-westward to join Cockles Lane and then along the crest of the high ground before dropping down to Locket's Hole on the Fleet shore.

The Wreck.

The facts about the voyage, the wrecking and the salvage of the *Golden Grape* come from the High Court of the Admiralty Inquiry held at Melcombe Regis in the Borough of Weymouth and Melcombe Regis from the 10th January 1641(2) until 28th March 1642. A total of 343 witnesses gave their depositions to the Court and they mentioned another 204 people. Of the witnesses 301 were on the beach at some time between Saturday 11 December 1641 and the following Wednesday.

On the 12th January 1641(2) the first witness, Arthur Grey, an innkeeper of Wyke Regis, deposed that he was on the seaward side on the beach when the *Golden Grape* was driven ashore and cast away where he stood and he looked on until the company of the ship came ashore, at which time some of the company wanted him to help them to a place of shelter for they were very cold, wet and faint. He offered to take them over the Fleet [a stretch of water between the beach and the mainland] in his boat and to guide them to his house in Wyke Regis where they might refresh themselves. At this, about five of the ship's company got into his boat and he carried them across. But before they climbed into the boat the steersman gave Grey a peg of silver to carry for him, which he did. After they landed on the mainland he continued to carry the peg of silver in the company of the crewmen to his house in Wyke Regis where the men and about four or five others of the ship's company stayed that night.

He then said that the steersman had delivered a bag of money to him and that an Irishman, one of the company of the ship then also delivered another bag of money to his wife and that the ship's Master also brought yet another bag of money into his house and delivered it to him. The money together with the peg of silver, (everything he had received) he then delivered to the Vice Admiral when it was called for, without taking out any part of it. He said that another of the company of the ship brought to him an old brass kettle and a copper spoon or ladle, which he still has. Grey said that he saw another of the crew whose name was William Phillis, but who was commonly called Little Will, bring a bag of coin into his boat, which Phillis took out again when they landed, but what Little Will did with it afterwards he doesn't know as before Will got to Grey's house, he had gone into the house of one Feaver of Bridge, within the parish of Wyke Regis. Finally he declared that he had not nor had in his custody nor in the custody of any other for his use any other or more of the money, plate, coin, goods or provisions of the ship except those items already declared, and one hundred pieces of eight which he kept for the diet, fire and entertainment of nine men of the *Golden Grape*'s company for three nights and four days.

Susannah Grey said that the bags had been put into a chest next to the bed in the chamber where the Master of the ship lay but by whom she didn't know.

Later that night with the Master's knowledge the same bags were taken out of the chest by her, and delivered to her husband who took them away and put them in another place, but she did not know where. A peg of silver was also brought out, but she never saw it again until it and, as far as she could remember, all the money was delivered to the Vice Admiral.

She also said that the trumpeter of the *Golden Grape* brought a great quantity of coin into her house, about half a peck she thought (equivalent to about 60 pieces of eight), which he took away with him again. She had no other coin or goods from the ship except for an old brass kettle, a ladle, and a hundred pieces of eight, which her husband kept in return for diet, fire, entertainment and lodging of nine of the ship's company for <u>four</u> days <u>and</u> nights.

Robert Coast the gunner said that after the *Golden Grape* was cast away and before she was quite broken to pieces, the boatswain's mate of the ship went aboard twice, and the first time brought out some gold pistoles (2 escudos coins or doubloons) in his hat, which he gave to Cornelius Van Berkham the steersman, who put them into Coast's pocket, saying "keep these and we will divide them between us". The boatswain's mate went aboard a second time and brought more pistoles of gold ashore in his hat, part of which he gave to Coast (they came to one hundred and five pistoles) and the boatswain's mate kept the rest for himself. Coast said that he later delivered all those pistoles that he had received from the boatswain's mate to Mr. Strode of Portland, who then delivered the same to the Vice Admiral.

Michael Hatherwick boatswain of the *Golden Grape* said that when the Golden Grape was cast on shore in the West Bay near the Isle of Portland, she was broken to pieces and the greatest part of the goods, moneys, plate, and merchandize lost except that salved by the country people nearby. He also said that he saved a small bag of pieces of eight (which had been opened before) in which were one hundred and twenty six pieces of eight, which John Peirce, George Allin, William Phillis and he shared between them, he had fifty one pieces, the other three each had twenty five pieces. He then claimed that the trumpeter of the ship later took out of the bag thirty-one pieces of eight leaving Hatherwick only twenty pieces. He had bought himself some clothes, and had spent the rest since coming to Weymouth.

In his initial statement to the inquiry, sailor Richard Rich of Barnstable, Devon, said that he was one of the company of the late ship called the *Golden Grape* and that in May he was shipped at Dover by the Master of the ship, Thomas Redwood, to go as Gunner's Mate in a voyage for Cadiz in Spain. When the *Golden Grape* was wrecked he saved a bag of money, which he gave to the ship's Master on the beach. After leaving the beach and travelling towards Weymouth, the boatswain gave him seven pieces of eight, and while following certain Dutchmen (who had been on board the ship as passengers) along the way he was given another five or six pieces of eight, which all went on clothes and other necessaries.

Walter Pyedwell, a Weymouth surgeon, said that shortly after the *Golden Grape* was cast away the ship's surgeon came to the "sign of Starre" in Weymouth where Pyedwell lived. (A reference in 1659 saying "the Chapel stairs near the sign of the Star" means the Star was near the foot of the steps leading to the Chapel fort). The surgeon bought a coat from him for six pieces of eight, which he took from his pocket. Pyedwell then said that in one of the rooms at the Star, Richard Rich, one of the company of the *Golden Grape,* took a bag of money from his breeches and counted out about sixty pieces of eight onto a table in front of him and Joane Bond, a maidservant in that house. When Richard Rich was re-examined he said he had forgotten to say in his previous statement that he had received from the surgeon of the ship about thirteen or fourteen pounds in pieces of eight, which he later gave to Mary Paine to keep for him.

Testifying on the 15 January 1641(2), Mary Paine of Melcombe Regis, a young single woman said that one day last week Richard Rich, one of the company of the *Golden Grape,* did deliver to her the bag of silver and gold, which is now produced to the commissioners, and did entreat her to keep it for him, but she said that the money Rich gave her was all in silver, and that she exchanged with the surgeon of the ship so much silver as amounted to the value of the gold now in the bag, it being in all between thirteen and fourteen pounds, consisting of forty six pieces of eight, a pistole of gold, and three pounds and nine shillings in other gold, which the Vice Admiral now took into his custody. She thought that the reason why Rich delivered the money to her was because there was some former acquaintance between them in Dover.

John Swetnam of Melcombe Regis, a woollen draper, said that about three weeks ago [the last week of December] he sold about five pounds worth of woollen cloth to the wife of Bartholomew Paine of Melcombe Regis, which she paid for in pieces of eight. Shortly after, either she or Mary Paine her daughter, exchanged with him about thirty or forty shillings in pieces of eight for English white money and gold but he said that he did not give her any pistole of gold, or any other foreign gold, only English money.

John Curteis of Melcombe Regis said that the mother of Mary Paine of Melcombe Regis paid him about three pieces of eight for making a cloak and other garments for both Richard Rich and Mary Paine.

James Smyth one of the company of the *Golden Grape*, said that he was shipped in Amsterdam by Derrick Redhoosd, and three other Dutchmen (whose names he didn't know); the owners of the *Golden Grape*; to go as boatswain's mate in her for Cadiz in Spain. One of the owners paid him more than one month's pay in advance. They sailed from Amsterdam on the fourth of May for Dover where Thomas Redwood was shipped by a factor (name of Peters) on behalf of the owners to go as Master of the ship for the voyage. They sailed outside the rocky bar of Sanlucar where two boats brought certain silver plate, bullion, and coin, which were loaded on board the ship, but he did not know who sent the same aboard or whither it was consigned.

Out of the stranded ship Smyth took six bags of coin and a peg of silver, which he threw ashore to the steersman and the gunner of the ship, and then went ashore himself. But soon after, the steersman and gunner wanted him to go aboard again, which he did, and then threw another three small bags of coin ashore to them. In the steerage room he picked up some pistoles of gold which he put in his cap and carried ashore with him, and delivered them to the steersman (but he wasn't sure how many).

The steersman gave them to the gunner to keep, willing him and Smyth to be silent and to say nothing of them and they would share the same between them. Again the steersman and gunner wanted him to go aboard the ship once more and to save as much more of the gold as he could find there, which he did, and brought them some more pistoles of gold (but again he didn't know how many) but he delivered them to the steersman once more, who likewise gave the same to the gunner to keep; only Smyth kept twenty one pistoles for himself, but after about three days, he delivered them to the Vice Admiral.

Smyth also said that while he was aboard the ship he took up sixteen pieces of eight which he found loose in the steerage, and which he also kept to himself, and that after he reached Weymouth, William Bushel, one of the ship's company, gave him forty more pieces of eight, with which he bought clothes and other necessaries. He stated that he still had seventeen pistoles of gold left in his custody and ten pieces of eight not yet spent, which he was ready to deliver.

John Peirce one of the company of the *Golden Grape* said that when he was at Cadiz, he was there shipped by Thomas Redwood Master of the Golden Grape to go as a sailor in her for the voyage to Dover. When the ship was wrecked on Chesil Beach he was very sick at that time, and because of that he took none of the gold, silver plate, money, coin or other goods or commodities out of the ship, but said that the cook of the ship had a long bag full of pieces of eight, and the surgeon another; the boatswain yet another, out of which the boatswain gave him twenty five pieces of eight. He spent part of the money on clothes for himself, and with the rest he paid a Mr. Gibson, a surgeon of Weymouth, for medicine, costing him about fifteen shillings.

William Phillis, one of the company of the *Golden Grape*, stated that he was servant to Henry Wallopp of Dover, but while his Master was away in May, his Mistress shipped him aboard the ship to go as a sailor for Cadiz. After the ship struck, but before she was all split, Phillis was ordered and directed by the Master to go aboard again, and once there he went into the cabin and picked up four or five bags of coin, which he threw off the ship to the Master and to some others of the company of the ship who were then ashore, after which (the ship breaking up more and more and Phillis fearing for his life) he quickly got to the shore, where he picked up a long bag of coin intending to carry it to a nearby village called Wyke Regis, but being weary and weak and on the way meeting with Owen Gibbons of Wyke with a horse, he delivered the said bag to Gibbons entreating him to carry it there for him, which Gibbons did, but to whose house he carried it Phillis didn't know.

Phillis also picked up in the ship about ten or twelve loose pieces of eight, which he put into the linings of a cap he was wearing, before putting it on again. While going towards Wyke Regis in the company of the Master of the ship (and the Master complaining of a pain in his head) Phillis put his cap on the Master's head, which the Master wore to Wyke Regis where he took off the cap from his head, and (feeling the money there) took out some of the pieces and left only five or six pieces in it and gave it back to Phillis who had since spent them. The boatswain of the ship had a bag of coin, out of which he gave Phillis twenty-five pieces of eight and with part of that he bought himself clothes to wear and other necessaries, the remainder he had also spent.

George Allen, one of the crew of the Golden Grape said that in May, he was shipped at Dover by the steersman of the ship, to go as a sailor in her for Cadiz. When the Golden Grape was forced ashore and broken to pieces, Allen barely escaped with his life. Afterwards as he was going towards Wyke Regis, the ship's cook gave him a bag of coin containing two hundred and thirty three pieces of eight, which he gave to the Master of the ship. On the way, while still going along on the beach, he saw the four Dutchmen, who had come on board as passengers, sharing a bag of coin between them and he demanded a part so they gave him six pieces of eight. Afterwards the boatswain of the ship gave him twenty-five pieces out of a bag of coin, and with part of that he later bought clothes and other necessaries for himself, and the remainder he had since spent.

Thomas Byrd the cook of the *Golden Grape* said that after the ship was cast on shore on the beach in the West Bay near the Isle of Portland, he with the boatswain, and the carpenter of the ship went aboard the wreck from where he took and threw ashore about six bags of coin, but then seeing a country man in a blue jerkin (whose name he didn't know), pick up one of the bags, he stopped throwing any more ashore, but carried two bags ashore with him on his back, but after a while, he was not able to carry both so gave one whole bag to an Irishman, one of the crew of the ship, who carried it away, but what he did with it Byrd didn't know. He carried the remaining bag to the town of Weymouth with all the money in it save for about forty pieces of eight, which he gave to certain people (unknown) to carry the bag for him. After being at Weymouth he delivered two hundred pieces of eight which were in the bag to the Master of the ship, and that was all the money that he had left after he had bought himself clothes to wear, of which he was in great need, and which cost him about three pounds.

Catharine Langar of Weymouth a widow said that Thomas Bird the cook of the *Golden Grape* came to her house in Weymouth the same night that the ship was cast away and took out and counted on the table in her house a great many pieces of eight, which John Senior's man of Melcombe Regis weighed. (John Fildew and Joseph Manders were also present). When the Master of the ship came to her house the next day he took the money from the cook and gave it to her to look after and shortly afterwards took it back from her again. She also said that the surgeon of the ship paid her three pieces of eight for his diet while he lay at her house, and gave her another piece of eight for attending to him; and that Rich one of that company had also paid her three pieces of eight for his diet, and gave her another piece of eight for attending him, and that one William, another of the company had done the same, and that was all the money that she received or had from any of the company of that ship.

James Cornish of Weymouth a woolen draper deposed that the day after the

Golden Grape was cast away Thomas Redwood, late Master of the ship, came to him (as he was and is one of the Constables of the Town) and desired him to search for monies taken out of the ship, whereon Cornish went with him to the house of Catharine Langar, a widow in Weymouth, where they found the cook of the ship from whom they took sixteen hundred reales [equivalent to 200 pieces of eight], which the Master had.

He also said that shortly afterwards he received from John Peirce one of the company of the ship thirty six shillings in pieces of eight for cloth, which he had sold to him to make him a suit of clothes, and that he received twenty-seven shillings in the same coinage from the boatswain of the ship and an Irishman, two others of the company of the ship for three waistcoats. He further said that the trumpeter of the *Golden Grape* told him that Arthur Grey's wife of Wyke Regis being privy to his hiding of one hundred and fifty pieces of eight in her garden had deceived him of one hundred and five pieces of them, because afterwards when he came to look for his money, there were only forty five pieces left, the rest had been taken away.

Agnes the wife of William Holmes a mariner of Weymouth said that on the same day at night that the *Golden Grape* was cast away the carpenter of the ship came along by her door in Weymouth very wet and in great distress and taking pity on him she let him into her house, where she provided victuals and clothes for him, and lodged him there. Soon afterwards he asked to borrow a purse, but she having none to lend, he took out of his pockets certain pieces of eight (but how many she did not know), which he put into a wooden dish that was there and gave them to her to lay up for him, which she did, putting them into a chest in the chamber where he lodged. She then said that shortly after the carpenter left her house secretly without giving her notice or so much as taking his leave and when she looked in the chest she found the dish there and thirty seven and a half pieces of eight piece in it, which she now produced and delivered to the Vice Admiral. She said that before the carpenter went away he had paid her thirty two shillings in pieces of eight for clothes that she had bought for him, but paid her nothing at all for his diet and lodging all the while he was there, nor for a waistcoat and some other necessaries, which she bought for him.

Owen Gibbons, a sailor of Wyke Regis, said that about nine o'clock at night on the same day that the *Golden Grape* was cast away he went there with Faithfull Angell of Weymouth, a labourer, and his brother Robert Angell of Wyke Regis where they saved seven barrels of raisins of the sun between them, which they carried from there in Robert Williams' boat to Wyke Regis and Gibbons said he still had the barrels. He also saved about a peck and half of loose wet fruit, which he also carried home with him. He added that the same night Arthur Grey's wife entreated him to ride his horse down there to fetch one of the company of the ship who was very sick, which he did, and when he got there he put John Peirce, the sick man, on his horse; and another of the ship's company called Little Will was present. One of them delivered a long double bag of coin to him, which he put onto the neck of his horse, and lead the horse directly to the house of Arthur Grey where he left Peirce and the bag of coin, which he believed was put into the chest in the chamber where more (Grey had said three in total) bags of money had been put before, and Peirce then gave him and another with him one piece of eight between them for their pains in helping him.

The time given by Gibbons of when the sailor was carried back differed with the next testimony of Nicholas Chapple of Wyke Regis, a sailor who said that on Saturday about two or three o' clock in the afternoon (the same day that the *Golden Grape* was cast away on the beach) as he was going there he met Owen Gibbons and two of the company of the ship with him, near a place called Bridge within the parish of Wyke Regis. One of the crew was sick and Gibbons had put him on his horse together with a double bag of money, which the sick man held fast in his hand on the neck of the horse. Gibbons lead the horse from there to the house of Arthur Grey in Wyke Regis in his company as Gibbons had asked him to return there with him. When they got there Chapple took the sick man down from the horse, and carried him into Arthur Grey's house, and the bag of money was then likewise taken down from the horse's neck and carried into the house (but by whom he didn't know). He said that he then carried the sick man up into a chamber in Grey's house, where he saw the money put into a chest that stood in the chamber, but by whom he did not know, but said that after the bag of money was put into the chest he saw Grey's wife shut and lock the chest. The sick man then took out of his pocket a piece of eight and gave it to him and Owen Gibbons between them for their pains in bringing him there. When he eventually got to the beach he picked up two or three ship's blocks and a small quantity of wet raisins of the sun.

As a result of Gibbons' testimony the innkeeper Arthur Grey of Wyke Regis, having formerly been examined, was now re-examined. He said when Owen Gibbons brought the sick man to his house, a double bag of money (besides those which Grey had delivered to the Vice Admiral) was then also brought into his house, and put into the chest standing in the chamber as mentioned in Gibbons' deposition. The next morning the steersman of the Golden Grape came to him and demanded the bag of money from him, which he gave to him in front of his wife. The steersman took the bag away and that was the reason why Grey had not mentioned it in his former deposition as he thought that the bag of money was the steersman's own money.

Susanna Grey wife of Arthur Grey was also re-examined and said that when Owen Gibbons brought the sick man to her husband's house she now very well remembers that a double bag of money was then also brought into the house and put into the chest in the chamber. She then went on to corroborate her husband's new testimony.

For the salvors a bag of 240 pieces of eight would have weighed 14 lbs or 6.5 kgs; a bag of 500 pistoles (2 escudos Spanish gold coins or doubloons) 7.5 lbs or 3.5 kgs; a jar of oil about 12 lbs or 6 kgs, and a barrel of raisins of the sun 92 lbs or 42 kgs.

William Lovell of Fleet a husbandman deposed that the same day that the *Golden Grape* was cast away on the beach he went there where he, together with Robert Tooledge, John Allin and Robert Bryer saved three barrels of raisins, which they carried to his house together with one of the company of the ship who was very sick (where this deponent kept the sick man seven or eight days, and then he was moved to Mr. Mohun's house where he remained until he died). Having refreshed the sick man and himself he went on the beach again where he and his company took out of the ship twelve more barrels of raisins of the sun, six of which one that named himself William Drake and the Mr. Vice Admirals servant, took from them, and left the other six with them for salvage. Lovell had one and when he was aboard the ship he took up a bag of money which was fast sealed, but he had opened it, and counting the money found there to be two hundred pieces of eight, of which he had 120, the other 80 he delivered to John Pollard of Fleet who was present with him when he found it. He also said that he and his company then saved the main bonnet sail of the ship, which afterwards they delivered to John Pope of Weymouth who demanded the same from them in the name of the Master of the ship. He said that Christopher Lovell of Fleet had in his custody the foreyard of the *Golden Grape*, which he had also helped to save.

Francis Spratt of Wyke Regis a husbandman said that on the night that the *Golden Grape* was cast away on the beach, he went there accompanied by Anthony Bryne, and William Stone, servants to Anthony Clapcott of Wyke Regis. There they salved seven barrels of raisins of the sun out of the ship, and while bringing them away, one William Lovell of Fleet (pretending he had the power from the Vice Admiral) took four barrels from them, and carried them away already having many more barrels in his custody. The remaining three, they carried them to Wyke Regis in a cart belonging to William Cade, his Master, and put them into his house where they still remained. He also said that Bernard and John Cade, two of William Cade's sons brought home two jars of oil that had been taken out of the ship.

George Chip a sailor of Wyke Regis said that the day after the *Golden Grape* was cast away he went on the beach where he met Robert Hunt of Wyke Regis, and his son and servant, who having saved ten barrels of raisins of the sun wanted his company to carry them over the Fleet in his boat, which they did, and Hunt gave them two of the ten barrels for their pains. Hunt carried the other eight barrels home to his house. Chip said that he and the rest of his company saved one more barrel of fruit, and they carried the three barrels to Wyke Regis in the plough of Mr. John Jeffries and then to his house where they yet remained, ready to be delivered.

Bartholomew Williams of Wyke Regis, sailor said that at about midnight of the same day that the *Golden Grape* was cast away, he went to the beach where he gathered up some loose raisins of the sun, which he put into his linen breeches and carried to his boat. He added that he and the company of his boat (Nicholas Williams, Henry Florry, John Curteis, Henry Lyne, and Nicholas Charles) loaded about twenty four jars of oil aboard the boat and carried them over the Fleet to the mainland, but who salved them he didn't know, [Robert Hunt's servant saved them] neither did he remember anybody who was in the boat except for the daughter of Robert Hunt of Wyke Regis. Of the oil, he and his company had twelve jars for their pains - two jars apiece, and he said that he had now delivered his two jars (one of which was not quite full) to Mr. Arthur.

Leonard Sandford a sailor of Wyke Regis said that the next morning after the *Golden Grape* was cast away he, together with John Andrews and Henry Pitt of Wyke Regis, went to the place where the ship lay and they saved eight barrels of raisins of the sun, two of which were taken from them by Richard Gilbert, John Dobye, and Jennings Attwool, of Portland, who staved one of the two barrels to pieces, the other they carried away with them to Portland. He and his partners carried the other six barrels to Wyke Regis where they remained.

Daniell Andrews of Wyke Regis, a fisherman said that on the same day that the *Golden Grape* was cast away he went on the beach and aboard the ship with an adze in his hand and once there, a wave crashed over him so violently on his back and bruised him so much that he came away without taking or saving any of the goods or provisions of that ship, but as he came away he picked up a shirt and in the sleeve were some letters, and a handkerchief which he carried to his house and delivered to his wife Joane. She showed them to John Hodder of Weymouth and another man, who having opened and perused them gave them back to her.

Thomas Grey of Wyke Regis a sailor said that the same day that the *Golden Grape* was cast away he went to the beach where he found a piece of a small rope belonging to the ship, two pieces of beef, a piece of leather, and a piece of a plot drawn in paper which he carried home with him. On the Monday following (being two days after) he went there again, where he met John Andrews of Wyke and others, who having salved six barrels of raisins of the sun, wanted him to carry them down the Fleet in his boat and they promised that he would have a share in them for his pains, but so far he had not received anything for his effort. Afterwards on the same day Richard Baily of Melcombe Regis and others in his company having saved seventeen barrels of raisins of the sun, three of which were broken, also wanted him to carry them over the Fleet for them, promising him the ninth part of the same for his pains, and having done it, they gave him one of the barrels, which he still had.

William Boyt of Wyke Regis a fisherman said that the same day that the *Golden Grape* was cast away, he went on the beach where he met with John Boyt, John Bayly, Bryant Feaver, William Bishopp the elder, William Bishopp the younger, Thomas Pitt, John Feaver and Nicholas Feaver of Wyke Regis and John Pope of Weymouth who all joining together, saved twenty two barrels of raisins of the sun, and twenty eight jars of oil, three sails (which the Master of that ship affirmed to be the mainsail the foretop sail and the mizzen sail) a great lantern, a small barrel of stinking butter, a wooden bowl with some spike nails in it, a screw to mount a piece of ordinance with all, & the rudder of a boat. All of the goods (save the three sails and the screw, the former of which are in the custody of John Bayly, and the latter in the hands of the Bryant Feaver) are in his custody, which, as he salved for the use of the proprietors, he was ready to deliver when required.

John Pope of Weymouth, a shoemaker said that he was on the beach with William Boyt and the rest of the company at the salving of the several parcels of goods and provisions. Pope had in his custody the compass and the short sword specified by William Bishopp the elder. He then said that he also took up there a full jar of oil and another half full, two hundred and fifty wet lemons and about fourteen or sixteen pounds of wet raisins. He also received the main bonnet sail belonging to the ship from one of Fleet.

Thomas Bayly a yeoman of Wyke Regis said that on the same day when the *Golden Grape* was cast away he went on the beach where he and his company saved fifteen barrels of raisins of the sun, twenty six jars of oil, three Flemish boxes with salves in them, two small sea chests, two chambers or murderers, and some small pieces of ropes. He added that when he had saved the oils he put all the jars into Nicholas Williams' boat wanting him to carry them over the Fleet for him to the mainland which Williams did, but he said that he never saw the oils or any part of them since, but he had since been told that Robert Hunt of Wyke Regis had fifteen of them in his custody. The rest of the goods and provisions he had in his possession and was ready to deliver them. He also said that Robert Falkoner and some others of Weymouth and Melcombe Regis afterwards brought fifteen more barrels of raisins of the sun to his house where they still remained.

John Bayle son of Thomas Bayly [note the lack of spelling consistency] of Wyke Regis, a yeoman deposed that on Sunday morning the day after the *Golden Grape* was cast away he was sent by his father with his plough, together with John Butcher, his father's servant, to fetch whatever goods they had saved the day before. He loaded fifteen barrels of raisins of the sun onto his plough for his father and for Robert Hunt of Wyke Regis, and fifteen other barrels of raisins of the sun for Robert Falkoner, Gregory Backway, and Henry or Christopher Bayly of Melcombe Regis, two small chests, two chambers, and some other small trifles, which they carried home in the plough to his father's house where they yet remain.

Ann the wife of Christopher Cowrage a sailor of Wyke Regis, said that being on the beach the same day that the *Golden Grape* was there cast away she met a boy, the servant of Andrew Mills of Wyke Regis, who then had a single bag of money under his arm which he had got out of the ship, which (being a bit too heavy for the boy to carry) she carried for him for a while, but then (being tired herself) she gave it back to the boy whole, just as it was when she received it from him. She then said that as the boy was carrying the bag of money homewards Richard Gilbert of Portland met him, and took the bag and money from him, promising to give the boy satisfaction for salving the same, but whether Gilbert gave the boy anything or not she did not know.

Robert Hunt of Wyke Regis a yeoman said that he had in his house in Wyke Regis seven whole barrels of raisins of the sun and another barrel almost full, which his son and servant salved on the beach, and another barrel of raisins of the sun which Thomas Loder of Weymouth had salved and left there, and fifteen jars of oil which his son and servant likewise saved, some small ropes, a pewter pot, and some broken pieces of the timber from the ship. All of which he was ready to deliver. His only claim to any other goods from the wreck was his share of the six barrels of raisins of the sun which Thomas Bayly and he had saved between them and which Thomas Bayly still had.

Thomas Hunt, son of Robert Hunt said that on the same day that the *Golden Grape* was cast away he went to the beach where he and Thomas Bayly of Wyke Regis saved six barrels of raisins of the sun, which Thomas Baily now had in his custody, and twenty six jars of oil, of which fifteen are in this deponent's father's house, the rest Nicholas Williams and his company kept as payment for carrying the jars across the Fleet in their boat. They then saved two small ship's chests, and two chambers, which Bayly also had in his custody. The next day he went there again where he and Henry Meech, his father's man, and Ann Hunt, his sister, saved some small pieces of ropes and ten barrels of raisins of the sun, one of which was not quite full, and they gave two of them to George Chipp and Henry Keilway of Wyke Regis for carrying the other eight in their boat over the Fleet. The eight barrels of fruit and pieces of ropes are in his father's house.

Jennings Attwool of the Isle of Portland a yeoman deposed that the same day that the *Golden Grape* was cast away on the beach he went there where he and his company saved twenty eight bolts of silk, two bags of silver plate, a loaf of silver bullion and two jars of oil. He also saved by himself one other bolt of silk, which he delivered to Daniell Peirce his father in law, who still had it his possession. He also saved a flag belonging to the ship, an astrolabe, a cross staff and a quadrant, all of which he had in his custody as well as the said two jars of oil. He had no other goods or provisions from the wreck save for only a small quantity of wet raisins, which he had carried home.

Francis Saveer of the Isle of Portland mason deposed that he went on the beach the same day that the *Golden Grape* was cast away and the following two days, whither when he came the first day he went aboard the ship where he took up a short piece of silk that was wrapped about a piece of timber in the ship, and eighteen rows of buttons, (which he now delivers to the Vice Admiral) two old coats, a jacket, an old shirt, an old red waistcoat and three or four bolts of iron, which he had at home in his custody, and in several trips he carried home to his house about seven pecks of wet raisins of the sun. He added that Luke Knapp his boy being there also took up and carried home two old jerkins and some old shirts (which his wife threw away as soon as they were brought home) and about a barrel of wet raisins of the sun the most part of which fruit he still had in his house, which is almost spoiled.

Thomas Bussell of Chickerell yeoman said that the same day that the *Golden Grape* was cast away on the beach he went there, and managed to board the ship where he saved two barrels of raisins of the sun (the head of one of them being beaten out, and many of the fruit taken away) two jars of oil and about half a bushel of loose fruit, which he had at home in his house and is ready to deliver. He then added that about **two days after that, when the ship was broken to pieces and quite carried away,** he went there again accompanied by Roger Dyker his servant, where Dyker took up in the sea near the place where the ship lay, a bag of money which he took from Dyke, carried home with him, but had since delivered to the Vice Admiral.

Peter Haught a fisherman of Weymouth deposed that on the day after the *Golden Grape* was cast away on the beach he went up the Fleet in the boat in the company of John Cotton, where Haught and his company saved twelve barrels of raisins of the sun, which they did put into the boat, and carried to Weymouth, where eight of the barrels were then delivered into the custody of Richard Pitt, and four into the custody of William Dry. Haught further said that the next day they went there again with the boat where Walter Bond loaded the boat with twenty three barrels of raisins of the sun which were carried for him in two journeys, over the Fleet and landed at a certain place called Foxholes near Wyke Regis, where they were left in the custody of Bond, but what he did with them he didn't know.

Walter Bond of Weymouth a fisherman deposed that the day after the *Golden Grape* was cast away on the beach he together with Symon More, Ralph Limbrey, William Chappell, and others of Weymouth went there where they saved and carried home with them three barrels of raisins of the sun, about half a jar of oil, and three other small barrels (but what is in them he did not know) all of which were in his custody. They also then brought home with them four other small barrels, which are in the custody of Symon More, and three other barrels of raisins of the sun and a barrel about half full, which are in the custody of Ralph Limbrey.

The next day (by the directions of the Master of the ship) they went there again where they saved thirty four barrels of raisins of the sun, whereof one was broken up by Alice Whittle of Weymouth and all the raisins taken out by the bystanders except about a quarter of the barrel, which he then took out and carried home in their handkerchiefs and pockets and another of the said barrels Mr. John Jeffries of Wyke took and kept because they had been landed on his ground. Twenty of the remaining thirty-two barrels were swiftly put into the cellar of Mr. Fabian Hodder, at whose house the Master lay, and the other twelve in the customs cellar of Weymouth.

He further said that they then brought with them to Weymouth **a cable, a hawser, two murderers [swivel cannon] and the fore shrouds of the ship, which were then also put into the custody of the said Mr. Hodder. They also brought to Weymouth seven pieces of ordinance belonging to the ship, which now lay in the streets there, and one Murderer, which was put into the house of William Wykes of Weymouth. They also brought to Weymouth with them the foremast, the bowsprit, a windlass, and a capstan, seventeen round shot, two anchors, two carriages, and a piece of a new shootcable about twenty fathoms in length, another piece of a cable about ten fathoms in length, and a piece of a hawser about six fathoms in length, which they put into the cellar of Leonard Helland** in Melcombe Regis and he said that he was ready to deliver all of the said goods.

Andrew Ebourne of Melcombe Regis mariner deposed that on the Tuesday after the *Golden Grape* was cast away on the beach he went there in the company

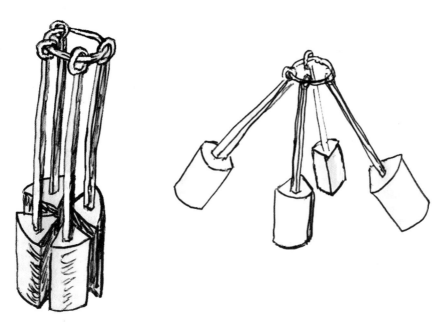

Diagrams of cross-bar-shot, or "star" shot, as folded and loaded into the cannon then expanding as it exits the cannon.
Three of the quadrants, one with remains of bar, discovered off Chesil Beach

of Thomas Damon and Roger Woodcocke of Melcombe Regis where they saved a piece of a junk about a fathom in length, a piece of a fore knight, two or three sheaves for blocks, and a murderer, which Thomas Damon now had.

Andrew Pitt a sailor of Weymouth said that the morning after the *Golden Grape* was cast away on the beach he went there together with John Cotton, William Dry, Peter Haught, Philipp Ashe, Andrew Cotton, **James Bond**, and Symon Watte, where they saved thirteen barrels of raisins of the sun which they carried to Weymouth and landed on the quay but one of the barrels was stolen from them there (but by whom he did not know). He said that eight of the barrels were put into his father, Richard Pitt's house and the other four into the house of William Drye.

Thomas Bayly a mason from Melcombe Regis said that he was on the beach with Robert Falkoner and his company at the saving of the goods and provisions which belonged to the *Golden Grape* expressed and mentioned in the depositions of Robert Falkoner and said that at the same time the company saved twenty four cross-bar-shot, a small top, and the foretopmast's shrouds belonging to the *Golden Grape*, which Walter Bond took from them into his custody and gave them three shillings in money for saving them.

Angel Wattes a carpenter of Melcombe Regis said that on the Tuesday after the ship was cast away on the beach he went there, where he saved one barrel of raisins of the sun, which while carrying it home on a horse, it fell accidentally from the horse onto the ground and the fruit fell out into the dirt. He gathered the raisins up again and put them into a sack, and carried it to his house where it is still. He had also been at the beach the day before, where he gathered up certain wet loose fruit, which he put into a bag, and lay it down on the beach, from where it was stolen together with the bag. He then took up a junk of a cable about twelve or sixteen fathoms in length, a shovel and some small pieces of iron about four pounds weight, the junk and shovel he had in his custody, but the iron was sold for about four or five pence.

William Winter a brewer of Weymouth said that on the day after the *Golden Grape* was cast away on the beach he went there where he helped to save eight barrels of fruit with James Hardey, Cake, the servant of Henry Coxe and Robert Pitt of Weymouth the barrels being left on the beach in the custody of Cake, Coxe's servant and James Hardey, who kept the same there until the next morning, at which time Winter went there again with the intention of carrying the fruit to Weymouth, but when he got there he found five of the barrels missing, which had been taken from those that had been looking after them, by Walter Bond, and Symon Mores of Weymouth, the other three Winter carried home to his house where they still remained.

Richard Baylye a mason of Melcombe Regis said that the day after the wreck he went there in the company of blacksmith Edward Pounston alias Hownsell of Melcombe Regis, and when they reached there they went aboard the ship out of which they took and saved eight barrels of raisins of the sun, which they laid on the beach, where one barrel was stolen from them, but by whom he did not know, another barrel they gave to William James of Melcombe Regis to carry the other six over the Fleet in his boat for them, which six barrels they carried home to their houses, four to his own house and two to Edward Hownsell's house. He said that he sold one of the barrels he had to **the wife of Mr. John Arthur** for which she paid him forty shillings, two of the others he still had whole at home, the fourth Mr. Richards one of the officers of the Custom House ordered him to open alleging that he thought it was a barrel of tent, out of which barrel some part had been taken but the rest is still there.

William Symonds of Portisham, a thatcher, said that on the Monday after the *Golden Grape* was wrecked on the beach, he went there and by the Fleet side he found two and a half barrels of raisins of the sun, which had been taken out of the ship, which he paid a boatman from Wyke Regis two shillings to carry them over the Fleet. Once across the Fleet he then met John Gillam of Portisham who was there with his cart, and who he asked him to carry the fruit to Portisham for him promising him one half for his pains. He said that he sold his part of the fruit, a whole barrel full to Doby, a blacksmith of Mounkton, for nineteen shillings.

Walter Sandford a weaver of Portisham deposed that the day after that the *Golden Grape* was cast away on the beach he went there in the company of Richard Halston of Corton and others. Halston wanted him to help save some of the barrels of raisins that were in the ship, which he did, altogether saving ten barrels of raisins, which Halston then carried to Corton in his cart and gave Sandford two barrels of wheat for his pains. He also said that being aboard the ship he took up some loose wet fruit there, which he put into the sleeve of his waistcoat and carried home.

John Ricketts, son of Walter Ricketts of Portisham, said that the day after the *Golden Grape* was cast away on the beach he went there where he and William Cake of Portisham saved eight barrels of raisins of the sun out of the ship, which they carried and laid on the beach, and left them there in the custody of John Woode servant to Thomas Meech of Portisham, yeoman, intending to fetch them from there the next morning, but he said that when they reached there the next morning the barrels of raisins had all been carried away. Wood told him that certain men of Weymouth came there and having beaten him took the barrels and carried them away.

Christopher Eyles a weaver of Portisham, said that on the Monday after the *Golden Grape* was cast away on the beach he went there where he bought a barrel of fruit from Robert Gawden of Portisham for three shillings and four pence, which he carried home on a horse that he had borrowed from Mrs. Galping the vicar's wife of Portisham for that purpose, to whom he gave one half of the barrel of fruit for hire of the horse.

John Symonds of Portisham, a yeoman, said that on the day after that the *Golden Grape* was cast away on the beach he went there accompanied by his maid servant and another of Anthony Hardey of Portisham, where the said maidens picked up some quantity of fruit, about a peck and a half each, which they put into their aprons and carried home with them. He said that his son Richard Symonds also saved one barrel of fruit, which his son carried home in his cart, and that he then carried another barrel for the widow Samways of Portisham. The barrels are at home in his house, as well as certain barrels for Thomas Harden and Henry Russell of the same place (but how many he did not know) and that he also carried one barrel for Robert George of the same place and likewise his son Richard then saved another barrel of fruit, which was emptied into sacks and carried home to his house on a horse. The next day, Monday, he went there again where he bought a barrel almost full of raisins of the sun from Thomas Loder of Weymouth for which he paid seven shillings. He emptied the fruit out of the barrel, and put it into bags and carried it home to his house. He said that his servant William Samways then also saved a jar of oil, which he had in his house, and a wallet of raisins of the sun, but what became of them he did not know.

Thomas Webber of Portisham husbandman said that on the Tuesday after the *Golden Grape* was cast away on the beach he went there where he helped save two masts of that ship, which he left there on the beach, and some pieces of timber part of the ribs of the ship, a great shot, a bottle of wine (about a pint and a half), some nails, and one spike.

Thomas Ploughman of Portisham, a husbandman, deposed that on the day after the *Golden Grape* was cast away on the beach he went there to see what Henry Thresher of Portisham had done with the horse, which his wife had lent to Thresher, and it was where Robert Lovell of Fleet gave about a peck of wet raisins of the sun to him, which he carried home with him.

Richard Symonds, son of John Symonds of Portisham, yeoman, said that the next day in the morning after the *Golden Grape* was cast away on the beach he went there in the company of Joseph, the son of Anthony Hardey of Portesham where they saved three barrels of raisins of the sun, which they carried home and put two of them in Anthony Hardey's house and the other in his father's house. He also said that he carried home in his father's plough seven other barrels of raisins of the sun for Robert George, Thomas Harden and Henry Russell of Portisham, one of which was for the widow Samwayes of Elwood [Elworth], which his father bought from her. He had nothing else except some loose fruit, which he carried home to his father's house in a sack on a horse.

John Rawlin, a mason of Waddon, deposed that on the day after the ship called the *Golden Grape* was cast away on the beach he went there where he found seven pieces of Spanish coin, which he exchanged with Susan Keat of Abbotsbury for about ten or eleven shillings, which he spent on his house, it being an old house.

Richard Samwayes of Portisham, husbandman, deposed said that on the day after the *Golden Grape* was cast away on the beach he went there in the company of Henry Mills of Portisham, where this deponent took up and saved a murderer belonging to the ship, which he put into a boat there and carried to Fleet to the house of Magdalen Allin widow, where it yet remains. He picked up a certain quantity of loose fruit there, which he put into his pockets and carried home with him.

Philip Ash, a sailor of Weymouth deposed that the day after the *Golden Grape* was cast away on the beach he went there in the company of John Cotton, Peter Haught and others where they saved thirteen barrels of the fruit of the sun out of the ship and carried them to Weymouth, where eight are in the custody of Richard Pitt, four in the custody of William Dry and one in the custody of John Allen.

Christopher Gibbs of the Isle of Portland, a mason, deposed that the same day that the *Golden Grape* was cast away on the beach he went there where he amongst others saved out of the ship thirty bolts of silk, one bag of silver plate containing twenty one pieces, another bag of silver plate containing twenty four pieces, and a peg of silver. Twenty-four of the bolts of silk with all the plate and the bag of silver were delivered to Mr. Vice Admiral, four of the bolts are in the custody of Mr. William Strode in Portland Castle, the other two pieces or bolts of silk are in the custody of Richard Gilbert of the island. He had at present in his custody a short piece of silk about two yards in length.

William Sweet the younger of the Isle of Portland, a mason, said that on the same day that the *Golden Grape* was cast away on the beach he went there where one bolt of silk was taken from him by Maximilian Mohun of Fleet esquire, and this deponent did then also save one jar of oil and about a bushel of raisins of the sun.

Thomas Wiggott of the Isle of Portland, a tailor, deposed that the day after the *Golden Grape* was cast away on the beach he went there in the company of Samuel Painter and Richard Peers of the said Island where they saved one barrel of raisins of the sun, which they broke up and divided between them and on the following day being Monday, he went there again where he bought another barrel of raisins of the sun from Philipp Benvile of Portland for four shillings. He carried it home and divided it with John Stone of Portland, whose horse he had borrowed to carry the barrel on, Stone paying him half the money paid out for the barrel.

Philipp Benvile of the Isle of Portland, a sailor, said that the day after the *Golden Grape* was cast away on the beach he went there where he with seven others of the said island in his company saved twelve barrels of raisins of the sun. Six of which Walter Bond of Weymouth received and had from them, the other six are in the custody of Mr. Fortune the porter of Portland Castle, and he then also saved one other barrel of raisins of the sun, which he sold to Thomas Wiggott of Portland for three shillings and ten pence.

William Hellyer a sailor of Abbotsbury said that on the same day that the *Golden Grape* was cast away on the beach he went there where he saved a barrel and a half of raisins of the sun, three jars of oil, one of which was not full, two pair of bandoliers, and a horn half full of powder. He also found on the beach one piece of eight and two small pieces of coin to the value of fifteen pence a piece or thereabouts. All of which, except only the money, are in the custody of Mr. Henry Garland, his Master.

Thomas Evans of Abbotsbury, a fisherman, said that on the same day that the *Golden Grape* was cast away on the beach he went there where he saved about the quantity of a barrel of raisins of the sun, which he took up loose and wet and two jars of oil one of which was only half full and that he had since used the other whole jar at his house. On the deck of the ship he found a little purse of money containing about twenty pieces of foreign coin, but he said that Joseph or James Gardner of Wyke Regis, Robert Angell of the same place, Jeffry Thistle of Fleet and Thomas Puckett of Abbotsbury took it from him by force leaving him only two of the pieces called testons which he now delivered to Mr. Arthur.

John Pollard of Abbotsbury, a husbandman said that his servant brought to his house a bottle of wine containing about two quarts, which he had saved out of the ship.

John Olliver a sailor of Abbotsbury said that the same day that the *Golden Grape* was cast away on the beach he went aboard the ship and saved two pieces of silks.

Nicholas Bussell of Chickerell, a husbandman, said that being aboard the ship he picked up a bag of Spanish coin, in which there were about two hundred pieces of eight, which he had in his custody and is ready to deliver. He helped save another bag of money, which his uncle Thomas Bussell had already delivered to the Vice Admiral.

Henry Nosciter a fisherman of Langton Herring said that the day after the *Golden Grape* was cast away on the beach he went there where he helped save six barrels of raisins, four of which were delivered to Mr. John Allin of Weymouth, the other two barrels Mr. Allin gave to him and Thomas Comage of Langton for saving the rest. He also took up a piece of a barrel in which were about thirty-six pounds of raisins, which together with the other barrel that he had, he sold for about seven shillings. He then bought one barrel and half of raisins from a woman of Steepleton (whose name he could not remember) for which he paid her twenty-four shillings, and sold the same again to John White of Sherborne for forty shillings.

Richard Buttler of Upwey in the county of Dorset, a husbandman, deposed that since the *Golden Grape* was cast away he bought several parcels of goods that came out of that ship. That is to say one barrel of raisins of the sun from William Lovell of Fleet for twenty shillings, one barrel of raisins from John Allin of Fleet for twenty shillings, one barrel of raisins from John Williams of Fleet for ten shillings, and one other barrel from Richard Damer of Little Waddon for which he paid him five shillings in money and carried home to his house another barrel for him, which was worth five shillings more. He said that Thomas Masterman of Upwey bought six barrels of raisins of the sun at Fleet, which he sold and sent to Sturminster Newton but to whom he did not know, and that Mr. Benjamin Bale of Upwey bought one barrel, Eugenius Vincent two barrels, Owen Hendey and Giles Hendey three barrels, and Walter Paty one barrel.

William Purchas a baker of Abbotsbury said that the same day that the *Golden Grape* was cast away on the beach he went there where he saved two barrels of raisins of the sun, which he emptied into four pots and carried them home, of which he sold a hundred and a quarter to a widow of Cerne for two and a half pence the pound, by which means he made fifty shillings besides all his charges.

He also saved two bolts of pieces of silks, one of which, being wrapped in a cape, John Pope of Weymouth took from him saying he was Mr. Vice Admiral's man, the other one he sold part to one of Taunton for six pounds and one shilling, and the other part, being twelve yards, to Captain Strangwayes for eighteen shillings.

John Hendey the younger of Langton deposed that he was on the beach the same day that the *Golden Grape* was cast away where he saved two bolts or pieces of silks, which he delivered to Mr. Mohun's son.

John Godding of Fleet said that the same day the *Golden Grape* was cast away he went on the beach where he saved out of the ship one bundle of plate weighing about thirty or forty pounds, which he delivered to Mr. Mohun being fast mayled, and that he did then also help to save four barrels of raisins of the sun, which were likewise delivered to Mr. Mohun.

Anthony Carter a sailor of Fleet deposed that he was on the beach the same night that the *Golden Grape* was cast away where he took up a bandolier and some fruit out of a barrel, which he carried home in his coat, he also said that Thomas Perkins servant to Mr. Mohun then showed him one piece of silver, which came out of the ship and the next day he together with Joseph Keat and Robert Allen saved eight barrels of raisins of the sun, which Walter Bond of Weymouth took from them and gave them no satisfaction at all for saving the same.

Henry Haywell of Abbotsbury, a fisherman testified that the day after the *Golden Grape* was cast away on the beach he, being hired by Mr. Nicholas Strangwayes, went down the Fleet with his boat in the company of his son Richard and Christopher Doby and his son Edward. They reached the shore of the Fleet near the wreck where Peter Ford put aboard the boat nine barrels of raisins, which Haywell and his company carried back to Abbotsbury and delivered to the house of Mr. Strangwayes. Haywell had also picked up on the beach about half a bushel of raisins, which he put into a bag and carried home with him.

Maximilian Mohun of Fleet, Esquire, being on the beach, said that a stranger brought to him a box taken out of the ship, the *Golden Grape* with letters in it and a book of account of Thomas Redwood Master of that ship, which he now delivered to the Commissioners. He also declared that he had in his custody a black piece of taffeta sarcenett, which he had caused to be dried, about seven or eight barrels of raisins, two of which are broken open, a chest belonging to one of the company of the ship in which is a handsaw, a chisel, and some other small trifles and a jar of oil, which are all the goods (as he remembered) that he had in his custody belonging to that ship. He said that he caused twenty-eight pieces of silk and two parcels of plate to be put together on the beach and preserved, but they were afterwards taken and carried away by some of the inhabitants of Portland.

Thomas Hayward of Abbotsbury, a fisherman, deposed that the Monday after the *Golden Grape* was cast away on the beach he went there where he took up about three pecks of raisins, which he carried home with him in a pair of fish pots on horseback.

Daniell Andrews a fisherman of Wyke Regis said being on the beach the same day the *Golden Grape* was cast away he saw Thomas Carter of Fleet have in his hand under his cap a bag of money, which Carter took away but how much he did not know.

Access to the wreck of the *Golden Grape* was either by boat across the Fleet waters or boats from Weymouth or Portland up the Fleet, or by foot along the Chesil Beach from either the Portland or Abbotsbury ends where the beach joins Portland to the mainland. The latter two communities had the advantage that anybody could make their way along the beach on foot and carry back what they could manage. Bags or sacks of raisins, the odd jar of oil, any loose coins, etc. It was also possible to take a horse along the beach to carry more or heavier goods back and several Abbotsbury men were on the beach the Saturday night of the wreck where they saved five barrels of raisins of the sun, which they emptied into sacks and carried home upon six horses, with no mention of crossing the Fleet.

An Abbotsbury man used a horse on the Sunday to carry home raisins that his wife and daughter had salvaged and another on the Monday filled fishpots carried on his horse to transport his share of the raisins. Another way would have been to cross Smallmouth by ferry from Wyke to Portland and then access the beach on foot but Austine, the keeper of the passage boat, was one of those on the beach on the first day, probably using his ferry boat, so perhaps an unlikely option. Whatever way they came, even the darkness and cold did not deter some as they were on the beach well into the night and a few (mainly servants) were left overnight to guard individual piles of salvaged goods before their Masters or others from their group came back in the morning to collect them.

At the subsequent enquiry 343 witnesses gave depositions of what part they had played in the salvage of the *Golden Grape*. Of the 132 people on the beach on the first day and night of the wreck there were 31 Portlanders, second in total number were the 22 men from Wyke Regis (expectedly high, being the nearest village), while the distant Abbotsbury had 20 there. Chickerell, Fleet, Langton Herring had 16, 12 and 11 respectively followed with 8 from Weymouth. As word of the wreck got out, the second day saw the further inland village of Portisham well represented as well as larger numbers of Weymouth and Melcombe Regis people.

Comparing the 301, mainly male, people on the beach for the five days from Saturday to Wednesday with the same year 1641 Protestation returns for males over the age of 18, gives representative figures for Langton Herring of 61%, Chickerell 55%, Fleet 41%, Wyke Regis 40%, Portland 36%, Portisham 24%, Weymouth 21%, Abbotsbury 19% and for Melcombe Regis 9%.

Ship or Village	Sat	Sun	Mon	Tue	Wed	Total	1641 Total Male > 18 Protestation Return figure	%age of over 18 Males at wreck	Miles from Wreck
Golden Grape	10	0	0	0	0	**10**			0
Abbotsbury	20	22	5	0	0	**47**	244	19%	7.03
Chickerell	16	5	1	0	0	**22**	40	55%	1.93
Corton	0	2	0	0	0	**2**			5.34
Fleet Gerards	12	1	0	0	0	**13**	32	41%	2.36
Waddon	0	1	0	0	0	**1**			5.34
Langton Herring	11	10	2	0	0	**23**	38	61%	3.90
Melcombe Regis	1	11	2	4	0	**18**	207	9%	2.10
Portisham	1	24	5	1	0	**31**	129	24%	6.15
Portland	31	18	4	0	0	**53**	147	36%	3.11
Shilvinghampton	0	1	0	0	0	**1**			4.85
Upway	0	0	0	1	1	**2**	103	2%	4.97
Waddon	0	6	0	0	0	**6**			5.34
Weymouth	8	19	5	4	0	**36**	175	21%	2.10
Wyke Regis	22	11	3	0	0	**36**	89	40%	0.87
	132	**131**	**27**	**10**	**1**	**301**			

This shows how important the wreck was to the local population especially when the other 204 people who are mentioned in those depositions are taken into account even allowing for the unknown number of women and children in those communities. Overall 26% of the total males over 18 were on the beach with a figure of over 38% of over 18 males involved in the wreck in some way.

Ship or Village	Female	Male	1641 Total Male > 18 Protestation Return figure	%age of over 18 Males	ALL
Golden Grape		14			14
Abbotsbury		62	244	25%	62
Blandford		1			1
Cerne		1			1
Chickerell	1	37	40	93%	38
Corton		6			6
Dorchester		1			1
Easter Compton		1			1
Elwood		1			1
Fleet	2	24	32	75%	26

Gerards Waddon		1			1
Kingston		1			1
Langton Herring		28	38	74%	28
Martinstown		1			1
Melcombe Regis	2	28	207	14%	30
Monkton		1			1
Portisham	4	50	129	39%	54
Portland	3	69	147	50%	72
Portland Castle		4			4
Sherborne		1			1
Shilvinghampton		3			3
Steepleton		1			1
Taunton		1			1
Upway		8			8
Waddon	1	8			9
Weymouth	5	60	175	34%	65
Wyke Regis	6	59	89	66%	65
Blank		51			51
Total	**24**	**523**			**547**
		Overall percentage		38%	

Occupation	Number	Percentage
others	142	26%
husbandman	80	15%
sailor	69	13%
fisherman	55	10%
trades	43	8%
servant	32	6%
mason	31	6%
yeoman	24	4%
son	19	3%
wife	14	3%
GG crew	10	2%
labourers	9	2%
widow	7	1%
daughter	6	1%
father	5	1%
sister	1	0%
	547	**100%**

The boatmen of Wyke were paid in kind to carry people over and their salvaged goods back across the Fleet to the mainland shore while others used boats to come down the Fleet waters from Chickerell, Fleet, Langton and Abbotsbury. Larger fishermen's boats were used to sail or row from Weymouth and Portland to pick up goods. Trows would have been used to cross the Fleet but it is probable that the larger and deeper lerrets, kept on the Chesil Beach and normally used for fishing off the seaward side would have been used to carry substantial amounts of plunder back across the Fleet as did other lerrets from Portland or Weymouth.

Once on the mainland, goods were taken home by individuals or by groups on foot, by horse or cart or any other means. Horses were either their own or borrowed or hired from another, on the understanding that any salvaged goods were then split with the horse's owner. Again carters were paid by splitting any salvaged goods in half shares while others in the days after the wreck brought their carts from Upwey and Portisham to buy salvaged goods such as barrels of raisins for their own use or to sell on at a profit to inland towns as far as away as Taunton and Sturminster Newton. The adjacent mainland landowners also charged a percentage of any goods landed on their land. As well as horses and carts, ploughs were used to carry barrels of raisins and jars of oil back home; 30 barrels of raisins as well as 26 jars of oil, two murderers and other items in the case of one Wyke yeoman. The goods must have been guarded between trips to nearby Wyke but another enterprising person took 7 barrels of raisins back to Portisham on a plough.

As well as goods being taken by rivals, some from Weymouth, including Walter Bond and Simon Mores, said they were the Vice Admiral's men acting on behalf of the ship's owners and confiscated a lot of goods, sometimes taking all of them, beating them if necessary but at other times allowing the salvors to keep part as a reward. Stronger companies of people such as the Christopher Gibbs' gang from Portland kept all of their substantial and very valuable booty; themselves having taken over the two bags of silver plate and bolts of silks gathered together by Maximilian Mohun's group from Fleet.

Gibbs gang of 11 consisted of a mixture of 7 masons (including himself) and 4 sailors. Somehow they managed to purloin the two bags of silver plate of 21 and 24 pieces as well as saving a loaf of silver and 30 bolts of silk.

From the details disclosed by the Captain and crew regarding the voyage, plus the depositions identifying exactly what was salvaged, the return cargo of the Golden Grape can be estimated to be worth at least £10,000, which is equivalent to £1 million today. But there seem to be omissions or at least some economy with the truth in the inquiry.

The captain of the *Golden Grape*, Thomas Redwood, who is meticulous in the details for the rest of the voyage regarding cargoes and shippers, is uncertain about the number of bags of pieces of eight that were loaded on board off Sanlucar de Barrameda and like the rest of his crew, suffers amnesia when asked who paid for the pepper with the bullion and silks.

The Portlanders, are the largest group on the beach on the first day and saved their full share of the barrels of raisins and took the bolts of silk and the two bags of silver plate from Mohune's Fleet men as well as saving a small silver cup, and the loaf of silver. Yet they only save roughly the same number of jars of oil as the Chickerell men who are half their number. Perhaps that is explained because they were concentrating on the more valuable cargo. Tellingly no silver coins are mentioned as being saved by any Portlander despite Richard Gilbert being accused of taking a full bag of pieces of eight from a boy, yet each of the other villages on the first day disclose finds of odd coins. The Portlanders were both on and went inside the ship where loose coin was found as they save a substantial amount of onboard shirts, breeches, coats, buttons, a musket, cartridges, powder and some of the ship's navigational instruments.

Wyke Regis innkeeper Arthur Grey and his wife Susannah are recalled and both admit they forgot to mention a double bag of money deposited at their dwelling in their first deposition. Crewman Richard Rich is recalled because of a discrepancy between gold and silver money spent by his Weymouth friend. A fellow villager accused Thomas Carter of Chickerell of having a small bag of coin under his cap as he walked away from the wreck but when Carter is recalled he denied this. Only 200 of the well over 500 gold pistole coins are accounted for.

The four Dutch passengers on the *Golden Grape*, who were possibly the original owners, are briefly spoken of by some of the crew because they obtained some pieces of eight from them as they walked back along the shore after the wreck carrying a bag of pieces of eight but that is the last time they are mentioned. Fabian Hodder, Mrs Arthur and John Arthur himself are not called upon to bear witness despite benefiting from the salvage.

Of the 400 jars of oil only 172 were salvaged from the wreck likewise only the equivalent of 535 barrels of raisins out of 1253 onboard were saved and there is no mention of saving the large wine barrels of tent and sack at the inquiry. Although the wreck was on the beach for two days before it broke up and its timbers started being salvaged, it must have been a calamitous grounding as 7 of the crew were killed in the wrecking either as she hit the beach by being thrown against its timbers or crushed by falling masts or indeed swept off the decks and drowned. There is no mention of what was done with the bodies or whether they were washed up later in Chesil Cove as normally happened to drowned sailors. Any deck cargo could have been washed off but even allowing for all that there is a yawning gap between what is saved and what was on board. The inquiry gives one of the most detailed accounts of a shipwreck and its salvage but the suspicion is that some people got more than they said from the wreck.

The distribution of the salvaged goods is as follows for firstly the non-bullion cargo, then the bullion cargo, mainly saved by the crew, and then a village breakdown of the ship's equipment and sundries.

Homeward Bound Cargo	Barrels of raisins of the sun	Jars of oil	Bolts of Silk	lemons	oranges	Ordnance, murderers, chambers
	1253	400	43			
Salvaged cargo by village						
Abbotsbury	55	8	2	12	4	
Chickerell	55	21				
Corton	13					
Fleet	53	2	1			
Gerrards Waddon						
Langton Herring	35	1	2	60		
Melcombe Regis	9			3		1
Portisham	75.5	3				1
Portland	19.5	23	30	29		
Shilvinghampton	1					
Waddon	7					
Weymouth	115.5	3		250		10
Wyke Regis	83	100				2
Unknown	3	11				
Equivalent barrels of loose raisins	11					
TOTAL	**535.5**	**172**	**35**	**354**	**4**	**14**

Homeward Bound	Peg of Silver	Loaf of silver	Bag of 500 gold coin pistoles	Bag of mixed pistoles and pieces of eight	Bags of pieces of eight	Other gold or silver	Bags of silver plate
Cargo	1	1	1	1	?	?	2

Salvaged Bullion

Chickerell					2 bags of 200 p8		
Portland	possible 1 peg of silver	1 loaf of silver				small silver cup	1 bag of 21 pieces, 1 bag of 24 pieces

CREW

Thomas Redwood						small gold neck chain	
Cornelius Van Berkham					bag of 525 p8		
Michael Hatherwick					small bag of 126 p8		
James Smyth	1 peg of silver		200		6 bags of p8, 3 small bags p8		
Thomas Byrd					8 bags each of 240 p8		
Richard Rich					bag of 200 p8		
William Phillis					5 bags		
4 Dutchmen					1 bag		
TOTAL	**1?**	**1**	**200**		**28**		**2**

Abbotsbury.
4 oranges, 12 lemons, bottle of wine about 2 quarts, 5 pieces of brass, old pair of breeches, knife, a bag of wool, and half a board being piece of the cabin, 10lbs of iron.

Chickerell.
Pound of wool, barrel of olives, given lb of wool by Welshman from Portland, John Stevens of Chickerell gave him a pound of wool for 3 p8, ounce of wool, piece of barrel of olives, 1/4 lb of wool, half pound of wool, paper book containing 3 quire of paper, 3 ozs. of wool, small firkin of olives sold for 2s, lock of wool, found piece of ship's rope in field.

Fleet.
Chisel, hammer, 150 nails, small barrel of powder, bandolier, main bonnet sail, Chris Lovell has foreyard, box of letters, an account book, black piece of taffeta sarcenet, crewman's chest containing handsaw, chisel etc, a musket.

Langton Herring.
Peck of lemons, 30 lemons, pair of iron tongues, old knife, earthen cup.

Melcombe Regis.
24 cross-bar-shot, small top, foretopmasts shrouds to Walter Bond for 4s, fathom of junk, piece of foreknight, 2 or 3 sheaves for blocks, 1 murderer, 3 lemons, a pump bolt, 2 chambers, piece of cable 3.5 fathoms, timbers of ship, only good for firewood, 12-16 fathoms of a junk of a cable, a shovel, small pieces of iron (4lbs).

Portisham.
6 lbs langar shot, yard and half of rope, small piece of cordage, 2 pieces of cordage, murderer, 2 masts, some timber (ribs), a great shot, bottle of wine of 1.5 pints, some nails & a spike, little wooden powder box, 3 pieces of cordage.

Portland.
Ship's flag, astrolabe, crossestaff, quadrant, musket, 29 lemons, compass, a cloak, a cartridge of powder, pewter pot, old coats, old pair of stockings, a bible, a cap, 2 old coats, 2 empty cartridges, 18 rows of buttons, 2 old coats, a jacket, old shirt, old red waistcoat, 3 or 4 bolts of iron, 2 old jerkins, some old shirts later thrown away, some wool, 2 pair of old breeches, 2 shirts.

Waddon.
80 needles in a paper.

Weymouth.
7 small barrels, cable, hawser, 3 murderers, fore shrouds, 7 pieces of ordnance, foremast, bowsprit, windlass, capstan, 17 round shot, 2 anchors, 2 carriages, piece of new shootcable (20 fathom) piece of cable 10 fathoms, piece of junk, piece of hawser, some other cannonballs etc., went to W Bond, 3 fathom of junk sold for 3s to Peter Joy, small pieces of timber, hawser, 250 lemons, bought 2 pieces of timbers from men at Fleet for 18d

Wyke Regis.
Shirt containing letters & handkerchief, small quantity of wool in a bag about

3-4lbs, 2 pair old canvas breeches, 4lbs of wool, 2 old pair of breeches, 3 Flemish boxes of salves, 2 small sea chests, 2 chambers (or murderers), some small pieces of rope, 3 sails (mainsail, foretopsail, mizzen sail) great lantern, small barrel of stinking butter, wooden bowl with spike nails, screw mount for ordnance, rudder of a boat, oar of boat, compass short sword, 2 or 3 blocks of ship, 2 ship's rugs, pillow, old brass kettle, copper ladle, piece of small rope, 2 pieces of beef, piece of leather, piece of plot drawn in paper, some small ropes, pewter pot, some timber from the ship, 8 fathoms or wrist diameter rope, hawser, piece of rope.
Unknown.
Purchas said Pymer saved 2 armfuls of wool.

The Ship

From the crew's statements given at the inquiry we know the Golden Grape was originally a Dutch ship and from the items salvaged from the wreck we know it had three masts; fore, main and mizzen, bonnet sails, bowsprit, spritsail top, foretopmast, windlass, capstan, the rowle from the whipstaff, 2 anchors, 17 round shot, 2 carriages, 7 pieces of ordnance, 2 chambers, 8 murderers, a great shot, and 24 cross bar shot.

Whipstaff with roller in the centre

Because of the war with Spain and the trade embargo there would have been a surfeit of Dutch merchantmen at the time and if you wanted a new ship the Dutch provinces could provide a fluit at 40% of the cost of an English ship.

The Golden Grape was probably a Dutch fluyt, fluit or flyboat as the English called it, a merchantman that could carry lots of goods with minimal crew, about a third of those needed for a comparable English ship. They were also made of Baltic pine rather than oak so were cheaper to build and lighter and thus faster through the water but the developments made by the Dutch in the rigging of the ship meant less crew were needed to sail them.

Fluyts had a tumblehome appearance, that is, the broad width of the ship was brought inwards up to her narrow decks and this was another reason the Dutch undercut freight rates on the Baltic trade. Until 1699 the toll for travelling through the Helsingor Sound, a narrow channel east of Denmark leading into the

Dutch fluyts from all angles in 1647

Baltic Sea, was based on a ship's deck area, so a narrow decked ship that swelled out beneath to hold all the goods would incur a lower toll than other types of ships of similar tonnage. It got its name because its tumblehome shape meant the aftercastle was by necessity very narrow and resembled the shape of the tall narrow bowled champagne wine glass known as a flute.

Fluyts ranged from two masted ships of 200 tons up to three masted ships of 500 tons and even some 800 tons ships. The larger ships as well as having three masts, had the innovations of a bowsprit carrying a spritsail, and fluyts of over 500 tons were fitted with a whipstaff instead of just a tiller, both of which the Golden Grape had hence the Golden Grape would have been of at least 500 tons if not larger. Some idea of her length and breadth can be gauged from the fact that a smaller 400 tons fluyt had a length of 115 feet (35 metres) and a beam of 22 feet (6.8 metres). Foreknights are mentioned as being saved from the *Golden Grape* and these probably refer to the two large timbers called knightheads, which supported the ends of the windlasses or the heel of the bowsprit. The wreck of a Dutch fluyt named as the *Lion,* because of the carving on the top of her rudder, was found in 2009 in the cold but preserving waters of the Baltic Sea. Abaft the fore and main masts were carvings of a man's head with a beard and helmet – the knightheads. The replica of Drake's *Golden Hind* in London also has carved knightheads.

The presence of bonnet sails that are laced on to the bottom of a sail means they can be easily removed rather than having to furl sails in the event of a storm so again fewer crew were needed.

Dutch Merchants supposedly bought the Golden Grape on behalf of a Captain John Holding of Dover but when they got there Holding was found to be "not at home" it was then to be sold to two Dover merchants and they recruited John Redwood as Captain. Even if the sale wasn't strictly genuine the Dutch Steersman Cornelius Van Berkham who had sailed her the 162 miles from Amsterdam to Dover was to be supplanted by an English Captain for the 1167 miles long voyage from Dover to Cadiz.

At Amsterdam several of the 16 crew who had been taken on there were English sailors. This was not unusual as many nationalities of sailors went where the money was, and during the seventeenth century the Dutch virtually monopolised the Baltic trade, most of the Mediterranean and certainly the East Indies trade where they eclipsed the Portuguese and English East India Companies. The Dutch could sail their lightly armed ships with minimal crew so they could undercut the freight rates of merchant ships from other countries. So successful were they that England adopted or copied Holland's mercantile methods and Dutch financiers set up the Bank of England in 1694 to finance William of Orange's debt when he took over the throne of England.

The Dutch then had twice the merchant fleet of England's and 9 times that of France.

In 1603 England had a population of 4.5 million, France 16 million in 1600, Spain

8 million in 1596 while the Dutch Republic had well under 3 million so they needed foreign sailors both for their merchant and naval fleets and this was also a reason why they generally made trade partners with countries rather than establishing Dutch settlements there.

However northern Holland ports such as Amsterdam usually recruited nearby Hanseatic (German) and Scandinavian sailors whereas southern ports of Middleburg and those in Zeeland had more English and a few French seamen. If the shippers wanted the Golden Grape to appear as an English ship to the Spanish and not a Dutch one, they would have indeed recruited more English sailors in Amsterdam than usual.

Some of the crew left once the Golden Grape had reached Cadiz but at least one English sailor was enlisted in Cadiz. Again this shows the multi-nationality of seamen at the time and the attraction of a chance to sail to the New World and make a fortune from Cadiz. Following Henry VIII's marriage to Katharine of Aragon, English trade with Spain had improved and Henry built a hostel for English sailors in Cadiz. Of the twelve sailors of the crew of twenty men and boys giving evidence at the inquiry only one man was Dutch, the other eleven men were English so at least half the crew were English, more than enough to pass as an English trading ship with an English Captain.

The increase of crew from 16 to 20 for the longer voyage to Cadiz was needed to give the crew enough breaks on the voyage and reflected the difference between the Baltic manning with the Mediterranean trade routes, but also the extra men could defend the ship from being boarded, the favoured means of attack by pirates. No coincidence that gunner's mate, Richard Rich was recruited at Dover. On board were swords, muskets, murderers or breech loading cannon, all primarily used for boarding a ship or deterring boarders. Even the cross bar shot could be a means of killing a large number of sailors, though primarily it was used to dismast an enemy so allowing the attacked ship to sail away rather than stand and fight against heavier numbered assailants. But unusually for a fluit merchantman she also had at least 7 pieces of ordnance, a number that would deter all but the largest privateer.

Crew

Thomas Redwood	Master
Cornelius Van Berkham	Steersman/Master's mate
Robert Coast	Gunner
Michael Hatherwick	Boatswain
James Smyth	Boatswain's mate
Richard Rich	Gunner's mate
Richard Gregory	Surgeon
Thomas Byrd	Cook

John Pierce	Sailor
William Phillis	Sailor
George Allin	Sailor
William Bushel	Crewman

According to Redwood of the total 20 crew, 7 men and boys drowned and witness John Lovell of Fleet said that a sick member of the crew was taken to Fleet House where he later died, so with the above 12 giving evidence at the subsequent inquiry all are accounted for Redwood's total of 20. There is no mention of the bodies being recovered but one would have expected them to wash up in Chesil Cove.

Apart from those listed above there were four Dutchmen as passengers, and amongst the crew of twenty was a trumpeter, and a carpenter.

Thomas Redwood was the Master and Captain of the Golden Grape from Dover to Cadiz and for the return voyage from Sanlucar de Barrameda, while Cornelius Van Berkham was Master for the initial voyage from Amsterdam to Dover. There he became Master's Mate and steersman or navigator, using the astrolabe, quadrant, compass, and crossstaff (all of which were salvaged from the wreck) to locate his ship's position.

Robert Coast, the gunner controlled the use of the guns on board, and supervised Richard Rich, the gunner's mate and other crew. He would have been in charge of the ship when it was engaged in a fight or a chase.

Michael Hatherwick, the bosun looked after the stores, the ropes for the rigging, cables, anchors, sails, flags, colours and pendants. A bosun used a silver whistle to catch the attention of the crew before conveying the Master's orders. He or James Smyth, the bosun's mate was in charge of the candles used throughout the confines of the ship, a serious duty considering the danger of fire on board ship.

Thomas Byrd, the cook victualled the crew, keeping the salt meat in water. He also used the fat from cooking to sell for candles. The green wood used to light his fire first thing created smoke that fumigated the forecastle and it was his duty to extinguish the fire with water as soon as a battle was announced. The crew would also have used his fire to dry their clothes.

The carpenter had to be adaptable in repairing the ship from leakages or battle or storm damage and would have had a full set of tools in his chest and ensured there was a supply of spare parts to repair masts, yards, the rudder and pumps. He would also need a supply of oakum, lead sheets, wood, canvas and tallow for leaks and sail repairs. Some ship's carpenters painted the spars and sails before battle with alum to make them non-inflammable.

Richard Gregory, the chirurgeon or surgeon was solely responsible for tending to the crew's ailments and accidents and would need to have knowledge of any foreign diseases likely to be encountered in the voyage.

Trumpeters were used on board ships to hail another ship, to signal and herald important people aboard and to blow a farewell when dignitaries left the ship. He

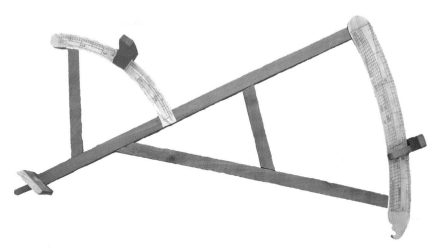

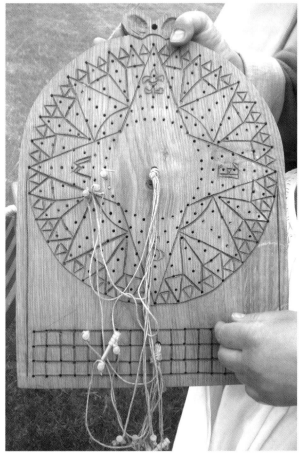

The backstaff or Davis quadrant (above) enabled seamen to take latitude readings from the sun or moon without looking directly into the sun but instead using the shadow of the sun on the common horizon vane, bottom left of the staff.

The traverse board (left) has two sections, the top recording the direction sailed while the bottom section of columns for different speeds is used to record the ship's speed every hour, taken from the ship's log, a knotted rope let out behind the ship. Pegs recording the direction sailed for each half hour were placed in each of the 8 rings starting from the centre until the 4 hour watch was complete and then a dead reckonong course could be plotted.

used his trumpet to attend the Captain, and entertain in the Captain's cabin during dinner, and also played music to encourage the crew in their tasks for example when weighing the anchor.

In Greek mythology mention is made of the trumpeter on board Odysseus's ship blowing a martial call to signal that they were under attack. Trumpeters together with drums were also common on Venetian galleys in the 15th Century both for signalling as well as for music. John Blanke, a black man, was trumpeter on Henry VIII's warship the *Mary Rose* where he was paid 8 pence a day.

A Master John Brewer was one of Drake's trumpeters who gave evidence against Hatton's man, Thomas Doughty who was tried and executed for sedition, during Drake's circumnavigation.

In Nicholas Rodger's The Safeguard of the Sea, he states that in 1582 all the Queen's ships were to have a trumpeter, and the largest ships a trumpeter who should have " a silver trumpet, and himself and his noise to have banners of silk of the admiral's colours. His place is to keep the poop, to attend the general's going ashore and coming aboard, and all other strangers or boats, and to sound as an entertainment to them, as also when they hail a ship, or when they charge, board or enter her".

Rodger goes on to say that in the 1630s the trumpeter still served a useful purpose not only for signalling but also in being in charge at the poop of the sailors working the mizzenmast's sails while the Master was in charge of the mainmast and the bosun the foremast.

It was not only just an English naval trait for in 1642 Abel Tasman, while on a Dutch East India ship off the coast of New Zealand, heard a trumpet-like sound from the Maoris on shore, to which his ship's trumpeter replied in kind.

In 1655 William Horner sailed as trumpeter aboard the merchant ship *Smyrna*, bound to the East Indies. According to his will, proved twenty years later, he left a silver trumpet worth six pounds and three shillings, as well as a brass trumpet with silver garnishing worth one pound, which suggests the former was for heralding duties, while the latter was the day-to-day one for signalling.

It seems therefore that the trumpeter on the Golden Grape would have been in charge of the poop and mizzenmast as well as for signals. Perhaps such unambiguous signalling helped when there was a mixed Dutch English crew speaking a different language, as well as clearly transmitting the Master's orders above the sound of crashing waves. The trumpeter would also have been there to create a good impression when heralding aboard the Spanish merchants to trade at Cadiz though possibly muted at Sanlucar.

Sailors such as William Phillis, John Pierce and George Allin, were usually able seamen who could undertake all the duties including those aloft, taking in sails, and who also attending the guns, while William Bushell, a crewman was probably a landsman or an elderly sailor no longer quite up to it and would swab the decks amongst other more menial duties, hence the piratical expression of swabs being the lowest class of men on board.

Outbound cargo.

Pepper.

The Spanish merchants had always got their supply of peppers via Lisbon when the Portuguese controlled the trade with the Moluccan Spice Islands in the East Indies but the Dutch had ousted them and the English East India Company from the East Indies (the English East India Company transferred their trade attentions to India). Now all pepper came from Holland and in the case of the Golden Grape it had been loaded at Amsterdam and was bound for Sanlucar, no doubt to be smuggled out to the Indies in the New World. In 1640 the price peaked at 694.2 maravedis per pound in Andalusia and in 1641 it was still 613, the highest two years in that century. With 34 maravedis equivalent to one real this means 18 reales to the pound or 2.25 pieces of eight (reales or £12) to the pound in weight.

Cornelius Van Berkham, the steersman who sailed the *Golden Grape* from Amsterdam to Dover states the amount of pepper loaded at Amsterdam and consigned to the un-named merchant(s) of Sanlucar is about 200 barrels of pepper. If we assume for dry goods that there are 3.28 bushels to a barrel and a bushel weighs 28 pounds this gives a staggering total value of 41,328 pieces of eight (about £10,500). When the two boats from the port meet them outside the bar of Sanlucar to unload the pepper they then load a bag of 500 pistoles of gold, many bags of pieces of eight, two bags of silver plate, a peg of silver, a loaf of silver, together with the silks and two bags of red wool in return. The whole exchange, with unknown merchants, unspecified bags of pieces of eight, and an unknown consignee for these return goods, appears to be a totally clandestine mission.

The "peg" of silver is probably a pig, misheard by the notary at the *Golden Grape* Inquiry maybe because of Van Berkham's Dutch accent and it then remains a "pegg" throughout the rest of the inquiry's statements. Pigs of different cast metals, lead, iron and silver are formed when ingots are cast in sand fed from a central reservoir (or sow) through small channels and the ingots are called pigs as they resemble pigs feeding off a sow. The small connecting channel can be broken off once they have cooled. A later 17th century shipwreck off Chesil Beach mentioned "most of the silver lost except for 7 sows (lumps of silver)" so the porcine connection is firmly established for silver ingots.

Other cargo.

As well as the pepper, they loaded "certain cordage, certain barrels of nails, a certain quantity of tallow and some blocks for rigging of ships" on board the Golden Grape at Amsterdam. When they reached Dover more cordage and certain parcels of copper were loaded aboard the Golden Grape before they sailed for Cadiz.

Cordage is the term that covers the ropes used in rigging sailing ships, their cables and hawsers. For a ship the size of the *Batavia*, a Dutch East India fluyt of 650 tons built in 1628, there would be 21 km (13 miles) of rope used aboard her.

The cordage loaded at Amsterdam would have come from the hemp cultivated in the western part of the central Netherlands. Not only was hemp used to make ropes but also sails and the Dutch built Golden Grape would have had both made from hemp. Canvas is a Dutch derivation of the Latin cannibis.

The cordage loaded at Dover could possibly have come from near to where the Golden Grape was wrecked. At the western end of Chesil Beach lies Bridport, which was famous from the time of King John for its rope making because its hinterland was ideal for growing both hemp and flax. In 1213 the Bridport rope makers had to work night and day to provide rope for King John's navy. Its importance was emphasised by a decree from Henry VIII that all hemp grown within 5 miles of the town was to be used to make rope for his navy. A more macabre use of rope was the hangmen's noose that was known as the Bridport dagger and which features in the aftermath of the wreck of the Golden Grape.

As shipping trade expanded in the 16th century Queen Elizabeth ordered that all landowners holding over 60 acres should grow hemp or face a £5 fine. Philip II of Spain followed suit to service his Indies shipping trade and navy. Obviously from the Golden Grape's outbound cargo, Spain needed more, or possibly cheaper, supplies.

The parcels of copper loaded at Dover could have originally come from the Falun mine of Sweden, which was producing 70% of the world's copper in the 17th century, in fact so plentiful was their supply of copper that from 1624 they produced copper as well as silver dalers as money, large sheets of copper to the equivalent values of the Spanish dollar coins. The 10 daler weighed 20 kg and it must have been a relief when they went out of circulation in 1776.

However the copper mines of the Lake District in England also produced copper from the late 16th century. Archaeologists working at the site of the Jamestown English settlement, established in America in 1607, found high arsenic traces by spectrometry in the copper they unearthed. It proved that the copper was not only European in origin but from England so the source of the parcels of copper on board the Golden Grape could have been English. If it had been Swedish the copper would have more likely to have been loaded at Amsterdam as the Dutch had a virtual monopoly of the Baltic trade. The Swedish copper daler sheet money does give us the price of copper as half a daler per kilogram of copper, so about 2 reales per pound.

Return Cargo.

Sherry sacke.

At Cadiz, Cornelius Williamson Heddah, a young merchant, loaded aboard the Golden Grape "twelve butts of sherryes sackes" on the Master's, the Gunner's and Master's Mate's account. John Jacob Fabiansa put on board four more butts of sacke on his own and his Amsterdam father's account. Sherryes sacke was the particular

Spanish white wine found in the area between the towns of Jerez de la Frontera, Sanlucar de Barrameda at the mouth of the river Guadalquivir, and El Puerto de Santa Maria, the small port opposite Cadiz.

When war with France prevented the English from buying their traditional Bordeaux wines the Spanish took the opportunity to put forward sherry sacke as a substitute. By 1491 all export tax on wine was abolished for English and Spanish ships trading at Sanlucar and in 1517 English merchants were allowed to establish themselves in the region and even to bear arms. Exports of sherries sacke or sacke grew until Henry VIII divorced Catherine of Aragon fermenting Spanish unrest with England. A great number of English merchants fled and the export of sherry slowed during the threat of the Spanish Armada however when Drake raided Cadiz in 1587 he captured 2,900 pipes of sherry, which helped bolster the demand for sherry. By the time James I had made peace with Spain, the English merchant colony at Sanlucar had been re-established and thus the demand for sherry continued. Sherry at this time was not fortified so the strength of the sherry sacke produced was a maximum of 16% ABV. A butt or pipe of sherry contains 105 imperial gallons.

Tent.

Tent was a Spanish red wine produced at that time in Galicia in north western Spain and in Malaga and as the latter was part of Andalusia the 3 pipes of tent loaded aboard the Golden Grape at Cadiz by Robert Coast, the ship's gunner on his own account, probably originated there.

Raisins of the sun.

The best raisins are the Malaga, muscatel or sun raisins, which were left to dry on the vine. These particular grapes do not drop when ripe but instead the stem twists and the grapes shrivel and become sweeter because the sugar intensifies as the water evaporates in the hot sun hence why they were known as "raisins of the sun" for the Golden Grape or listed as "raisins solis" when S. Mico imported them into Weymouth in 1649 and even today they are known as sun dried raisins.

Cadiz merchants Martin Laderoon De Gavarre and Anthony De Swasse loaded 1019 barrels of raisins of the sun onto the Golden Grape bound for a certain Careiles and other merchants of Havre de Grace in France and a further 234 barrels of raisins of the sun were loaded by fellow Cadiz merchant Albertus Martin to be delivered to Garratt Vanteene and Edward Peters of Dover.

Olive oil.

Cadiz merchants Martin Laderoon De Gavarre and Anthony De Swasse loaded 400 jars of olive oil on board the Golden Grape and these were consigned, again, to a certain Careiles and other merchants of Havre de Grace in France.

Spurred by the demand from the Indies, which caused the price of wheat in Spain to double, olive oil to triple and wine to increase eightfold in the 15th century, the

Guadalquivir Valley was planted with cereals, wines and olives for sale not only in Seville but also for export to Northern Europe and the Indies. In the 16th century Seville produced 7.1 million kilos of olive oil. Apart from cooking, salet oyle or olive oil was used to spread on bread, in the soap industry, in sealing wax, in rush lights and in cloth finishing. Taken with wine it was said to ease kidney stone pain and a saucer of salet oyle (or salad oil) down the throat was a traditional English cure for snakebites. For sailing ships and colonial outposts such as Virginia and Jamaica, olive oil replaced butter as it lasted longer on the voyage and in the hotter climate colonies.

In 1960 John Coggin classified Spanish olive oil jars, made in or around Seville from the 16th and 17th centuries, as being of three types. Type A oblong jars were normally used for wine and held a Castilian wine arroba of 4.26 gallons whereas late 16th century type B globular jars held half an oil arroba or 1.65 gallons. Type C carrot shaped jars held 0.57 gallons. As Coggin is writing in a Yale University publication I have assumed he refers to US gallons and have converted litres to US gallons where necessary, which seems to confirm that they are indeed US gallons.

When I was searching the web for a photographic example of a Spanish oil jar I eventually came across mention of one that had been trawled up near Wolf Rock, 4 nautical miles south west of Lands End, and which had been presented to the Penlee House Gallery & Museum, who very kindly allowed me to take some photographs of it while it was on display at the National Maritime Museum Cornwall in Falmouth.

I sent the photographs to Dr Andrew Fitzpatrick of Wessex Archaeology to ask if he could help give a more precise type identification and date and according to their medieval pottery expert Lorraine Mepham.

"This example is a Spanish olive jar of fairly common type – these jars were made not only in or around Seville but also in Portugal, in an area centred on the Alentejo (the so-called Merida ware); the Seville types are more common. A three-fold typology (types A, B and C) was defined by Goggin (1960). This example is almost identical to one in the collection of the Museum Boymans-Van Beuningen in Rotterdam (Hurst *et al*. 1986, fig. 29.80), which is described as a small version of Goggin's type A large jar, which was used for wine, although it is also very close to his type B globular jar for olive oil. The difference seems to be in the base – the type A has a pointed base while the type B is rounded. The collared rim, however, is of type B, and matches examples found on Armada wrecks; also, the shoulder is not rounded, which Goggin considered to be a late feature. The Museum Boyman's-Van Beuningen olive jar (which is a Merida type) is dated broadly to the 17th century, which would fit with the 1641 date for the wreck."

References

Goggin, J.M., 1960, *The Spanish Olive Jar: an Introductory Study*, Yale University Publications on Anthropology 62

Hurst, J.G., Neal, D.S. and van Beuningen, H., 1986, *Pottery Produced and Traded in North West Europe 1350-1650*, Rotterdam Papers 4

A fine half arroba example holding 6.25 litres, (which again equates to 1.65 US gallons) was found on the Armada ship the *Trinidad Valencera* wrecked off the coast of Donegal. Olive oil jar shards have been found on Spanish shipwrecks off Florida and at English settlement sites in Virginia as well as in Exeter where olive oil was used in Exeter cloth finishing. Sixteenth century records apparently show that olive oil was predominately shipped in either one arroba or half arroba jars and if we assume those on the Golden Grape in 1641 were type B half arroba jars of 1.65 US gallons then the 400 jars totalled 660 US gallons (550 Imperial gallons or 2,500 litres) where one gallon was said to be enough to keep a man supplied for a year.

Silk.

The 43 bolts of taffeta silks loaded aboard the Golden Grape at Sanlucar would have come from either Seville or Granada. The Moriscos (Muslims who stayed and had been forced to convert to Catholicism after the Moors had been defeated and forced out of Southern Spain) had irrigated the land and produced silk throughout Andalusia from their Mulberry Tree plantations for many years. Doubts about their true Christianity in the second half of the 16th century lead to a rebellion in Granada in 1571 and their eventual forced move to the north of the country where they could not aid a Muslim invasion from Africa.

Christians took over the industry with disastrous results. Where three Moriscos had earned a good living, one Christian was barely scraping by and silk output fell. Eventually production increased and by 1603 there were 3,000 silk looms in Granada. Fernando Garrido's research shows a similar decline in Seville where there had been 1600 silk weavers' looms at the beginning of the 16th Century but this had fallen to 300 looms by the end of the 17th century. By 1616 the last of the Moriscos had been forced out of Spain, thus exacerbating the enmity of the Barbary "Turks".

Oranges & lemons.

Though not mentioned as being loaded aboard the Golden Grape, the oranges and lemons salvaged from the wreck would have come from the area directly around Seville and could have been shipped by the crew on their own account just as in the 1960s my father always brought back punetts of tomatoes or small barrels of Jersey potatoes when he was Chief Engineer on the British Rail Channel Islands ferries returning to Weymouth.

Gold and silver.

Sir Francis Drake historian and explorer, John Thrower, took photographs of El Camino Real (The Royal Road) when he left his companions on a hill and ventured down the track and found a rare piece of surviving paving on the Camino Real. The narrow mule track ran through the jungle from Panama on the Pacific coast, across the isthmus first to the Caribbean Sea port of Nombre de Dios, and then, after

Drake had sacked the town and successfully attacked the silver bearing mule train in 1573, it was diverted to Portobello. Thrower's photograph was taken on the part of the Camino Real common to both destinations. By 1597 the inhabitants of Nombre de Dios had relocated to Portobello, which was a far more secure haven and soon had two forts guarding it against attack.

The Camino Real was literally a funnel of silver from the New World of Spanish South America to the Old World of Spain and thence beyond. Silver bars, plates, pegs of silver, silver coinage in the form or pieces of eight, four, two, one, and half reales disgorged through it. The veritable mountain of silver discovered in 1545 at Potosi in the Vice Royalty of Peru (now Bolivia) produced millions of coins over two centuries. These, as well as bars of silver, were loaded on llamas and taken down from the Andes to the port of Arica and then loaded aboard ships northward to Panama.

When news that the yearly Tierra Firme Fleet from Spain had arrived at either Nombre de Dios or after Drake's raid, at Portobello (in the time of the Golden Grape), the silver bullion and coinage gathered together at Panama was loaded on to a 100 string of mules and taken over the Camino Real to one of those ports. There it was loaded onto the Spanish Treasure fleet, which would sail to Havana to await the New Spain Fleet bringing riches from Mexico and the Yucatan before sailing back together to Spain.

Silver bars should have been stamped with quinto marks to show the Royal tax of a fifth had been paid and they were accounted for by the ship's silvermaster but many bars, pegs, wedges or ladles of silver were smuggled on board without the mark, having paid no tax. Spanish South American merchants had travelled to the ports where, amid the yearly Fleet fairs, they purchased return goods for the settlers in South America. Nombre de Dios swelled from 200 inhabitants to over 5,000 at fair times.

These return goods, many of them smuggled out from Spain, were transported back the same way as the silver had come out, even as far as Potosi, which at the time was one of the richest cities in the world. Its churches and shrines were bedecked in silver. If there was room stones were carried back by mule to pave the Camino Real because even in the dry season it was still a tortuous route that became impossible during the wet winters.

Gold escudos, particularly the two escudos known as pistoles or doubloons had already been shipped from the Nuevo Reino mint of Santa Fe de Bogata and loaded on board the fleet at Cartegena.

It was this illicit trade in smuggled bullion and coins from the South America treasure fleets that paid for the pepper on board the *Golden Grape* at Sanlucar de Barrameda while the pepper etc., from her was smuggled out to Portobello for the rich Spanish South American merchants and silver mine owners.

Salvage

The Golden Grape was wrecked on the Chesil Beach in Dorset, a bank of pebbles stretching from Portland westwards for 18 miles to Burton Cliffs and a beach that physically links the "Isle" of Portland to the mainland at Abbotsbury. Behind the beach runs a lagoon starting from the Smallmouth inlet from Portland Roads, the expanse of sea between Portland and Weymouth. From Smallmouth the salty waters of the Fleet become less and less tidal and more and more brackish the nearer the lagoon gets to its termination at Abbotsbury. On the way it passes the villages of Wyke Regis, Chickerell, Fleet, and Langton Herring all situated near to its mainland shore. At this time most of their inhabitants survived as husbandmen or fishermen and there were strict demarcations along the beach between which marks each village's fishermen could fish.

As well as fishing in the Fleet and off the Chesil Beach there was also a harvest from the sea in the form of flotsam and jetsam, of cargoes washed from the decks of ships or from shipwrecks themselves. The bay was a trap that ensured any floating objects, maybe oranges or lemons, timbers etc., would eventually wash up at some point of the beach. The Dorset author Thomas Hardy labelled the waters off Chesil Beach "Deadman's Bay", as often the bodies of shipwrecked sailors or passengers would be found washed up on the shores of the beach. It was natural when there was a storm for people to beach comb the shore and for Innkeeper Arthur Grey to have gone over the Fleet from the shore at Wyke to the beach in his trow (a flat bottomed boat made to navigate the shallow mudflats of the Fleet waters) to see if anything had been washed up.

He was there when the *Golden Grape* came ashore and, luckily for the crew, was washed high up on the beach. Otherwise the loss of life would have been much greater if the ship had stuck on the shore and broken up in the surf from the pounding of the waves and the barrage of the pebbles thrown against it in the maelstrom. Not only does the surf break even the sturdiest of ships in a short time, be they wooden or even later iron or steel, but it is virtually impossible for victims to struggle or swim ashore unaided. The undertow created as the mountainous waves recede draws the pebbles back out like a moving carpet for anybody standing on it. As it does so it lifts those pebbles up and swirls them around as if the pebbles and the victim were in the drum of a huge washing machine with the pebbles pummelling their bodies. Bodies, dead or alive, that have made it to shore have been denuded of all clothes save for a cuff or collar, and literally beaten black and blue and one survivor in a later shipwreck in the late 18th century was mistaken for a woman of colour so badly bruised was she.

On the day it was Grey who offered the Captain and crew shelter at his inn at Wyke and took them and their salvage over the Fleet in his boat. Others from nearby flocked to the beach to see what they could find and word swiftly got further and further out during the day and the days following. Not only Wyke people were there at the start but from Portland also, some of whom may have seen the ship in trouble

Sail boats in the Fleet, the Smallmouth rope ferry, and Portland in the distance

and seen it strike the shore and made there way along the beach. Then people came from villages along the Fleet and from Weymouth and Melcombe Regis and the day after people from even further out at Abbotsbury, Waddon and Upway.

After all these people had got their salvage and managed to keep their goods from others they had to get them home somehow. People who had come on foot carried raisins away in their aprons, jerkins, and bags or whatever piece of clothing they could make into a bag. Some managed a jar of oil or even a barrel but what of a number of full barrels of raisins or jars of oil? In order to get them home they had to band together either as people from the same village or possibly in groups either that were fishing crews or smuggling crews for some of these groups proved well organised. If they had no boat they had to pay a boatman to carry the goods across the shore to the mainland giving the boat crew one barrel out of every six and sometimes pay the landowner in kind to land them on his land. Once on the mainland shore of the Fleet they still had to get the goods home. Some individuals had horses, one person borrowed the vicar's horse from Abbotsbury, other local groups from Wyke used a farmer's plough to load the goods on and carry them off and some even brought carts from as far a field as Corton and Abbotsbury.

What has to be remembered is the generally poor state of the roads at this time. It was said at the time that if you drew a line from the Wash to Gloucester and then a curve down to Weymouth, the area inside would cover where heavy wheeled traffic was well established in the early 17th Century. However wagons, even if available, were usually banned in the winter as they badly cut up what were little more than packhorse tracks and made them impassable and if a cart could be used in the rainy winter it was limited by decree to carrying one ton only and could harness no more than 5 horses to it. Most of England was encouraged to use packhorses between All Saints Day and May Day. Indeed so bad were carts for damaging the road surfaces that they were banned from the wooden quays at Weymouth and Melcombe Regis and iron studded or rimmed wheeled carts were banned from crossing the wooden bridge linking the towns so maybe most carts, instead of spoked wheels banded by an iron tyre, had solid wooden wheels like the carts depicted in illustrations of Portland carrying stone.

Walter Bond had his group's goods carried by boat across to Foxholes, a lower part of the mainland shore with tracks into Weymouth. There he either arranged for carts to carry the salvaged goods on the flatter ground all the way from there into Weymouth or reloaded the goods onto Weymouth boats to take them back by sea to Weymouth Quay. Other locals paid to have their bulky spoils carried down the Fleet waters to the ferry at Smallmouth and again other groups came with their boats from either Weymouth or Portland to load the goods and row or sail them back to Weymouth Quay or Portland Castle.

Local landowner and Squire, Maximilian Mohun, together with his son and men, rowed down the Fleet Lagoon from the village of Fleet to the scene of the wreck and salvaged many things, heaping them up on the beach and then taking some items back up the Fleet to his Manor House near the village of Fleet. Likewise Sir John Strangways the landowner at Abbotsbury, whose family had rights to wreck on parts of the Chesil Beach, sent a boat full of his men down the Fleet to salvage what they could. He vehemently insisted that he had a moiety (or equal part) of any salvaged goods from at least one man in Langton.

Salvage since then.

In April 1981 a solid silver "pebble", picked up from Chesil Beach and known locally as a "Duckey Stone" was auctioned at Duke's Auction Rooms in Dorchester. It was about five inches in diameter and weighed 37 ounces and came from local jeweler John Vincent's collection. When I examined it prior to the auction, there were no marks and it seemed as if a ladle had scooped out some molten silver to produce a hemispherical silver lump on cooling. The lack of marks would suggest it was smuggled silver.

One story, which may be apocryphal, is that a duck shooter found it one day on the beach and took it to a blacksmith to make into lead shot but the blacksmith recognized it as silver and gave him some ready made lead shot in exchange. On his deathbed the blacksmith is said to have admitted what he'd done to his friend and asked his forgiveness. This was duly given but the duck shooter said "what riles I is that if only you'd opened your mouth afore we could have had cartloads of them". Another story is that Portland fishermen used them as doorstops.

It certainly wasn't a single event as in 1848 it was reported "A large piece of silver, weighing about 60 ounces (called a Duckey stone by the Portlanders) was found a few days since on the Portland Beach, by a poor man. A number of these lumps of silver have been found there at various times; it is thought that there is a great many still left, the remains of wreck many years since".

A different slant was put on the meaning of duckey stone in 1897. "Frequently nuggets of silver have been found. These are known locally as "ducky stones" so called from the fact that on one occasion a finder of one of these lumps of silver, being ignorant of its value, used to play a game of 'ducky' which consists of each player throwing a stone at one belonging to one of the players, which is placed on a big stone or rock - a favourite pastime in the good old days."

1827 was obviously another good year for finds from Chesil Beach. "During the last week in consequence of a violent gale of wind from the West, which caused a great convulsion in the tremendous beach of Portland, many pieces of ancient coin, bars of gold & silver, supposed to have been buried in the wreck of the Dutch buccaneering vessel *Hope*, which was lost there near 100 years ago, have been picked up by many people of that island, Wyke, etc. Several other valuable articles in silver, bowls, spoons etc., have also been found, likely to have been on board the *Alexander*, East Indiaman, and the *Colville*, West Indiaman, that were unfortunately lost on that part of the coast".

The fact that the *Hope*, a Dutch West Indiaman wrecked in 1749 is mentioned is due to it being well known as having £50,000 of treasure on board. By the time of its wreck there were newspapers to report the wreck, the salvage and the subsequent court cases for stealing from the wreck. In comparison by the 1820s very little was written or known about the Golden Grape, which was much nearer the Portland and Wyke end of the beach than the *Hope*. This book is the first time the full enquiry into the *Golden Grape* has been published. The other wrecks are mentioned because the *Alexander* was wrecked off Wyke in 1815 and the *Colville* in Chesil Cove in 1824 so they were still fresh in the public's mind and thus supposedly accounted for the location of finds on the beach there.

Mention of gold bars was confirmed when we talked with local seine fishermen who said that brass bars with funny marks on them had been picked up on the beach over the years. The marks they described are the ones stamped on the Spanish South American gold bars.

In 1988 a local pensioner metal detecting on Chesil Beach found two gold 2 escudo cobs coins known as pistoles or doubloons, minted at the Sante Fe de Bogata mint and later an 8 escudos gold cob coin from the Lima mint, the latter as good as any found on the 1715 Spanish Fleet wrecked off Florida. A truly sumptuous coin that I advised him not to sell for less than £2,500 at the time but now worth about £10,000. I know one dealer got in touch but he told him that he was keeping it for his son.

Chapter 3 After the Wreck

English Civil War.

The war between the Parliamentarians (Roundheads) and Royalists (Cavaliers) started in 1642 and finally ended in 1651. The Parliamentarians tried King Charles the First for treason and the King was executed by beheading on 30 January 1649(50). His son, later to be King Charles the Second was exiled to France.

Oliver Cromwell rose to commander of the Parliamentarian Army then later ruled the protectorate from 1653 to 1659.

Dorset participants.

Parliamentarians (Roundheads)

Colonel William Sydenham – Governor of Weymouth & Melcombe Regis
Major Francis Sydenham – William's younger brother
Captain John Arthur – merchant and ship owner of Melcombe
Vice Admiral Sir William Batten
Sir William Waller – Major General

Royalists (Cavaliers)

Fabian Hodder – merchant and ship owner of Melcombe
Anne Hodder- Fabian's wife
Henry Rose – chandler of Melcombe
John Cade - sea captain
John Mills - town constable
Sir Lewis Dyve - Sergeant-Major-General in Dorset, based in Sherborne Castle
Sir William Hastings - Governor of Portland Castle
General George Goring - Lieutenant General of Horse
Elizabeth Wall – go between
Walter Bond - fisherman of Hope or Ope, Weymouth
John Dry - tanner of Weymouth
Thomas Samways – tailor of Melcombe
Philip Ashe a sailor of Weymouth
Leonard Symonds
William Philips – shoemaker of Weymouth
Richard Mighill - Irish mercenary
John Hodder – mercer of Melcombe and brother of Fabian Hodder
Humphrie Weld – wealthy Londoner who bought Lulworth Castle in 1641
Maximilian Mohun – Squire of Fleet. (Name pronounced Moon hence Moonfleet)
Robert Mohun – son of Maximilian
Sir John Strangways – MP. Owner of Abbey lands at Abbotsbury
Giles Strangways – Colonel, son of Sir John Strangways

Civil War – Treachery, Battle, and a Hanging

Fabian Hodder's standing in the local community was reflected by the fact that in 1639-40 while George Churchey was the Mayor of Weymouth, Fabian Hodder was Treasurer of the Town, and though Mayors come and go, a Treasurer tends to stay on, so he was a man of power and influence in the local community.

After the shipwreck and salvage of the Golden Grape in December 1641 and the subsequent Court of Inquiry, which continued until 28th March 1642, there was constant unrest between King Charles and Parliament and this eventually led to outright Civil War in August 1642. The twin ports of Melcombe and Weymouth together with the Portland Roads anchorage were of importance because of their location on the south coast. Supplies could easily be shipped in via them and ships brought in to add firepower not to mention reinforcements either by ship's personnel or by the transportation of troops. The Parliamentarians were first to hold the towns and immediately started fortifying them. The Chapel above the harbours on the Weymouth side was made into a fort and there was already one at the Nothe, this to command the approach to the twin ports and also to cover some of Portland Roads. Meanwhile Melcombe had forts and gates added to safeguard it from attack by land from the north and from the west via the Backwater and of course it had the drawbridge to Weymouth as its southern defence. As early as 1625 "the walls of the Blockhouse are to be built up with stone, and a Purbeck stone platform to be made for the two guns on the North". In 1626 the towns have had an additional gun platform built on both the Weymouth and the Melcombe Regis sides and in 1641 the total number of cannon was 15 demi culverins and 7 sakers.

Meanwhile Fabian Hodder had his own trouble with Parliament in the autumn of 1642 because of one of his business transactions. He appears to have disguised a cargo of Fullers Earth as tobacco-pipe clay so avoiding the duty.

"House of Commons Journal Volume 2: 28 October 1642
"Transporting Fullers Earth."
Resolved, upon the Question, That Wm. Padner and William Wayte, Comptrollers and Officers of the Customs in the Port of Poole, be forthwith sent for, as Delinquents; for suffering the Bark the *Black Dogg* of Weymouth, freighted with Twenty Tons of Fullers Earth, under Colour of Tobacco-pipe Clay, to pass; and not to take Bonds, as they ought to do, that it would not pass or unlade in any Port out of the King's Dominions.
Resolved, That Fabian Hodder be forthwith sent for, as a Delinquent; for endeavouring to transport a Bark, freighted with Fullers Earth, to Rotterdam in Holland.
Ordered, that the Bark called the *Black Dogg* of Weymouth, freighted with Fullers Earth, now in the Port of London, be stayed by the Officers of the said Port, until this House take farther Order: And that the Examination of the whole Business be

Portland Castle; boats in the Fleet; Smallmouth Ferry house & Wyke Church

referred to the Committee for the Customs".

Unfortunately there is no record of what further action was taken against the ship or against Fabian Hodder regarding this transgression. This wasn't to be the last time that Fabian Hodder was to have trouble in Poole, but as in this instance, the authorities proved to be negligent in their duties and one has to wonder if it was due to incompetence or being bribed to look the other way.

The small ports of Weymouth and Melcombe Regis were fought over and changed hands several times during the Civil War but in June 1644 they had been retaken by the Parliamentarian Roundheads and together with Sandsfoot Castle, were governed by Colonel William Sydenham, whilst the Royalists, under the command of Sir William Hastings, held Portland.

It was in February 1645 that Hastings was informed that there was a conspiracy afoot to take the ports of Weymouth and Melcombe Regis back into Royalist control. He was told that the leader of the conspiracy was a leading Melcombe councillor and merchant called Fabian Hodder, the same merchant mentioned in the wreck of the Golden Grape and the same person who gave shelter in his house to the Captain of the Golden Grape. Hodder's wife Anne had sent a letter to Sir Lewis Dyve at Sherborne saying that the towns were ripe for taking from the Roundheads and that they would need his support to carry it off. Dyve had already been ordered by the King to take Weymouth for the Crown so he was a willing ally and promised to bring 1500 of his men from Sherborne to support the attack on Weymouth and Melcombe Regis from the north. He sent orders to Sir William Hastings at Portland to aid the uprising with an attack from Portland on the southern flank of Weymouth.

His messenger was Elizabeth Wall, the same woman used by Anne Hodder to deliver her letter to Dyve. He ensured that Hastings would take his words seriously by giving Elizabeth Wall a tongue token, used to prove the person carrying it was close to the Royalist hierarchy. It was a token with the King's head on one side and his initial on the other and was small enough to be hidden under the tongue if the messenger was stopped by the Parliamentarian Roundheads. Hastings knew his duty and promptly endorsed the plan. In the coming days Elizabeth Wall conveyed messages between Sherborne and Portland to finalise the details and crucially to set the time and the date.

It was to be midnight on Sunday 9th February 1645. The sermon summoning the conspirators to Portland Castle that afternoon was given on the Sunday morning at St Andrews Church, the church that stood above Church Ope Cove. Part of the royalist force at Portland, together with Portlanders themselves, was to report for duty to Portland Castle by five o'clock that afternoon. Of the one hundred and twenty that turned up, half were to go by boat and the rest by land to attack Weymouth.

As well as wearing white handkerchiefs tied around their arm so they could recognize friend from foe they needed a password on that pitch-black night. Mark Vine states in his book "The Crabchurch Conspiracy" that the password Crabchurch came from an area of Portland.

In 1693 Captain Greenville Collins published his British Coastal Pilot series of charts around Britain. On number 12, covering the South Dorset coast including Weymouth and Portland, there is "Crab" marked on the map just inland from Church Ope Cove. The Royalists were in the church and Crab was nearby so why not "Crabchurch" as the password as it would certainly be peculiar to Portland?

So where does Crab come from? Apparently there was a pier in Church Ope Cove and a cart track down to the beach where there was a thriving fishing community. Inigo Jones shipped Portland Stone out from there for his buildings in London in the 1620s and when he died, Sir Christopher Wren took over, until the pier, and with it the cart track, was washed away in a landslip in the 1670s. The "crab" was used to pull the boats up the beach. In this instance crab is a capstan where the bars are inserted right through the top of the barrel instead of into the pockets of a drumhead in a conventional capstan and hence would look like a crab from above. This theory is confirmed by Collins' chart of Brighton where he states "a town that standeth by the seaside on a Beach. There are many vessels [that] belong to it, which they heap up with Crabs [capstans] on the dry Beach."

Church Ope Cove with boat haulage

The conspirators within Melcombe and Weymouth were to be the key to the twin assaults. Hodder's associate, our old friend from the Golden Grape salvage, Walter Bond, was entrusted to guide the force of Royalists from Portland to attack the Nothe Fort by boat. Bond is described, as the "Hope fisherman" so presumably he worked and lived from what is now the in-filled Hope Square but which, in those days, was a cove or Ope on the Weymouth Harbour shoreline, also known locally as the hole.

The 60 men, consisting of part of the Royalist force and supplemented by fierce hardy Portlanders, would probably have been rowed from Portland Castle in 5 or 6 lerrets, and led by Walter Bond to the chosen landing place, which would have been out of sight of Sandsfoot Castle, Bincleaves Fort as well as the Nothe Fort.

Lerrets are double-ended boats up to 21 feet in length and 7 feet in beam, that were later used primarily off the Chesil Beach for fishing, and recovering flotsam and jetsam, including of course, buoyed smuggled goods. Depending on size they were usually either four or six oared (though there were some eight oared ones too) and used thowl pins rather than rowlocks, and the handle end of the oar was weighted with a block of wood called a copse nailed to the oar both to balance the oar and with a hole in it to take the thowl pin. Each lerret, cleared of fishing nets and depending on size, would be able to carry between 10 and 12 men including the rowers. (In 1877 two lerrets were launched off Chesil Beach to go to the aid of the iron hulled ship *Avalanche*, sinking after a collision in the Channel and the lerret crews of 7 in each boat, managed to bring back 12 survivors between them, making a total of 13 people in each of these six oared versions). Obviously the lerret would go slower because of such a load but also because there would have been less room for the oarsmen to row as normal, possibly the oarsmen cut down to 4 or 2.

Lerrets with sails at Chesil Cove

For Bond and the Portland boatmen it would have taken about an hour, or an hour and a half, to row across Portland Roads on that dark cold February night, the thowl pin mounts leathered and greased to cut down on extraneous noise from rowing. Any Roundheads stationed at the three fortifications would have had to be extremely keen, after seven months of stable Parliamentary rule, to keep a lookout on such a night, rather than take shelter inside.

I have stood on the shore between the Nothe Fort and Newton's Cove when the racing gigs, with 6 oarsmen and a cox/steersman, are racing between each point and but for the cox calling out encouragement there would have been no noise at all. According to lunar and tide programs, which can work out the times and phases of the moon and tide at that time, the moon was in its last quarter, and wasn't due to rise until 2:45 a.m. that Sunday night/Monday morning so, as one would expect, the date and time had been carefully planned to take the enemy unawares on a pitch black night. Plus the high tide was due at 00:16 so the current would have taken the lerrets northbound from Portland Castle to Newton's Cove at a rate of at least half a knot to aid the oarsmen and they would have landed before midnight on the top of the tide and right under the cliff so lessening the vulnerable distance to cover between the boat and shore. On a dark cold February night it would be possible to land in Newton's Cove and be ashore without anybody knowing and then take the Bincleaves Fort above the Cove before moving onto the Nothe Fort.

We do know Weymouth fishermen had lerrets at this time because in June 1618 Matthew Knott, James Bush, Adam Cuttler, T. Ilkins, Christmas Peteres and others rowed out from "Waymouth Key" to the north then turned back to Portland Roads where they took "three men in a lirret on board a barque in the Roads". They made 2 trips to supply what turned out to be a pirate vessel, with mutton, butter, and four or five gallons of beer, receiving a barrel of flour, two kettles, two coverlids and two shillings in exchange. So this lerret had a crew of at least 5 and was carrying 3 passengers in it together with some supplies, this again supports the notion that a load of 10 or 12 men was entirely possible for a lerret. William Simpson's map of "Waymouth" in 1626 shows lerrets fishing with seine nets off Chesil Beach.

While those royalists came by lerrets to attack the Nothe and Bincleaves forts, the others came by land and John Dry, a tanner from Weymouth, arranged for the ferryman at Smallmouth to bring them across by his ferry. This was probably still the same "Austine the ferryman" mentioned in the Golden Grape inquiry. Once on the mainland they made their way for a surprise attack on Chapelhay Fort from the rear using the lanes and byways. The only habitation to avoid from Smallmouth to the Chapel Fort was Sandsfoot Castle. Between them, the two Royalist forces managed to take both major forts and also the smaller one at Bincleaves, overlooking Newton's Cove.

Meanwhile local tailor Thomas Samways was set to open the gate to Melcombe so Dyve could attack the Roundheads' garrison in Melcombe at the same time. Hodder had already gone around on the day trying to bribe as many local people to fight with them as possible and offered them the sum of £5 as the inducement but there were only a few takers. Those that did take the money joined a group of Royalists, from the villages north of Melcombe, namely Upwey, Broadwey, Preston and Sutton Poyntz, who were waiting at Radipole to join with Dyve's force. They waited in vain, for crucially it wasn't until noon the next day that Dyve finally arrived.

The moonless night would have made things worse for Dyve coming the 30 miles from Sherborne. It was reckoned that horses could be ridden at 5 mph in winter daylight (7 mph in summer when tracks were less muddy etc) so it would have taken 6 hrs in daylight and possibly double that at night in the pitch black? Dyve was a cavalry officer but were there also foot soldiers and even carts or wagons as well? Both would have slowed things up even more. Sunset was 5:35 pm on that Sunday night so if they wanted the cover of darkness that would have been their setting off time. However 12 hours late is still pretty hard to believe. Was Dyve's heart really in this fight, a fight forced on him rather than his own idea?

With the element of surprise totally lost and the Melcombe attack consequently postponed, Dyve's force joined Hastings' men to clear any vestiges of Parliamentarian resistance in Weymouth and to consolidate their position. Colonel William Sydenham had already retreated back to Melcombe to regroup and consider his options while the Royalists besieged them. The surprise Royalist attack had also been a personal setback as well as a military one, as his brother Major Francis Sydenham suffered fatal wounds when he lead a counter attack to retake the Chapel Fort.

Sydenham and his 900 men were now surrounded in Melcombe by a far greater Royalist force that was bombarding them with musket shot and cannon shot. Sydenham replied in kind even sending a raiding party across in boats to set Royalist boats and houses in Weymouth alight. His previous call for the Royalist destruction of Melcombe housing to be abated had been ignored but after this reprisal raid there was no more wanton destruction from the Royalists.

During this siege, Vice Admiral Batten in the *James* and another man o' war managed to land 200 sailors from Poole directly onto the beach and Sydenham's forces were further supplemented when 100 horsemen broke through the Royalist cordon. Sydenham even managed to break out and attack a small Royalist force at Radipole and later even brought 900 sheep into Melcombe to feed the garrison and the inhabitants. (In January 1646 "Andrew and Johan Milles were reimbursed £82 for 12 cows, 10 sheep, 4 other beasts, 110 sheep, and 40 lambs, which were taken from them by the soldiers near the garrison of Weymouth in the time of the troubles." This money would come from the estates of the eventually defeated Royalists).

A large force of Royalists lead by General George Goring then came down from Dorchester and made a great show of strength both in numbers and noise, putting fear into the inhabitants of Melcombe, however far from actually attacking they went back to Dorchester. Why risk losing experienced fighting men when they could besiege Melcombe instead.

On the 25th February the Parliamentarians from Melcombe intercepted some supply wagons destined for Weymouth and in beating off the accompanying Royalist horsemen; they managed to capture one or two wagons of food to divert to Melcombe. Sir Lewis Dyve observed these events from the Chapel Fort and he immediately reacted by sending out 100 soldiers to reinforce the Royalist party. Sydenham on seeing this, and once the Royalist foot soldiers were far enough away, seized the opportunity to lower the drawbridge from Melcombe and send out 150 musketeers under the command of Major Wilson and Captain Langford, who proceeded to clear the Royalists out of their way and then attacked the Chapel Fort, where after 30 minutes of hard hand to hand fighting they managed to take the fort with only the loss of one man. They took many prisoners, amongst them a Lt. Colonel, a Major, 3 Captains, 3 Lieutenants and 100 inferior officers and common soldiers. At least six Royalists lay dead, amongst them Philip Ash, but now Colonel William Sydenham had Weymouth and the Chapel Fort back under his command. The Royalist, Sir Lewis Dyve had escaped to Wyke with his men and then took his force off to join Goring in Dorchester where, to his great embarrassment, he would have to break the bad news.

The bridge linking the towns of Melcombe Regis and Weymouth was a wooden one of 17 arches with a central drawbridge of two leaves, and depending on the size of the boats going through to the backwater, either one or both leaves would be raised, the fixed charge being 6d for one and 12d for both. Sydenham had raised the drawbridge leaf on the Melcombe side to stop the Royalists coming across after they had taken Weymouth and subsequently lowered it to send 150 musketeers across to Weymouth to take Chapelhay when the opportunity presented itself.

Town Bridge with "stairs" to the Chapel Fort

This would suggest that the leaf on the Weymouth side was already down. It could have been due to previous damage, as the bridge was continually being repaired because of boat collision or just wear and tear such as repair of the "wheel and ramer" or "new ropes" being required. Sydenham cutting the lifting ropes on the Weymouth leaf as he retreated could also have caused it, if so he would have made sure that any attempts to replace the Weymouth ropes were thwarted by his musketeers who could hide behind Melcombe's raised drawbridge and pick off any Royalists attempting to renew their ropes. It seems remiss of the Royalists that they neither noticed any activity before the lowering of the Melcombe drawbridge nor prevented the 150 Roundhead musketeers surging across the narrow bridge. They had, after all, been bombarding Melcombe before so they had the range.

Local Civil War historian Mark Vine suggests that the bombardment of Melcombe Regis originally came from some Royalist supporting ships anchored in the Ope, perhaps even one of Fabian Hodder's ships, firing westwards across the harbour. The cannon ball lodged in the wall in Maiden Street would support this trajectory. Equally the cannon ball could have been fired from the Nothe if they had turned the cannons around but these were primarily to protect the ports from enemy ships and this is less likely. The theory is that these Royalist ships were destroyed when they were set on fire by Sydenham's retaliatory attack by small boats and consequently there was then no artillery to prevent Sydenham's breakout across the bridge. Certainly the cessation of the Royalist bombardment after Sydenham's attack reinforces the theory.

Sydenham recognised the weakness and put the bridge out of action after retaking Weymouth to prevent Goring using it for his attack and the bridge wasn't repaired until 1651, presumably the previous rope ferry was used until then.

Sydenham knew that another Royalist assault was certain to take place but he didn't know when and the Royalists still held the Nothe and Bincleaves Forts so he was already vulnerable on his eastern flank in Weymouth. In the interim Admiral Batten brought in another 100 men to bolster Sydenham's force to 1300.

On the 27th February Sydenham's Roundheads came across a Royalist deserter who soon told them that he had overheard the Royalist attack being planned for that very night so there was frantic reinforcing of defences to be done and a strategy to be worked out. Sydenham had a barricade built behind the town's gate at Weymouth. This was somewhere near the Boot Hill end of the High Street or near Love Lane, which was immediately east of the Old Town Hall, and is described as "by the West Gate". Sydenham fully expected it to be stormed so built a second barricade at the far end, the eastern end, of the High Street.

Sure enough Goring and all his forces turned up at Midnight with one part set to attack Melcombe and a second to attack Weymouth. The Melcombe assault was a lacklustre affair but the Weymouth attack was a far more resolute one. Goring's men stormed the western gate and as expected then took the first barricade and swarmed down the High Street in the full expectation of the quick victory but Sydenham now had them where he wanted them and a hail of musket balls flew down upon them from all the houses together with a barrage of both musket balls and cannon balls from the more substantial barricade at the end of the street. The leading men were decimated and more and more poured forward over the bodies to share the same fate.

Sydenham's force then came out to take the Royalists on in hand-to-hand combat and Goring's men finally retreated out of Weymouth.

Flush with success the Parliamentarians were then confronted by their colleagues fleeing from Captain Thornhill's fort situated just to the east of the town bridge where they had been routed by the 300 strong Royalist Irish mercenaries from the Nothe Fort. Sydenham stiffened the Roundhead resolve and together they marched down towards the Irish on the quay where they quickly retook Thornhill's Fort and pushed the Irish back towards where they had come from. In their haste to escape many of the Irish fatally blundered into the swampy waters of the Ope or the "hole" and in February the cold sea and cloying mud would have had no mercy for them, Sydenham's force certainly didn't. Those that hadn't drowned were put to the sword or shot by musket ball. It is said that about 250 Irish men died there that night.

The east end of the ancient High Street Weymouth.

Ope with a pinnace being fitted out

Soon after, the remaining Royalists at the Nothe and Bincleaves Forts fled to join Goring and Dyve at Wyke and although Sydenham expected yet another attack from Goring's still superior numerical force it failed to materialise because as soon he heard the news that a Parliamentarian force had entered Dorset, Goring fled first to Dorchester and thence to Taunton, while Dvye went back to the comparative safety of Sherborne Castle. Sydenham had proved himself a resolute and very gifted commander unlike the experienced Cavalry Officer Dyve who had failed to arrive on time for the first attack and subsequently made a vital mistake to lose the Chapel Fort.

In fairness the advantage the moonless night gave to the Portland men coming by boat and attacking the Nothe Fort, would have made travelling on horseback from Sherborne that much harder but one gets the impression that Sydenham would have made it if it had been the other way around.

As well as the death of Philip Ash, news soon came to the Royalists that fellow conspirators Leonard Symonds and William Philips had also been killed in the fighting. Philips was the owner of the house, "seventy staires" below Chapelhay, where the conspirators had originally started out from with such high hopes and both Ashe and Philips were two of the salvors of the Golden Grape. Philips, described as a shoemaker in the Golden Grape Inquiry, had accompanied Walter Bond when he went to the wreck the second time so was no doubt in the Hodder clique even before the idea of a conspiracy was put forward.

After their victory in retaking both towns and retaining Sandsfoot Castle, Sydenham convened an inquiry to try the conspirators they had caught and who had been imprisoned on board Admiral Batten's ship in the harbour. These were Walter Bond, Thomas Samways, John Mills the town constable, Richard Mighill, and John Cade the Royalist ex Sea Captain and town alderman, possibly the same John Cade who had been Mayor in 1635.

Being an Irishman would have been held against Mighill because of alleged atrocities by the Irish Catholics against the English and Scottish protestant settlers in Ireland. Mighill pre-empted his fate by hanging himself with a rope on board the ship, but the gibbet awaited the rest of the prisoners and on the 3rd March 1645 they were duly taken up to the Nothe.

Having admitted his part in the conspiracy, John Cade was first to be hanged. Then Walter Bond and Thomas Samways were brought forth and were met with the sight of Cade's body still hanging there. Both had their charges read out to them but before sentence could be passed they both pleaded for their lives and Sydenham in an act of mercy allowed them to be taken back to gaol to cogitate on their actions and maybe to be persuaded to implicate others. Finally the town constable John Mills was brought forward. No pleading from him and in a final act of defiance he threw himself from the ladder without even recourse to God's forgiveness. Perhaps both Cade and Mills knew any pleas would go unheard, for Sydenham probably took Mills' actions as an affront to him personally, Mills being the town constable and as such a supposed upholder of the law.

Cade meanwhile would have known the enmity that Sydenham held for Fabian Hodder and Sydenham shared that enmity equally with Hodder's wife Anne, nee Cade. If indeed John Cade was related to Anne Hodder, perhaps her brother or her father, this was the perfect chance of revenge on her as a woman and on her own family who had jointly caused the uprising and in which Sydenham's own brother Francis had died. The main absentee from this event was the principle instigator of the Crabchurch Conspiracy Fabian Hodder, who had escaped from the scene of the defeat, possibly by boat. However Hodder was eventually arrested and imprisoned at Poole and knowing this, Sydenham was probably salivating at the prospect of bringing him back to be hanged in the most exemplary manner to complete his revenge.

Just as in the case of the Fullers Earth aboard the *Black Dogg* ship when he had circumvented the tax from the authorities at Poole back in 1642, so Hodder was once again set to get the better of them. Hodder managed to escape from the gaol and the implication is that he bribed his way to freedom. Certainly Hodder was both a prosperous merchant and a ship owner and the trade between Weymouth and Poole was a thriving one for both ports and Hodder would have had the contacts at Poole as well as further afield. If there were palms to be greased he would know, both who, and how to do it. His commercial standing would have ensured that even if he didn't have the money on him to bribe them for his escape from gaol it would be guaranteed by his friends, or family and perhaps in this case by his fellow Royalists. Bribes were commonplace especially when local smugglers were caught. It was only the lesser smugglers who were arraigned in court; the others paid their way out of gaol.

Certainly the animosity between Sir Lewis Dyve, the Royalist commander at Sherborne and Colonel William Sydenham the Parliamentarian Governor of the twin towns of Weymouth and Melcombe would have ensured that Dyve would do his utmost to get Hodder free for he knew that of all the conspirators the vengeance that Sydenham wanted to mete out most of all was on Hodder.

After the Roundheads had finally defeated the Royalists and Charles had fled to France, compensation was required from the vanquished in favour of those on the side of the victors. In 1648 one such instance concerned the back pay due to loyal Roundhead, Lieutenant Colonel Barrett Lacey, and he was duly recompensed, not with money, but by being ordered to take that part of the old barque, the *Mary* of Weymouth and her tackling, "which belongeth unto Fabyan Hodder, a delinquent".

Fabian Hodder is earlier mentioned in 1646 when it is recorded that sailor John Bure overheard a conversation outside the George Inn on the quay in Melcombe, between John Jourdain and local bailiff and justice of the town, Henry Rose. Jourdain said to Rose "you are a cavalier and as bad as Fabian Hodder or worse, and a two faced knave". Rose replied that he would "throw down all again" and Jourdain's rejoinder was "thou art a double faced man and Fabian Hodder is an honester man than thou".

Jourdain may well have been right in his judgement of Rose as he would have been a close ally of Hodder's for it seems that Henry Rose was brother in law to Fabian Hodder for Hodder had married Anne Cade at St Mary's Church, Melcombe on 23rd May 1633, followed by Henry Rose marrying Dorothy Cade at the same venue on 27th November 1634. The family link is further substantiated in a will of Melcombe merchant John Cade dated 9th June 1659 appointing the merchants Fabian Hodder and Henry Rose as his executors. This can't be the same John Cade hanged at the Nothe but surely he is a relative of Anne Cade and who better to have as executors of a merchant's will than fellow merchants and probably uncles? It's also confirmation that Fabian Hodder was back in 1659 possibly having noted the way things were going politically after the resignation of Richard Cromwell in May 1659 and the subsequent refusal of Parliament to recognise the Protectorate in the same month. By the next year things had indeed changed dramatically as on 25th May 1660 Charles II arrived at Dover followed on the 29th by a triumphal entry into London.

In September 1648 some Weymouth townspeople had protested that there were "malignants" in office and Gabriel Cornish, who had been Master of Ordnance for the King resigned as alderman on 3 November 1648. This was followed in early 1649 by the resignation of six other aldermen, ex mayor George Churchey, the brother in law of Francis Gape the Town Clerk; James Giear a Mayor in 1640, Henry Rose, who is mentioned as having been a sergeant for the King, thus proving Jourdain right; Richard Harrison, John Hodder and Alexander Clatworthy. After the restoration of the monarchy, the six Weymouth aldermen, who had resigned in 1649, were restored in October 1662 together with Fabian Hodder. Hodder was back in office, even if a little poorer. Henry Rose had indeed been duplicitous as he had supplied the Roundheads from his chandlery during their occupation of Weymouth but it didn't stop him being made Mayor in 1660-61.

It is apparent that in 1676 Fabyan Hodder is in charge of Portland Castle, the former Royalist headquarters on Portland for on 22nd May 1676 he writes to the Honourable Humphrie Weld at Weld's eponymous address in London, namely Weld House in Weld Street, saying that one of the porters at the Castle has moved out into his own house to live but comes back to act as a porter to show any gentleman around who wishes to see the Castle. Hodder then states that regarding Weld's lawsuit against the executors of Sir Edward Sydenham for the profits of Portland, there is nothing worth a penny there except a horse that is hired out at 13 shillings and 4 pence per annum (roughly a halfpenny a day). This is obviously in reference to the restitution of Weld's fortune as a Royalist supporter who had suffered when the Parliamentarians took power and gave away his assets to the Roundheads. This Sydenham was of Giddy Green in Essex and Weld had persuaded Charles II that Edward Sydenham had not done all he could against the Parliamentarians. Charles II had already dismissed Sir Edward Sydenham from his office of Captain of Portland Castle and appointed Humphrie Weld instead, as well as making Weld Captain of Sandsfoot Castle.

The accounts of Portland Castle for the period 10th April 1677 until 25th March 1679 confirm that Fabyan Hodder is Captain Lieutenant there and paid at the rate of 12d per day and that his net pay for the two years, less 16 days, and less pendage and debenter is £35 and 2 shillings and 7.5 pence. The gunner and also the porter are paid at the rate of 8d a day while the 5 soldiers are paid at 6d per day.

The numerical strength of the Castle had decreased since 1661 when there was both a Captain and a Lieutenant and eleven soldiers and gunners and also when the pay for them was considerably more, but it looks as if Hodder was being seen right by the ruling Royalists, with an appointment of standing and some revenue but leaving plenty of time for Hodder to carry on with his own business ventures.

The next known event in Fabian Hodder's life is his second marriage, to Mary Taylor, when they were married on the 10th August 1681 by licence at Wyke Regis.

Confirmation of his first wife Anne's death comes in his will dated 20th September 1681.

> **"In the name of God Amen I**
> Fabian Hodder of Weymouth and Melcombe Regis in the county of Dorset merchant the twentieth day of September in the thirtie third yeare of the reigne of Our Soveriegne Lord Charles the Second by the Grace of God of all England Scotland France and Ireland King Defender of the Faith ? and in the yeare of Our Lord One thousand six hundred eightie and one being of perfect memorie and remembrance praised be God doe make and ordaine this my last will and testament ? and forme following (viz)
>
> First I bequeath my soul into the hands of Almightie God my Maker hoping that through the mercy ? and passion of Jesus Christ my only Saviour and Redeemer to receave ? all pardon and foregiveness of all my synns and as for my bodie to be buried in Christian Buriall at the direction of my executrix hereafter in ? nominated in the Church within the towne of Melcomb Regis as neare to my former wife Ann as shall be convenient. Item whereof my former wife Ann of late deceased did in her lifetime give unto several relations and friends as she thought fitt I the said Fabian Hodder doe ratifie allow and confirme what my said wife Ann did soe doe and I doe freely give and bequeath and my desire is that such friends and relations shall have such summes of money and other goods and chattels as my said wife Ann did give in her lifetime and by her paper ? to that purpose may appeare.
>
> Item I doe also give and bequeath to everyone of those friends and relations that my former wife Anne gave to (as by her paper may appear) as much in value to each of them as my said wife gave to each of them, to be payd in lawfull English money. Item I doe give to my Sonn in Law Richard Hodder the summe of five pounds of lawfull money of England.
>
> Item all the rest of my Goods chattels implements of household Leases Lands and Tenements whatsoever I doe hearby freely give and bequeathe unto my now loving wife Mary her heires and assignes forever, upon Condition that shee shall pay all my debts and bequests and make her sole Executrix of this my last Will and Testament revoking all other wills and testaments by mee formerly made. In witness whereof I the said Fabian Hodder have hereunto put my hand and seale the day and yeare first above written Fabyan Hodder Sealed signed and published in the presence of Elizabeth Lacortnce? the marke of Mary Roberts. Geor. Vincent."

It is interesting to see the date of the will expressed both in the year of the reign of Charles II and also in the year of our Lord, Jesus Christ. This is confirmation of his strong royalist belief, as it does not seem to be mandatory for other wills of the time. Hodder obviously calculates the reign of Charles II from the death of Charles I in January 1649, which on the face of it would make it the thirty second year of his reign, however England was still using the Julian calendar for civil records and the New Year did not start until Lady quarter day, 25th March, so legally Charles I died in January 1648 and hence why it is stated as the thirty third year of the reign of Charles II in Hodder's will.

In his will Hodder leaves all his goods to his second wife Mary, save for the goods, chattels and money already promised by his first wife Anne to friends and relations in her paper, presumably the paper being her will. His only other family bequest is to his "sonn in law" Richard Hodder for the amount of £5. At this time son in law could also mean stepson. Presumably the rest of his family had been catered for in Anne's wishes. He also asks to be buried in the church in Melcombe Regis (St Mary's) as near to his former wife Anne as possible and this and the confirmation of her bequests underlines the love and respect he must have held her in.

It was she after all, who sent the letter, via the messenger Elizabeth Wall, to Sir Lewis Dyve at Sherborne Castle, asking for his support for the conspiracy. If she was also related to the Royalist ex Sea Captain and fellow conspirator John Cade, one wonders if she was the power behind her husband or at least a partner, for she left a will and her husband Fabian honoured her bequests as an equal. Certainly Sydenham charged both "Fabian Hodder and his wife for intelligencers and traitors" in equal measure and John Cade was certainly a local man, being listed as Lieutenant in the Melcombe militia in 1632 and later becoming an Alderman of the town and even Mayor in 1635/6, so he could very well have been related to Anne. Mark Vine, in his book on the Crabchurch Conspiracy, states Cade is an ex Royalist Sea Captain and as such, and if he is also related by marriage, it is surely safe to assume he had strong business ties with Hodder in his guise as ship owner and merchant.

Cade's status was not forgotten after his hanging in 1645, for on the 22nd September 1647, Thomas Snow, a cooper was admitted as a Freeman of the Borough of Weymouth because he qualified by marrying the daughter of a freeman, in this case he "married the daughter of Mr. Cade, one of the late aldermen of this towne; admitted freeman" no disbarment here or mention of why Cade was the late alderman.

Nor was Cade's widow and family forgotten as the Committee of Dorset, set up to redistribute monies from Royalists to Parliamentarians and to judge on hardship appeals, granted her the sum of 40s a year for three years to clothe her three children. Captain Arthur was ever present on the committee so perhaps he was instrumental in seeing a fellow sea captain's family looked after despite being on opposing sides.

How did the others who either took part in or were mentioned by the witnesses in the salvage of the cargo from the Golden Grape fare?

In 1646 Maximilian Mohun senior and junior of Fleet are declared delinquents and the father is imprisoned in Weymouth. The Mohun's land, valued at £160, was sequestered and Mrs Mohun had to plead to the Dorset Standing Committee before they let her have Fleet Farm back as a tenant, it having being let to a Robert Stephens for a rent of £70 a year, in the interim.

When the Royalist-held Portland Castle surrendered in 1646, another son, Robert Mohun, like the other soldiers and inhabitants of the Castle, was allowed to depart with all arms, horses, and property and to go back to his home. No slinking out ashamedly, they came out with all their possessions with the sound of drums, colours flown high, armed to the teeth – literally, for they had bullets in their mouths and the match alight ready to fire their matchlock muskets. One of the terms of surrender was that the previous Governor of Portland when the Parliamentarians had it, Captain John Arthur, would not be reinstated. Those signing the peace deal on behalf of the island of Portland were: - Thomas Salway, William Dyer, Thomas Weare, Robert Gillow, Thomas Wiggat and Christopher Gibbs, the latter two had been involved in the salvage of the *Golden Grape*. Captain Robert Mohun died in 1667 but lived to see the lands restored to the family when Charles II gained the throne. When Charles II later imposed a hearth tax of 2 shillings a hearth, Maximilian Mohun back at Fleet House, had to pay for twelve when the average for dwellings in Fleet village was one, possibly two hearths, so it shows what a great house it was.

Mohune's Fleet House, now the present day Moonfleet Hotel

Sir John Strangways of Abbotsbury had lost his house, burnt down when the Roundheads attacked Abbotsbury in November 1644. He was subsequently captured with his son Giles at the siege of Sherborne in 1645 and imprisoned in the Tower of London for three years. Giles was also imprisoned in the Tower and only released when the family paid £10,000. He later became MP for Bridport after the restoration.

Sir John Miller also known as Meller, of Little Bredy and Winterborne Came, and an MP, was also declared a delinquent because of his Royalist support and had his estate sequestered in 1645. "Sir John Miller's man" had been at the wreck.

John Hodder who had acted as a representative of older brother Fabian on the Chesil Beach at the salvage of the Golden Grape, had arranged to send all his valuables out of the town to a friend, one John Vincent, who lived at Broadway, in case Hodder's Weymouth house was pillaged by marauding troops of either side in the forthcoming battle over the town. When it came to getting them back Vincent said they had been plundered by escaping Royalists on their way out of town after their final assault in 1645. They had dug up his floorboards, found Hodder's property and the only thing left was some money, twenty two shillings and sixpence scattered about the floor the next day.

Hodder didn't believe him and took it to court where the full extent of the loss was detailed as £175 in money, two silver beer bowls worth £9, one great silver beaker worth £5, four dozen silver spoons worth £16, a sugar dish or plate worth 20 shillings, a gilt silver bowl worth 35 shillings and 14 gold rings worth £25, together with two silver dishes, five silver spoons, a wine bowl, a silver whistle and chain and other articles. The outcome is not recorded but John Hodder was either defrauded by a friend or robbed by the very forces he supported.

Like his brother he was not to be kept down for long. In the Weymouth apprentice and freeman records John Hodder and his wife Elizabeth take on several apprentices between 1649 and 1653 and they are variously described as merchant, grocer or mercer (dealer in cloth), perhaps he was all three, so it would appear that John continued to do well in Weymouth, even just a short time after the Crabchurch Conspiracy.

The last we hear of the tailor Thomas Samwayes is being pardoned from being hanged at the Nothe and then returned to prison. What of his fellow conspirator Bond?

In 1662 on the restoration of Charles II, an Act of Parliament was made to reward surviving loyal royalists who had fought for Charles I. Walter Bond of Weymouth is granted a yearly pension and though the amount is not given it would have been between 20 and 40 shillings a year.

The Wyke Regis burial register states that on December 20th 1677, a Walter Bond was buried at Wyke Regis. The church at Wyke Regis was the church for the whole of Weymouth and if it is the same Walter Bond he was certainly a Weymouthian, living as he did as a fisherman at Hope.

As one would expect with his later namesake there is some confusion regarding the youthful salvor, James Bond, mentioned in the wreck of the Golden Grape for there are two entries in the burial register at Wyke Regis: -
the first entry gives "January 13 1681 James Bond"
the second entry "February 06 1686 James Bond".

But as an enemy of the later namesake might have said "you only die once Mr Bond".

What of the structures? The forts in Melcombe and Weymouth were pulled down. All the stone from Cold Harbour Fort except the great ashlar stones and those to the west, which were kept as a sea defence, and almost all of the New Fort, Mountjoy Fort and Nothe Fort and also the Chapelhay Fort except for a few stones, were sold for £51 and 1 shilling.

A large stone Nothe Fort was later built in 1872 as a defence against the threat of invasion by Napoleon III. Blockhouse Lane and Governors Lane survive as street names in Melcombe as for a while did Francis Street leading up to Chapelhay in Weymouth. Civil War historian Mark Vine believes the latter street was named after Major Francis Sydenham as a mark of respect in the area where he fought and died though there is mention of "8 properties on the south side of Francis Street" in the 1617 Weymouth rent returns.

Sandsfoot Castle seemingly left isolated when the Royalists attacked from Portland both by land and sea, soon lost any importance, probably due to cliff erosion below it. In 1701 there is an order to take stone from Sandsfoot Castle to repair the bridge in Weymouth. Ironic as it is said stone taken from Bindon Abbey was used to help build Henry VIII's Sandsfoot Castle after his dissolution of the Monasteries. This recycling of building material confirmed its usefulness was already over for it was abandoned as a fort in 1665 just being used as a store until 1691.

However apparently there is one thing that did survive from the Civil War battles. A cannonball, fired perhaps from the Royalist ships in the Ope in Weymouth, still resided near to the quay in the wall of the one of the Tudor buildings in Maiden Street, Melcombe Regis. For health and safety reasons a wooden replica now replaces this, while the lower floor of the building is presently a public convenience.

The Chairman of the Golden Grape Inquiry was Captain John Arthur and he was appointed as both the Vice Admiral of Dorset and as Captain of "Sandy Fort" (Sandsfoot Castle) in 1644. A Captain John Arthur is mentioned as leading a Parliamentarian company of military during the first year of the Civil War serving in the Portland campaign. He is then mentioned as owning the vessel *King David* in 1643. In 1646 Captain John Arthur is one of the Dorset Standing Committee deciding who has to pay for their Royalist support and on the other hand doling out the self same money to repay Parliamentarians any costs that they had incurred.

As Collector of Customs and as a fellow merchant in his own right, Captain Arthur would have known local merchant and ship owner Fabian Hodder well. Perhaps this is why Hodder, who was the prime organiser and maybe the major beneficiary of the salvage and who gave shelter to the Captain of the *Golden Grape*, was never called to give his deposition to the Golden Grape Inquiry. If Arthur knew everything about Hodder (well almost all) it was also probable that Hodder knew everything about Arthur.

What we do know is that Richard Baylye of Melcombe Regis had sold one barrel of raisins from the wreck of the Golden Grape "to the wife of Mr John Arthur for wich she payed him forty shillings" thus compromising John Arthur's role in charge of the Inquiry. Funnily enough she too was not called as a witness. (However she must have died between 1641 and 1648 as "Capt. John Arther & Mistress Katherin Foard married 18th October 1648" at Melcombe Regis. His previous marriage had been on 11 May 1634 to a Rebecca Brummell, presumably the same wife mentioned in the Golden Grape Inquiry). Arthur was a man of many hats and he remained at least Vice Admiral of Dorset until 1653 and became Mayor of Weymouth in 1650-51.

In view of Arthur's appointment as Head of Customs, he would have known that Hodder had been caught trying to smuggle fullers earth and no doubt as ship owner and merchant that wasn't the first or last time. The Bussell family of Weymouth later married into the Hodder family and in 1838 when the local ship the *Dove* owned by a Peter Bussell was wrecked on Chesil Beach she was described as a smuggler, perhaps carrying on earlier family tradition, as smuggling was rife during the Tudor and Stuart times.

In 1635, privateering promoters, Thomas Gyear, mayor in 1630 and an MP, Thomas Waltham, of Melcombe, and John Blachford, of Dorchester were heavily fined for conspiring together to avoid payment of customs at Poole and Weymouth, despite several of their ships having received Admiralty commissions. The fines don't seem to have been paid immediately, if ever, as in 1651 the Sheriff mentions the fines, two of £2,000 and one of £3,000 as being outstanding. (Using the National Archives historic currency converter, that gives a buying power figure for today of £177,000 and £266,000 respectively).

What the salvage of the *Golden Grape* and the subsequent Crabchurch Conspiracy show is that Hodder was a powerful and a well organised man. His plan to take the twin towns of Weymouth and Melcombe Regis back under Royalist rule was a sound one and only foiled by Sir Lewis Dyve's failure, for whatever reason, to arrive as required at midnight. If he had, the remaining Parliamentarians under Colonel William Sydenham would have been defeated and forced out of Melcombe Regis as well as out of Weymouth. Dyve's delay allowed Sydenham the time and security to use his undoubted military acumen to finally defeat the Royalist force superior in both numbers and location on the heights of Weymouth. Again Dyve made a vital mistake in sending troops out to the wagon attack, which depleted his defensive forces and allowed Sydenham to retake Weymouth.

Had Hodder's plan worked, the Royalists would have had a secure port on the south coast available to King Charles to bring across a French Army to the Royalist stronghold of the southwest. The Duke of Monmouth used such a plan in 1685 when he landed with his 80 or so supporters from Holland at nearby Lyme Regis to take on James II for the throne of England. Monmouth's plan failed for lack of support but Charles I had much bigger support in the country and would also have brought a substantial French army with him by means of the superior ports of Weymouth and Melcombe Regis. William of Orange later proved the point when he landed at

Brixham with an army of 11,000 infantry and 4,000 cavalry on 5 November 1688 to take the English throne from James II.

Not only do we have the most comprehensive record of a treasure wreck on the Chesil Beach, describing the voyage, the wreck, the way the local population made a living and their hierarchy, but also some of the participants are then caught up in one of the most turbulent times for the country let alone for Weymouth and Melcombe Regis. A civil war pitting friend against friend and family against family that would confirm the governance of this land from absolute monarchy to elected representatives.

One way or another Hodder certainly made money from the wreck of the Golden Grape and it was he who planned the conspiracy and gave out money to buy support for it. Perhaps if the *Golden Grape* hadn't have been wrecked just 8 months before the Civil War, Hodder and his supporters would not have had enough money to fund the conspiracy three years later.

Chapter 4 Artefacts

Sydenham's Armada Plates

The seabed off Chesil Beach changes depending on the effect of hurricane or gale force storms, which carve out the bottom just as much and as quickly as they create a new profile of the beach. Within hours it can change back after giving tantalising glimpses of what lies on the sea floor.

The sand pebble margin can move in and out from the shoreline and in 1980 a whole swathe of the seabed was totally denuded of pebbles after a hurricane. At a depth of 15 metres, and 100 metres from the shore, a 20 metres width of the seabed showed the underlying clay where once pebbles had been. This extended for at least a mile along the direction of the shore, while ships' anchors, usually buried and not seen by me in 15 years of diving, stood out from their now meagre covering of pebbles. Part of a side of an iron sailing ship ran into the beach and while drift diving along the swathe of clay I discovered the wreck of a second world war P40 fighter lying upside down, still armed with four wing machine guns and its wheels folded neatly into the wings.

Such large scale denuding is exceptional but the seabed was always changing in different ways along the beach. One part of the beach, say off Langton Herring, could have tons of pebbles pulled out to sea exposing the wreck of an iron steamer more than usual, while the wreck of an iron sailing ship off Ferrybridge was covered up more. The change in depth of pebbles never seemed to be uniform along the beach.

That is why you can dive the same wreck, the same part of the seabed time after time, and often in limited visibility and then suddenly something new appears. One evening I was solo diving and doing the usual wreckage tour looking for anything new as well as for crabs and particularly lobsters that might lie under the wreckage. I drifted shoreward a little way from the wreck but suddenly I spotted something in the murk and swam over to find a round metal object just lying on top of the pebbles. It was a small grey metal plate with a bumpy bottom or centre boss, overall about six inches in diameter and it looked either pewter or silver.

I examined it as closely as possible but could see no marks and there was none of the usual concretion on it, so making sure there was nothing else lying around I grasped it tightly in my hand and swam into shore and fairly strode up the beach, got changed and rowed back over the Fleet. I was so excited I had to show it to somebody and drove around to my usual dive buddy Les Kent and his partner Julie.

On the top of the plate/dish it had a purplish patina and it wasn't until later when we found silver pieces of eight newly exposed on the clay that we recognised this to be a usual occurrence with exposed silver. It didn't look like pewter to us so I took it to a local jeweller who did a test for silver and he confirmed that it had silver in it. From research I identified it as a "bumpy bottom plate, an armada dish, a Drake plate" and the British Museum dated it around the 16th or 17th century. I could find plenty of pewter examples in the books but no silver ones until -

in October 2010 two silver parcel gilt Armada dishes came up for auction at the Somerset auction house of Lawrences in Crewkerne, Somerset. They were two of five missing dishes from an "Armada Service" of 31 dishes and plates that had been discovered in the early 1800s. The two 8 inch diameter dishes sold for a total of £161,000 ($100,000) mainly because of their provenance and remarkable condition.

When the Spanish Armada attacked England in 1588 a John Harris commanded 35 men onboard a ship called the *Adwyse* and his relative, William Harris, paid £50 towards England's defence. It is said that as a reward they shared in the spoils from that Armada defeat and this went towards the cost of commissioning another 15 dishes and 7 plates to add to the existing family collection of silver gilt dishes, which were dated between 1581 and 1582. These latter ones were dated between 1599 and 1602, which perhaps suggest that the money actually came from trading or ongoing privateering against the Spanish, if not piracy.

Later the family plates were engraved with the coat of arms of Sir Christopher Harris, Vice Admiral of Devon, on the left of the shield, and the arms of his wife Mary Sydenham of Somerset on the right, hers being "argent, three rams passant sable". Sir Christopher was friend to Sir Walter Raleigh and Sir Francis Drake and was related by marriage to Sir Richard Grenville. Mary's niece, Elizabeth Sydenham became Drake's second wife in 1585.

In 1645 during the Civil War Sir Christopher's royalist great nephew, fearing being overwhelmed by the Parliamentarian forces, hid the Armada Service and other family valuables in a cave on Dartmoor. There they remained until the Christmas of 1827 when three labourers, employed to enlarge the cave for use as a potato store, stumbled upon the hoard. Returned to the family, 26 of the 31 Armada Service plates and dishes were sold in 1885 and again in 1911 when they fetched a world record sum of £11,500 before being purchased in 1992 by the British Museum, where they are now displayed.

Apparently it is rare for Elizabethan silver to have survived the English Civil War when much was either pillaged or melted down by each side to pay the troops and fund the war. Such pieces, either survived from being hidden on land or come from shipwrecks like the silver spice dish recovered from off Chesil Beach. Silver dealer and Antiques Roadshow expert Alastair Dickenson, who had bought the two dishes at Lawrences auction on behalf of a collector, dated the one I found off Chesil Beach at around 1610. Apparently the lack of marks is not unusual for that time in England but this could also indicate that it is foreign, perhaps similar to the contents of the bags of Spanish plate loaded aboard the Golden Grape at Sanlucar.

As well as the Civil War connection it is probable that Mary Sydenham was a relative of Colonel William Sydenham, who features in the Crabchurch Conspiracy, as his Sydenham family had moved from Somerset to Wynford Eagle and both families have ancestors born at Drimpton and both share the same arms of "argent, three rams passant sable".

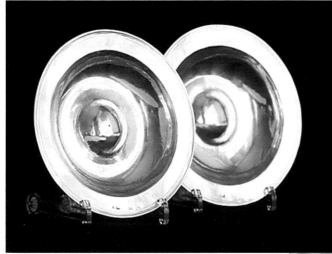

Two of the Harris Sydenham hoard of silver Drake or Armada dishes and plates. All have the bumpy bottom in the centre so they sit flat on a table.

Close up of the Harris & Sydenham Arms (three rams) on the above dishes

The silver bumpy bottom, Armada or Drake dish recovered from Chesil Beach and dated as circa 1610

Merchant's Seal Ring

Regular newspaper reports of treasure finds from Chesil Beach after storms, of gold and silver bars, dollars, crowns, guineas, wedges of silver, silver duckey stones, bowls and spoons, go back as far as the 1820s. In February 1897 for instance, "On Sunday a fisherman named White found a gold ring and a dollar" and in the 1920s this appeared in the local paper.

"Treasure hunting; Southern Times, March 3rd 1923:
The recent heavy seas and abnormally low tides have altered the configuration of the beach and laid bare stretches of the former ocean bed normally submerged. Finds have included jewellery and coins, the latter comprising sovereigns and silver dollars. The sovereigns are reckoned to come from the wreck of the Royal Adelaide and the dollars from a Spanish treasure ship lost in the bay during the Armada."
One such historic find of treasure came to light in 2010.

"A medieval gold merchant's seal ring. The circular bezel with merchant's seal to the centre, the shank with Latin text "O Mater dei Memento Mei" (O Mother of God Remember Me) the shank terminating in scrolling shoulders circa 1450.

Provenance: Apparently discovered on Chesil Beach by the vendor's grandfather in the mid 1920s and thence by descent. Rings of this type were worn by merchants not entitled to a coat of arms but whose mark was widely recognised within the trade. Most were produced in bronze or silver making this gold example extremely rare. Estimate £2,000-3,000"

The above is taken from Duke's (The Dorchester Fine Art Saleroom) Auction catalogue for a Silver, Jewellery and Watches sale held on Thursday June 17th 2010 where the ring sold for £16,730.

From Internet research there is another merchant's seal ring, again in gold, of a design with a similar 4 but with F beneath it and that has been identified as belonging to a German merchant and dated 1564. These two rings, together with the design of the Scinde District Dawk, a postage stamp showing the early mark of the East India Company established in 1600, share this "sign of four". All three have a short vertical stroke through the horizontal tail of the 4, while the central vertical stroke is extended downwards terminating in a horizontal stroke, which in the case of the ring found on Chesil Beach, bisects the O beneath it. This O could be an initial for the merchant who lost it.

The "sign of four" is derived from the Christian symbol Chi Rho (XP) based on Greek letters for Christus Rex, and the 4 was later modified to a reverse 4 in the medieval period. Apparently the Christian "sign of 4" is common to the majority

1 The Camino Real (Royal Road). Literally a funnel of silver and gold

TANDEM SI

2 Sir Christopher Hatton sponsor of Sir Francis Drake's circumnavigation voyage. Note the red and yellow colours of Hatton's arms top right of the picture as they are the colours that the Pelican was repainted in and Drake renamed the Pelican as the Golden Hinde in honour of his sponsor because it sits atop Hatton's arms.

3 Golden Hinde replica in Hatton's colours.

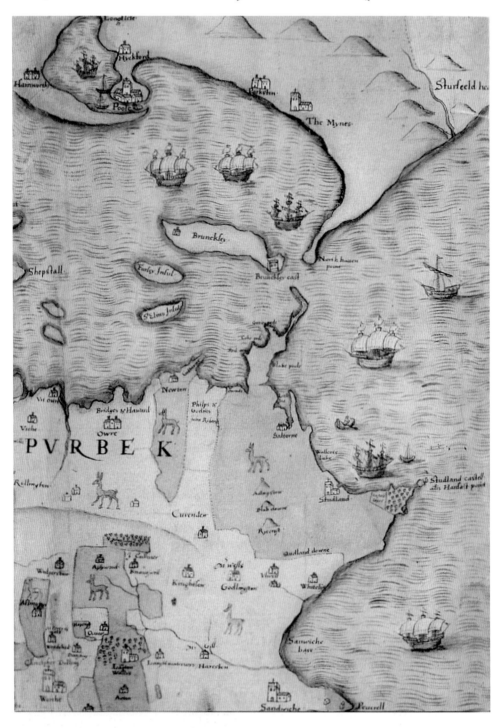

4 Ralph Treswell's 1585 map of Purbeck, Studland & Poole

5 Studland Bay, the pirates' safe haven in Dorset

6 Re-enactment Royalist dinner at Humprie Weld's Lulworth Castle

7 Henry Strangwish, pirate

8 Drake's Colours.

Top Row l to r: Colonel; Lt. Colonel, and Sergeant-Major's flags, the latter with wavy pile in top left corner

Bottom Row l to r: Three Captain's flags in seniority left to right

9 Lulworth Civil War re-enactment showing Sergeant- Major's flag with wavy pile

3 ships ride at anchor in Portland Road with 5 flying the red English ensign. One has the additional white wavy pile from canton to corner. This is typical of Army flags used later in the Civil War. A Dutch ship is being fired on or saluted, The white flag portion has been inked in at a later date

10 Portion of Simpson's 1626 map of Weymouth

11 Anti personnel swivel guns or "murderers"

12 Looking from Portland with Chesil Beach linking to the mainland again at Abbotsbury, top left, and Deadman's Bay left of the beach. The road to Weymouth runs to the right over the present Ferry Bridge, middle right, where the rope ferry bestrode the inlet to the Fleet Lagoon. The white ramp, the narrow point of the mainland left of centre, is where the Bridging Camp meets the Fleet Lagoon, built over the sandy bay of Locket's Hole in the 1920s. The *Golden Grape* was wrecked opposite that point in Deadman's Bay. Portland Harbour (Portland Roads) is the foreground sea.

True description of the Situation

Chesil Beach curves to Portland with the Fleet Lagoon between it and the
mainland and the rope Ferry across the Passage linking the lagoon to the sea.

Weymouth and Melcombe Regis, 1626

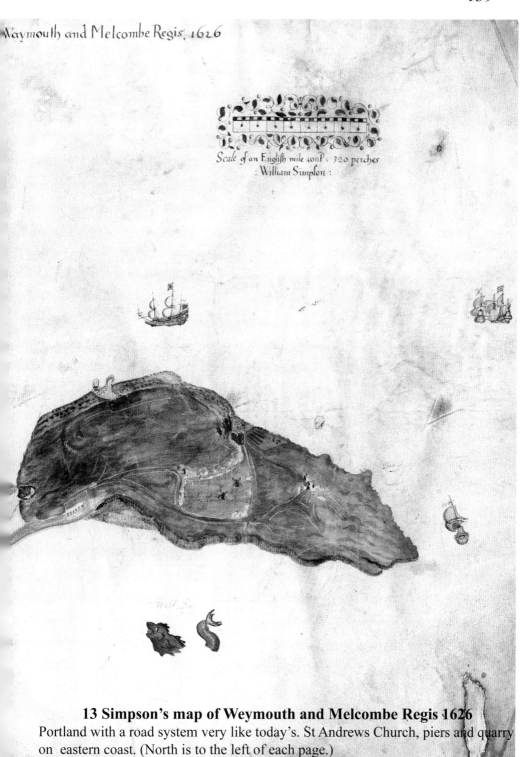

Scale of an English mile conP; 320 perches
: William Simplon :

13 Simpson's map of Weymouth and Melcombe Regis 1626
Portland with a road system very like today's. St Andrews Church, piers and quarry
on eastern coast. (North is to the left of each page.)

14 Trows on the Fleet shore, the first two made by Royston Mowlam

15 Bridge Lane, still a narrow track, up towards Wyke

16 Wyke Church & village with Chesil Beach leading to Portland

17 Seine fisherman Royston Mowlam in the last lerret on Chesil Beach

18 The Fleet Lagoon from St Catherine's Chapel at Abbotsbury. Lockets Hole was on the landward side of the narrowest point in the distance.

19 Spanish Andalusian olive oil jar recovered from the sea off Wolf Rock, Cornwall, similar to those loaded on board the *Golden Grape* at Cadiz

20 Gibbons leads a sick crewman on his horse with another crewman with a double bag of coin. 21 Barrels of raisins and olive oil jars on Weymouth Quay.

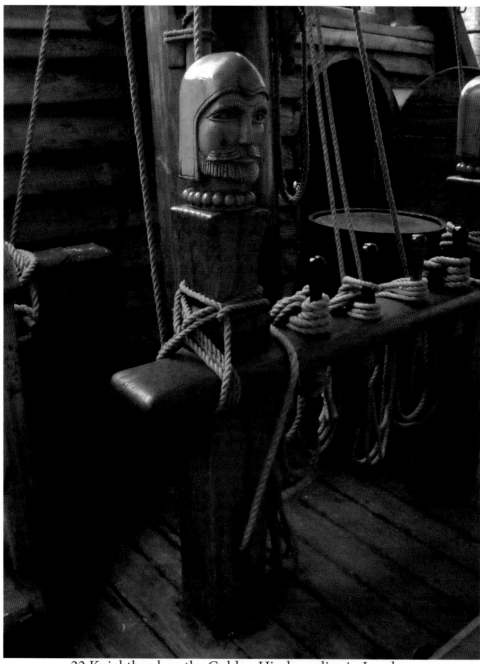

22 Knighthead on the Golden Hinde replica in London

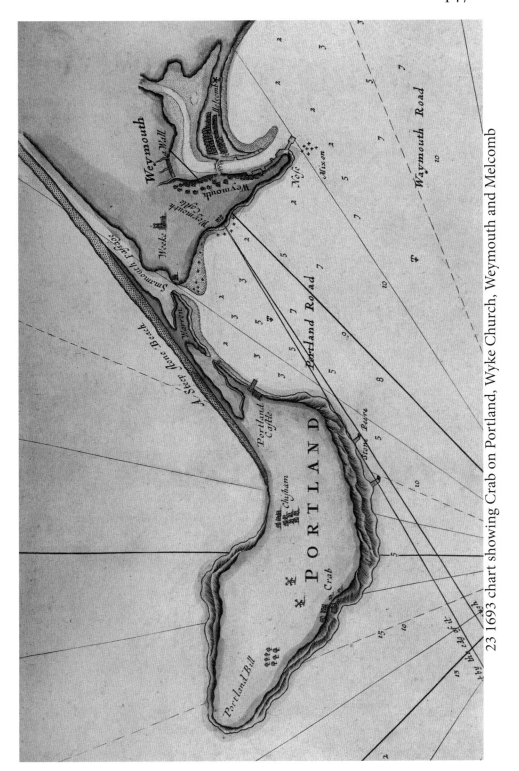

23 1693 chart showing Crab on Portland, Wyke Church, Weymouth and Melcomb

24 This 1773 town map with bridge where it was in 1641 shows the Ope, a cove also known as the Hole, where the Irish Mercenaries were killed. c (top left) is the Blockhouse Fort., m (centre right) is the Queen Elizabeth or Nothe Fort and l (bottom centre shows the Lookout minor fortification.

Bond and the Portlanders landed between it and the Nothe Fort before taking both while land forces took the Chapel Fort.

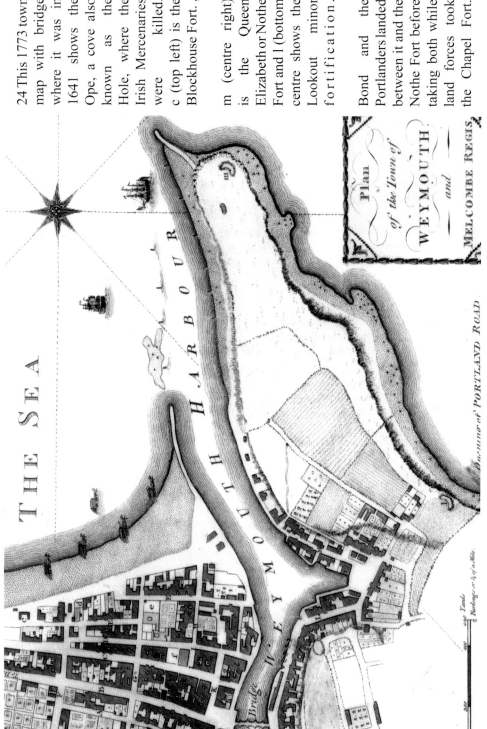

Plan of the Town of WEYMOUTH and MELCOMBE REGIS

THE SEA

HARBOUR

WEYMOUTH

On coming of PORTLAND ROAD

25 The reefs in Newtons Cove show at low tide where Bond and the Portlanders were to attack the Lookout and Nothe Forts so the attack was set for midnight with the high tide at 00:15 and the reefs would have been covered as in the photograph below. It would be important to get as close to the cliff for the attack rather than have men disembarking at low tide and stumbling over the rocks that pitch black night, the resultant noise exposing them in the larger killing ground between the boat and the cliff.

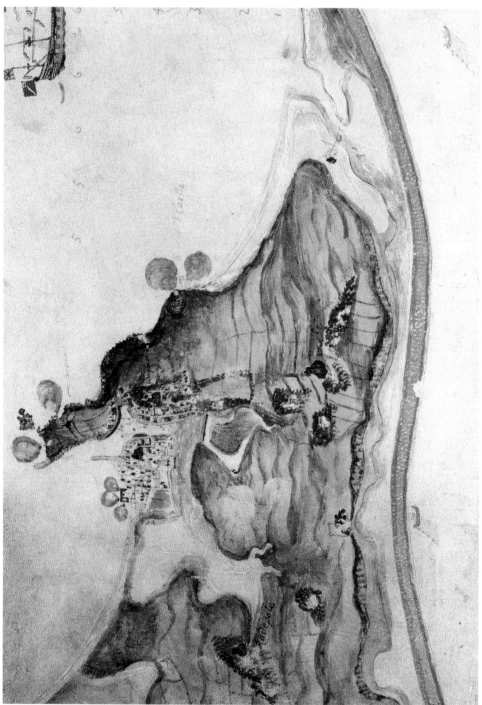

26 Two lerrets seine fishing off Chesil Beach. Wyke Church, Melcombe &
Weymouth Chapels, Blockhouse and Nothe Forts & Sandsfoot Castle all firing.

27 Bond and Samways are confronted by the body of John Cade hanging as they are brought forward for their sentence, but they successfully pleaded for their lives. The re-enactment by the English Civil War Society features historian Mark Vine as the Roundhead overseeing their trial.

28 The hanging of Royalist John Cade on the Nothe

29 Cannonball embedded below top window in Tudor building in Melcombe Regis

30 This Armada dated Tudor House backed onto the Ope and was probably built for a shipbuilder and possibly owned by Thomas Giear, Mayor of Weymouth in 1616

31 Les Kent, left, and myself in the 1970s comparing cannonballs from what we thought was the treasure ship De Hoop wrecked off Chesil Beach in 1749. The first of many cannon shipwrecks we found in Deadman's Bay. Photo taken by his partner Julie Kent who supported us on diving and metal detecting days and with hut and equipment repairs.

32 Merchant's seal ring, reflection shows the wax image.

33 John Butcher with 16th Century hackbut

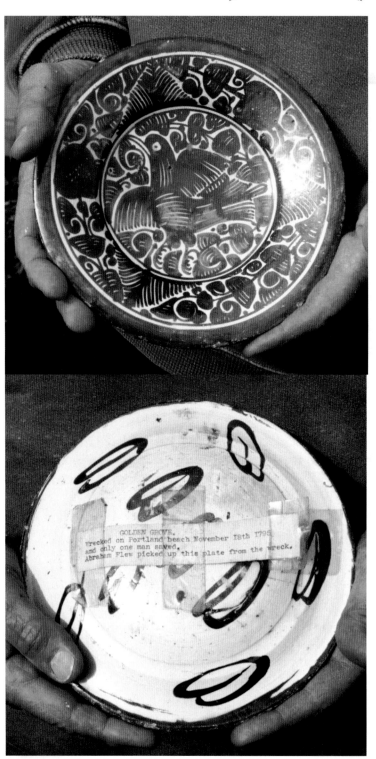

34 Spanish lustreware plate from Valencia s u p p o s e d l y salvaged from the wreck of the *Golden Grove,* an English outbound transport, in 1795 but of much earlier date and possibly salvaged from the homeward bound *Golden Grape* returning from Cadiz in 1641.

Typewritten note says *"Golden Grove* wrecked on Portland Beach November 18th 1795 and only one man saved. Abraham Flew picked this plate from the wreck."

Abell Flew and also a Robert Flew were both involved in the salvage of the Golden Grape so perhaps the name was misread when retyping the original handwritten note.

35 Silver pieces of 8, 4, 2, & 1 and 36 below, a gold 8 escudos and 2 doubloons or pistoles, showing obverse & reverse sides, all from Chesil Beach

37 Les Kent metal detecting for coins & artefacts

38 Author with the original High Court of the Admiralty Inquiry document in the Map and Large Document Reading Room at The National Archives, Kew

39 Bar of silver, pieces of eight, gold pistoles or doubloons

40 Sidescan sonar (left) showing at least 7 cannon-like objects on "palm of hand". This shows a different type of sea bottom to the surrounding bottom, possibly showing underlying iron concretion.

41 Bottom photo confirms embedded iron cannon with cascabel to left of photo and the white line running along the barrel to the muzzle. Perhaps cannons are easier to spot by sidescan than visually underwater.

of marine merchants' marks. When the East India Company was formed it was still usual for each merchant or Company of Merchant Adventurers to have their own mark that included the "Sign of Four". The Christian sign was there to ward off evil spirits including the dangers of shipwreck and piracy. The beseeching script on the ring "O Mother of God Remember Me" reinforces that merchant's plea.

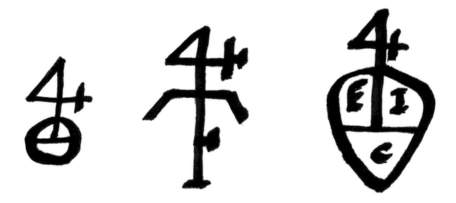

Sign of 4, marine merchants' marks

Unsurprisingly from its location on Chesil Beach, we know the ring probably came from a marine merchant, and that the ring and its plea did not save him from shipwreck but may or may not have saved him from death there. We can surmise that the four marine merchants from Amsterdam on board the Golden Grape would have had similar seal rings and although this ring is dated circa 1450, a ring of that quality and presumably with goodwill built up over years in the business, would have passed down through generations.

Roman amphora

One evening after work during the summer diving season I had rowed down the Fleet, walked my kit over the Chesil Beach and prepared to solo dive off the seaward side of Chesil Beach. As I washed my mask out in the water and put it on the rubber seal sitting over my top lip split slightly from the effect of perishing. I hesitated pondering whether to continue despite the leak of water into the mask and the consequent continual need to use some of my air to blow the water out of the mask. I decided that the effort of rowing all that way and climbing over the beach with all my diving gear meant that I should try, even if the dive was shorter and more uncomfortable than usual.

Would it be worth all the effort? It was. The fascination is that you never know what you will find. I swam out quite a way on the bottom to the margin where the pebbles meet the sand. This was usually good for flatfish and also wreckage from ships seemed to collect there. No doubt over the years the heavy seas had washed some wreckage out by sliding over the pebbles from their initial grounding on the shore until embedding in the softer sand.

With the lateral current, I glided above the bottom keeping a keen eye out for the slightest sign of fish or wreckage when a short curve in the sand caught my attention. I swam down to it and carefully wafted the sand from it. It had a round hole and appeared stone like. I turned it over and it was obviously the broken neck of a jar with stubs where the handles had been broken off it.

Originally it was thought to be the neck of a roman amphora dated about 50BC but recently it was identified by Andrew Fitzpatrick of Wessex Archaeology, an expert on Amphora, as a first or second century Roman amphora of Dressel type 20, which was used to ship olive oil from southern Spain, from the province of Baetica, basically modern Andalucia. He considered that "their tops were often cut off to allow the vessel to be reused so it could simply have been thrown over the side. There are also some fragments of Dressel 20 from Yarmouth Rhodes, Isle of Wight, which are interpreted as indicating portage rather than a wreck."

Dressel Type 20 Amphora

17 cms rim diameter

Amphora neck found upside down on the sand pebble margin

Whether the neck points to it just being thrown over the side, or possibly a wreck (Roman coins have been found on the beach nearby) it is worth investigating but it is a strong coincidence that I found this neck of a Roman amphora about a quarter of a mile from where the *Golden Grape* wrecked and which was also carrying Spanish Olive Oil in jars from Andalucia.

Bronze Hackbut

One summer's evening in the early 1970s, John Butcher was once again on his own drift diving with the tide along the Chesil Beach between Wyke and Chesil Cove. The water was crystal clear and at twenty feet off the bottom and with the same visibility in each direction John could clearly see a considerable swathe of seabed just by turning his head from side to side as the current took him. So swimming in and out along the sand-line where the pebbles merge into sand and thence to the ripples of sand further out, he had his eye out for either flatfish or any signs of wreckage, something he had done many times before. Suddenly John's trained eye spotted a straight line on the bottom and he immediately swam down towards it to investigate. With his heart beating faster as he got closer he realised that it was indeed man-made rather than natural, and he couldn't believe his luck when he could see that it was a small bronze cannon just lying in the pebbles.

What to do? John looked around and could see what looked like a heap of cannons in the distance but he was wary of leaving the bronze cannon and going any closer in case he couldn't find it again in the tide and the good but still limited underwater visibility. All he could make out was the fact that they seemed to have a ring above the breech suggesting naval cannon rather than land cannon. John quickly cleared around the bronze cannon and let the disturbed silt wash away in the tide, and he could now see the octagonal lines of it, the swell of its muzzle and how long it really was, about 3 feet. He eased it clear of the bottom, and then he literally weighed up his options. It was heavy but one person could manhandle it to the shore. Leave it and come back to it? He might not find it again or another diver might do so in the meantime. The common maxim was to never leave it if it could be retrieved. A long swim into the beach along the bottom was the alternative. John checked his air gauge, he didn't want to have to jettison it midway to the beach if his air ran out and not be able to find it once more. (This was before the advent of buoyancy aids/life jackets to lift him and it off the bottom).

He judged that he had just about enough air to swim it in if all went well but as soon as he started to swim in towards the shore, the weight of the cannon in his arms dragged him face down into the bottom, so John decided to take off his fins and walk along the bottom stooped and leaning into the lateral tide. Eventually he was near the edge of the beach and crawled up the last mounds of pebbles before his head broke the surface and he knew he had done it. He edged the cannon up to safety and then got himself up there. It had been a long way cradling the cannon in his arms but now the realisation and elation of what he had found flooded over him. It was every diver's dream to find a bronze cannon and he had done it, the first such find along the Dorset coast. Seemingly walking on air he strode over the beach and eventually got back to his car with the cannon.

When he got it home and inspected it closely there was very little sea growth and the bronze was clean of the encrustation of pebbles and grit that usually forms on some objects underwater. How old was it and what type of cannon was it exactly? Were their any others still out there amongst that heap of cannons he had seen in the distance nearby? How could he get there again without being followed, for word would soon get out? All these questions needed answers.

John took pictures of the cannon and got in touch with Rodney Alcock the conservator at the Dorset County Museum who identified it as a German hackbut, an anti-personnel weapon used on the poop deck or gunwale to fire down on boarders attacking the ship or to clear them from the decks. The tubular socket at the breech end held a wooden arm or tiller that fitted in to it so the cannon could be aimed. It was octagonal along its entire length tapering from breech to muzzle where it had a raised moulding, it also had a bronze firing pan seen on the right side of the breech in the photograph and a triangular recoil stop to hang over the gunwale or other suitable ship's cross member but there were no marks of maker etc. However experts dated it as being around 1500. At the time I saw a photo of a similar hand cannon, which had been found in a Scottish Castle, shown in Harold L. Peterson's book "The Book of the Gun" and that was dated about 1475.

A similar German bronze hackbut again dated circa 1500, came up for sale at a Christie's auction in November 2005. It had a similar triangular recoil stop, was again octagonal, though it was in stages rather than a straight line throughout its length of 30 ¾ inches (78.1cm). It also had a tubular socket for the tiller and a bronze firing pan (cover missing) and the estimated auction price was 3 to 4,000 pounds. Back in the 1970s John's cannon went for auction and is reputed to have sold for £800 to a member of a well-known rock group of the time.

John never found another bronze cannon and never found the heap of cannons he had seen in the distance because he was being followed as I can attest, for we had heard of the cannon and seen it on display so knew he was diving on a good wreck. When one day I spotted his diving group's Mini Moke filling up with petrol as we passed a local garage I, with Les Kent my diving buddy in the passenger seat, pulled over and then followed them all the way to Burton Bradstock before losing them down a side turn. Nefarious times.

A couple of years ago I bumped into John, now in his 60s and I asked him where he had actually found the cannon as there were two versions doing the rounds, and he said "I'll show you" so I picked him up the next day and after we had climbed to the top of Chesil Beach he pinpointed the spot and recounted the above story of how he had found it. I think he knew the game was up, because about three months later he died, no doubt taking many other secrets with him, but what a game!

Spanish Plate

In 2003 despite my initial reluctance, as I had heard most of them before, I attended a day's series of Maritime talks at Dorset County Museum because my friend Rodney Alcock had arranged them. Rodney had been a source of great knowledge regarding my wreck finds both in the history and in the conservation of them. It was Rodney who had conserved a 10 feet long iron cannon lifted by Royal Navy helicopter from the Guns Site that we were working on in 1974. It was identified as a 17th Century Swedish Finbanker.

The talks however turned out to be very interesting and during a lunch break I happened to ask a chap stood nearby if he was enjoying them. He was indeed, especially the one covering Christian's Fleet where six ships from his convoy had been wrecked on Chesil Beach in 1795. He had my full attention, as I, with some colleagues, owned five of those wrecks.

His interest came from the fact that one of his ancestors from Portland had picked up a plate from one of the wrecks. I quickly went through all the 6 wrecks and when I said *Golden Grove* he said, "Yes, that's it". He said the plate was still in the family and that his brother who lived away had it and he would be interested to know about our diving on Christian's wrecks. I asked if I could photograph it for my wreck research and giving him my phone number he said he would get his brother to bring it down when he next visited. I cursed that I hadn't taken his phone number as I was impatient to see it but sure enough a call came to say he would be coming down that week and could they come over?

The plate was dark red with a bird in the centre surrounded by patterns and on the back were a series of whorls again in red on the white background. The back also had some printed text sellotaped on to it and this had apparently replaced the original hand written text. It read: -
"*Golden Grove*
Wrecked Portland Beach November 18th 1795
and only one man saved.
Abraham Flew picked this plate from the wreck".

The brother said it had been identified as a Spanish plate but was of a much earlier period than the 1790s, the time of the wreck of the *Golden Grove* when 7 drowned while another 18 of those on board survived but the ship went to pieces shortly after she struck the beach. I was pleased to be allowed to take photographs of it and thought nothing more about it. Abraham Flew had been mentioned in other wreck reports as the tide surveyor around the time of Christian's wrecks but when I transcribed the Inquiry into the wreck of the *Golden Grape* from old Secretary Hand writing to modern writing I came across an Abell Flew, a mason from Portland. He had been to the wreck, which was accessible for 4 days and admitted only that he had picked up a peck of raisins from a barrel there. A Robert Flew, yeoman of Portland, had been on board the *Golden Grape* and had picked up two books amongst other things.

Could the old hand written note on the back have been misattributed when typed up? Was it *Golden Grape* instead of *Golden Grove* and was it an ambiguous A. Flew or R Flew, or was Abraham mistaken for Abell? Did this much earlier Spanish plate indeed come from the *Golden Grape* on its way back from Cadiz in Spain? It was accessible for 4 days after it was wrecked, while 150 years later the hired transport *Golden Grove,* which was taking stores out from England to the West Indies, was dashed to pieces shortly after striking the beach.

Once again I asked Andrew Fitzpatrick of Wessex Archaeology for help and their ceramics expert, Lorraine Mepham said the dish "is Late Valencian Lustreware, the last flowering of the Spanish lustreware tradition. This is dated broadly to the period from circa 1475 into the 17th century, although rare from the late 16th century. During this phase of production, the motifs used became somewhat debased from the intricate foliage and geometric designs previously used; coarse drawn birds, such as the example seen here, are typical of the 17th century. There is a comparable example of this date in the Museum Boymans-Van Beuningen (Hurst et al. 1986, plate 10). If this dish were in fact from the *Golden Grape*, and not the *Golden Grove*, it would certainly fit with the wreck date of 1641".

Either way it would not have been surprising for the *Golden Grape* to have such valued lusterware plates onboard. Similar but earlier lustreware plates found on the Studland Bay Wreck helped identify her as a possible Spanish shipwreck dated between 1500 and 1525.

Silver Bar, gold Pistoles & silver Pieces of Eight

All the above have been found either on or off the Chesil Beach either in the past or since the advent of the aqualung for divers and metal detectors for use either on the beach or underwater.

Silver pieces of 8, 4, 2, and 1 recovered off Chesil Beach

Chapter 5 The *Golden Grape* Inquiry

Background

The High Court of Admiralty was established to deal primarily with questions of piracy or spoil. This gave the right to ship owners to appeal to the court for recompense if pirates had taken their ship or cargo or in this case if, after being wrecked, the cargo or goods had been salvaged. Owners had to prove that they were entitled to the return of the goods or the value of the goods.

The Inquiry would be held by the appropriate Vice Admiral for that part of the coast where the incident took place or the port into which the prize ship was taken, if either came under their jurisdiction. Between 1640 and 1642 the Vice Admiral for Dorset, which had jurisdiction over Weymouth & Melcombe Regis, was Francis Cottingham, Baron Cottingham. There was a vacancy until 1644 when John Arthur became the Vice Admiral until 1653.

It was Captain John Arthur who was appointed Chairman of the High Court of Admiralty Inquiry into the wreck and salvage of the *Golden Grape*. John Ellis was the other overseer of the Inquiry together with the Public Notary, Francis Cape. The Inquiry commenced at Melcombe Regis on Monday 10th January 1641(2) and the last deposition was taken on Monday 28th March 1642, the new year commencing on Lady Day, 25th March.

The first week was a full week from Monday to Saturday, the first two days were spent hearing the detailed testimony of the crew of the Golden Grape followed between Wednesday and Friday with people from Wyke Regis being examined and a mix of mainly Portesham and one or two Melcombe Regis and Weymouth witnesses on the Saturday.

In subsequent weeks the court heard testimony on only 2 or 3 days per week except for the 4th week when there are 5 days. Mainly Weymouth and Melcombe Regis witnesses are heard from in the second and third weeks before the people from Portesham and Waddon testify from the 1st February until Wednesday the 9th February when Portlanders turn up for four days of testimony. On the 16th the people from Abbotsbury and neighbouring Corton, and Shilvinghampton together those witnesses from Chickerell, Fleet, Langton Herring and odd ones from Upway fill the days up to 4th March.

There is then a long break until 28th March 1642 when the last witness, a man from Upway bears testament and the Inquiry finishes.

I have transcribed the full Inquiry from the 17th century Secretary Hand into present day script but I have left the lack of a spelling convention even between the surnames of father and son in the same sentence, and other idiosyncrasies as they are, because I believe it to be so rich in the way it is written and reflects such hard times. It shows how words are transformed and derived, e.g. sithence into since, plus there is the full genealogical history of the populace at that time, and the everyday history of prices and availability of goods and services then.

Each sheet of parchment is numbered at the foot of the first side only, so I have added a number on the reverse corresponding to the first side, e.g. 6, and the reverse side 6R, to act as a reference. At the end of the transcription I have added an index to first the witnesses and then the people mentioned in the text based on these Inquiry page numbers.

I have added a glossary below to show the units of measurement and the coinage used then and to explain words that occur in the inquiry.

Glossary for High Court of the Admiralty Inquiry

Measures of capacity

1 gallon	4.55 litres
four gills	one pint
two pints	one quart
four quarts	one gallon
two gallons	one peck
four pecks	one bushell
eight bushels	one quarter or 2 stones
firkin	small wooden barrel containing nine gallons
barrel	contains 36 gallons of liquid
pipe or butt	a large cask containing 105 gallons

Coinage

British new penny (p)	2.4 old pennies (d)
Piece of eight	Spanish silver coin of 8 reales later known as a dollar
Teston or Testoon	a coin with Henry VIII's head on one side, minted in Tudor times worth 12d or 5p
Pistole or Doubloon	a Spanish gold 2 escudos coin
Groat	English coin worth 4d or just over 1.5p
Shilling	English coin worth 12d or 5p

Golden Grape Inquiry text

accompt	account
aeze	could be either an adze or an axe
astrolabe	an instrument to measure the latitude of the ship's position by sun or star
bed sacke	mattress, hence to go to bed - "hit the sack"

bolt	roll of material, for silk, a lea or skein is 120 yards
bonnet	additional sail attached to the courses
cable	a thick rope
chamber	room or a charge inserted in the breech of a cannon
chirurgeon	surgeon from the 14th century Anglo Norman surgien and Old French cirurgien. The Latin chirurgia and Greek kheirurgia
compass	it uses the magnetic field of the Earth and the alignment of a magnet to determine the Magnetic North Pole and so set a ship's course.
cordage	the lines and rigging of a vessel
courses	the sails on the lower yards of a ship to which bonnet sails could be attached.
cross bar shot	this could refer to expanding star shot, which when fired from a cannon spreads out like a cross with a quarter of the cannon ball on each arm.
cross staff	for measuring the altitude of a heavenly body, first used at sea in the 16th century.
deposition	the giving of testimony upon oath in a court of law
fathom	six feet or just under two metres
fore knight	this could be a reference to two large timbers called knightheads, which supported the ends of the windlasses or the heel of the bowsprit
gunwale	the rail around the deck on which light swivel cannon were mounted.
hellyer	tiler
husbandman	a tenant farmer or small freeholder up to 50 acres earning about £15 pa
inholder	inn keeper
junk	piece of old rope
labourer	earning about 1 shilling (5p) per day.
langar shot	langrel or langrace, was shot fired from a cannon consisting of bolts, nails, and other pieces of iron fastened together or enclosed in a canister, and was used at sea for tearing sails and rigging, but also used by privateers as an anti personnel weapon.
moiety	one of two parts
murderer	a swivel hand cannon usually mounted on the gunwale, used as an anti personnel weapon
pillowbeer	pillow case
porquett	pocket, from Anglo Norman, poket a little bag and pone bag, and from medieval Dutch poke for bag, hence pig in a poke.
quadrant	or back staff is used with a compass card to measure direction
quire	a collection of leaves of parchment or paper, folded one within the

	other, in a manuscript or book.
rode	road, as in Portland or Cadiz Roads, a sheltered area of sea where ships can ride at anchor
salve	ointment for wounds
sarcenet	fine soft silk fabric used for clothing, ribbons etc.
sawyer	person who saws timber
sithence	later becoming since, from the Old English siththan (literally meaning "after that")
smale	small
spent	used up or exhausted
Squire	Lord of the manor earning about £450 pa
taffeta	a thin lustrous plain weave fabric of silk especially for women's clothes
tent	a Spanish red wine
thither	towards that place, in that direction
top	a platform giving more support to the topmast in square rigged ships
topmast vane	narrow pennant, strip of bunting, or pendant mounted on a spindle indicating the wind direction.
whensoever	whenever
whipstaffe	the wooden vertical lever attached to the tiller by which the helmsman steered the ship from a higher deck.
Yeoman	Freehold farmer of 50 acres earning £45 pa with some up to £200 pa

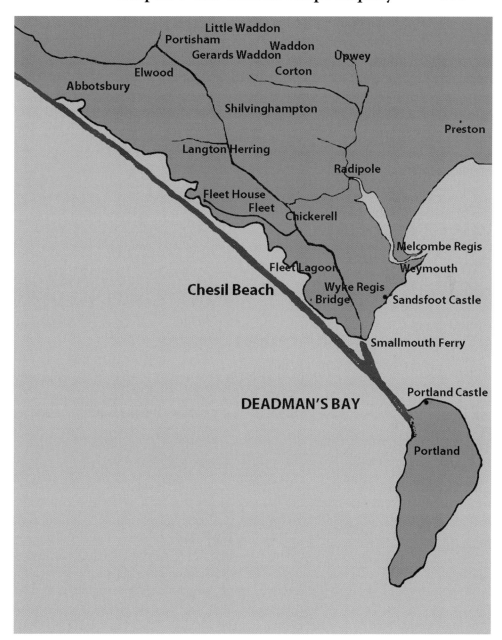

The towns and villages surrounding Chesil Beach where the *Golden Grape* was wrecked opposite Bridge, in Deadman's Bay. People attending the wreck from Portland and Abbotsbury were followed by those across the Fleet waters at Wyke, Chickerell, Fleet, and Langton Herring. Others from outlying villages together with Weymouth and Melcombe Regis arrived in great numbers the following day.

High Court of Admiralty Inquiry

Depositions taken at Melcomb Regis in the Borough of Waymouth and Melcomb Regis in the County of Dorset; the tenth day of January 1641, before us, whose names are subscribed by virtue of the commissioners before expressed Francis Cape notary public being then also present:

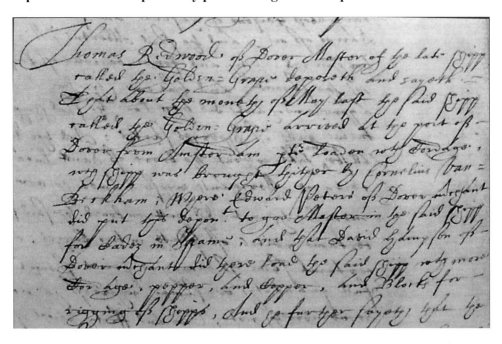

Thomas Redwood of Dover Master of the late shipp called the Golden Grape deposeth and sayeth that about the moneth of May last the said shipp called the Golden Grape arrived at the port of Dover from Amsterdam part loaden with cordage wich shipp was brought thither by Cornelius Van Berkham; where Edward Peters of Dover merchant did put this deponent to goe Master in the said shipp for Cadez in Spaine, and that David Hampson of Dover merchant did there load the said shipp with more cordage, pepper, and copper, and blocks for rigging of shipps, and he further sayeth that the said shipp stayed in Dover about three weeks, at wich time this deponent and the rest of the company of the said shipp (being twenty in all, of whome part came in the said shipp from Amsterdam, the residue (being about eight or nine) this deponent shipped at Dover) went on in her voyage for Cadez aforesaid, part of the said loading (vizt) the copper, cordage, and blocks being consigned to Martin Laderoon De Gavarre, and the residue (vizt) the pepper to a merchant of Saint Lucar whose name he now remembreth not, wich were delivered to them accordingly

1

and this deponent further saieth that the said Martin Laderoon De Gavarre, with

Anthony De Swasse and Albertus Martin did there relade the said shipp with these goods following (vizt) the said Martin Laderoon De Gavarre and Anthony De Swasse did put on board the said shipp a thousand and nineteen barrells of raisins of the sunne, and fower hundred jarres of oile, and the said Albertus Martin two hundred thirty and fower barrells of raisons of the sunne, and that one Cornelius ... a yongue merchant did then load aboard the said shipp twelve butts of Sherryes sackes: And this deponent allsoe saieth that without the barre of Saint Lucar certaine merchants whose names he now remembreth not did putt on board the said shipp certaine peices of plate in two bagges, and a certaine sume of money in peices of eight, the full quantity or sume thereof he now remembreth not, two and forty pieces of silke, two bagges of redwooll, a pegg of silver bullion, and a loafe of silver bullion, five hundred pistolles in one bag and certaine other gold mixed with peices of eight the certaine sume of wich he now remembreth not, And this deponent likewise sayeth that the thousand and nineteen barrels of raisons of the sunne, and the oyles were consigned to one Careiles and other merchants of Haver dugrace in France, and the other raisons of the sunne to Garratt Vanteene

1R

and Edward Peters of Dover, and part of the plate and silkes to certaine merchants of Roane in France whose names he new remembreth not, and the residue of the plate and the wools for the same place, but the sackes were to be disposed of by this deponent, and Robert Coast, gunner of the said shipp, and he further saieth that he knoweth noe other owners of the said shipp save onely Robert Garland of London merchant and the said Edward Peters of Dover, merchant And moreover this deponent sayeth that uppon the eleaventh day of December last by extremity of fowle weather the said shipp was forced on shore uppon the beach in the West Bay of Portland Island where shee was broken to peices, seaven men and boyes drowned, and the greatest parte of the goods moneys plate and loading lost save onely such as were salved by some of the company of the said shipp, and by other people of the Country who by force and violence tooke and caryed the same away. And this deponent alsoe sayeth that he received since the said shipp was cast away from Richard Gregory chirurgeon of the said shipp fiftie peices of eight, and from the cooke of the said shipp two hundred peices of eight; And that he did putt about his necke a smale gold chaine, wich he yet hath; And that he hath noe other goods or moneys in his hands or custody, belonging to the said shipp save certaine gunns and some parte of the provisions of the said shipp wich now lye uppon the key of Waymouth, and are in the

2

cellar of Mr. Fabian Hodder of the same towne in whose house this deponent lodgeth And lastly this deponent sayeth that his bills of loading of all the said goods, his letters of advice and other letters were all lost att such time as the said shipp was cast away.

Cornelius Van Berkham of Amsterdam Mariner Masters Mate of the said shipp called the Golden Grape deposeth and saieth that about the beginning of May last Henricke and Derricke Doomers, two brothers living in Amsterdam, did putt this deponent and about fowerteen or fifteen men more into the ship called the Golden Grape, and told him that they had bought the said shipp for one John Holding of London: and then sent this deponent and the said shipp and company with certaine cordage, about two hundred barrells of pepper, certain barrells of nailes, a certaine quantity of tallow, and some blockes loaden aboard the said shipp to Dover to take in the said Holding to goe Master in her for Cadez in Spaine whither she was bound with those goods and loading: Whither when they came (not finding the said Holding there) Garratt Vanteen and Edward Peters, merchants, told

2R

this deponent that they were owners of the said shipp and thereuppon did put Thomas Redwood to goe Master in her for that voyage: And he further saieth that during his stay att Dover David Hampson merchant did load aboard the said shipp some more cordage and certaine parcels of copper, and from thence sayled directly for Cadez where they delivered all the said goods (except the pepper) unto Martin Laderoon De Gavarre, and Albertus Martin, and the pepper to a merchant of Saint Lucar whose name he now remembreth not. And moreover this deponent saieth that the said Martin Laderoon De Gavarre att Cadez aforesaid did load aboard the said shipp one thowsand and nineteen barrells of raisons of the sunne, and three hundred ninety and six jarres of oile (but for whose accompt this deponent knoweth not) And that the said Albertus Martin did loade aboard the said shipp two hundred thirty and fower barrells of raisons of the sunne to be delivered unto the beforenamed Edward Peters And that one Cornelius Heddah did load aboard the said shipp twelve butts of sacke for the accompt of the said Redwood, the Gunner, and himselfe, And that one John Jacob did put aboard the said shipp fower butts of sacke for his owne accompt and his fathers who liveth in Amsterdam, And that a certaine merchant (whose name this deponent knoweth not) did putt on board the said shipp two bagges of wooll, And that the said gunner had three pipes of tent for his owne accompt loaden there likewise, And this

3

deponent further saieth that when the said shipp was come without the barr of St Lucar certain merchants (unknowne) did deliver aboard the said shipp, three and fortye peices of taffata, a bagg of redwooll more, five hundred pistolls of gold in a bagg many baggs of peices of eight (the certaine quantity or sume whereof he knoweth not) a pegg of silver, a loafe of silver, two bags of silver plate, but to whome the same were consigned, or for whose accompt the same were this deponent doth not know. And this deponent alsoe saieth that, sayling towards Dover in their course homewards, the said shipp by extremity of foule weather was driven on shore on the beech in the West Bay neere the Island of Portland, where she was broken to peices and the said goods and loading all castaway and lost, save such as some of their owne company and many inhabitants of the villages adjacent did by violence take and cary away. And this deponent further sayeth that he saved the pegg of silver which was delivered to Arthur Grey of Wyke Regis, and a bagg of peices of eight being neer about five hundred twenty and five peices amounting to fower thousand and two hundred Ryalls, wich he also delivered to the said Grey: And that he hath none of the goods moneys, or provisions of the said shipp at present in his custody or in the custody of any to his use more then before he hath expressed. And lastly this

3R

deponent saieth that shortly after the said shipp was cast away one James Smith the boatswains mate of the said shipp did in this deponent's presence bring on shore certaine pistolls of gold in his hatt wich he put into the pocquett of Robert Coast the gunner of the said shipp, and that he went aboard the second time and brought more pistolls of gold from thence, wich he kept to himselfe, saying, that he would keep something for his owne use.

Robert Coast, gunner of the late shipp called the Golden Grape deposeth and saieth that the said shipp called the Golden Grape doth belonge unto Wesseilhen Normen, and unto Henricke and Derricke Doomers of Amsterdam, and to Derricke Peterson Rodhoost of Parmarent who are owners of the same, And that in the moneth of Aprill last this deponent was by Cornelius Van Berkham steersman of the said shipp (by the direcions of the said Wesseilhen Norman) shipped to goe gunner in her in her intended voyage for Cadez in Spaine, and that the said Norman payed this deponent two moneths pay in hand. And he further saieth that about the fowerth day of May following this deponent and about fifteen or sixteen men more in the said shipp departed from Tessell and sailed for Dover, the said shipp being

4

in parte laden with pepper, blocks and cordage, and consigned to Mr. Hampson and Mr. Peters of Dover who were appointed to put in one John Holding to goe Master in the said shipp for that voyage to Cadez, but (he being from home) the said Mr. Hampson and Mr. Peters did put Thomas Redwood in his steed to goe Master in her. And this deponent further sayeth that at Dover they tooke in a certaine quantity of cordage, tallow, and copper to make up the full loading of the said shipp, and about the midst of June following departed from there and sayled directly to Cadez aforesaid, where they unloaded all the said goods (save the pepper) and delivered the same to Martin Laderoon De Gavarre, and the pepper was taken out of the said shipp without the bar of St. Lucar. And this deponent alsoe sayeth that the said Martin Laderoon De Gavarre did loade aboard the said shipp in the harbour of Cadez a great quantity of oyle and raisons of the sunne the certainty whereof, and whither or to whome they were consigned he knoweth not; And that Albertus Martin did there alsoe load aboard the said shipp about two hundred and forty barrells of raisons of the sunne, but to whose accompt this deponent alsoe knoweth not And that Cornelius Williamson Heddah did there put aboard the said shipp eight butts of sacke for the accompt of a merchant of Roane whose name this deponent knoweth not, and fower butts of sacke more for the accompt of the said

4R

Master and this deponent And that John Jacob Fabiansa did put aboard the said shipp fower other butts of sacke for the accompt of the said Merchant of Roane, And this deponent did then alsoe putt aboard the said shipp for his owne accompt three pipes of tent, And that the said de Gavarre did then putt aboard the said shipp two bagges of red wooll. And this deponent further sayeth that when the said shipp was come without the barre of St. Lucar there was brought aboard the said shipp certaine taffata's, a bagg of redwooll, and a great quantity of money and plate, the particulars whereof, or whose the said goods and plate were, or to whome consigned he knoweth not. And moreover this deponent sayeth that as they were in their course sayling homewards the said shipp was by fowle weather cast a shore on the beech in West Bay neer the Isle of Portland where she was by the violence of that tempest broken in peices, and the goods all lost, save onely such as were salved by the company of the said shipp and by certaine country people living neere who in multitudes came thither and caryed away great quantityes of the same. And this deponent further sayeth that after the said shipp was cast away and before she was quite broken to pieces the boatswaines mate of the said shipp did goe aboard twice, and att the first time brought thence certaine pistolls of gold in his hatt wich he delivered to Cornelius Van Berkham the steersman, who did put them into this deponent's pocquett, saying to this deponent keep these and we will divide them betwen us, and then the said boatswaines mate

5

went aboard the second time and brought more pistolls of gold ashore in his hatt, parte of wich he delivered to this deponent (wich he afterwards counting found to be an hundred and five pistolls) and the residue the said boatswaines mate kept to himselfe, And lastly this deponent sayeth that all those pistolls wich he received from the said boatswaines mate he did afterwards deliver to Mr. Strode of Portland, who hath since delivered the same to the Viceadmiral. And that this deponent hath not in his owne custody nor in the custody of any other person to his use any more gold, silver, or other goods or provisions of or belonging to the said shipp.

Michael Hatherwick boatswaine of the late shipp called the Golden Grape deposeth and sayeth that uppon the fifteenth day of March last he was shipped into the said shipp called the Golden Grape by the steersman Cornelius Van Barkham and by Wesseilhen Norman one of the owners thereof, and that Henrick and Derrick Doomers and Derrick Peterson Redhoosd are the other owners of the said shipp And that about the end of April following this deponent and the rest of his company (being

5R

sixteen in all) did load aboard the said shipp to the use of the said owners certaine cordage, pepper, tallow and blocks for the rigging of shipps, with wich about the fowerth of May following they putt in at Dover with intent to take in John Holding to goe Master in the said shipp in their voyage for Cadez, but when they came to Dover there was more cordage and more copper putt aboard the said shipp to make up her loading, and then Thomas Redwood was putt to go Master in her (the said Holding not being then there) but by whome this deponent knoweth not: From whence they sailed directly to Cadez, where they unloaded all the said goods (save only the pepper wich they delivered att the barre of St. Lucar) unto Martin Laderoon de Gavarre; And this deponent further saieth that the said Martin Laderoon de Gavarre and other Merchants did there reload aboard the said shipp great quantityes of raysons of the sunne neer about thirteen hundred barrells, fower hundred jarres of oyle, sixteen butts of sacke and three pipes of tent in the harbour of Cadez, but for whose accompt this deponent knoweth not. And that when the said shipp was come without the barre of Saint Lucar there was brought aboard her three baggs of redwooll, certaine plate, and moneys three and forty peices of taffata's, but who sent the same aboard or whither or to whome the same were consigned this deponent doth not know, onely it was reported by the Spaniards that they were to go to Halver dugrace in France. And this deponent further saieth that in their course homeward the said shipp by extremity of fowle weather was cast on shore in the West Bay neer

6

the Isle of Portland, where she was broken in peices and the greatest part of the said goods, moneys, plate, and merchandize lost save only such as was salved by the country people neer. And this deponent alsoe sayeth that he did save a smale bagg of peices of eight (wich had been opened before) in wich were one hundred and six and twenty pieces of eight, wich John Peirce, George Allin, William Phillis and this deponent shared between them, of wich this deponent had one and fiftye peices, and the other three had five and twenty peices a peice; and he further saieth that the trumpetter of the said shipp did afterwards take out of the bagg one and thirty of these peices that this deponent had, wich he caryed away with him, and left to this deponent only twenty pieces, with part of wich he hath bought him clothes the remainder he hath spent since his coming to Waymouth. And lastly he saieth that he hath not nor ever had any other or more of the goods, moneys, or provisions of or belonging to the said shipp.

6R

Deposicons taken at Melcomb Regis aforesaid the eleventh day of January in the year before named before us whose names are subscribed by virtue of the commissioners before expressed Francis Cape notary public being then also present.

Richard Rich of Barnestaple in the county of Devon, saylor deposeth, and sayeth that he was one of the company of the late ship called the Golden Grape and that he was shipped att Dover by Thomas Redwood Master of the said shipp about the moneth of May last to goe Gunners Mate in a voiage for Cadez in Spain, in wich voyage he went with the said Master and company and unloaded the said shipp att Cadez and att the barre of Saint Lucar. And in the rode of Cadez the said shipp was in parte loaden againe, and consigned or ordered to sail for Haverdugrace in France (as this examinant hath heard) And that without the barre of St. Lucar there was brought and putt aboard the said shipp money and plate the certaine sume or quantity whereof, to whome it was consigned or by whome putt on board this deponent doth not know. Wich being there taken in they loosed from thence and sayling in their course homewards the said shipp was by violent stormes and tempestuous weather driven a shore upon the beech in the West Bay neer the Isle of Portland where she was broken to peices. Att wich time this deponent did save a bagg of money out of the said shipp wich he delivered unto

7

the Master of the said shipp uppon the beech. And this deponent further saieth that shortly after he departing from the beech and travailing towards Waymouth the boatswain of the said shipp gave him seaven pieces of eight, and that following certain Dutchmen (that came in the said shipp as passengers) that way he tooke up five or six peices of eight more, with all wich he hath bought him clothes and other necessaryes. And lastly this deponent sayeth that he hath not nor had either in his owne custody or in the custody of any other to his use any other or more of the goods, plate, or money out of or belonging to the shipp.

James Smyth one of the company of the said shipp called the Golden Grape deposeth and sayeth that he was shipped by one Derrick Redhoosd and three other Dutchmen (whose names he knoweth not) in Amsterdam, owners of the said shipp called the Golden Grape to goe boatswaynes Mate in her for Cadez in Spaine, one of wich owners payed him there one moneths

7R

pay in hand from whence uppon the fowerth day of May last they departed and sailed to Dover where Thomas Redwood was shipped by a factor for the said owners (whose name is Peters) to goe Master of the said shipp in the said voyage. From wich place they departing sailed to Cadez where they unloaded all the goods out of the said shipp. (save onely certaine barrells of pepper wich were taken out and delivered at the barre of Saint Lucar.) And this deponent further sayeth that the said shipp was reloaden againe in the rode of Cadez by some Spanish and Flemish merchants with fruit and oyles, and some wines for the use of the said Master and company. From whence (after they had there taken the said goods aboard the said shipp) they removed without the barre of Saint Lucar where was brought in two boats certaine silver plate, bullion, and coine wich was there putt on board the said shipp, but who sent the same aboard or whither it was consigned this deponent doth not know. And this deponent also saieth that after they had taken in those goods there they loosed from thence and sayled directly homewards, but by the way violent and tempestuous winde and weather arising did drive the said shipp a shore upon the beech in

West Bay neer the Isle of Portland where she was by the violence of that tempest

8

broken to pieces. Out of wich ship this deponent (as yet remaining aboard) did take six bags of coine and a pegg of silver, wich he threw ashore unto the steersman and the gunner of the said shipp, and then went a shore himselfe. Soone after wich the said steersman and gunner did desire this deponent to goe aboard the said shipp againe, wich he accordingly did, from whence he did then throw ashore to them three small baggs of coine more, and tooke up in the steerage roome certain pistolls of gold which he putt in his capp and caryed ashore with him, and delivered the same to the steersman (but the certain number of them he knoweth not) who gave them to the gunner to keep, willing him and this deponent to be silent and to say noething of those, and they would share the same between them. After wich the said steersman and gunner desired this deponent to go aboard the said shipp againe and to save soe much more of the gold as he could there finde, wich he did, and brought thence some more pistolls of gold (but how many he knoweth not) wich he delivered to the said steersman alsoe, who likewise gave the same to the said gunner to keep; only this deponent kepte one and

8R

twenty pistolls to himselfe wich about three days after he delivered to the Viceadmiral who then required the same from him. And this deponent also sayeth that whiles he was aboard the said shipp he did take up sixteen peices of eight wich he found loose in the steerage, wich he kept to himselfe, and that after he came to Waymouth William Bushell, one of the company of the said shipp delivered him this deponent forty peices of eight more, with wich he hath bought him clothes and other necessaryes. And he likerwise saieth that he hath seaventeen pistolls of gold left in his custody and tenn peices of eight not yett spent wich he is ready to deliver, And lastly he hath sayeth that he hath not in his owne custody nor in the custody of any other to his use any other or more of the gold, silver, plate, bullion, or other goods or provisions of or belonging to the said shipp.

John Peirce one of the company of the said shipp called the Golden Grape deposeth and sayeth that he being att Cadez in Spaine was there

9

shipped by Thomas Redwood Master of the said shipp to goe as a sailor in her for Dover. Whereuppon he went aboard the said shipp. And he saieth that in sayling thitherwards the said shipp by violent stormes and tempestuous weather was forced on shore upon the beech in the West Bay neer the Isle of Portland where the said shipp by the extremity of the said storme was broken to peices and the most parte of her loading perished. And this deponent further sayeth that he (being at that time very sick tooke none of the gold silver plate money coine or other goods or comodityes out of the said shipp. But saieth that the cook of the said shipp had a longe bagg full of peices of eight, and the chirurgeon another; And that the boatswayne had another, out of wich he gave this deponent five and twenty peices of eight, with parte of wich this deponent did buy clothes for himselfe, and with the residew did pay one Mr. Gibson, a chirurgeon of Waymouth for phisike, the sume that he payed him being fifteen shillings or thereabouts. And lastly he saieth that he hath not nor had either in his owne custody or in the custody of any other to his use any other or more of the goods moneys or provisions of the said shipp.

9R

William Phillis one of the company of the ship called the Golden Grape deposeth and saieth that he being a servant to Henry Wallopp of Dover was by his Mistresse (in the absence of his Master) in May last there shipped to goe as a saylor in the said shipp the Golden Grape for Cadez in Spaine, to wich port he went accordingly, and returning homewards the said shipp by foule weather was forced ashore uppon the beech in the West Bay neer the Isle of Portland, where she was broken to peices. But before she was all splitt this deponent by the order and directions of the Master of the said shipp did adventure to goe aboard againe, whither being come he went into the cabin and did take up there fower or five bagges of coine, which he threw of the shipp unto the said Master and some others of the company of the said shipp who were then a shore, After wich (the shipp breaking more and more and the deponent in danger of his life) he made haste and gott to the shore, where he tooke up a longe bagge of the said coine intending to cary the same with him to a village neer called Wyke Regis, but being weary and weak and meeting with one Owin Gibbons of that place by the way, with an horse this deponent delivered the said bagge to him entreating him to cary it thither for him, wich the said Gibbons undertooke to doe, but to whose house there he caryed the same this deponent knoweth not. And he further saieth that he tooke up in the said shipp about tenn or twelve loose peices of eight wich he putt into the lyninges of

10

a capp which he then wore, and that goeing towards Wyke Regis aforesaid in the company of the said Master of the shipp (and the said Master complayning of a paine in his head) this deponent did put his capp on the said Masters head, who did weare the same to Wyke Regis aforesaid, whither being come the said Master tooke of the said capp from his head, and (feeling the said money there) tooke out some of the said peices and left onely five or six peices therein and then delivered the same to this deponent who hath since spent the same. And this deponent further sayeth that the boatswaine of the said shipp having a bagg of coine wich he tooke out of the said shipp did give this deponent five and twenty peices of eight out of the said bagge, with part of wich he hath bought him clothes to weare and other necessaryes, the remainder he hath spent. And lastly this deponent sayeth that he hath not nor had in his owne custody nor in the custody of any other to his use any other or more of the gold silver plate wares merchandizes or provisions of or belonging to the said shipp.

10R

George Allen one of the company of the shipp called the Golden Grape deposeth and sayeth that in May last he was shipped att Dover by the steersman of the said shipp to goe as a saylor in her for Cadez whither he went in the said shipp, and there having unloaden the goods that were in her, and she being reloaden did depart thence and sett saile to come homewards, but by the way by reason of very violent stormes the said shipp was forced a shore upon the beach in the West Bay near the Isle of Portland where she was broken to peices, out of wich this deponent hardly escaped with his life. And he further sayeth that afterwards as he was goeing towards Wyke Regis a village neer the place where the said shipp was cast away the cooke of the said shipp did deliver unto this deponent a bagge of coine in wich were two hundred thirty and three peices of eight wich this deponent delivered to the Master of the said shipp, And that by the way goeing alonge upon the beech he espyed fower Dutchmen who came in the said shipp as passengers sharing a bagg of coine between them of whome this deponent demanding a parte they gave him six peices of eight. And he further saieth that afterwards the boatswaine of the said shipp having a bagge of coine gave this deponent five and twenty peices parte thereof, with some of wich money he hath bought clothes and other necessaryes for himselfe, the remainder he hath spent since. And lastly he sayeth that he hath not nor had in his custody nor in the custody of any other to his use any other or more of the goods money plate coine or merchandizes of or belonging to the said shipp.

11

Deposicons taken at Melcomb Regis aforesaid the twelfth day of January in the year before named before us whose names are subscribed by virtue of the commissioners before expressed Francis Cape notary public being then also present.

Andrew Pitt of Wyke Regis in the County of Dorsett yeoman deposeth and saieth that about two dayes after that the shipp the Golden Grape was cast away upon the beech in the West bay near the Isle of Portland he went from his house to the Fleet side neer the said beech where he saw three barrels of fruit lyeing wich had been taken out of the said shipp and an halser belonging to her and many persons neer the same, but who they were he knoweth not nor what became of the said fruit, onely the halser was afterwards halled up by two sonns of the widow Heminges of Waymouth and brought into the backside of this deponent and thence left, where it now remaines, and wich he is ready to deliver. And this deponent further sayeth that he hath not nor had in his custody nor in the custody of any other to his use any more or other of the goods or provisions of or belonging to the said shipp save onely about a pecke and halfe of wett raysons wich his daughter being ther tooke up and brought home to his house.

11R

Arthur Grey of Wyke Regis aforesaid in the said County of Dorsett Alehouskeeper deposeth and saieth that he was att the sea side uppon the beech in the West bay att such time as the ship called the Golden Grape was there driven a shore and cast away where he stood and looked on untill the company of the same ship were come ashore uppon the said beech, att which time some of the company desired this deponent to helpe them to some place of succour for that they were very cold wett and faint, whereuppon the deponent offered them his boat to wafte them over the Fleet within the said beech between that and the maine land and to guide them to his house in Wyke Regis aforesaid, where they might refresh themselves, whereuppon about five of the said company came into his boat and he caryed them over. But the said deponent saieth that before they came to the boat the steersman of the said ship delivered this deponent a pegge of silver to cary for him wich he did. And after they were landed on the Maine he tooke the said pegge of silver and caryed the same in the company of the men of the said shipp unto his house in Wyke Regis aforesaid, where the said men and about fower or five others of that company lay that night. And the said deponent further sayeth that the said steersman delivered unto him this deponent a bagge of money, And that an Irishman one of the company of the said shipp did alsoe then deliver to this deponents wife another bagge of money

12

And that the Master of the said shipp did then alsoe bring into the deponents house another bagge of money and delivered the same alsoe to him this deponent. All wich money together with the said pegg of silver he hath heretofore confessed to have received and (uppon comand) hath delivered the same to the Viceadmirall without taking out or deteyning any part thereof. And the said deponent further saieth that another of the company of the said shipp did bring and deliver unto him an old brasse kettle and a copper spoone or ladell wich are now in his custody. And he further saieth that one other of the company of the said shipp whose name is William Phillis but comonly called little Will did in this deponents presence bring into his boat a bagg of coine, wich att their landing he took thence againe, but what he did with it afterwards this deponent doth not know (the said little Will goeing into the house of one Feaver of Bridge within the parish of Wyke Regis aforesaid before he came to this deponents house) And lastly this deponent sayeth that he hath not nor had in his custody nor in the custody of any other to his use any other or more of the money, plate, coine, goods or provisions of the said shipp save only those that are before declared, and one hundred pieces of eight wich he kept in his custody for the dyett fier and entertainment of nine men of that company for three nights and fower dayes.

12R

Susanna Grey the wife of the aforesaid Arthur Grey deposeth saieth that uppon the day that the shipp called the Golden Grape was cast away there was brought into her husbands house in Wyke Regis one bagge of coine by the Master of the said shipp, another bagg of coine by the steersman, and another bagg of coine by an Irishman one of the company of the said shipp. Which baggs were put into a chest in the chamber where the said Master lay standing by his beds side, but by whome she knoweth not. And that afterwards the same night (the said Master being in his bedd and knowing thereof) the same baggs (as she thinketh) were by her taken out of the said chest, and delivered to her husband who caryed the same away and putt them in some other place, of wich she know not. And that a pegge of silver was alsoe brought thither, but she never saw the same untill it was delivered to the Viceadmirall. And she further sayeth that all the said money (to her best remembrance) hath been heretofore delivered the said Viceadmirall And she allsoe sayeth that the trumpetter of the said shipp did allsoe bring into her house a great quantity of coine (about half a peck as she guesseth wich he tooke away with him againe, this deponent having noe part thereof. And lastly she saieth that she hath noe other coine or goods of the said shipp save onely an old brasse kettle, a ladle, and an hundred pieces of eight wich her husband kept in satisfaccon for dyet and lodging of nine of the company of the said shipp for fower dayes and nights.

13

Thomas Byrd cooke of the ship called the Golden Grape deposed saieth that after the said shipp was cast on shore upon the beech in the West Bay neere the Isle of Portland this deponent, the boatswaine, and the carpenter of the said shipp went aboard the same ship from whence this deponent tooke and threw a shore about six baggs of coine, and then seeing a country man in a blew jerkin (whose name he knoweth not) to take up one of the said bagges he did forbeare to throw any more thither, but tooke two baggs with him, wich he caryed ashore, and kept them awhiles on his backe, but (not being able to cary both he delivered, one whole bagg to an Irishman one of the company of the said shipp, who caryed the same away, and what he did with it this deponent knoweth not And he further saieth that he carried the bagg that was left with him unto the towne of Waymouth and all the money in it save about forty peices of eight wich he gave to certaine people (unknown) to cary the said bagg for him. And that after his being att Waymouth he delivered two hundred peices of eight wich were in the said bagg unto the Master of the said shipp, and that was all the money that he had left after he had bought him clothes to weare, of wich he stood in great want, and wich cost him about three pounds, And this is all the money or goods that he had out of the said shipp, or belonging to the same.

13R

Mary Smart the wife of Nicholas Smart of Wyke Regis saylor, deposed sayeth that the next day after that the shipp called the Golden Grape was cast away she went uppon the beech there, where she tooke up about fower pounds of wett raisons of the sunne wich she putt into the boat of one Nicholas Williams to be caryed home for her, from whence they were taken, but by whome she knoweth not. And that she hath not, nor had in her owne custody nor in the custody of any other to her use any other of the goods wares or merchandizes, of or belonging to the said shipp.

Anthony Winter of Wike Regis aforesaid saylor deposed saieth that the next day after the shipp called the Golden grape was cast away on the beech in the West bay he went thither where he tooke up certaine wett raisons, wich he putt into a bag that he had there with him, and caryed home to his children who have since eaten the same. And that he hath not nor had any other or more of the goods or provisions of or belonging to the said shipp.

Owen Gibbons of Wyke Regis aforesaid saylor deposed sayeth that about nine of the clock in the night of the same day that the ship called

14

the Golden Grape was cast away on the beech in West bay neere the Isle of Portland he went thither where he saved seaven barrells of fruit wich he hath in his custody and is and will be ready to deliver the same, and about a peck and halfe of loose wett fruit wich he allsoe caryed home with him. And he further saieth that he was by the wife of Arthur Grey of Wyke Regis the same night intreated to ryde downe his horse thither and to fetch them one of the company of the said shipp who was then very sicke, wich he did, and being come thither did put John Peirce (the sicke man uppon his horse, one other of the company called little Will being then present. And he further saieth that one of them did deliver to him a longe double bagg of coine, wich he did putt uppon the necke of his horse, and soe did lead the said horse directly to the house of the said Arthur Grey, where he left the said Peirce and the said bagg of coine, wich this deponent doth believe was putt into the chest in the Chamber there where mor bags of money had been putt before, And that the said Peirce did then give this deponent and another that was there with him one piece of eight between them for their paines. And lastly this deponent sayeth that he hath not nor had any other or more of the goods money or provisions of the said shipp then he hath before in this his deposicon sett forth.

14R

John Murrey of Wyke Regis aforesaid fisherman deposeth saieth that early in the morning the next day after the said shipp called the Golden Grape was cast away on the beech in the West bay neer the Isle of Portland this deponent went thither, where he tooke out of a barrell that then lay uppon the beech about three pecks of raisons of the sunne, and putt them into a bagg wich he caryed home with him to Wyke, part whereof he hath there spent, and the remainder he hath sold to John King of Melcomb Regis for five shillings (wich money he now payeth to Mr Arthur) And he further saieth that he hath not nor had any other or more of the goods wares or provisions that were belonging to the said shipp.

Henry Harvest of Wyke Regis aforesaid husbandman deposeth sayeth that the Monday after the shipp called the Golden Grape was cast away on the beech in the West bay he went thither in the company of the Master of the said shipp and of Mr Charity and Mr. Hodder of Waymouth with whome he returned againe. And that uppon the Saturday before his wife was there and brought thence about three parts of a pecke of wett raysons of the sunne wich she caryed home, where viewing them she found a great deale of gravell and sand amongst them. And that was all the goods of the said shipp wich he, his wife, or any of his people, or any other to his use had or have to this deponents knowledge.

15

Francis Spratt of Wyke Regis aforesaid husbandman deposed sayeth that upon the same day att night that the ship called the Golden Grape was cast away uppon the beech in the West bay neer the Isle of Portland he went thither accompanyed with Anthony Bryne and William Stone servants to Anthony Clapcott of Wyke Regis aforesaid, whither upon they came they salved out of the said shipp seaven barrells of raysons of the sunne, and bringing them away one William Lovell of Fleet (pretending he had the power from the Vice Admirall) tooke fower from them, and caryed them away having then many more barrells in his custody, the residew being three this deponent and the others that went with him caryed to Wyke Regis aforesaid in a cart of William Cades this deponents Master, and putt them into his house where they yet remaine. And this deponent further saieth that Bernard Cade and John Cade two of the sonnes of the said William Cade did att the same time bring into the said William Cades two jarres of oyle that were taken out of the said shipp. And lastly this deponent sayeth that he hath not nor had any other or more of the goods wares or provisions of or belonging to that shipp.

George Chip of Wyke Regis aforesaid saylor deposeth saieth that uppon the next

15R

day after the shipp called the Golden Grape was cast away he went uppon the beech where he mett with Robert Hunt of Wyke Regis, and his sonne and servant, who having saved tenn barrells of raysons of the sunne desired this deponent and his company to cary the same over the Fleet in his boat, wich they accordingly did, and for their paines the said Hunt gave them two of the said tenn barrells, and the rest the said Hunt caryed home to his house. And this deponent further saieth that he and the rest of his company did save one barrell of fruit more, wich three barrells they caryed to Wyke Regis in the plough of Mr John Jeffries and to his house where they yet remaine, and are and shalbe ready to be delivered. And lastly this deponent sayeth that he hath not nor had any more or other of the goods or provisions of or belonging to the said shipp

Thomas Peck of Wyke Regis aforesaid laborer deposed saieth that uppon the same day that the ship called the Golden Grape was cast away he went to the beech where he did take up some loose wett raysons about twelve pounds in weight, wich he did put into the sleives of his coat and cary home with him. And that he was there againe the Monday following and then gathered up a bundle of wood peices of the said shipp wich he caryed home to make firewood. And that he hath not nor had

16

any other or more of the goods or provisions of or belonging to that shipp.

Bartholomew Williams of Wyke Regis saylor deposed sayeth that about twelve of the clock in the night of the same day that the shipp called the Golden Grape was cast away he went to the beech where he tooke up certaine loose raisons of the sunne wich he put into his linine breeches and caryed to his boat. And he further saieth that he and the company of his boat (vizt) Nicholas Williams Henry Florry John Curteis Henry Lyne and Nicholas Charles did take aboard the said boat about fower and twenty jarres of oyle, and caryed the same over the Fleet to the Mayne Land, but who salved the same this deponent knoweth not, neither doth he remember any body that was in the said boat that he knew save onely the daughter of Robert Hunt of Wyke Regis: Of wich oile this deponent and his company had twelve jarres for their paines (vizt) two jarrs apeice, and this deponent hath the said two jarrs wich he had, and now delivereth the same to Mr. Arthur, of wich one is not quite full. And lastly this deponent sayeth that he hath not nor had either in his owne custody or in the custody of any other to his use anyother or more of the goods or provisions of or belonging to that shipp.

16R

James Gardiner of Wyke Regis aforesaid fisherman deposed saieth that upon the same day that the shipp called the Golden Grape was cast away he went uppon the beech and soe aboard the said shipp (wich was then neer broken to pieces) where he tooke out of a barrell about a peck and halfe of raisons of the sunne wich he put into a bagg and caryed with him home. An he further sayeth that att the same time he saved out of the said shipp two shipp rugges and one pillow, wich he caryed home likewise, and also one whole barrell of raisons of the sunne wich he caryed to his brother Robert Geales house in Wyke Regis where he left the same, all wich he is and wilbe ready to deliver. And he further saieth that he then tooke up alsoe two pieces of Spanish coine, one of wich is halfe a piece of eight, and the other a teston, wich he now produceth and delivereth to Mr. Arthur. And lastly he saieth that he hath not nor had in his owne custody nor in the custody of any other to his use any more or other of the goods moneys or provisions that were in the said shipp.

Nicholas Charles of Wyke Regis aforesaid saylor deposed saieth that he went uppon the beech the same day that the shipp called the Golden Grape was there cast away where he tooke up two jarres of oyle, and certaine loose wett raysons of the sunne wich he putt

17

into his breeches and caryed home with him wich two jarres of oyle he hath yett att home in his house and is and wilbe ready to deliver the same. And that he hath not nor had in his owne custody or in the custody of any other to his use any other or more of the goods or provisions of or belonging to that shipp.

William Wareham of Wyke Regis aforesaid saylor deposed saieth that uppon the next day after that the shipp called the Golden Grape was cast away he went uppon the beech, where this deponent together with Alexander Lea, George Chipp and Henry Kellway did save three barrells of raisons of the sunne wich they caused to be caryed to the house of Mr. John Jeffries in Wyke Regis aforesaid where they yett remaine ready to be delivered. And he further saieth that he hath not nor hadd in his owne custody nor in the custody of any other to his use any other or more of the goods or provisions of or belonging to that shipp.

Alexander Geale of Wyke Regis aforesaid fisherman deposed saieth that the next day after that the shipp called the Golden Grape was cast away he went uppon the beech where he tooke up a smale

17R

quantity of wett raisons of the sunne wich he caryed home in his capp. And that he hath not nor had any other or more of the goods or provisions of or belonging to that shipp.

Leonard Sandford of Wyke Regis aforesaid saylor deposed saieth that on the next day in the morning after that the shipp called the Golden Grape was cast away uppon the beech in the West Bay neere the Isle of Portland he this deponent together with John Andrews and Henry Pitt of Wyke Regis aforesaid did goe to the place where the said shipp lay where they saved eight barrells of raisons of the sunne two of wich barrells were taken from them by Richard Gilbert, John Dobye, and Jennings Attwooll, of Portland, who staved one of the said two barrells to peices the other they caryed away with them into Portland, the other six barrells this deponent and his said parteners caryed to Wyke Regis aforesaid where the same doe yett remaine. And this deponent further saieth that he hath not nor had in his custody nor in the custody of any other to his use any other or more of the goods or provisions of or belonging to the said shipp.

18

John Andrews of Wyke Regis aforesaid fisherman deposed saieth that on the next day in the morning after the shipp called the Golden Grape was cast away he went to the beech in the company of Henry Pitt and Leonard Sandford where they saved eight barrells of raisons of the sunne, two of wich were taken from them by Richard Gilbert, John Doby and Jennings Attwooll of Portland the other six this deponent and his said partners caryed home with them where they yett remaine. And he further saieth that he hath not nor had any other or more of the goods or provisions of or belonging to that shipp.

Henry Pitt of Wyke Regis aforesaid saylor deposed saieth that the next day after the shipp the Golden Grape was cast away he went to the beech in the company of Leonard Sandford and John Andrews where they saved eight barrells of raysons of the sunne, two of wich were taken from them by Richard Gilbert, John Doby and Jennings Attwooll of Portland the other six this deponent and his said parteners caryed home with them, where they yett remaine. And he further sayeth that he hath not nor had any other or more of the goods or provisions of or belonging to that shipp.

18R

Deposicons taken at Melcomb Regis aforesaid the thirteenth day of January in the year before named before us whose names are subscribed by virtue of the commissioners before expressed Francis Cape notary public being then also present.

Robert Angell of Wyke Regis aforesaid sailor deposed sayeth that upon the same day that the shipp called the Golden Grape was cast away uppon the beech in the West bay neer the Isle of Portland he this deponent together with Faithful Angel his brother and Owen Gibbons of Wyke Regis went thither in consortshipp to save some of the goods of the said shipp, whither being come they saved seaven barrells of raisons of the sunne, wich they caryed to the said Owen Gibbons his house in Wyke Regis aforesaid in whose custody they yett remaine; And this deponent further saith that he being aboard the said shipp did take up there two old paire of canvas breiches wich he hath in his custody and is ready to deliver. And lastly he saieth that he hath not nor had in his custody nor in the custody of any other to his use any more or other of the goods or provisions of or belonging to the said shipp.

Daniell Andrews of Wyke Regis aforesaid fisherman deposeth and sayeth that uppon the same day that the shipp called the Golden Grape

19

was cast away he went uppon the beech and soe aboard the said shipp with an Aeze in his hand whither being come, a wave of the sea came and lighted so violently on his back and bruised him much, soe that he forthwith came away without taking or saving any of the goods or provisions of that shipp, onely he sayeth, that as he came away he took up a shirt, in the sleive of wich there were some letters, and an handkerchiefe wich he caryed to his house and delivered to his wife.

Thomas Grey of Wyke Regis aforesaid sailor deposed saieth that the same day that the shipp called the Golden Grape was cast away he went to the beech where he took up a peice of a small rope belonging to the said shipp, two peices of beefe, a peice of leather, and a peice of a plott drawne in paper wich he caryed home with him. And he further saieth that uppon the Monday following (being two dayes after) he went thither againe, where he mett with John Andrews of Wyke and others, who having salved sixe barrells of raysons desired this deponent to cary the same down the Fleet in his boat & promised that he should have a share in them for his paines, wich he accordingly did, but hath not yet received any thing for his paine And he further sayeth that (afterwards) the same

19R

day Richard Baily of Melcomb Regis and others in his company having saved seaventeen barrells of raisons of wich three were broken did likewise desire this deponent to cary the same over the Fleet for them, promising him the nineth parte of the same for his paines, wich he having performed, they gave this deponent one of the said barrells which he yett hath in his custody. And lastly he saieth that he hath not nor had in his custody nor in the custody of any other to his use any other or more of the goods or provisions of or belonging to the said shipp.

William Boyt of Wyke Regis aforesaid fisherman deposed sayeth that the same day that the shipp called the Golden Grape was cast away he this deponent went uppon the beech where he mett with John Boyt, John Bayly, Bryant Feaver, William Bishopp the elder, William Bishopp the yonger, Thomas Pitt, John Feaver and Nicholas Feaver of Wyke Regis and John Pope of Waymouth who ioyning all together did there save two and twenty barrells of raysons of the sunne, eight and twenty jarres of oyle, three sailes (wich the Master of that shipp affirmeth to be the Main=saile the fore= top saile and the mizne saile) a great lanterne, a small barrell of stinking butter, a wooden

20

bole with some spyke nails in it, a skrew to mount a peice of ordinance withall, & the rudder of a boat: All which goods (save the three sails and the skrew, the former of wich are in the custody of the said John Bayly, and the latter in the hands of the said Bryant Feaver) are in the custody of this deponent wich, as he salved for the use of the proprietors soe he is and will be ready to deliver the same whensoever thay shalbe required from him. And lastly he saieth that he doth not remember of any other goods of the said shipp that are in his custody or in the custody of any other to his use save onely those that before in this his deposicon he hath declared.

John Bayly of Wyke Regis aforesaid husbandman deposed saieth that he was present with William Boyt uppon the beech att the saving of the severall parcells of goods and provisions specifyed in the deposicon of the said William Boyt, of wich the sayles are in the custody of this deponent, and he is ready to deliver the same. And he saieth that he hath not nor had in his owne custody nor in the custody of any other to his use any more or other of the goods or provisions of or belonging to the said shipp.

20R

John Boyt of Wyke Regis aforesaid fisherman deposed sayeth that he was present with William Boyt and the rest of the company by him in his deposicon named att the saving of the severall parcells of goods and provisions belonging to the shipp called the Golden Grape expressed in the said deposicon; And he further sayeth that he did then save the oare of a boat then wich he hath in his custody. And that he hath not in his custody nor in the custody of any other to his use any other or more of the goods or provisions of or belonging to the said shipp.

Bryant Feaver of Wyke Regis aforesaid saylor deposeth and sayeth that he was present with William Boyt and the rest of the company by him in his deposicon named att the saving of the severall parcells of goods and provisions belonging to the shipp called the Golden Grape in the said deposicon expressed, of all wich the skrew onely is in the custody of this deponent and he is ready to deliver the same. And he alsoe sayeth that he hath not nor had either in his owne custody or in the custody of any other to his use any other or more of the goods or provisions of or belonging to the said shipp.

21

William Bishop the elder of Wyke Regis aforesaid husbandman deposeth and sayeth that he was present with William Boyt and the rest of his company named in his deposicon att the saving of the severall goods and provisions belonging to the Golden Grape expressed in the said deposicon. And further he sayeth that there was one jarr of oyle more then saved wich Mr. John Jeffries of Wyke Regis aforesaid tooke from them for groundage because they had putt the same on shore, upon his ground, And a compasse, and a short sword wich are in the hands of John Pope one of the said company. And lastly he sayeth that he hath not nor had in his custody nor in the custody of any other to his use any more or other of the goods or provisions of or belonging to the said shipp.

William Bishop the yonger of Wyke Regis aforesaid husbandman deposeed sayeth that he was presente upon the beech with William Boyt and the rest of the company named in his deposicon att the saving of the severall goods and provisions belonging to the Golden Grape expressed by him & others of their company in their deposicons. And that he hath not in his custody nor in the custody of any other to his use any other or more of the goods or provisions belonging to that shipp.

21R

Thomas Pitt of Wyke Regis aforesaid husbandman deposed saieth that he was present uppon the beech with William Boyt and the rest of his company in his deposicon named att the saving of the severall goods and provisions expressed by him and others of the said company in their deposicons. And he further sayeth that he hath not in his custody nor in the custody of any other to his use any other or more of the goods or provisions of or belonging to the said shipp.

John Feaver of Wyke Regis aforesaid saylor deposed sayeth that he was present uppon the beech with William Boit and the rest of his company in his deposicon named att the saving of the severall goods and provisions belonging to the shipp called the Golden Grape expressed by him and others of that company in their deposicons. And he further sayeth that he hath not, nor had in his custody or in the custody of any other to his use any other or more of the goods or provisions of or belonging to the said shipp.

22

Nicholas Feaver of Wyke Regis aforesaid saylor deposed sayeth that he was present uppon the beech with William Boyt & the rest of the company in his deposicon named at the saving of the severall goods in the said deposicon & others of the said company expressed. And he further sayeth that he hath not in his owne custody nor in the custody of any other to his use any other or more of the goods or provisions of or belonging to that shipp.

John Pope of Waymouth shoomaker deposed sayeth that he was present uppon the beech with William Boyt and the rest of the company by him in his deposicon named att the salving of the severall parcells of goods & provisions expressed by him and others in their deposicons, of wich this deponent hath in his custody the compasse and the short sword specifyed by William Bishopp the elder in his deposicon. And he further sayeth that he this deponent tooke thence alsoe a jarre of oyle full and another halfe full, two hundred and halfe of wett lymons and about fowerteen or sixteen pounds of wett raysons. And that he likewise received from one of Fleet the maine Bonnett saile belonging to the said ship. And lastly that he hath not nor had either in his owne custody or in the custody of any other to his use any other or more of the goods or provisions of or belonging to the said shipp.

22R

Joane the wife of Daniell Andrews of Wyke Regis aforesaid fisherman deposed sayeth that the same day that the shipp called the Golden Grape was cast away the said Daniell Andrews her husband went to the beech from whence returning againe he brought home with an handkercheife and a shirt in wich were some letters wich this deponent tooke forth and shewed to John Hodder of Waymouth and another man, who having opened and perused the same redelivered them to this deponent, wich letters she not knowing what to doe with all did afterwards. And she further sayeth that she hath not nor had any other or more of the goods or provisions of or belonging to that shipp.

John Lyne of Wyke Regis aforesaid fisherman deposed sayeth that the same day that the shipp called the Golden Grape was cast away he went to the beech where she lay, where this deponent saved two jarres of oyle wich he hath in his custody and is ready to deliver the same. And he further saieth that he hath not nor had any more or other of the goods or provisions belonging to that shipp.

Thomas Bayly of Wyke Regis aforesaid yeoman deposed sayeth that uppon the same day after the shipp called the Golden Grape

23

was cast away he went uppon the beech where he and his company did save fifteen barrells of raysons of the sunne, sixe and twenty jarres of oyle, three flemish boxes with salves in them, two small sea chests two chambers or murderers and some small peices of ropes, And he further sayeth that when he had saved the said oyles he put all the said jarres into the boat of Nicholas Williams desiring him to cary the same for him over the Fleet unto the Maine Land wich the said Williams undertook to doe, but this deponent sayeth that he never saw the said oyles nor any parte thereof since, only he sayeth that he hath been told that Robert Hunt of Wyke Regis aforesaid hath fifteen of them in his custody, the residew of the said goods and provisions this deponent sayeth that he hath in his possession and is and will be ready to deliver the same. And he likewise sayeth that Robert Falkoner and some others of Waymouth Melcomb Regis did afterwards cause fifteen barrells more of raysons of the sunne to be brought into this deponents house where they yett remaine. And lastly he sayeth that he hath not in his owne custody nor in the custody of any other to his use any other or more of the goods or provisions of or belonging to the said shipp.

23R

John Bayle sonn of Thomas Bayly of Wyke Regis aforesaid yeoman deposed sayeth that uppon Sunday morning being the next day after the shipp called the Golden Grape was cast away he was sent by his father together with John Butcher his fathers servant with his plough to fetch some such goods as they had saved the day before, where he did loade into his said plough fifteen barrells of raysons of the sunne for his said father and for Robert Hunt of Wyke Regis aforesaid, and fifteen other barrells of raysons for Robert Falkoner, Gregory Backway, and Henry or Christopher Bayly of Melcomb Regis, two smale chests, two chambers, & some other smale trifles, wich they caryed home in the said plough to his fathers house where they yett remaine. And that he hath not nor had to his owne use any of the goods or provisions belonging to the said shipp.

John Butcher servant to Thomas Bayly of Wyke Regis aforesaid yeoman deposed sayeth that he this deponent and his Masters sonn John did Sonday morning goe with his said Masters plough, and did bring home with them the several parcells of goods menconed in the deposicon of the said John Bayly wich they delivered att his said Masters house, And that this deponent hath not nor had to his owne use any of the goods or provisions belonging to that shipp.

24

Ann the wife of Christopher Cowrage of Wyke Regis aforesaid saylor deposed saieth that she being upon the beech the same day that the shipp called the Golden Grape was there cast away she mett with a boy the servant of Andrew Mills of Wyke Regis aforesaid who then had single bagge of money under his arme wich he had gotten out of that shipp, wich (being somewhat too heavy for the boy to cary) this deponent caryed for him a whiles, but then (being wearyed herselfe) she delivered the same to the boy whole as it was when she received it from him. And she further sayeth that as the said boy was carying the said bagg of money homewards one Richard Gilbert of Portland mett with him, and tooke the said bagg and money from him, promising to give the said boy satisfaccon for salving the same, but whether the said Gilbert gave him any thing or not this deponent knoweth not. And she allsoe saieth that whiles she was upon the beech neer the said shipp she gathered together and tooke up about twelve pounds of wett raysons of the sunne, wich she caryed home with her, and hath sithence spent the same. And lastly she sayeth that she hath not nor had in her owne custody nor in the custody of any other to her use any other or more of the goods or provisions of or belonging to the said shipp.

24R

Nicholas Chapple of Wyke Regis aforesaid saylor deposed sayeth that upon Saturday about two or three of the clock in the afternoon (it being the same day that the shipp called the Golden Grape was cast away upon the beech) as this deponent was goeing thither he mett with Owen Gibbons of Wyke Regis aforesaid, saylor and two of the company of the said shipp with him near a place called Bridge within the parish of Wyke Regis aforesaid, one of wich being sicke the said Gibbons did putt him uppon his horse together with a double bagg of money wich the said sicke man held fast in his hand uppon the neck of the said horse, from whence the said Gibbons did lead the said horse to the house of Arthur Grey in Wyke Regis aforesaid in the company of this deponent (he being by the said Gibbons entreated to returne thither with him) whither being come this deponent tooke downe the said sicke man from the horse, and caried him into Arthur Grey his house, and the said bagg of money was then likewise taken downe from the horse necke and caried into the said house (but by whome this deponent knoweth not) And this deponent sayeth that he did alsoe cary the said sicke man up into a chamber in the said Grey's house, where he saw the said money putt into a chest that stood in the said chamber, but by whome he knoweth not yet sayeth, that after the said bagge of money was putt into the said chest he saw the said Grey's wife shutt and locke the chest thereuppon. And he further sayeth that the said sicke man gave this deponent and the said Gibbons a peice of eight between them for their paines in bringing him thither, wich peece he tooke

25

out of his pocquett. And lastly this deponent sayeth that when he was upon the beech he tooke up there two or three blocks of the shipp and a smale quantity of wett raisons of the sunne And that that he hath not nor had either in his owne custody nor in the custody of any other to his use any more or other of the goods or provisions of or belonging to that shipp.

Robert Hunt of Wike Regis aforesaid yeoman deposed sayeth that he hath in his custody in his house in Wyke Regis aforesaid seaven whole barrells of raisons of the sunne and another barrell allmost full, wich his sonne and servant did salve uppon the beech, and another barrell of raysons of the sunne with Thomas Loder of Waymouth salved and left there, and fifteen jarres of oyle wich this deponents sonne and servant likewise saved, some smale ropes, a pewter pott, and some broken peices of the timber of the said shipp. All wich he is and will be ready to deliver. And that he hath not nor had either in his own custody or in the custody of any other to his use any other or more of the goods or provisions of or belonging to the said shipp, save only his part of sixe barrells of raysons of the sunne wich Thomas Bayly and this deponent saved between them and wich are in the custody of the said Thomas Bayly.

25R

Thomas Hunt sonn of the aforesaid Robert Hunt deposed saieth that uppon the same day that the ship called the Golden Grape was cast away he went to the beech where he and Thomas Bayly of Wyke Regis aforesaid did save sixe barrells of raisons of the sunne, wich the said Thomas Baily hath now in his custody, and sixe and twenty jarres of oyle, of wich fifteen are in this deponents fathers house, the residew Nicholas Williams and his company in whose boat the same were putt to be caried over the Fleet doo deteine from them, they likewise saved then two smale shipp chests, and two chambers, wich the said Bayly alsoe hath in his custody. And this deponent further saieth that the next day he went thither againe where this deponent Henry Meech his fathers man and Ann Hunt his sister did save tenn barrells of raysons of the sunne one whereof was not quite full, of wich they gave two to George Chipp and Henry Keilway of Wyke Regis for carying the other eight in their boat over the Fleet, and some smale peices of ropes, wich eight barrells of fruit and peices of ropes are likewise in this deponents fathers house. And lastly he saieth that he hath not had in his custody nor in the custody of any other to his use any other or more of the goods or provisions of or belonging to the said shipp.

Henry Meech servant to Robert Hunt of Wyke Regis aforesaid deposeth and sayeth that

26

uppon the same day that the ship called the Golden Grape was cast away he went to the beech where he this deponent, with Thomas Hunt his Masters sonne and Thomas Bayly of Wyke Regis aforesaid did salve sixe barrells of raysons of the sunne two chambers and two smale shipp chests wich are in the custody of the said Thomas Baily, and sixe and twnety jarres of oyle, of wich fifteen are in the house of the said Robert Hunt this deponents Master, the residew Richard Williams of Wyke Regis aforesaid and his company doe deteine for caryeing the same over the Fleat in their boat. And that he hath not nor had in his custody nor in the custody of any other to his use any other or mores of the goods or provisions of or belonging to the said shipp.

Ann Hunt daughter of Robert Hunt of Wyke Regis aforesaid deposed saieth that uppon the next day after that the shipp called the Golden Grape was cast away she together with Thomas Hunt her brother and Henry Meech her Fathers man did goe to the beech where they did save out of the said shipp tenn barrells of raysons of the sunne whereof eight her father hath in his custody the other two they gave to the boatman George Chipp and his company for carying them in their boat over the Fleat. And that she

26R

hath not had in her custody nor in the custody of any other to her use any other or more of the goods or provisions of or belonging to the said shipp.

Andrew Mills of Wyke Regis aforesaid yeoman deposeth and saieth that uppon the same day that the shipp called the Golden Grape was cast away he went to the beech, where this deponent with John Mills his brother, Mathew Allenn the younger, and Austine the keeper of the passage boat did salve between them seaven barrells of raisons of the sunne a rope about eight fathom in length and about the bignes of this deponents handwrest and one jarre of oyle, wich goods this deponent hath in his custody. And that he hath not nor had either in his owne custody or in the custody of any other to his use any other or more of the goods or provisions of or belonging to the said shipp.

27

Deposicons taken at Melcomb Regis aforesaid the fourteenth day of January in the year before named before us whose names are subscribed by virtue of the commissioners before expressed Francis Cape notary public being then also present.

William Stone servant to Anthony Clapcott of Wyke Regis aforesaid yeoman deposed saieth that about two of the clock in the morning of the next day after the shipp called the Golden Grape was cast away he this deponent together with Francis Spratt and one Winter servants to William Cade of Wyke Regis aforesaid yeoman and Anthony Bryne of the same place went over the Fleat uppon the beech where they salved seaven barrells of raysons of the sunne out of the said shipp and layd them uppon the beech, where one Lovell of Fleet tooke fower of the said barrells from them, and left them onely three wich they caryed to Wyke Regis aforesaid, and did put the same into the said William Cade his house, And this deponent also then take up a peice of a rope belonging to the said shipp wich he hath yett in his custody And that he hath not nor had any other or more of the goods or provisions of that shipp save only some wett raisons wich he caryed home in his pocquett.

27R

Anthony Bryne of Wyke Regis aforesaid fisherman deposed saieth that about two of the clock in the morning of the next day after the ship called the Golden Grape was cast way he went to the beech together with William Stone servant to Anthony Clapcott of Wyke Regis aforesaid and Francis Spratt and one Winter servants to William Cade of the same place, where they did salve out of the said shipp seaven barrells of raysons of the sunne wich they layd uppon the beech where one Lovell of Fleat tooke fower of those barrells from them, the other three they caryed to the house of the said William Cade where they doe yett remaine; And this deponent further saieth that he hath not nor had any more or other of the goods or provisions of the shipp save onely a smale quantity of wett raysons wich he caryed home in his pocquett.

Arthur Grey of Wyke Regis aforesaid having been formerly examined and now reexamined deposeth and sayeth that att such time as Owen Gibbons before examined did bring the sicke man in his deposicon menconed, to this deponents house, a double bagg of money

28

(besides those wich this deponent heretofore deliver to the Vice admirall) was then alsoe brought into his house, and putt into the chest standing in the chamber menconed in the said Gibbons his deposicon. And that the next morning the steersman of the said shipp the Golden Grape came to this deponent and demanded of him the said bagg of money wich this deponent then delivered to the said steersman in the presence of his wife, wich he caried away with him out of this deponents house, and this deponent saw the same noe more. And the reason why this deponent did not expresse this in his former deposicon is because he thought that the said bagge of money was the said steersman's owne money.

Susanna Grey wife of the said Arthur Grey having been formerly examined and now reexamined deposeth and sayeth that att such time as Owen Gibbons before examined did bring the sicke man in his deposicon mencioned to her husbands house she doth now very

28R

well remember that a double bagg of money was then alsoe brought into the said house and put into the chest standing in the chamber in the said Gibbons his deposicon mencioned, but by whome she remembreth not; And this deponent alsoe well remembreth that on the next morning the steersman of the said shipp the Golden Grape did call to the said Arthur Grey this deponentes husband for the said bagg of money, wich her said husband did then deliver unto him, but what the said steersman did with the same she doth not know. And that the said bagg of money was a bagg of money more and besides those wich her said husband did before deliver to the Viceadmirall.

Mary Angell the wife of Thomas Angell of Wyke Regis aforesaid fisherman deposeth and saieth that upon the same day that the shipp called the Golden Grape was cast away upon the beech she went thither, where she tooke up a small quantity of wooll in a bagg (out of wich some others that were there had pulled a great part) wich she hath since dryed, and doth guesse that it weighs about three or fower pounds, wich she hath att home in her house, and is ready to deliver the same whensoever it shalbe required; And she tooke

29

up then allsoe a jarre of oile the greatest part of which was leaked out, and a smale quantity of wett fruit that lay loose upon the beech wich she caryed home with her. And that she hath not nor had either in her owne custody or in the custody of any other to her use any other or more of the goods or provisions of or belonging to the said shipp.

Faithfull Angell of Waymouth aforesaid labourer deposeth and saieth that upon the same day at night that the shipp called the Golden Grape was cast away upon the beech he went thither together with Owen Gibbons and Robert Angell of Wyke Regis, where they salved seaven barrells of raisons of the sunne between them wich they caryed frome thence in the boat of Robert Williams unto Wyke Regis aforesaid, and putt the same into the house of the said Owen Gibbons where they doe yett remaine. And he further saieth that he did not take up neither had nor had either in his owne custody or in the custody of any other to his use any other or more of the goods or provisions of the said shipp, save onely a smale quantity of wett fruit wich he tooke up there & caryed home with him.

29R

Robert Geale of Wyke Regis aforesaid saylor deposeth and saieth that upon the same day att night that the ship called the Golden Grape was cast away he went to the beech together with James Gardiner of Wyke Regis aforesaid where they saved one barrell of raisons of the sunne wich is now in this deponents house and shalbe delivered whensoever it shall be required. And that he hath not nor had either in his own custody or in the custody of any other to his use any more or other of the goods or provisions of that shipp save only a smale quantity of wett raisons of the sunne wich he tooke up on the beech and caryed home in his pocquett.

Henry Lyne of Wyke Regis aforesaid fisherman deposeth and sayeth that about midnight after the shipp, the Golden Grape was cast away he went to the beech in a boat in the company of Bartholomew Williams and others where he gathered up a smale quantity of loose wett raysons of the sunne, and caryed them to the said boat; att wich time the sonne of Robert Hunt of Wyke Regis aforesaid did bring and putt into the said boat many jarres of oyle (but the certaine number of them he knoweth not) to

30

be caryed over the Fleet to Wyke side promising them halfe for their paines of wich this deponent had two jarres wich are now in his father John Line's house in Wyke Regis aforesaid ready to be delivered. And that he hath not nor had any other or more of the goods or provisions of or belonging to the said shipp.

John Curters of Wyke Regis aforesaid fisherman deposeth and sayeth that about midnight after the shipp called the Golden Grape was cast away he went up to the beech in a boat in the company of Bartholomew Williams and the rest of his company whither being come a servant to Robert Hunt of Wyke Regis aforesaid did put aboard the said boat divers jarres of oyle (but how many this deponent knoweth not) with this deponent and his company caryed over to Wyke side where they were landed. Two jarres whereof this deponent had for his paines in rowing in the said boat, one of wich (not being full) he hath since spent, the other he hath sold to astranger for three shillings. And that he hath not nor had any other or more of the goods or provisions of or belonging to the said shipp.

30R

Deposicons taken at Melcomb Regis aforesaid the fifteenth day of January in the year before named before us whose names are subscribed by virtue of the commissioners before expressed Francis Cape notary public being then also present.

Thomas Michell of the Island of Portland in the County of Dorset yeoman deposeth and saieth that the same day that the shipp called the Golden Grape uppon the beech neer the said Island he went thither in the company of many other Islanders where he did help save with them eight and twenty peices of silke; And this deponent did by himselfe save two jarres of oyle and another peice of silke wich he delivered to Daniell Peirce of the said island this deponents father in law, who hath the same in his custody. And this deponent further saieth that he hath not either in his own custody or in the custody of any other to his use any other or more of the goods or provisions of the said shipp save onely a smale quantity of wett raisons of the sunne wich he tooke up uppon the beech and caryed home with him.

Daniell Peirce of the Isle of Portland aforesaid yeoman deposeth and saieth that the

31

same day that the shipp the Golden Grape was cast away he went uppon the beech where he had two bolts of silke delivered unto him the one by Thomas Michell and the other by Jennings Attwoll his sonnes in law, wich he hath in his custody and is ready to deliver. And that he hath not nor had in his custody nor in the custody of any other to his use any more or other of the goods or provisions of or belonging to that shipp.

Jennings Attwooll of the Isle of Portland aforesaid yeoman deposed sayeth that the same day that the shipp called the Golden Grape was cast away uppon the beech he went thither where he and his company did save eight and twenty bolts of silke, two bagges of silver plate a loafe of silver bullion and two jarres of oyle, And this deponent did alsoe save by himselfe one other bolt of silke wich he delivered to Daniell Peirce his father in law, who hath the same yett in his custody; And he did alsoe save a flag belonging to the said shipp, an astrolab a crossestaffe and a quadrant wich he hath in his custody as allsoe the said two jarrs of oyle And that he hath not in his custody nor in the custody of any other to his use any more or other of the goods or provisions of that shipp save only a smale quantity of wett raysons wich he caryed home with him.

31R

Francis Saveer of the Isle of Portland aforesaid mason deposed saieth that he went uppon the beech the same day that the ship called the Golden Grape was cast away and two daies following, whither when he came the first day he went aboard the said shipp where he tooke up a short peice of silk that was wrapped about a peice of timber in the shipp, and eighteen rowes of buttons (wich he now delivereth to the Viceadmirall) two old coates, a jackett, an old shirt, an old red wastcoat and three or fower bolts of iron wich he hath at home in his custody, And that he did alsoe att the said severall times take up and cary home to his house about seaven pecks of wett raisons of the sunne. And he further saieth that Luke Knapp his boy being there alsoe did take up and cary home two old jerkins and some old shirts (wich this deponents wife threw away soe soone as they were brought home) and about a barrell of wett raisons of the sunne the most parte of wich fruit this deponent hath yett in his house, wich is almost spoyled And that he hath not had in his owne custody nor in the custody of any other to his use any more or other of the goods or provisions of or belonging to the said shipp.

Walter Pyedwell of Waymouth aforesaid chirurgeon deposed saieth that shortly

32

after the shipp the Golden Grape was cast away the chirurgeon of that shipp came to the signe of Starre in Waymouth aforesaid where this deponent liveth, and being there did buy of this deponent a coat for wich he payed him six peices of eight wich he tooke out of his pocquett And this deponent further sayeth that Richard Rich one of the company of that shipp did in a chamber of the said house in the presence of this deponent and of one Joane Bond a maid servant in that house take out of his breeches a bagg of money wich he did open and tell upon the table, and (as this deponent doth remember) he had in all about three score peices of eight And more he cannot say concerning the said shipp or goods.

Richard Rich one of the company of the ship the Golden Grape having been before examined, and now reexamined deposeth and sayeth that he had of the chirurgeon of the said shipp about thirteen or fowerteen pounds in peices of eight (wich before in his former deposicon he had forgotten to expresse) which money this deponent delivered to Mary Paine a young woman living in Melcomb Regis to keep for him. And that he hath not nor had any other or more of the moneys that was in the said shipp save onely what he hath before declared.

32R

Mary Paine of Melcomb Regis single woman deposeth and saieth that Richard Rich one of the company of the shipp the Golden Grape did one day the last weeke deliver unto her the bagg of silver and gold, wich is now produced to the comissioners, and did intreat her to keep it for him, but she sayeth that the money the said Rich did deliver to her was all in silver, and that she did exchange with the chirurgeon of the said shipp soe much silver as amounteth to the valew of the gold now in the said bagge, it being in all between thirteen and fowerteen pounds (vizt) forty and sixe peices of eight, a pistoll of gold, and three pounds and nine shillings in other gold, wich the Viceadmirall now taketh into his custody. And she further sayeth that the said Rich did not att any time deliver unto her any other or more money, and she doth conceive that the reason why the said Rich did deliver the said money to her was for that there was some former acquaintance between them in Dover.

Bartholomew Paine of Melcomb Regis aforesaid hellyer deposed sayeth that he doth not know of any money that Mary Paine his daughter had from Richard Rich of from any other person, nor of any money that she hath or had in her custody.

33

Deposicons taken at Melcomb Regis aforesaid the seventeenth day of January in the year before named before us whose names are subscribed by virtue of the commissioners before expressed Francis Cape notary public being then also present.

John Swettnam of Melcomb Regis aforesaid woollen draper deposed saieth that about three weekes since he did sell unto the wife of Bartholomew Paine of Melcomb Regis aforesaid hellyer soe much woollen cloth as came to about five pounds for wich she payed him in peices of eight, And that either she or Mary Paine her daughter did shortly after exchange with him about thirty or forty shillinges in peices of eight, for wich he gave the valew in English white money and gold but he saieth that he did not deliver unto her any pistoll of gold, or any other foraigne gold, only English money.

Richard Stradling of the Isle of Portland aforesaid labourer deposed sayeth that the same day att night that the shipp the Golden Grape was cast away uppon the beech he went thither, whither when he came he went

33R

aboard the said shipp where he did take up some loose raysons with wich he filled his pocquetts, And that he and three others (whose names this deponent knoweth not, but they are well knowne to Thomas Daniell of Waymouth) living att Wyke Regis did take out of a bagg certaine quantityes of wooll, part whereof they caryed away with them, and left this deponent a parte to himselfe in the said wooll=bagg wich this deponent caryed home alonge with him to Portland, where he did hyde the same, but in what place he refuseth to relate, but sayeth that afterwards he took the same out of that place where he had hidden it, and did putt in a bagg wich he borrowed of Emanuell Hendey of Portland in whose house this deponent lodgeth And that he then brought thence alsoe a jarre of oyle wich he sold to Richard Gilbert of Portland aforesaid for fower shillings. And lastly he sayeth that he hath not in his custody nor in the custody of any other to his use any more or other of the goods or provisions of or belonging to the said shipp.

Thomas Allen of Fleat in the County of Dorsett yeoman deposed saieth that the same day that the shipp called the Golden Grape was castaway uppon the beech he went thither, whither when he came he went aboard the said shipp where he did take up a chizell and an hammer, an hundred

34

and halfe of nailes, and fower barrells of raisons of the sunne wich Thomas Carter of Fleat and this deponent did save between them, and alsoe one other barrell of raisons of the sunne wich this deponent saved himselfe, one jarre of oyle and a little barrell of powder all wich he hath in his custody and is ready to deliver, And he further saieth that John Allen his kinseman did then allsoe take up about halfe a bushell of wett raisons of the sunne, wich are allsoe att home in this deponents house, And lastly he saieth that he hath not nor had in his owne custody or in the custody of any other to his use any more or other of the goods or provisions of or belonging to the said shipp save only one peice of eight, two halfe peices of eight, and a peice of french money wich he found uppon the beech about a weeke after, and hath now delivered to the Viceadmirall.

Thomas Bussell of Chickerell in the said County of Dorsett yeoman deposed saieth that the same day that the shipp called the Golden Grape was cast away uppon the beech he went thither, whither uppon he came he went aboard the said shipp where he did save two barrells of raysons of the sunne (the head of

34R

one of them being beaten out, and many of the fruit taken away) two jarres of oile and about halfe a bushell of loose fruit, wich he hath att home in his house and is ready to deliver And this deponent further saieth that about two daies after that the said shipp was broken to peices and quite caried away he went down thither againe accompanied with Roger Dyker his servant, where the said Dyker did take up in the sea neer the place where the said shipp lay a bagg of money wich this deponent took from him and caryed home with him, but hath since delivered the same to the Viceadmirall. And lastly this deponent saieth that he hath not nor had in his custody nor in the custody of any other to his use any more or other of the goods or provisions of or belonging to the said shipp.

Joseph Keat of Fleat aforesaid sailor deposed saieth that the same day that the shipp called the Golden Grape was cast away uppon the beech he went thither, whither when he came he went aboard that shipp where he tooke two old paire of breeches and about bushell of loose raysons of the sunne wich he caryed home with him And that he hath not nor had in his custody nor in the custody of any other to his use anymore or other of the goods or provisions of or belonging

35

to that shipp save onely certaine smale peices of brasse money wich he found scattered about the shipp, neither doth he know of any other person or persons that have or had any money out of that shipp.

Catharine Langar of Waymouth aforesaid widow deposed saieth that Thomas Bird the cook of the shipp called the Golden Grape came to her house in Waymouth the same night that the said shipp was cast away did take out and tell uppon the table in her said house a great many peices of eight wich John Seniors man of Melcomb Regis did there weigh for (John Fildew and Joseph Manders being there alsoe present And that the Master of the said shipp cominge thither the next day took the said money from the cook and delivered the same to this deponent to keep, wich the said Master shortly after fetched from her againe And she alsoe saieth that the chirurgeon of the said shipp did pay her three peices of eight for his dyett while he lay att her house, and gave her another peice of eight for attending him; and that Rich one of that company did likewise pay her three peices of eight for his dyett, and gave her another peice of eight for attending him, and that one William another of the said company did the like, wich is all the money that this deponent received or had from any of the company of that shipp.

35R

Walter Bond of Waymouth aforesaid fisherman deposed saieth that the next day after the shipp the Golden Grape was cast away on the beech he together with Symon More, Ralph Limbrey, William Chappell, and others of Waymouth went thither where they did save and carye home with them three barrells of raisons of the sunne, a jarre of oyle about halfe, and three other smale barrells (but what is in them this deponent doth not know) all wich are in the custody of this deponent; And they did alsoe then bring home with them fower other smale barrells wich are in the custody of the said Symon More, and three other barrells of raysins of the sunne and a barrell about halfe full wich are in the custody of the said Ralph Limbrey And this deponent further saieth that the next day (by the directions of the Master of the said shipp) they went thither againe where they did save fower and thirty barrells of raysons of the sunne, whereof one was broken up by Alice Whittle of Waymouth and all the raysins taken out by the standers by save about a quarter parte of the same wich this deponent tooke out and caried home in their handkerchiefs and pocquetts and another of the said barrells Mr John Jeffries of Wyke took, and keepeth away because the same were landed uppon his ground; twenty of wich two and thirty barrells were forthwith putt into the cellar of Mr. Fabian Hodder att whose house the said Master lay, and the other twelve in the customers cellar of Waymouth aforesaid And this deponent further sayeth that they then brought with them to Weymouth a

36

cable, a hauser, two Murderers and the fore shroudes of the said shipp wich were then alsoe putt into the custody of the said Mr. Hodder, And he further saieth that they alsoe then brought to Waymouth seaven peices of ordinance that did belong to the said shipp which now layd in the streets there, and one Murderer wich was putt into the house of William Wykes of Waymouth aforesaid And he further saieth that they did alsoe then bring to Waymouth with them the foremast, the boaspritt, a windlace, and a capstan seaventeen round shott, two anchors, two cariages, and a peice of a new shootcable about twenty fathom in length wich did belong to the said shipp; and another peice of a cable about tenn fathom in length, and a peice of an halser about six fathom in length, wich they putt into the cellar of Leonard Hellard in Melcomb Regis And lastly this deponent sayeth that he hath not in his custody nor in the custody of any other to his use anyother or more of the goods or provisions of or belonging to the said shipp; and that he is and will be ready to deliver all such of the said goods wich are or were in his custody and heretofore delivered.

Symon More of Melcomb Regis aforesaid saylor deposed saieth that he was present at

36R

the saving and bringing home of the severall goods and provisions that did belonge to the shipp called the Golden Grape declared and expressed by the said Walter Bond in his deposicon, and doth acknowledge that he hath the fower smale barrells in the said deposicon menconed in his custody, and allsoe two chambers wich he is ready to deliver And that he hath not had in his custody nor in the custody of any other to his use any more or other of the goods or provisions of or belonging to the said shipp.

Ralph Limbrey of Waymouth aforesaid fisherman deposed saieth that he was present att the saving and bringing home of the severall goods and provisions that did belong to the shipp called the Golden Grape declared and expressed by the said Walter Bond in his deposition, and doth acknowledge that he hath the three barrells and halfe of raysins of the sunne in the said deposition mentioned wich he is ready to deliver And that he hath not nor had in his custody nor in the custody of any other to his use any more or other of the goods or provisions of or belonging to the said shipp save only one jarre of oile wich one Thomas Parmiter saved and delivered to this deponent to cary for him, wich is now in this deponents house.

37

William Philips of Waymouth aforesaid shoomaker deposed saieth that he was present att the saving and bringing home of the severall goods and provisions that did belong unto the shipp called the Golden Grape (the second time that the said Walter Bond went to the beech) wich the said Bond hath declared and expressed in that part of his deposition, And that this deponent and some others did then alsoe save an halser wich was left in the custody of Andrew Pitt of Waymouth. And that he hath not nor had in his custody nor in the custody of any other to his use any other or more of the goods or provisions of or belonging to the said shipp.

Walter Chappell of Waymouth aforesaid sailor deposed sayeth that he was present with Walter Bond att the saving and bringing home of the severall goods and provisions that did belonge to the shipp called the Golden Grape expressed in the said Walter Bond's deposicon, And that he hath not nor had in his custody nor in the custody of any other to his use any more or other of the goods or provisions of or belonging to the said shipp.

37R

Edward Martin of Waymouth aforesaid sailor deposed saieth that uppon the Monday after the shipp called the Golden Grape was cast away uppon the beech he was present there with Walter Bond and his company att the saving and bringing home of the goods and provisions that did belonge to the said shipp on that day wich the said Walter Bond hath before declared and expressed in his examination And that he hath not nor had in his custody nor in the custody of any other to his use any other or more of the goods or provisions of or belonging to that shipp.

Joseph Maunders of Waymouth aforesaid shoomaker deposed saieth that he hath seen Richard Rich one of the company of the shipp called the Golden Grape who lodged in this deponents house to have about seaven or eight peices of eight, wich is the greatest number that ever he saw him have; And that the said Rich hath lodged, and dyetted in this deponents house about a moneth, but whether he hath paied anything for the same or how much he hath paied this deponent doth not know.

38

Deposicons taken at Melcomb Regis aforesaid the twentieth day of January in the year before named before us whose names are subscribed by virtue of the commissioners before expressed Francis Cape notary public being then also present.

Richard Clerke servant to Thomas Mims of the isle of Portland yeoman deposed saieth that about fower or five dayes after that the said shipp called the Golden Grape was cast away Richard Stradling of the said Island labourer did bring unto this deponents Masters house some wett wooll in a bagg, whereof how much there was this deponent doth not certainly know, but doth conceive that the same might weigh about eight or nine pounds, wich hath ever since there remained untill that now Richard Gilbert servant to Mr Viceadmirall hath by his comand fetched the same thence.

William Wykes of Waymouth aforesaid joyner deposed saieth that uppon the Monday after that the shipp called the Golden Grape was cast away on the beech he was there present with Walter Bond att the saving

38R

of the goods hereafter mentioned (vizt) seaven peices of ordinance, two anchors, a winlace, a capstan, a foremaste, a boaspritt, a peice of a cable about twenty fathom in length, two cariages, and seaventeen round shott being parcell of the said shipps provisions, And that he did then alsoe save one barrell of fruit wich William Minterne, Angel Watte, and William Hardey of Melcomb Regis tooke from him. And that he hath not nor had in his own custody nor in the custody of any other to his use any more or other of the goods or provisions of or belonging to the said shipp save onely a smale quantity of wett raysons of the sunne, and two peices of the timber of the said shipp wich he bought of some of Fleat for eighteen pence.

Richard Browne of Waymouth aforesaid mariner deposed saieth that he was present with the said William Wikes att the saving of the severall parcells of the provisions that did belonge to the shipp called the Golden Grape and declared in the said William Wykes his deposicon And that he hath not nor had in his custody nor in the custody of any other to his use any other more of the goods or provisions of or belonging to the said shipp.

39

Deposicons taken at Melcomb Regis aforesaid the twenty first day of January in the year before named before us whose names are subscribed by virtue of the commissioners before expressed Francis Cape notary public being then also present.

Robert Flew of the Isle of Portland aforesaid yeoman deposeth and saieth that the same day att night that the shipp called the Golden Grape was cast away uppon the beech he went thither, whither being come he went aboard the said shipp where he took up a certaine quantity of wooll, it being (as he guesseth) six pounds in weight or upwards, and about a peck of raysins of the sunne, three jarres of oyle of wich this deponent have two and Ralph Bunne of the said island (who was then with him) hath one, two bookes, a lambskin, and a smale quantity of turpentine, And that afterwards the same night this deponent & the said Ralph Bunne and his wife did alsoe save one whole barrell of raysins of the sunne between them And that he hath not nor had in his custody or in the custody of any other to his use any other or more of the goods or provisions of or belonging to that shipp.

39R

Ralph Bunne of the Isle of Portland aforesaid yeoman deposed sayeth that uppon the same day att night that the ship called the Golden Grape was cast away uppon the beech he went thither whither when he came he went aboard the said shipp where he did take up a certaine parcell of wooll (the full weight whereof he doth not know) wich he wrapped up in his coat and caryed home with him, he alsoe tooke up there a jarre of oyle wich he alsoe caryed home with him, and hath eaten some part thereof since, and about three pecks of raysins of the sunne wich he tooke out of a barrell that Robert Flew of the said island and this deponent had saved between them; And he further saieth that att the same time he tooke up there about tenn oranges and lymons and a topmast vane wich vane he hath att his house And that he hath not nor had in his custody or in the custody of any other to his use any other or more of the goods or provisions of or belonging to the said shipp.

Gilbert Downing of Waymouth aforesaid mariner deposed saieth that uppon the Monday morning after that the shipp called the Golden Grape was cast away uppon the beech he was goeing thither and by the way as he went between Wyke Regis and

40

the said place he mett with Faithfull Angell of Waymouth and a brother of his that lives at Wyke Regis, by the water syde with six barrells of raysins of the sunne in their keeping, wich barrells they caryed from thence unto an house in Wyke Regis aforesaid (but whose house it is this deponent doth not know And this deponent sayeth that he did not take upp there, nor hath, nor had in his custody or in the custody of any other to his use any of the goods or provisions of or belonging to the said shipp.

Morgan Guilliams of Melcomb Regis aforesaid shipp carpenter deposed sayeth that shortly after the shipp called the Golden Grape was cast away uppon the beech he went thither two severall times, where att the first time this deponent with Morgain Millett his servant and Stephen Powlett of Melcomb Regis aforesaid did save two barrells of raysins of the sunne, wich being wett they broke open, and taking out the raysins thence did putt the same in linine baggs, and in their breeches, and soe caryed them home uppon an horse, where they did divyde them between them, this deponent and his said servant having two parts of the same and

40R

the said Stephen Powlett one part And this deponent further saieth that att the second time that he was uppon the beech he saved the roller of the whipstaffe and a peice of timber part of the said shipp wich he caryed to his house where they doe yett remaine. And lastly this deponent sayeth that he hath not nor had in his owne custody or in the custody of any other to his use any other of the goods or provisions of or belonging to that shipp.

Arthur Gardiner of Waymouth aforesaid sailor deposed saieth that shortly after the shipp called the Golden Grape was cast away uppon the beech as this deponent was goeing towards that place he saw eight barrells of raysins of the sunne lye open in veiw in a certaine place called Fox=holes being neer the water side within the parish of Wyke Regis, but he saw nobody with them nor neer the said place, wich this deponent lefte there without taking any part of the same, nor doth he know who putt them there or caryed them thence, And that he hath not nor had in his custody nor in the custody of any other to his use any part of the goods or provisions of or belonging to the said shipp.

41

Deposicons taken at Melcomb Regis aforesaid the twenty fourth day of January in the year before named before us whose names are subscribed by virtue of the commissioners before expressed Francis Cape notary public being then also present.

Agnes the wife of William Holmes of Waymouth aforesaid mariner depsoed sayeth that uppon the same day at night that the shipp called the Golden Grape was cast away the carpenter of the said shipp came alonge by her dore in Waymouth aforesaid very wett and in great distresse uppon where she taking comiseration did call him into her house, where she provyded victualls and clothes for him, and lodged him there; who soone after his coming in thither demanded of this deponent to borrow a purse, but she having none to lend, he tooke out certaine peices of eight (but how many she knoweth not) out of his pocketts, wich he putt into a woodden dish that was there and gave them to this deponent to lay up for him, wich she did putting them in a chest in the chamber where he lodged. And she further sayeth that shortly after the said carpenter was gonn

41R

from her house (of wich she knew not for he went away secretly with out giving her notice of soo much as taking his leave) she looking into the said chest found the said dish there and seaven and thirty peices of eight and a halfe peice of eight in it, wich she now produceth and delivereth to the Viceadmirall. And this deponent saieth that before the said carpenter went away in such secret manner as aforesaid he payed this deponent two and thirty shillinges in peices of eight for clothes that she had bought for him, but payed her noething att all for his dyett and lodging all the whiles he was there, nor for a wastcoat and some other necessaryes wich she bought for him & wich he had from her during his being in her house. And lastly this deponent saieth that she doth not know of anymore or other money that the said carpenter hath or had, neither hath she anyother in her custody.

Thomas Mines of the Isle of Portland aforesaid yeoman deposed sayeth that shortly after the shipp called the Golden Grape was cast away Richard Stradling of the same island labourer did bring unto this deponent a certaine parcell of wooll in a bagg wich he prayed this

42

deponent to lay up for him, wich this deponent promised to doe, but before he did lay up the same he caused it to be weighed, and it was then tenn pounds by weight And this deponent further sayeth that whiles he was wanting from home the said Stradling (as he doth conceive) knowing where this deponent had layed the said wooll, came provately and tooke part of the said wooll out of the bagg and putt in another place, whereof this deponent mistrusting and being told that the wooll found in the bag did not weigh full tenn pounds he searched neer the place where he had layed the bagg where he found (as he thinketh the remainder of the said wooll wich he hath in his custody and is ready to deliver And this deponent further sayeth that since the said shipp was cast away Alice the wife of Charles Mathews a souldyer of Portland Castle did bring to this deponent about a pound of wooll and a jarre of oyle, for wich she had from him two bushells of wheat, and this deponent was to keep the said wooll and oyle untill she brought him tenn shillings for his wheat. And he alsoe sayeth that Richard Clerk his servant did bring to this deponents house a certaine quantity of loose wett fruit, wich is spent. And that he hath not nor had any other or more of the goods or provisions of or belonging to the said shipp.

42R

Andrew Ebourne of Melcomb Regis aforesaid mariner deposed saieth that uppon the Tuesday after that the shipp the Golden Grape was cast away uppon the beech he went thither in the company of Thomas Damon and Roger Woodcocke of Melcomb Regis aforesaid where they did save a peice of a junk about a fathom in length, a peice of a fore knight two or three sheaves for blocks and a murderer, which murderer the said Thomas Damon hath in his custody. And that this deponent hath not nor had in his custody nor in the custody of any other to his use any other or more of the goods or provisions of or belonging to that shipp.

Roger Woodcocke of Melcomb Regis aforesaid mariner deposed saieth that he was present with Andrew Ebourne and Thomas Damon uppon the beech the Tuesday after the shipp called the Golden Grape was cast away where they did save a peice of an old junk, a murderer wich the said Damon hath in his custody and two or three other smale peices of the wrecke of the said shipp, And this deponent did there take up a small quantity of raysins of the sunne there wich he caryed home in a bagg And that he hath not nor had in his custody nor in the custody of any other to his use any more or other of the goods or provisions of that shipp.

43

Ralph Trivett of Melcomb Regis aforesaid saylor deposed saieth that uppon the Tuesday after the shipp called the Golden Grape was cast away uppon the beech he went thither where he together with Morgane Guilliams and his servant Martin White and Giles Powlett a peice of cable about three fathom and halfe in length which they sold to David Helland of Melcomb Regis for fower shillinges (of wich the said Morgane Guilliams had noe parte) And they did alsoe then save divers peices of the timber wrecke of the said shipp soe much as fower men were able to cary, wich were good for nothing but firewood And that he hath not nor any other or more of the goods or provisions of or belonging to the said shipp.

William Drewer of Waymouth aforesaid sailor deposed sayeth that the next day after that the shipp called the Golden Grape was cast away he went to the beech with Robert Falkoner, two of the Baylyes and three others of Melcomb Regis where they saved fower and twenty barrells of raisins of the sunne, of wich the said Robert Falkoner hath in his

43R

custody about six or seaven barrells the rest are in the house of Thomas Bayly of Wyke Regis, two murderers, a chamber, seaventeen or eighteen round shott the foreshrouds, the spritsaile topp and two great blocks wich Walter Bond of Waymouth tooke into his custody, and a peice of a junk wich this deponent hath, and alsoe a peice of an halser wich was put into the celler of Leonard Gillard in Melcomb Regis, And that he hath not nor had in his custody nor in the custody of any other to his use any more or other of the goods or provisions of or belonging to that shipp.

Andrew Pitt of Waymouth aforesaid sailor deposed saieth that the next morning after that the shipp called the Golden Grape was cast away uppon the beech he went thither together with John Cotton William Dry, Peter Haught, Philipp Ashe, Andrew Cotton, James Bond, and Symon Watte where they did save thirteen barrells of raisins of the sunne wich they caryed to Waymouth and landed uppon the key there, where one of the said barrels was stollen away from them (but by whome this deponent knoweth not) And this deponent sayeth that eight of the said barrells were put into the house of Richard Pitt this deponents father and the other fower into the house of the said William

44

Drye, And this deponent further saieth that they did att the request of John Allen the elder at the same time cary home for him one barrell of raisins of the sunne wich they delivered unto him at his house in Waymouth And that this deponent and some others with him did then alsoe salve an halser belonging to the said shipp wich they left att the house of Andrew Pitt in Wyke Regis And lastly this deponent saieth that he hath not nor any more or other of the goods or provisions of or belonging to the said shipp save only a certaine quantity of loose fruit wich he caryed home in his pocquett.

Morgain Hemmings of Waymouth sailor deposed saieth that about three daies after that the shipp called the Golden Grape was cast away uppn the beech he together with Andrew Pitt and George Bastin of Waymouth went thither where they did salve an halser belonging to the said shipp wich they caryed to the house of Andrew Pitt in Wyke Regis where it yett remaines And that he hath not nor had in his custody nor in the custody of any other to his use any more or other of the goods or provisions of or belonging to the said shipp.

44R

Robert Falkoner of Melcomb Regis aforesaid hellyer, deposed saieth that the next day after that the shipp called the Golden Grape was cast away uppon the beech, this deponent together with Thomas Bayly, Christopher Baily, Gregory Backway, Giles Fowler, John Damarick and William Drewer of Melcomb Regis went thither, where they did save fower and twenty barrells of raysins of the sunne, of wich fifteen are in the house of Thomas Bayly of Wyke Regis, sixe are in this deponents custody, two they gave to one Cope a boatman for carying the same over the water, & one they gave to one Grey of Wyke Regis for carying the same thither And this deponent alsoe sayeth that att the same time they salved two murderers the fore shrouds of the said shipp, some great shott, the capp of the foremast and one chamber wich Walter Bond of Waymouth aforesaid hath in his custody And lastly this deponent saieth that he hath not nor had in his custody nor in the custody of any other to his use any more or other of the goods or provisions of or belonging to the said shipp.

Thomas Bayly of Melcomb Regis aforesaid mason deposed saieth that he was present uppon the beech with Robert Falkoner and his company att

45

the saving of the goods and provisions wich did belonge to the shipp called the Golden Grape expressed and mentioned in the deposicons of the said Robert Falkoner And further this deponent sayeth that att the same time the saied company did alsoe save fower and twenty crosse=bar=shott, a smale topp, and the foretopmasts shrouds belonging to the said shipp wich Walter Bond named in the said deposicon tooke from them into his custody and delivered unto them three shillings in money for saving the same, and then told them that what more money was coming to them for saving the said goods they should save And lastly this deponent saieth that he hath not nor had in his custody nor in the custody of any other to his use any more or other of or belonging to the said shipp.

Gregory Backway of Melcomb Regis aforesaid sailor deposed saieth that he was present upon the beech att the saving of the severall goods and provisions that did belonge to the shipp called the Golden Grape mentioned and expressed in the deposicons of Robert Falkoner and Thomas Bayly wich were delivered as in their said deposicons is declared And that this deponent hath not nor had any more or other of the goods or provisions of or belonging to the said shipp.

45R

Christopher Bayly of Melcomb Regis aforesaid mason deposed saieth that he was present upon the beech with Robert Falkoner and his company att the saving of the severall goods and provisions menconed and expressed in the depositions of the said Robert Falkoner and Thomas Bayly wich did belonge to the shipp called the Golden Grape, And that this deponent hath not nor had any other or more of the goods or provisions of or belonging to the said shipp.

John Damarick of Melcomb Regis aforesaid butcher deposed saieth that he was present with Robert Falkoner and the rest of his company upon the beech att the saving of the fower and twenty barrells of raisins of the sunne out of the shipp called the Golden Grape expressed in the deposition of the said Robert Falkerner But he cannot speak of any of the provisions of the said shipp that then were salved by the said company for that soe soone as the said barrells were saved this deponent was appointed to watch and keep them safe that they might not be stollen away, And he further saieth that he hath not nor had in his custody nor in the custody of any other to his use any more or other of the goods or provisions of or belonging to the said shipp.

46

Deposicons taken at Melcomb Regis aforesaid the twenty sixth day of January in the year before named before us whose names are subscribed by virtue of the commissioners before expressed Francis Cape notary public being then also present.

Roger Haught of Waymouth aforesaid shipp=wright deposed saieth that uppon the same day that the shipp called the Golden Grape was cast away uppon the beech Agnes the wife of William Holmes of Waymouth aforesaid did send for this deponent to her house where was then the carpenter of the said shipp, whither when this deponent was come the said carpenter desired him to goe aboard the said shipp and (if he could) to save his chest of tooles, wich he said was worth seaven pounds, wich this deponent promised to doe, and was goeing thither accordingly: but being come neer he espyed another shipp loaden with canara wynes then driving on shore uppon the said beech wich made this deponent leave of his intended iourney, and to goe, and save the men of that shipp, wich he did: And this deponent further saieth that he came not to the shipp called the Golden Grape att all, nor hath in his custody nor in the custody of any other to his use any of the goods or provisions belonging to that

46R

shipp save only one barrell of raisins of the sunne wich Isaak Haught this deponents sonn saved and layed in this deponents house where the same doth now remaine.

John Cotton of Waymouth aforesaid mason deposed saieth that the next day after that the shipp called the Golden Grape was cast away uppon the beech this deponent with some other boatmen went in his boat up the Fleet thither, whither being come Peter Haught of Waymouth aforesaid and the rest of his company did putt aboard the said boat twelve barrells of raysins of the sunne wich were caryed in the said boat to Waymouth, where eight of the same barrells were delivered into the custody of Richard Pitt, and fower into the custody of William Drye And this deponent further saieth that uppon the Monday following he went thither againe in his said boat, where Walter Bond and his company did putt aboard the said boat three and twenty barrells of raysins of the sun wich this deponent caryed for him and landed at a place called Foxholles neer Wyke Regis, but what the said Bond did with the same afterwards this deponent knoweth not And lastly this deponent saieth that he hath not in his custody nor in the custody of any other to his use any part of the goods or provisions of the said shipp.

47

Peter Haught of Waymouth aforesaid fisherman deposed sayeth that uppon the next day after that the said shipp the Golden Grape was cast away uppon the beech this deponent went up the Fleet in the boat and in the company of John Cotton thither, where this deponent and his company did save twelve barrells of raysins of the sunne, wich they did putt into the said boat, and cary to Waymouth, where eight of the said barrells were then delivered into the custody of Richard Pitt, and fower into the custody of William Dry And this deponent further saieth that the next day they went thither with the said boat againe where Walter Bond did put aboard the said boat att two severall times three and twenty barrells of raisins of the sunne which were caryed for him over the Fleet & landed att a certaine place called Foxholes neer Wyke Regis, where they were left in the custody of the said Bond, but what he did with them this deponent knoweth not. And lastly this deponent saieth that he hath not in his custody nor in the custody of any other to his use any more of the goods or provisions belonging to that shipp.

47R

Richard Pitt of Waymouth saylor deposed sayeth that he hath in his custody eight barrells of raisins of the sunne wich Andrew Pitt this deponents sonne did help to save out of the shipp called the Golden Grape lately cast away upon the beech And lastly this deponent hath not in his custody nor in the custody of any other to his use any other or more of the goods or provisions of or belonging to that shipp.

Isaak Haught the sonne of Roger Haught of Waymouth aforesaid shippwright deposed sayeth that upon the day after that the shipp called the Golden Grape was cast away upon the beech this deponent went thither where he with the help of another boy did save two barrells of raisins of the sunne, one of which John Allin the elder of Waymouth tooke from this deponent there presently, the other a woman of Wyke Regis caryed home for this deponent to his fathers house in Waymouth where the same yett remaines And that he hath not nor had in his custody nor in the custody of any other to his use any more or other of the goods or provisions of or belonging to the said shipp.

48

Ralph Lock of Waymouth aforesaid hellyer deposed sayeth that upon the Tuesday next after the shipp called the Golden Grape was cast away upon the beech this deponent together with his wife & John Paule of Waymouth aforesaid went thither where they took up an old junke about three fathom in length wich this deponent caryed home and sold to Peter Joy of Melcomb Regis for three shillinges And he further saieth that he hath not nor had in his custody nor in the custody of any other to his use any other or more of the goods or provisions of or belonging to the said shipp.

Angel Wattes of Melcomb Regis aforesaid carpenter deposed sayeth that the Tuesday next after that the shipp the Goldin Grape was cast away upon the beech this deponent went thither, where he saved one barrell of raisins of the sunne, wich in carying towards his home upon an horse fell accidentally from the said horse upon the ground in the dirt, by occasion whereof the said barrel was broken to pieces and all the fruit that was in the same fell out into the dirt, wich notwithstanding this deponent gathered up againe and putt into a sacke,

48R

and caried the same to his house where it yet remaines And this deponent further saieth that he was att the said beech the day before alsoe, where he gathered up certaine wett loose fruit wich he putt into a bagge, and lay up there upon the beech, from whence it was stollen together with the said bagge, And that he then tooke up a junke of a cable about twelve or sixteen fathom in length, a shovell and some smale peices of iron about fowre pound weight, wich junk and shovell he hath in his custody, but the iron was sold for about fowre or five pence, And lastly this deponent saieth that he hath not nor had in his custody nor in the custody of any other to his use any other or more of the goods or provisions of or belonging to the said shipp.

Robert Munday of Waymouth aforesaid fisherman deposed saieth that uppon the Tuesday after the shipp called the Golden Grape was cast away uppon the beech he went thither in his boat where he saved a smale peice of timber parte of the broken peices of the said shipp, worth fower pence or thereabouts, and that his child did then take upp about seaven or eight pound of raisins of the sunne wich he caried home with him And that this deponent hath not nor had either in his custody or in the custody of any other to his use any more or other of the goods or provisions of that shipp.

49

James Cornish of Waymouth aforesaid woollen draper deposed saieth that the next day after that the ship called the Golden Grape was cast away Thomas Redwood late Master of the said shipp came to this deponent (being then and yet one of the Constables of the said Towne) and desired him to search for moneys taken out of the said shipp, whereuppon this deponent went with him to the house of Catharine Langar widow in Waymouth aforesaid where they found the cook of the said shipp from whome they took sixteen hundred ryalls wich the said Master had And this deponent alsoe sayeth that shortly after he this deponent did receive from John Peirce one of the company of the said shipp sixe and thirty shillinges in peices of eight for cloth wich this deponent sold unto him to make him a suite of clothes, And that he received seaven and twenty shillings in the like coine from the boatswaine of the said shipp and an Irishman two other of the company of the said shipp for three wastcoats And this deponent further saieth that the trumpetter of the said shipp told him this deponent that Arthur Grey's wife of Wyke Regis being privy to his hyding of one hundred and fiftye peices of eight in her garden had deceived him of one hundred and five peices thereof, for that

49R

when he came afterwards to looke for his money there were left onely five and forty peices the rest beinge taken away, And he further saieth that he doth not know of the disposing of any other or more peices of eight or of any other coine taken out of the said shipp And that he hath not nor had either in his owne custody or in the custody of any other to his use any of the goods or provisions of or belonging to the said shipp.

Edward Courtney of Melcomb Regis aforesaid mason deposed saieth that the next day after the shipp called the Golden Grape was cast away uppon the beech this deponent went thither where he tooke upp about tenn or twelve pounds of wett raisins of the sunne wich he caried home alonge with him And that he hath not nor had either in his owne custody or in the custody of any other to his use any more or other of the goods or provisions of that shipp.

Thomas Samwayes of Melcomb Regis aforesaid taylor deposed saieth that uppon the Monday next after that the shipp called the Golden Grape was cast away uppon the beech this deponent went thither where he bought of Robert

50

Falkoner of Melcomb Regis aforesaid part of a barrell of raisins of the sunne for wich he paied him five shillinges, wich he brought home with him; And that he alsoe bought of Robert Smith of Waymouth a certaine quantity of loose fruit for wich this deponent payed him two shillings, and that this deponent tooke up some loose fruit there wich he caried home with him alsoe And that he hath not nor had any other or more of the goods or provisions of or belonging to the said shipp.

John Milles of Waymouth aforesaid taylor deposed saieth that the next day after that the shipp called the Golden Grape was cast away uppon the beech this deponent together with Andrew Mills his brother Benedict Grey, Walter Winter, George Wayman, Austine the ferryman att Portland & Mathew Allin of Waymouth went thither where they did save seaven barrells of raisins of the sunne which are in the house of the said Andrew Mills in Wyke Regis And this deponent further saieth that he hath not nor had in his custody nor in the custody of any other to his use any other or more of the goods or provisions of or belonging to the said shipp.

50R

Deposicons taken at Melcomb Regis aforesaid the twenty seventh day of January in the year before named before us whose names are subscribed by virtue of the commissioners before expressed Francis Cape notary public being then also present.

Nicholas Gilbert of Melcomb Regis aforesaid cobler deposed saieth that uppon the next day after the shipp called the Golden Grape was cast away uppon the beech this deponent went thither where he took up a certaine quantity of loose fruit wich he putt into a bagg and caried home with him, and the bolt of a pumpe and three lymons, And that he hath not nor had in his owne custody nor in the custody of any other to his use any more or other of the goods or provisions of that shipp.

Robert Smyth of Waymouth aforesaid labourer deposed saieth that he was uppon the beech the next day after the shipp called the Golden Grape was cast away where he tooke up a certaine quantity of loose fruit parte of wich he sold to Thomas Samwayes of Melcomb Regis for two shillinges the rest he caried home to his house and hath since spent the same And that he hath not nor had any more or other of the goods or provisions of or belonging to the said shipp.

51

Nicholas Sangar of Waymouth aforesaid sailor deposed saieth that the next day after that the shipp called the Golden Grape was cast away uppon the beech this deponent went thither where he tooke up about a peck of loose fruit wich he putt into a bagg and caryed home with him And that he hath not nor had any other or more of the goods or provisions of or belonging to the said shipp.

Symon Wattes of Melcomb Regis aforesaid sailor deposed saieth that upon the next day after that the shipp called the Golden Grape was cast away uppon the beech this deponent went thither together with John Cotton of Waymouth and his company where they did save thirteen barrells of raisins of the sunne and one barrell that was open att one end, nine of wich they forthwith caryed home and landed uppon the key in Waymouth where one of those barrells was conveyed away by Philip Ash of Weymouth (as this deponent hath heard) the other eight were putt into the house of Richard Pitt; the residew of the said barrells they left at the passage house by the way, fower of wich they afterwards fetched to Waymouth and put into the house of William Dry, the other that was open was emptyed by

51R

certaine women (as this deponent hath alsoe heard) and all the fruit caryed away And that this deponent hath not in his custody nor in the custody of any other to his use any other or more of the goods or provisions of or belonging to the said shipp.

Andrew Cotton of Waymouth aforesaid mason deposed saieth that the same day att night that the shipp called the Golden Grape was cast away uppon the beech this deponent went thither in the company of John Cotton his father and others where they did save twelve barrels of fruit, eight of wich were put into the house of Richard Pitt and the other fower into the house of William Dry of Waymouth And that this deponent hath not nor had in his custody any of the goods or provisions of or belonging to the said shipp.

William Dry of Waymouth aforesaid mason deposed saieth that the next day after the shipp the Golden Grape was cast away uppon the beech this deponent went thither in the company of John Cotton and others where they did save twelve barrells of fruit, eight whereof are in the house of Richard Pitt and the other fowre in this deponents house And that he hath not nor had in his custody nor in the custody of any other to his use any other or more of the goods or provisions of or belonging to the said shipp.

52

Deposicons taken at Melcomb Regis aforesaid the thirty first day of January in the year before named before us whose names are subscribed by virtue of the commissioners before expressed Francis Cape notary public being then also present.

Samuel Tackle of Waymouth aforesaid baker deposed saieth that uppon the next day after that the shipp called the Golden Grape was cast away uppon the beech this deponent went thither, whither he being come did goe aboard the said shipp and there with the helpe of his two servants did save three barrells of raisins of the sunne wich were caryed to this deponents barne in Weymouth aforesaid where they yet remaine And that one of his servants did then alsoe cary to this deponents house certaine loose fruit in a pillowbeer wich he took up there at that time And this deponent further sayeth that uppon the Monday following he went thither againe where he tooke up another barrell of raisins of the sunne in the wash of the sea, which he did there break open and take out the fruit & putt the same into bagges and soe cary it home to his house And that he hath not in his owne custody nor in the custody of any other to his use any more or other of the goods or provisions of or belonging to the said shipp.

52R

Edward Samwayes of Waymouth aforesaid tanner deposed saieth that the same day that the shipp called the Golden Grape was cast away uppon the beech he went thither where he tooke up a certaine quantity of loose fruit wich he did putt into his pocquetts and carye home with him And that he hath not nor had in his custody nor in the custody of any other to his use any other or more of the goods or provisions of or belonging to the said shipp.

Peter Cornelius of Waymouth aforesaid mariner deposed sayeth that uppon the Munday after the shipp called the Golden Grape was cast away uppon the beech he went thither accompanyed with his servant, George Evans and Martin Hamond of Waymouth and the servant of the said Martin Hamond, where this deponents said servant did fill a bagg with raysins of the sunne wich were taken out of a barrell that was given to the said George Evans for caryinge some other fruit over the Fleet in his boat, wich he caryed home to this deponents house: And that the said George Evans did then fill another bagg with raysins out of the said barrell, and the servant of the said Martin Hamond another bagg wich were caryed to their severall

53

dwellinges And that the said deponent hath not nor had in his custody nor in the custody of any other to his use any other or more of the goods or provisions of or belonging to the said shipp.

William Winter of Waymouth aforesaid brewer deposed sayeth that uppon the next day after that the shipp called the Golden Grape was cast away uppon the beech he went thither where he did help to save eight barrells of fruit together with James Hardey **(blank)** Cake, the servant of Henry Coxe, and Robert Pitt of Waymouth aforesaid wich were left uppon the beech in the custody of the said Cake, James Hardey and the said Coxe his servant who kept the same there untill the next morning, att wich time this deponent went thither againe with intention to cary the said fruit to Waymouth, but when he came thither he found five of the said barrells wanting, wich were taken from those that had them in keeping by Walter Bond and Symon Mores of Waymouth, the other three this deponent caryed thence to his house where they doe yett remaine, and wich he is and wilbe ready to deliver when they shall be required from him And this deponent alsoe saieth that he hath not nor had any other or more of the goods or provisions of or belonging to that shipp.

53R

James Hardey of Waymouth aforesaid sawyer deposed sayeth that he was present with William Winter of Waymouth att the saving of eight barrells of raysins of the sunne, wich he together with one Cake and a servant of Henry Coxe were appointed to keep untill the next morning but this deponent saieth that in the night time Walter Bond & Symon Mores of Waymouth with others came and tooke five of the said barrells from them, the other three the said William Winter the next day caryed to his house in Waymouth And that this deponent hath not nor had in his custody nor in the custody of any other to his use any other or more of the goods or provisions of or belonging to the said shipp.

John Curteis of Melcomb Regis aforesaid taylor deposed saieth uppon the Munday next after the shipp called the Golden Grape was cast away uppon the beech he went thither where he tooke up a smale quantity of wett raysins of the sunne wich he caryed home with him And that he hath not nor had any more or other of the goods or provisions of or belonging to the said shipp. And this deponent further saieth that the mother of Mary Paine of Melcomb Regis did pay or allow unto him this deponent about three peices of eight for making a cloke and other garments for one Richard Rich one of the company of the said shipp and the said Mary Paine.

54

Richard Baylye of Melcomb Regis aforesaid mason deposed sayeth that the next day after that the shipp called the Golden Grape was cast away uppon the beech he went thither in the company of Edward Pounston alias Hownsell of Melcomb Regis aforesaid blacksmith, whither when they were come they went aboard the said shipp out of wich they took and saved eight barrells of raysins of the sunne, wich they layed uppon the beech, where one barrell was stollen from them, but by whome this deponent knoweth not, another barrell they gave to William James of Melcomb Regis aforesaid to cary the other sixe for them over the Fleet in his boat, wich sixe barrells they caryed home to their houses (vizt) fower to the house of this deponent and two to Edward Hownsells house; And this deponent sayeth that he sold one of the barrells wich he had to the wife of Mr. John Arthur for wich she payed him forty shillinges, two of the others he hath att home whole, the fourth Mr. Richards one of the officers of the Custome house did cause this deponent to open alleadging that he thought it was a barrell of tent, out of wich barrell some parte hath been taken, the residew remaines yett there And lastly this deponent saieth that he hath not nor had any other or more of the goods or provisions of or belonging to that shipp.

54R

Edward Pownston alias Hownsell of Melcomb Regis aforesaid blacksmith deposed sayeth that he was present uppon the beech with Richard Baily of Melcomb Regis mason att the saving of the barrells of raysins of the sunne menconed & expressed in the deposition of the said Baily, two of wich barrells this deponent hath in his custody but whether the said barrells are full or not this deponent knoweth not yett saieth that he tooke none of the fruit out of them And that he hath not in his custody nor in the custody of any other to his use any more or other of the goods or provisions of or belonging to the said shipp.

George Allinn of Waymouth aforesaid fisherman deposed saieth that he was uppon the beech the next day after that the shipp called the Golden Grape was cast away where he did take upp about two bushels of wett raysins of the sunne, wich he did cary home in bagges att his backe att two several times where they doe yett remaine And that he hath not nor had in his custody nor in the custody of any other to his use any more or other of the goods or provisions of or belonging to the said shipp.

55

Deposicons taken at Melcomb Regis aforesaid the first day of February in the year before named before us whose names are subscribed by virtue of the commissioners before expressed Francis Cape notary public being then also present.

Nicholas Williams of Wyke Regis aforesaid fisherman deposed saieth that uppon the same day att night that the shipp called the Golden Grape was cast away uppon the beech he went up the Fleet in his boat thither where he had two jarres of oyle from Robert Hunt of Wyke Regis aforesaid for his paines in carying other jarres of oyle and other goods for the said Hunt over the Fleet wich he had salved out of the said shipp, one of wich jarres is since broken and all the oyle leaked out, the other this deponents wife Sarah Williams hath sold in the town of Waymouth for fower shillinges And that this deponent hath not in his custody nor in the custody of any other to his use any more or other of the goods or provisions of or belonging to the said shipp.

Thomas Angell of Wyke Regis aforesaid fisherman deposed saieth that uppon the same day that the shipp called

55R

the Golden Grape was cast away uppon the beech he and his wife went thither, where his said wife did save about fower pounds of wooll wich she hath delivered to Mr. Arthur. And that this deponent did then save two old paire of breeches and some smale quantity of wett **blank** And that he hath not nor had in his custody nor in the custody of any other to his use any more or other of the goods or provisions of or belonging to the said shipp.

William Symonds of Portisham in the County of Dorsett aforesaid thatcher deposed saieth that uppon the Munday after that the shipp called the Golden Grape was cast away uppon the beech he went thither, where by the Fleet side he found two barrells and halfe a barrell of raysins of the sunne which had been taken out of the said shipp, wich this deponent caused to be caryed over the Fleet in a boat of Wyke Regis for wich he payed the boatman two shillinges. And this deponent further saieth that when he came over the Fleet he mett with John Gillam of Portsham who was there with his cart, whome this deponent desired to cary the said fruit for him to Portsham aforesaid and promised him the one halfe for his paines, wich the said Gillam performing this deponent and he divyded the said fruit between them, And this deponent further saieth that he sold his parte of the same fruit (being an whole barrell full unto **(blank)** Doby of Mounkton blacksmith for nineteen shillings And that he hath not nor had any other or more or other of the goods or provisions of or belonging to the said shipp.

56

John Gillam of Portisham aforesaid husbandman deposed saieth that uppon the Monday after the shipp called the Golden Grape was cast away uppon the beech he went with his cart and two horses to the Fleet side neer that place with intent to buy some of the goods that were salved out of the said shipp for his money, but being come thither he mett with William Symonds of Portisham aforesaid who having in his custody two barrells and halfe of raysins of the sunne desired this depononet to cary the same home for him in his cart and promised to give this deponent one of the said barrells for his paines, wich this deponent accordingly performed, and being come home he received one of the said barrells wich he sold to one Woodford of Easter Compton for five and thirty shillings wanting two pence And that he hath not nor had in his custody nor in the custody of any other to his use any more or other of the goods or provisions of or belonging to the said shipp.

Deposicons taken at Melcomb Regis aforesaid the third day of February in the year before named before us whose names are subscribed by virtue of the commissioners before expressed Francis Cape notary public being then also present.

Walter Sandford of Portisham aforesaid weaver deposed saieth that

56R

the next day after that the shipp called the Golden Grape was cast away uppon the beech he went thither in the company of Richard Halston of Corton and others whither being come the said Halston desired this deponent to help him to save some of the barrells of raysins that were in the said shipp, wich this deponent accordingly did, and there did help him to save tenn barrells of raysins wich the said Halston caryed to Corton in his cart and gave this deponent two barrells of wheat for his paines And this deponent alsoe sayeth that being aboard the said shipp he tooke up certain loose wett fruit there wich he put into the sleive of his wastcoat & caryed home with him And that he hath not nor had any more or other of the goods or provisions of or belonging to the said shipp.

John Ricketts sonne of Walter Ricketts of Portisham aforesaid deposed saieth that the next day after that the shipp called the Golden Grape was cast away uppon the beech he went thither where he and William Cake of Portisham aforesaid did save out of the said shipp eight barrells of raysions of the sunne, wich they caryed and layed upon the beech, and there left the same in the custody of one John Woode servant to Thomas Meech of Portisham aforesaid yeoman, intending to fetch the same from thence the next morning, but this deponent saieth that the next morning when they came thither the said barrells of raysins were all caryed away the said Wood telling this deponent that

57

certaine men of Waymouth came thither and having beaten him did take the said barrells and cary the same away from him And this deponent further sayeth that he did then save two small peices of cordage and certaine loose fruit out of the said shipp wich he caryed home with him, and that George Tooledge this deponents fathers servant being there alsoe did save some loose fruit which he putt into **blank** and caryed home with him, but the certaine quantity of the same this deponent knoweth not And lastly this deponent saieth that he hath not nor had in his custody nor in the custody of any other to his use any more or other of the goods or provisions of or belonging to the said shipp.

Christopher Eyles of Portisham aforesaid weaver deposed sayeth that uppon the Monday after that the shipp called the Golden Grape was cast away uppon the beech he went thither where he bought of Robert Gawden of Portisham aforesaid a barrell of fruit for wich he payd the said Gawden three shillings and fower pence, wich barrell this deponent caryed home uppon an horse that he had borrowed of Mrs Galping the vicars wife of Portisham aforesaid for that purpose, to whome he gave the one halfe of the said barrell of fruite for hire of the said horse And that

57R

the other halfe (the same being wett) this deponent hath spent parte of it in his house the residew he hath bestowed on his friends And that this deponent hath not nor had in his custody nor in the custody of any other to his use any more or other of the goods or provisions of or belonging to the said shipp save only a smale quantity of loose wett raysins of the sun wich he then took up uppon the beech and caryed home with him.

John Symonds of Portisham aforesaid yeoman deposed saieth that uppon the next day after that the shipp called the Golden Grape was cast away uppon the beech he went thither accompanyed with a maid servant of his owne and another of Anthony Hardey of Portisham aforesaid, where the said Maydens did take upp some quantity of fruit, about a pecke and a halfe each, wich they putt into their aprons and caryed home with them And this deponent saieth that his sonne Richard Symonds did then alsoe save one barrell of fruit wich this deponent caryed home in his cart, and that he caryed then another barrell for the widow Samways of Portsham aforesaid, wich barrells are att home in his house, and certaine barrells for Thomas Harden and Henry Russell of the same place (but how many he knoweth not) and that he alsoe caryed one barrell for Robert George of the same place and likewise that this deponents said sonne Richard Symonds did alsoe then save another barrell of fruit wich this deponent did emptie out into sacks and cary home to his house uppon an horse And this deponent further

58

sayeth that uppon the next day being Monday he went thither againe where he bought of Thomas Loder of Waymouth a barrell almost full of raysins of the sunne for wich he payed him seaven shillings wich fruit this deponent emptyed out of the said barrell, and did putt the same into bagges and soe caryed it home to his house And he further saieth that William Samways this deponents servant did then alsoe save a jarre of oyle wich this deponent hath in his house, and a wallett of raisins of the sunne, but what became of them this deponent knoweth not And lastly this deponent saieth that he hath not nor had in his custody nor in the custody of any other to his use nor doth know of any more or other of the goods or provisions of that shipp.

Thomas Webber of Portisham aforesaid husbandman deposed saieth that uppon the Tuesday next after that the shipp called the Golden Grape was cast away uppon the beech he went thither where he did helpe save two Mastes of that shipp wich he left there uppon the beech, and some peices of timber parte of the ribbs of the said shipp, a great shott, a bottle of wyne about a pinte and a halfe, some nayles, and one spyke, and that he bought there some other smale peices of timber of some that had saved the same for & wich he payed three shillinges And this deponent further

58R

sayeth that his sonne William Webber did allsoe there save a barrell of fruit wich this deponent hath in his custody and a peice of a cable wich is in the custody of John Hendey of Langton And lastly this deponent saieth that he hath not nor had in his custody nor in the custody of any other to his use any more or other of the goods or provisions of or belonging to the said shipp.

John White of Portisham aforesaid sailor deposed saieth that uppon the next day after that the shipp called the Golden Grape was cast away uppon the beech he went thither in the company of Richard Halston of Corton Walter Sandford and two of the said Halstons servants where they did save thirteen barrells of raysins of the sunne, wich were caryed by boat over the Fleet and there landed; where the said Halston said that three of them were stollen away, the other tenn barrels the said Halston caryed in his cart to Corton and gave this deponent two bushells of wheat and eighteen pence in money for his paines And that this deponent hath not nor had in his custody nor in the custody of any other to his use any more or any other of the goods or provisions of or belonging to the said shipp.

Thomas Meech of Portisham aforesaid yeoman deposed saieth that he was not uppon the beech att all, neither hath he, nor had any of the goods or provisions belonging to the shipp called the Golden Grape.

59

Deposicons taken at Melcomb Regis aforesaid the fourth day of February in the year before named before us whose names are subscribed by virtue of the commissioners before expressed Francis Cape notary public being then also present.

Augustine Trew of the parish of Wyke Regis aforesaid saylor deposed saieth that uppon the same day next that the shipp called the Golden Grape was cast away uppon the beech he went thither in the company of Andrew Mills of Wyke Regis aforesaid and others, where they saved between them seaven barrells of raysins of the sunne, and a rope: wich are in the custody of the said Andrew Mills, And this deponent did alsoe save some smale quantity of loose fruit to him selfe wich was afterwards stollen from him uppon the beech And that he hath not nor had in his custody nor in the custody of any other to his use any more or other of the goods or provisions of or belonging to the said shipp.

Henry Kellway of Wyke Regis aforesaid saylor deposed sayeth that uppon the Monday next after the shipp called the Golden Grape was cast away uppon the beech he went thither together with William Wareham, Alexander Lea, and George

59R

Chipp of Wyke Regis aforesaid where they saved one barrell of raysins of the sunne, and that Robert Hunt of the same place gave unto this deponent and his said company two barrells more of raysins of the sunne for their paines in carying eight barrells for him over the Fleet, wich three barrells of fruit they caryed to the house of Mr. John Jeffries of Wyke Regis aforesaid where they doe yett remaine And that this deponent hath not nor had in his custody nor in the custody of any other to his use any more or other of the goods or provisions of or belonging to the said shipp.

Henry Flory of Wyke Regis aforesaid fisherman examined sayeth that he being in the boat with Nichlas Williams of Wyke Regis and others att the carying of certaine jarres of oyle for Robert Hunt of the same place over the Fleet had two jarres of oyle for his paines, wich he hath in his custody, and that he did then alsoe take up uppon the beech there a smale quantity of loose raysins of the sunne wich he hath att home in his house And that he hath not nor had either in his owne custody or in the custody of any other to his use any more or other of the goods or provisions of or belonging to the shipp called the Golden Grape.

John Hardey sonn of Anthony Hardey of Portsham aforesaid yeoman deposed saieth that uppon the Monday next after the shipp called the Golden Grape was cast away uppon the beech

60

he went to the Fleet side neer, where he saw many barrells of fruit broken up and caried but by whome he knoweth not, onely he saieth that John Symonds of Portsham did cary in his plough about nine barrells of fruit home to his house but how he did depose of them this deponent doth not know that And he alsoe saieth that one Gillam of Portsham had alsoe there some barrells of fruit but how many this deponent doth not know And that this deponent hath not nor had in his custody nor in the custody of any other to his use any of the goods or provisions of or belonging to the said shipp.

Thomas Ploughman of Portsham aforesaid husbandman deposed sayeth that uppon the next day after that the shipp called the Golden Grape was cast away uppon the beech he went thither to see what Henry Thresher of Portsham did with the horse wich this deponents wife had lent unto him where Robert Lovell of Fleet gave unto this deponent about a pecke of wett raysins of the sunne, wich this deponent caryed home with him And that he hath not nor had any more or other of the goods or provisions of or belonging to that shipp.

Margery Michell of Portisham aforesaid widow deposed saieth that she was not uppon the beech att all, but that

60R

Thomas Michell her sonne did bring to her house from thence in a sacke between two and three bushells of wett raysins of the sunne, A bushell whereof she sold to a carier (whose name she now remembreth not) for eight shillings And that she hath not nor had any more or other of the goods or provisions of the shipp called the Golden Grape.

William Cake of Portsham aforesaid husbandman deposed sayeth that the next day after that the shipp called the Golden Grape was cast away uppon the beech he went thither in the company of Richard Wilkins of Portsham, where John Ricketts of Portsham and this deponent ioyning together did save eight barrells of raisins of the sunne which they caryed over the beech to the Fleet side and there appointed John Wood servant to Thomas Meech to watch and keep the same, and the next morning certaine men of Weymouth pretending themselves to be the Viceadmiralls men (one of wich is named Pope) tooke them from the said Wood, but what is become of them this deponent knoweth not And that the same morning the said Ricketts and this deponent had three bagges filled with wett raisins of the sunne wich they caried to Walter Ricards of the said Ricards his fathers house in Portsham aforesaid where they gave this deponent about a bushel of the said fruit for his paines, wich he kept untill they were almost spilt with lyeing, and then sold twenty pound weight of the loose fruit to Mr. John Samford of Portsham for halfe a crowne, the rest were spoiled and

61

spent by this deponent And he further (**blank)** that when he was upon the beech he took up a langar shott wich he caryed home with him and sold to Robert Philips of Portesham for a penny a pound in weight the same being almost six pound in weight And that this deponent hath not nor had in his custody nor in the custody of any other to his use any more or other of the goods or provisions of that shipp.

John Meech of Portsham aforesaid weaver deposed sayeth that the next day after that the shipp called the Golden Grape was cast away upon the beech he went thither where out of certaine peices of barrells that there lay he took about halfe a barrell of raisins of the sunne wich he caried home some in his wallett wich fruit he hath spent in his house in the Christmas time And he saieth that then he took up alsoe a smale peice of cordage of that shipp wich he likewise caried home with him And that he hath not nor had in his custody nor in the custody of any other to his use any more or other of the goods or provisions of or belonging to the said shipp.

John Hazard alias Wallis sonne of Elizabeth Hazard alias Wallis of Portsham aforesaid widow deposed sayeth that the next day after that the ship

61R

called the Golden Grape was cast away upon the beech he went thither where he took up about halfe a bushel of wett raisins of the sunne wich he putt into a bagg and caried home to his mother who hath since spent the same in her house And that this deponent hath not nor had any more or other of the goods or provisions of that shipp.

Thomas Sandford of Portsham aforesaid husbandman deposed sayeth that the next day after that the shipp called the Golden Grape was cast away upon the beech he went thither in the company of John Meech, John Thresher sonn of Henry Thresher, Hugh Michell and Thomas Michell all of Portsham aforesaid where this deponent did save one barrell of raisins of the sunn, wich some of Waymouth (whose names he knoweth not) took from him, and that he took up there some loose fruit wich he putt into the sleive of his coat and caried home with him And that he hath not nor had any more or other of the goods or provisions of that shipp And this deponent further saieth that the said Hugh Michell and John Thresher did cary three barrells of raisins of the sunne over the Fleet, but what they did with the same afterwards this deponent knoweth not.

Richard Symonds sonn of John Symonds of Portsham aforesaid yeoman deposed saith that the next day in the morning after that the

62

shipp called the Golden Grape was cast away uppon the beech he went thither in the company of Joseph the sonne of Anthony Hardey of Portsham aforesaid where they did save three barrells of raisins of the sonn wich they caried thence & putt two of them in the said Anthony Hardey's house and the other in this deponents fathers house And this deponent further saieth that he did alsoe cary home in his said fathers plough seaven other barrells of raisins of the sunn for Robert George, Thomas Harden and Henry Russell of Portsham aforesaid, one of wich was for the widow Samwayes of Elwood wich this deponent's said father bought of her And this deponent lastly saieth that he hath not nor had in his custody nor in the custody of any other to his use any more or other of the goods or provisions of or belonging to the said shipp save only certaine loose fruit wich he caried home to his said fathers house in a sacke upon an horse.

John Sattford of Portsham aforesaid husbandman deposed saith that the next day in the morning after that the shipp called the Golden Grape was cast away uppon the beech he went thither in the company of Henry Russell and John Meech, where this deponent did take up a halfe a pecke of wett raisins

62R

of the sunne wich he caried home alonge with him And that this deponent hath not nor had in his custody nor in the custody of any other to his use any more or other of the goods or provisions of or belonging to the said shipp.

John Winter of Portsham aforesaid husbandman deposed saith that the next day after that the shipp called the Golden Grape was cast away uppon the beech he went thither where he tooke up and saved about a pecke of wett raisins of the sunne and two or three smale peices of cordes wich he caried home with him And that he hath not nor had any more or other of the goods or provisions of or belonging to the said shipp.

Andrew Urry sonne of Henry Urry of Portsham aforesaid husbandman deposed saieth that the next day after that the shipp called the Golden Grape was cast away uppon the beech he went thither where he tooke out of a barrell about halfe a bushell of raisins of the sunne wich he put into a bagg and caryed home with him to his fathers house, parte of wich were there spent, the rest were given and sent to William Samwayes of Martinstowne And this deponent saieth that he hath not nor had in his owne custody nor in the custody of any other to his use any more or other of the goods or provisions of or belonging to the said shipp save onely two oringes.

63

Robert George of Portsham aforesaid husbandman deposed sayeth that the next day after that the shipp the Golden Grape was cast away uppon the beech he went thither where he saved a barrell of wett raisins of the sunne wich John Symonds of Portsham aforesaid caryed home for him in his cart, seaven pecke of wich this deponent sold to a stranger for fowrteen shillings, the residue he hath spent And that he hath not nor had in his custody nor in the custody of any other to his use any more or other of the goods or provisions of or belonging to the said shipp

William Hawkins of Portsham aforesaid husbandman deposed saieth that the next day in the evening after that the shipp the Golden Grape was cast away uppon the beech he went thither in the company of William Bellett and Henry Bellett of Portsham aforesaid where they did save a barrell of raisins of the sunn which they caried to Chickerell to a kinsemans house of the said Belletts where they left the same, but this deponent saieth that the said Bellett hath since taken the said barrel thence and hath carried the same to Blandford where he delivered it to a daughter of his to sell for him there, and did promise this deponent

63R

part of the provenue thereof, but this deponent hath as yet received noething from him And this deponent further saieth that they did then alsoe finde a bagg full of raisins wich they shared amongst them whereof this deponent had about a pecke and halfe to his parte wich he caried home with him and hath since spent And that this deponent hath not nor had in his custody nor in the custody of any other to his use any more or other of the goods or provisions of or belonging to the said shipp.

William Webber sonn of Thomas Webber of Portsham aforesaid husbandman deposed saieth that the same day at night that the shipp called the Golden Grape was cast away uppon the beech he went thither in the company of John Tooledge of Langton where this deponent did save one barrell of fruit and a smale quantity of fruit in another barrell wich he caried to the house of Magdalen Allin widow in Fleet, and there left them; where afterwards in the night time the said barrell was broken open and parte of the fruit taken thence, but yett this deponent that there was enough left in both to make up one whole barrell, wich he took thence and caried to his fathers house in Portsham aforesaid And that this deponent hath not nor had in his custody nor in the custody of any other to his use any more or other of the goods or provisions of or belonging to that shipp save onely a little woodden boxe to put powder in.

64

Deposicons taken at Melcomb Regis aforesaid the fifth day of February in the year before named before us whose names are subscribed by virtue of the commissioners before expressed Francis Cape notary public being then also present.

Richard Rose of Waddon in the County of Dorsett aforesaid husbandman deposed saieth that uppon the next day after that the shipp the the Golden Grape was cast away uppon the beech he went thither where he saved two barrells of raisins of the sunne wich Richard Halston of Waddon aforesaid caried home in his cart for this deponent one of wich barrells hath been since opened and a good parte of the fruit spent in this deponents, the remainder of that and the other barrell are yett in this deponents house wich he is ready to deliver And that this deponent hath not nor had in his custody nor in the custody of any other to his use any more or other of the goods or provisions of or belonging to the said shipp.

Richard Dimon of Waddon aforesaid husbandman deposed saieth that uppon the next day after that the shipp called the Golden Grape was cast away uppon the beech he went thither where he

64R

saved two barrells of fruit, one of wich was there taken from him by some of Waymouth (whose names he knoweth not) the other this deponent sold to one Buttler of Upway a caryer for five shillings And that this deponent hath not nor had in his custody nor in the custody of any other to his use any more or other of the goods or provisions of or belonging to the said shipp.

Robert Symonds of Waddon aforesaid husbandman deposed saieth that uppon the next day after that the shipp called the Golden Grape was cast away uppon the beech he went thither where he together with Richard Rose of Waddon did save a barrell of raisins of the sunn wich had taken salt water and oile, wich this deponent caried over the Fleet where it was broken open by the servant of one Patye of Upway and others whose names this deponent knoweth not, and parte of the said fruit taken by them away, the remainder this deponent caried whome to his house, a great part whereof because it was oyly and had taken salt water this deponent hath since given away, and hath spent the rest And that this deponent hath not nor had in his custody nor in the custody of any other to his use any more or other of the goods or provisions of or belonging to the said shipp.

Hugh Browne of Portsham aforesaid husbandman deposed saieth that the next day after that the shipp called the Golden Grape was cast away upon the beech he went thither where he took up about three pecks of raisins of

65

the sunne which he putt into his wallett and caryed home with him where he and his family have spent the same And that Agnes Browne this deponents daughter being then there alsoe did take up about halfe a pecke of the same fruit wich she alsoe caried home to this deponents house where the same hath likewise been spent And that this deponent hath not nor had any more or other of the goods or provisions of or belonging to that shipp.

Thomas Wills of Portsham aforesaid labourer deposed saieth that upon the next day after that the shipp called the Golden Grape was cast away upon the beech he went thither where he took up about halfe a bushel of fruit, wich he did put into a linine bagg that he caryed thither with him for that purpose and caryed the said fruit home with him where he hath since spent the same And that he hath not nor had any more or other of the goods or provisions of or belonging to the said shipp.

Thomas Harding of Portsham aforesaid miller deposed saieth that upon the next day after that the shipp called the Golden Grape was cast away upon the beech he went thither where

65R

he together with Henry Russell of Portsham and John Wills of Chickerell did save three barrells of raisins of the sunne wich they caried to the house of William Wey in Chickerell aforesaid where they doe yet remaine. And this deponent further saieth that he did then alsoe save two other barrells of raisins of the sunne which were caried to Portsham in the cart of John Symonds of one of wich barrells this deponent could make but eighteen pence in money, the other barrell he spent and sold out the said raisins by the pound weight of wich he made in all a mark or thereabouts And lastly this deponent saieth that he hath not nor had in his custody nor in the custody of any other to his use any more or other of the goods or provisions of or belonging to the said shipp.

Robert Rawlin of Waddon aforesaid Mason deposed saieth that he was uppon the beech all three next dayes together after that the shipp called the Golden Grape was cast away where in all he had about halfe a pecke of raisins of the sunne given unto him (but by whome he knoweth not) wich he caryed home to his house and hath since spent the same, and that he did there alsoe finde in a paper about fower score needells wich he likewise caried home with him And that he hath not nor had in his custody nor in the custody of any other to his use any more or other of the goods or provisions of or belonging to the said shipp.

66

John Rawlin of Waddon aforesaid Mason deposed saieth that uppon the next day after the shipp called the Golden Grape was cast away uppon the beech he went thither where he tooke seaven pieces of Spanish coine wich he exchanged with Susan Keat of Abbotsbury for about tenn or eleaven shillinges wich money this deponent spent on her house being an olde house And that he hath not nor had any more or other of the goods or provisions of or belonging to the said shipp save only about halfe a peck of raisins of the sunne wich were given to this deponent by one of Abbotsbury whose name he knoweth not.

William Hendey servant to William Farre of Shilvinghampton in the said county of Dorsett yeoman deposed saieth that uppon the next day after that the shipp called the Golden Grape was cast away uppon the beech he went thither where he tooke up certain loose fruit and some other fruit out of a barrell in all about halfe a barrell wich he putt into a bagge that he had there with him and caryed home to his said Masters house where this deponent putt parte of the same fruit intohis celler and part in his said Masters barne uppon the floor there And this deponent further saieth that

66R

he did then alsoe there take up a smale peice of a rope parte of the cordage of the said shipp And that he hath not nor had in his owne custody nor in the custody of any other to his use any more or other of the goods or provisions of or belonging to the said shipp.

Robert Battin of Waddon aforesaid husbandman deposed saieth that uppon the next day after that the shipp called the Golden Grape was cast away uppon the beech he went thither where he this deponent and Agnes Battin his sister did save two barrells of raysins of the sunne wich Richard Halston of Corton did cary home for them in Mr. Stockers plough And this deponent further saieth that he sold the barrell of raisins wich he had unto Mr. Richard Yardley that married Mistres Perkins daughter of Dorchester for thirty shillinges, but doth not know what his said sister hath donn with the other barrell that was hers or how she hath disposed thereof. And that he hath not nor had in his custody nor in the custody of any other to his use any more or other of the goods or provisions of or belonging to the said shipp.

67

Deposicons taken at Melcomb Regis aforesaid the seventh day of February in the year before named before us whose names are subscribed by virtue of the commissioners before expressed Francis Cape notary public being then also

present.

Richard Samwayes of Portsham aforesaid husbandman deposed saieth that uppon the next day after that the shipp called the Golden Grape was cast away upon the beech he went thither in the company of Henry Mills of Portsham aforesaid, where this deponent took up and saved a murderer belonging to the said shipp, wich he putt into a boat there and caryed to Fleet to the house of Magdalen Allin widow, and there left the same, where it yett remaines And that he then took up a certaine quantity of loose fruit there wich he putt into his pocketts and caried home with him And that he hath not nor had in his custody nor in the custody of any other to his use any other or more of the goods of or belonging to the said shipp.

Edward Baily servant unto Samuell Tackle of Waymouth aforesaid baker deposed saieth that the next

67R

day after that the shipp called the Golden Grape was cast away upon the beech he went thither with Nicholas Preston his fellow servant where they together with the said Samuell Tackle their Master did save three barrells of raysins of the sunn wich they did putt into a boat and cary to Waymouth to his said Masters house where they doe now remaine And that this deponent hath not nor had in his custody nor in the custody of any other to his use any more or other of the goods or provisions of or belonging to the said shipp.

Alice Williams the wife of William Williams of Waymouth aforesaid saylor deposed saieth that upon the Tuesday next after the shipp called the Golden Grape was cast away she went to a place called the New=works neer to the said beech where she tooke out of a barrell that Walter Bonds boy of Waymouth aforesaid had opened about six pounds and halfe of raisins of the sunne, wich she hath since spent and given away, and that she then tooke up certaine peices of iron weighing about tenn pounds and halfe and a board being a peice of the cabbin of the said shipp wich she caryed home with her And that she hath not nor had in his custody nor in the custody of any other to her use any more or other of the goods or provisions of or belonging to the said shipp.

68

John Pount of Waymouth aforesaid sailor deposed saieth that the next day after the shipp called the Golden Grape was cast away upon the beech he went thither in the company of Joane the wife of Roger Chipp and Ann the wife of Ralph Locke and of Alice this deponents daughter where they did save out of the said shipp eight barrells of raisins of the sunn, wich they putt uppon the beech and leaving the same in the custody of Robert Smyth of Waymouth went home to Waymouth that night; And that the next morning they returned thither againe, whither upon they came all the said barrells and fruit were caryed away but by whome this deponent knoweth not And this deponent futher saieth that he then tooke out of a peice of a barrell about seaventeen or eighteen pounds of raisins of the sunn wich he caryed home with him, and hath since spent And that he hath not nor had in his custody nor in the custody of any other to his use any more or other of the goods or provisions of or belonging to the said shipp.

Philip Ash of Waymouth aforesaid sailor deposed saieth that the next day after the shipp called the Golden

68R

Grape was cast away uppon the beech he went thither in the company of John Cotton, Peter Haught and others where they did take out of the said shipp and save thirteen barrells of the fruit of the sunn wich they caryed to Waymouth, whereof eight are in the custody of Richard Pitt, fower in the custody of William Dry and one in the custody of John Allen And that this deponent hath not nor had in his custody nor in the custody of any other to his use any more or other of the goods or provisions of or belonging to the said shipp.

Deposicons taken at Melcomb Regis aforesaid the eight day of February in the year before named before us whose names are subscribed by virtue of the commissioners before expressed Francis Cape notary public being then also present.

Robert Gawden of Portsham aforesaid husbandman deposed saieth that the next day after the shipp called the Golden Grape was cast away uppon the beech he went thither in the company of William Thresher

69

of Portsham aforesaid where they did save two barrells of raisins of the sunn one of wich this deponent had for his parte, wich he sold to Peter Ford of Abbotsbury for fower shillinges, the other barrell the said Thresher had. And this deponent further saieth that he did then alsoe save two other barrells of fruit one of wich was there taken from him by some that pretended right to the same but what their names are he knoweth not, the other he sold to Christopher Eyles of Portsham aforesaid for three shillings and six pence, wich money the said Eyles hath not yet payed to this deponent, And this deponent alsoe saieth that he then took up there a peice of a rope about a yard & halfe in length, and about a pecke of loose fruit, wich fruit he putt into a bagg and caryed home with him where he hath since spent the same And lastly this deponent saieth that he hath not nor had in his custody nor in the custody of any other to his use any more or other of the goods or provisions of or belonging to the said shipp.

Henry Williams of Shillvinghampton in the County of Dorsett aforesaid yeoman deposed saieth that

69R

the next day after the shipp called the Golden Grape was cast away uppon the beech he went thither where he tooke out of the said shipp and saved one barrell of fruit wich was taken from him but by whome he knoweth not. And that he bought there of certaine persons whose names he knoweth not about a peck of loose fruit, wich he caryed home with him and have since spent And that he hath not nor had in his custody nor in the custody of any other to his use any more or other of the goods or provisions of or belonging to that shipp.

Henry Russell of Portsham aforesaid sailor deposed saieth that the next day after the shipp called the Golden Grape was cast away uppon the beech he went thither in the company of Thomas Harden, John Laine, Bartholomew Crews, John Wills and the brother of the said Harden being all of Portsham aforesaid where they did save fowerteen barrells of raisins of the sunn, seaven of wich they delivered to William Lovell of Fleet, the other seaven they divided between them, three of wich are on the possession of John Wills of Chickerell, two the said Harden his brother, and his man had between them, two barrells this deponent had, one of which he sold to Sir John Miller's man Abraham for two & thirty shillings, the other being broken and part

70

of the fruit taken out, this deponent tooke out the rest wich was about a bushel wich he caryed home to his house and hath since spent the same And that he hath not nor had in his custody nor in the custody of any other to his use any more or other of the goods or provisions of or belonging to the said shipp.

Deposicons taken at Melcomb Regis aforesaid the ninth day of February in the year before named before us whose names are subscribed by virtue of the commissioners before expressed Francis Cape notary public being then also present.

Richard Doby of the Isle of Portland aforesaid sailor deposed saieth that he went uppon the beech the same day that the ship called the Golden Grape was cast away where he saved about a pecke of raisins of the sunn wich he putt into a bagg and nineteen lymonds wich he caryed home with him; And that att another time he took upp a compasse belonging to the said shipp wich he hath now in his custody And that he hath not nor

70R

had in his custody nor in the custody of any other to his use any more or other of the goods or provisions of or belonging to the said shipp.

John Doby of the Isle of Portland aforesaid sailor deposed sayeth that he was uppon the beech the same day that the ship the Golden Grape was there cast away, where he in the company and by the help of others did save out of the said shipp eight and twenty bolts of silke and certaine peeces of plate, but how many there were of them he knoweth not, wich were shortly after delivered to the Viceadmirall. And this deponent further saieth that he did then allsoe take up and save a smale peice of silke about two or three yards in length wich he did deliver unto Christopher Gibbs of the said Island, And that he then alsoe saved about a peck of raisins of the sunn and two jarres of oyle wich he hath still in his custody and is ready to deliver And that this deponent hath not nor had in his custody nor in the custody of any other to his use any other or more of the goods or provisions of or belonging to the said shipp.

Robert Benvile of the Isle of Portland aforesaid mason deposed saieth

71

that the same day that the ship called the Golden Grape was there cast away uppon the beech he went thither where he amongst others did save out of the said shipp two bagges of silver plate, a pegg of silver, and eight and twenty bolts of silke wich were delivered to Christopher Gibbs of the said Island And that this deponent did then allsoe save two jarres of oile and about a peck of raisins of the sunne wich he caryed to his owne house and hath in his owne custody And that he hath not in his custody nor in the custody of any other to his use any more or other of the goods or provisions of or belonging to the said shipp.

Christopher Gibbs of the Isle of Portland aforesaid mason deposed saieth that the same day that the ship called the Golden Grape was cast away uppon the beech he went thither where he amongst divers others did save out of the said shipp thirty bolts of silke one bagg of silver plate conteyning one and twenty peices, one other bagg of silver plate conteining fower and twenty peices, and a pegg of silver, fower and twenty of wich bolts of silke with all the said plate and the bagg of silver were delivered to Mr Viceadmirall, fower of the said bolts are in the custody of

71R

Mr. William Strode in Portland Castle the other two peices or bolts of silke are in the custody of Richard Gilbert of the said island. And this deponent hath att present in his custody a short peice of silke about two yards in length And that he hath not in his custody nor in the custody of any other to his use any more or other of the goods or provisions of or belonging to the said shipp.

James Benvile of the Isle of Portland aforesaid mason deposed saieth that he was present with Christopher Gibbs of the said island uppon the beech att the saving of the plate and other goods expressed in the deposicon of the said Christopher Gibbs out of the shipp the Golden Grape And that this deponent did then allsoe save about halfe a bushell of raisins of the sunne, a jarre of oyle and a muskett wich he is ready to deliver And that he hath not in his custody nor in the custody of any other to his use any more or other of the goods or provisions of or belonging to the said shipp.

Percivall Hendey of the Isle of Portland aforesaid sailor deposed saieth that he was present uppon the beech with Christopher Gibbs of the said island and his company at the saving of the plate and other goods out of the shipp the Golden Grape wich

72

are expressed in the deposicon of the said Christopher Gibbs And that this deponent did then alsoe save one capp, two old coats, and two jarres of oyle wich he hath in his custody And that he hath not in his custody nor in the custody of any other to his use any more or other of the goods or provisions of or belonging to the said shipp.

Edward Doby of the Isle of Portland aforesaid sailor deposed sayeth that he was present uppon the beech with Christopher Gibbs of the said island att the saving of the plate and other goods out of the shipp the Golden Grape wich are expressed in the deposicon of the said Christopher Gibbs And that this deponent did then alsoe take up about a pecke of loose raisins of the sunne and tenn lymonds And that he hath not in his custody nor in the custody of any other to his use any more or other of the goods or provisions of or belonging to the said shipp.

Robert Peirce of the Isle of Portland aforesaid mason deposed sayeth that he was present uppon the beech with Christopher Gibbs of the said island att the saving of the plate and other goods

72R

out of the shipp called the Golden Grape wich are expressed in the deposicon of the said Christopher Gibbs And that this deponent did then alsoe take up about a yard of silke and halfe a pecke of raisins of the sunne wich he hath in his custody. And that he hath not in his custody nor in the custody of any other to his use any more or other of the goods or provisions of or belonging to the said shipp.

John Pierce of the said Isle of Portland mason deposed saieth that he was present uppon the beech with Christopher [Gibbs] of the said island and his company att the saving of the plate and other goods out of the shipp called the Golden Grape menconed and expressed in the said Gibbs his deposicon And that he hath not in his custody nor in the custody of any other to his use any more or other of the goods or provisions of or belonging to the said shipp.

John Elliott of the Isle of Portland aforesaid mason deposed saieth that he was present with the said Christopher Gibbs and his company uppon the beech att the saving of the severall goods and peices of plate out of the shipp called the Golden

Grape menconed and expressed in the deposicon of the said

73

Christopher Gibbs And that this deponent did then alsoe take up and save one jarre of oyle, a cloak, a cartridge of powder and about halfe a bushell of loose raisins of the sunne wich he hath in his custody And that he hath not in his custody nor in the custody of any other to his use any more or other of the goods or provisions of or belonging to the said shipp.

Alexander Attwooll of the Isle of Portland aforesaid mason deposeth saieth that he was present uppon the beech with the said Christopher Gibbs and his company att the saving of the plate and other goods out of the shipp called the Golden Grape menconed and expressed in the deposicon of the said Gibbs And that this deponent did then alsoe take up and save a peice of silke about two or three yards in length two jarres of oyle and a smale quantity of loose raisins of the sunne And that Robert Attwooll this deponents sonne did then alsoe take up about a peck of raisins of the sunne wich are in the custody of this deponent And this deponent saieth that he hath not in his custody nor in the custody of any other to his use any more or other of the goods or provisions of or belonging to the said shipp.

73R

John Elliott the younger of the Isle of Portland aforesaid mason deposed saieth that he was present uppon the beech with the said Christopher Gibbs and his company att the saving of the plate and other goods menconed in the said Gibbs his deposicon out of the shipp called the Golden Grape And this deponent did then allsoe take up one smale silver cupp wich he how delivereth and one pewter pott, a yard of silke or thereabouts, an old coat, an old paire of stockins, a bible, and about halfe a bushell of raisins of the sunne wich he hath in his custody And that he hath not in his custody nor in the custody of any other to his use any more or other of the goods or provisions of or belonging to the said shipp.

Robert Attwooll of the Isle of Portland aforesaid mason deposed saieth that uppon the same day that the shipp called the Golden Grape was cast away uppon the beech he went thither where he tooke up a jarre of oile and about halfe a bushell of raisins of the sunne wich he caryed home to his house And that he hath not in his custody nor in the custody of any other to his use any more or other of the goods or provisions of or belonging to the said shipp.

William Sweet thelder [the elder] of the Isle of Portland aforesaid mason deposed saieth that

74

he was uppon the beech the same day that the shipp called the Golden Grape was cast away where he did save two paire of old breeches two shirts and a smale quantity of raisins of the sunne wich he caried home with him to his house And that he hath not in his custody nor in the custody of any other to his use any more or other of the goods or provisions of or belonging to the said shipp.

William Sweet the younger of the Isle of Portland aforesaid mason deposed saieth, that upon the same day that the shipp called the Golden Grape was cast away uppon the beech he went thither where one bolt of silke wich was presently taken from him by Maximilian Mohun of Fleet esquire, and this deponent did then allsoe save one jarre of oyle and about a bushell of raisins of the sunne And that he hath not in his owne custody nor in the custody of any other to his use any more or other of the goods or provisions of or belonging to the said shipp.

Robert James of the Isle of Portland aforesaid labourer deposed

74R

saieth that he was uppon the beech when the shipp called the Golden Grape was cast away where he did take up and save about halfe a bushell of raisins of the sunne and three jarres of oyle wich he caryed home with him, one of wich jarres he hath sithence sold to Mrs. Strode of Portland Castle for two shillinges, parte of another he sold to Ann Benvile widow for fifteen pence, and the rest he hath spent And that he hath not nor had in his custody nor in the custody of any other to his use any more or other of the goods or provisions of or belonging to the said shipp.

William Housely of the Isle of Portland aforesaid mason deposed saieth that uppon the same day that the shipp called the Golden Grape was cast away uppon the beech he went thither where he did take up and save two jarres of oile and about a pecke of loose fruit, and two empty cartridges wich are still in his custody And that he hath not nor had in his custody nor in the custody of any other to his use any more or other of the goods or provisions of or belonging to that shipp.

Richard Peirce of the Isle of Portland aforesaid mason deposed sayeth that the next day after the shipp called the Golden Grape was cast away uppon the beech he went thither where he together with William Wiggott

75

and Samuel Painter of the said Island did save one barrell of raysins of the sunne, wich they brake upp and divided between them, of wich this deponent had about halfe a bushell to his parte And that he hath not nor had in his custody nor in the custody of any other to his use any more or other of the goods or provisions of or belonging to the said shipp.

Zackell Spurling of the Isle of Portland aforesaid mason deposed saieth that uppon the same day that the shipp called the Golden Grape was cast away uppon the beech he went thither where he did take up and save a jarre of oyle and about halfe a bushell of raisins of the sunne wich he took out of a barrell, wich goods he hath since spent but wilbe answerable for the value of the same And that he hath not nor had in his custody nor in the custody of any other to his use any more or other of the goods or provisions of or belonging to the said shipp.

Josias Portland of the Isle of Portland aforesaid mason deposed saieth that the same day that the shipp called the Golden Grape was cast away uppon the beech he went thither where he tooke out of a

75R

barrell about twenty pounds of raisins of the sunne wich he hath since spent in his house, but will be lyable to pay the valew of them. And that he hath not in his custody nor in the custody of any other to his use any more or other of the goods or provisions of or belonging to the said shipp.

Deposicons taken at Melcomb Regis aforesaid the eleventh day of February in the year before named before us whose names are subscribed by virtue of the commissioners before expressed Francis Cape notary public being then also present.

Andrew Attwooll of the Isle of Portland aforesaid sailor deposed saieth, that uppon the same day that the shipp called the Golden Grape was cast away uppon the beech he went thither where he take up and save about a barrell of raisins of the sunne wich he caryed home with him And that he hath not in his custody nor in the custody of any other to his use any other or more of the goods or provisions of or belonging to the said shipp.

Symon Barrett of the Isle of Portland aforesaid labourer deposed saieth that uppon the Monday next after the shipp called the Golden Grape was cast away uppon the beech he

76

went thither where he tooke up and saved about halfe a barrell of raisins of the sunne wich he caryed home with him And he hath not nor had in his custody nor in the custody of any other to his use any more or other of the goods or provisions of or belonging to that shipp.

Owen Lano of the Isle of Portland aforesaid yeoman deposed saieth that uppon the next day after that the shipp called the Golden Grape was cast away uppon the beech he went thither where he tooke up and saved about a pecke of raisins of the sunne wich he caryed home with him. And the next day he went thither againe where he together with the gunner of the said ship, Robert Wiggott, Owen Peirce, Benjamin

Peirce, Robert Flew, William Jennings, Edward Peirce, Zachell Jennings and Robert Byatt of the said island did save three barrells of raisins of the sunne of wich the said gunner had one whole one to his part the other two were divided between this deponent and the persons before named And that this deponent hath not nor had in his owne custody or in the custody of any other to his use any more or other of the goods or provisions of or belonging to the said shipp.

Abell Flew of the Isle of Portland aforesaid mason deposed saieth that upon the Monday next after that the shipp called the Golden Grape was cast away upon

76R

the beech he went thither where he did take out of a barrell about a pecke of raisins of the sunne wich he caryed home with him And that he hath not nor had in his custody nor in the custody of any other to his use any more or other of the goods or provisions of or belonging to that shipp.

John Flew of Portland aforesaid sailor deposed saieth that the same day that the shipp called the Golden Grape was cast away upon the beech he went thither where he did save and take up about halfe a bushell of raisins of the sunne wich he caryed home with him. And that the day following he went thither againe where he tooke up about a pecke and halfe of the like fruit wich he likewise caryed home with him And that he hath not nor had in his custody nor in the custody of any other to his use any more or other of the goods or provisions of or belonging to that shipp.

Owen Attwooll of the Isle of Portland aforesaid saylor deposed saieth that the same day that the shipp called the Golden Grape was cast away upon the beech he went thither where he tooke out of a barrell about halfe a bushell of raisins of the sunne wich he caryed home with him. And that he went thither againe another time and then tooke up about a pecke of raisins of the sunne wich he likewise caryed home to his house and hath since spent the same And that he hath not nor had in his custody nor in the custody of any other to

77

his use any more or other of the goods or provisions of or belonging to that shipp.

Thomas Wiggott of the Isle of Portland aforesaid taylor deposed saieth that the next day after that the shipp called the Golden Grape was cast away upon the beech he went thither in the company of Samuel Painter and Richard Peers of the said Island where they did save one barrell of raisins of the sunne wich they caryed home and divided between them And that the day following being Monday this deponent went thither againe where he bought of Philipp Benvile of the said island another barrell of raisins of the sunne for wich this deponent payed fower shillings wich he caryed home and divyded with John Stone of the said island whose horse this deponent had borrowed to cary the said barrell on, the said Stone paying this deponent halfe the money payed for the same And that this deponent hath not nor had any more or other of the goods or provisions of or belonging to that shipp.

Thomas Stoodleigh of the Isle of Portland aforesaid mason deposed saieth that uppon the next day after that the shipp called the Golden Grape was cast away uppon the beech he went

77R

thither where he tooke out of a barrell about a bushell of raisins of the sunne wich he caried home with him And that he hath not nor had any more or other of the goods or provisions of or belonging to that shipp.

Abraham Stoodleigh of the Isle of Portland aforesaid mason deposed sayeth that the next day after the shipp called the Golden Grape was cast away uppon the beech he went thither where he tooke out of a barrell about a bushell and halfe of raisins of the sunne wich he then caried home with him And that he hath not nor had in his custody nor in the custody of any other to his use any more or other of the goods or provisions of or belonging to that shipp.

Angell Stoodleigh of the Isle of Portland aforesaid mason deposed saieth that the next day after that the shipp called the Golden Grape was cast away uppon the beech he went thither where att two several times he did take up and save about a bushell of raisins of the sunne wich he caried home with him And that he hath not nor had in his custody nor in the custody of any other to his use any more or other of the goods or provisions of or belonging to the said shipp.

78

Thomas Stoodleigh of the Isle of Portland aforesaid mason deposed saieth that uppon the next day after that the shipp the Golden Grape was cast away uppon the beech he went thither where he tooke upp and saved out of a barrell about a pecke and halfe of raisins of the sunne wich he caried home with him And that he hath not nor had any more or other of the goods or provisions of that shipp.

Samuel Painter of the Isle of Portland aforesaid mason deposed saieth that the next day after that the shipp the Golden Grape was cast away he went upon the beech in the company of Thomas Wiggott and Richard Peirce of the said Island where they saved one barrell of raisins of the sunne wich they divided between them And that this deponent hath not nor had in his custody nor in the custody of any other to his use any more or other of the goods or provisions of or belonging to that shipp.

William Benvile of the Isle of Portland aforesaid sailor deposed saieth that uppon the Monday after that the shipp called the Golden Grape was cast away uppon the beech he went thither together with some other company in a boat where

Philipp Benvile and some others of that island having saved twelve barrells of raisins of the sunne did put six of them into the said wich this deponent & his said company did cary in the said boat unto Portland Castle where they left the same in the custody of Mr Fortune the porter of the said castle, the other six barrells were delivered unto Walter Bond of Waymouth And that this deponent hath not nor any of the goods or provisions att all belonging to the said shipp.

Philipp Benvile of the Isle of Portland aforesaid sailor deposed saieth that the next day after the shipp called the Golden Grape was cast away uppon the beech he went thither where he with seaven others of the said island in his company did save twelve barrells of raisins of the sunne. Sixe of wich Walter Bond of Waymouth received and had from them, the other sixe are in the custody of Mr Fortune the porter of Portland Castle, And that this deponent did then alsoe save one other barrell of raisins of the sunne wich he sold to Thomas Wiggott of the said island for three shillings and tennpence And that this deponent hath not nor had in his custody nor in the custody of any other to his use any more or other of the goods or provisions of or belonging to the said shipp.

79

Richard Benvile of the Isle of Portland aforesaid sailor deposed saieth that he was in the company of the before named Philip Benvile and did help save the twelve barrells of raisins of the sunne expressed in the deposicon of the said Philipp Benvile wich were disposed of as the said Philip Benvile hath in his said deposicon declared And that this deponent did att the same time alsoe save about a pecke and a halfe of raisins of the sunne wich he caried home to his owne house And that he hath not nor had in his owne custody nor in the custody of any other to his use any more or other of the goods or provisions of or belonging to the said shipp the Golden Grape.

Joell Hynde of the Isle of Portland aforesaid sailor deposed saieth that he was uppon the beach in the company of Philip Benvile and did help save out of the shipp the Golden Grape the twelve barrells of raisins of the sunne in the said Benviles deposicon menconed wich were disposed of as the said Benvile hath in his said deposicon expressed And that this deponent hath not nor had any more or other of the goods or provisions of or belonging to that shipp.

Robert Newcome of the Isle

of Portland aforesaid husbandman deposed saieth that he was uppon the beach in the company of Phillip Benvile and did helpe save out of the shipp the Golden Grape the twelve barrells of raisins of the sunne mencoed in the deposicon of the said Benvile wich were in such manner disposed of as the said Benvile hath deposed And that this deponent hath not nor had any more or other of the goods or provisions of that shipp.

William Comben of the Isle of Portland aforesaid sailor deposed saieth that he was uppon the beach in the company of Philip Benvile where he did helpe save out of the shipp the Golden Grape the twelve barrells of raisins of the sunne menconed by the said Benvile in his deposicon wich were disposed of in such manner as the said Benvile hath deposed And that this deponent hath not nor had any more or other of the goods or provisions of that shipp.

Andrew Comben of the Isle of Portland aforesaid husbandman deposed saieth that he was uppon the beach in the company of Philip Benvile where he did helpe save out of the shipp called the Golden Grape the twelve barrells of raisins of the sunne menconed by the said Benvile in his deposicon wich were disposed of in such manner

80

as the said Benvile hath deposed And that this deponent did then alsoe take up and save about a pecke of loose raisins of the sunne wich he caried home to his house And that he hath not nor had any more or other of the goods or provisions of or belonging to that shipp.

Philip Owfley of the Isle of Portland aforesaid mason deposed sayeth that he was uppon the beach in the company of Philip Benvile and did helpe save out of the shipp called the Golden Grape the twelve barrells of raisins of the sunne by the said Benvile menconed in his deposicon wich were disposed of as the said Benvile hath before declared And that this deponent hath not nor had any more or other of the goods or provisions of or belonging to the said shipp.

John Comben of the Isle of Portland aforesaid husbandman deposed saieth that he was uppon the beach in the company of Philip Benvile at the saving of the twelve barrells fruit by him in his deposicon menconed wich were disposed of as the said Benvile hath before declared And that this deponent hath not nor had any more or other of the goods or provisions of or belonging to that shipp.

80R

Bartholomew Comben of the Isle of Portland aforesaid husbandman deposed saieth that uppon the Monday after that the shipp called the Golden Grape was cast away uppon the beech he went thither where he took up about a pecke of raisins of the sunne wich he caryed home with him And that he hath not nor had any more or other of the goods or provisions of or belonging to that shipp.

Giles Peirce of the Isle of Portland aforesaid sailor deposed saieth that he was not att all neer the shipp called the Golden Grape neither hath he any of the goods or provisions of that shipp, only this deponents wife being there did help cary home raysins of the sunn for her father in law Robert Byett to his house in Portland aforesaid.

Edward Peirce of the Isle of Portland sailor deposed saieth that upon the same day that the shipp called the Golden Grape was cast away uppon the beech where he with the helpe of Owen Lano, of the said island, and others did save two barrells of raisins of the sunn one of wich Walter Bond of Waymouth had from them, the other they divided between them And that this deponent hath not nor had in his owne custody nor in the custody of any other to his use any more or other of the goods or provisions of or belonging to the said shipp.

81

William Pitt servant to Edward Owfley of the Isle of Portland aforesaid mason deposed saieth that the next day after that the shipp called the Golden Grape was cast away uppon the beech he went thither where he did save a smale quantity of wett fruit and two jarres of oile wich he caryed home and delivered to his said Master And that this deponent hath not nor had any more or other of the goods or provisions of or belonging to the said shipp.

Depositions taken at Melcomb Regis aforesaid the fourteenth day of February in the year before named before us whose names are subscribed by virtue of the commissioners before expressed Francis Cape notary public being then also present.

John Stone of the Isle of Portland aforesaid yeoman deposed saieth that he was not uppon the beech att all neer the place where the shipp the Golden Grape was cast away, neither hath he nor had he any of the goods or provisions of or belonging to that shipp save only a smale parcell of raisins of the sunne wich he bought of Thomas Wiggott of the said island for wich this deponent paid him two shillings

81R

William Jennings of the Isle of Portland aforesaid mason saieth that the same day that the shipp called the Golden Grape was cast away uppon the beech he went thither where he with seaven or eight others did save out of the said shipp three barrells of raisins of the sunne, one of wich Walter Bond, the Masters Mate and the Gunner of the said shipp tooke from them, the other two (whereof one was broken and not full) they shared between them And that this deponent did then alsoe take up and save neer about a pecke of loose fruit wich he caryed home with him And that he hath not nor had in his custody nor in the custody of any other to his use any more or other of the goods or provisions of or belonging to that shipp.

Richard Elliott of the Isle of Portland aforesaid sailer sayeth that the next day after that the shipp called the Golden Grape was cast away uppon the beech he went thither where he tooke up and saved about a pecke of raisins of the sunn wich he caryed home with him And that he hath not nor had any more or other of the goods or provisions of or belonging to the said shipp.

Alice Mathews the wife of Charles Mathews of the Isle of Portland aforesaid yeoman deposed saieth that the same day att night that

82

the shipp called the Golden Grape was cast away uppon the beech she went thither, where she did take up and saved about a pecke of loose fruit and two jarres of oyle a good parte of wich was leaked out, and two pounds of wooll or thereabouts wich she caried home with her, And that the next day after she went thither againe where she tooke up and saved about halfe a bushell more of loose fruit, wich she caryed home together with a wallett of fruit for the Porters boy of the Castle And that about a week after she bought for one Myms of the said island a jarre of oyle of Elizabeth Coles for wich this deponent payed her fower shillinges, wich jarre of oile together with a pound of the wooll or neer thereabouts she delivered unto the said Myms And that the other pound of wooll she sold to a stranger gentleman that came thither with Mr. John Allenn of Waymouth for two shillings and sixepence And lastly this deponent saieth that she hath not nor had in her custody nor in the custody of any other to her use any more or other of the goods or provisions of or belonging to the said shipp.

82R

Depositions taken at Melcomb Regis aforesaid the sixteenth day of February in the year before named before us whose names are subscribed by virtue of the commissioners before expressed Francis Cape notary public being then also present.

William Clerk of Abbotsbury in the said County of Dorsett yeoman deposed saieth that uppon the next day that the shipp called the Golden Grape was cast away uppon the beech he went thither where he tooke up and saved about halfe an hundred of loose fruit wich he putt into a bagge and caryed home with him uppon an horse And that the next day following he went thither againe where he saved and had five barrells of raisins of the sunne wich are now in his house, and wich he is ready to deliver And that he hath not nor had in his custody nor in the custody of any other to his use any more or other of the goods or provisions of or belonging to the said shipp.

Richard Rose of Abbotsbury aforesaid blacksmith deposed saieth that uppon the next day after that the shipp called the Golden Grape was cast away uppon the beech he went thither where he tooke up and saved a jarre of oile and about six pounds of loose raisins of the sunne wich he caried home with him And that uppon the day following he went thither againe where he bought and had of Jeffery Singer of Fleet three barrels of raisins of the sunne for wich this

83

deponent paid him fower shillings a barrell all wich this deponent hath att home in his house and is and will be ready to deliver. And that he hath not nor had in his custody nor in the custody of any other to his use any more or other of the goods or provisions of or belonging to the said shipp.

Jeffry Buck of Abbotsbury aforesaid roper deposed saieth that uppon the next day after that the shipp called the Golden Grape was cast away uppon the beech he went thither where he tooke up and saved about fower score pound weight of loose wett fruit wich this deponent caried to Waymouth and delivered to Mr John Senior for Mr. Viceadmirall who gave this deponent twenty pounds of the same backe againe And that this deponent hath not nor had in his custody nor in the custody of any other to his use any more or other of the goods or provisions of or belonging to the said shipp.

William Hellyer of Abbotsbury aforesaid sailor deposed saieth that uppon the same day that the shipp called the Golden Grape was cast away uppon the beech he went thither where he tooke upp and saved a barrell and a halfe of raisins of the sunn, three jarres of oyle, one of

83R

which was not full, two paire of bandeliers, and an horne halfe full of powder; And this deponent allsoe found uppon the beech one peice of eight and two smale peices of coine of the value of fifteen pence a peice or thereabouts All wich particulars save onely the money are in the custody of Mr Henry Garland this deponents Master And that this deponent hath not nor had in his custody nor in the custody of any other to his use any more or other of the goods or provisions of or belonging to the said shipp.

Marc Jolliff of Abbotsbury aforesaid yeoman deposed saieth that uppon the same day att night that the shipp called the Golden Grape was cast away uppon the beech he went thither where he together with William Newman, John Thresher and Nicholas Porter of Abbotsbury aforesaid did save six barrells of raisins of the sunne, wich raisins they tooke out of the said barrells and putt into sackes, wich they caryed to Abbotsbury aforesaid and there divyded the same between them, and those wich this deponent had for his parte are att home in his mothers house And this deponent alsoe saieth that he did then save two jarres of oile wich are likewise in his mothers house And that he hath not in his custody nor in the custody of any other to his use any more or other of the goods or provisions of or belonging to the said shipp.

84

William Hillary of Abbotsbury aforesaid husbandman deposed saieth that uppon the Munday after that the shipp the Golden Grape was cast away uppon the beech he went thither where he bought a barrell of raisins of the sunne by the meanes of Robert Tooledge of Fleet for wich this deponent was to pay five shillings, three shillings whereof he payed in hand, the other two shillings he hath yett in his custody, wich fruit he caryed home and sold to severall persons of wich he made in all about eight shillinges And that he hath not nor had any more or other of the goods or provisions of or belonging to the said shipp.

Thomas Evans of Abbotsbury aforesaid fisherman deposed saieth that uppon the same day that the shipp called the Golden Grape was cast away uppon the beech he went thither where he saved about the quantity of a barrell of raisins of the sunne which he thence tooke up loose and wett and two jarres of oile one of wich was but halfe full and that this deponent hath since spent the other remaines whole att his house And that uppon the decke of the said shipp this deponent found a little purse of money wherein he conceiveth there were about twenty peices of foraigne coine, wich he tooke up, but he saieth

84R

that one Joseph or James Gardner of Wyke Regis Robert Angell of the same place, Jeffry Thistle of Fleet and Thomas Puckett of Abbotsbury aforesaid tooke the same from this deponent by force leaving this deponent onely two of the said peices called testons wich he now delivereth to Mr. Arthur And that this deponent hath not nor had in his custody nor in the custody of any other to his use any more or other of the goods or provisions of or belonging to the said shipp.

William Doby of Abbotsbury aforesaid tailor deposed saieth that uppon the next day after that the shipp called the Golden Grape was cast away uppon the beech he went thither where he tooke up and saved a barrell of raisins of the sunne, and about fifty pounds of loose fruit of the same kinde wich was wett, wich he caried home with him, and afterwards sold the said barrell to Mr. John Michell of Kingston for sixe and twenty shillinges and eight pence And that this deponent hath not nor had any more or other of the goods or provisions of or belonging to the said shipp.

Walter Baily of Abbotsbury aforesaid fisherman deposed saieth that uppon the next day after that the shipp called the Golden Grape was cast away uppon the beech

85

he went thither where he saved a barrell of raisins of the sunn wich he broke open, took out the fruit, putt the same into bagges & soe caryed it home; where afterwards he sold the same to severall persons parte for two pence, and parte for three half pence the pound, but how much he made of it in all he knoweth not And this deponent hath not nor had any more or other of the goods or provisions of that shipp.

John Laverock one of the Porters of his Majestys Castle of the Isle of Portland deposed saieth that upon the same day that the shipp called the Golden Grape was cast away uppon the beech he went thither where he tooke up and saved three jarres of oile, and a certaine quantity of raisins of the sunn out of a barrell wich this deponent did put into the sleeves of his coat and soe cary home (his coat being much torne in striving to helpe save the goods of the said shipp) one of the jarres of oile this deponent delivered to one Mr Dowe of the said island, the other two remaine in the custody of this deponent And that this deponent hath not nor had in his custody nor in the custody of any other to his use any more or other of the goods or provisions of or belonging to the said shipp.

85R

William Newman of Abbotsbury aforesaid Inholder deposed saieth that upon the same day att night that the shipp called the Golden Grape was cast away uppon the beech he went thither where he tooke certaine raisins of the sunn out of two barrells wich he putt into sacks and caried home with him, where it yet remaines, And this deponent did then alsoe take up and save one jarre of oyle and about one hundred of lymons And that he hath not nor had in his custody nor in the custody of any other to his use any more or other of the goods or provisions of or belonging to the said shipp.

Nicholas Porter of Abbotsbury aforesaid channdler deposed saieth that upon the same day att night that the shipp called the Golden Grape was cast away uppon the beech he went thither in the company of Marc Joliff and others where they tooke up and saved five barrells of raisins of the sunne, wich they emptied into sacks and caried home uppon six horses, where they did divide the same between them, of wich this deponent had the thirteenth part, wich (as he conceiveth) are not full halfe an hundred weight but neer thereabouts And that upon the Monday following he went thither againe where he tooke up and saved about forty lymons and two peices of ropes belonging to that shipp wich he hath att home in his house And that this

86

deponent hath not nor had in his custody nor in the custody of any other to his use any more or other of the goods or provisions of or belonging to the said shipp.

Thomas Puckett of Abbotsbury aforesaid fisherman deposed saieth that upon the Monday after that the shipp the Golden Grape was cast away uppon the beech he went thither where he tooke up and saved about an hundred weight of wett fruit, wich he hath att home in his house save only a smale quantity thereof wich his children have eaten And that he hath not nor had in his custody nor in the custody of any other to his use any more or other of the goods or provisions of or belonging to the said shipp.

John Pollard of Abbotsbury aforesaid husbandman deposed saieth that he was not uppon the beech att all or after the shipp the Golden Grape was there cast away but saieth that Thomas Miller this deponents servant went thither twice, and brought thence att those two severall tymes about two bushells of wett raisins of the sunne, all wich are in this deponents house save onely some smale quantity thereof wich this deponents children have since eaten, and wich this deponent hath since spent in his house

86R

And this deponents said servant did allsoe bring to this deponents house a bottle of wyne conteyning about two quarts wich he saved out of the said shipp. And that this deponent hath not nor had in his custody nor in the custody of any other to his use any more or other of the goods or provisions of or belonging to the said shipp.

John Durdant of Abbotsbury aforesaid carpenter deposed saieth that the next day after that the shipp called the Golden Grape was cast away upon the beech he went thither with his brother William Durdant where they saved eight barrells of raisins of the sunne, one of wich in cariage homewards fell downe in the dirt wherewith it was wett and allmost spoiled, wich is since spent, and that one of the other barrells was not quite full, wich this deponent hath in his custody together with the other sixe barrells, and wich he is and will be ready, to deliver And that this deponent hath not nor had in his custody nor in the custody of any other to his use any more or other of the goods or provisions of or belonging to the said shipp.

William Durdant of Abbotsbury aforesaid fisherman deposed saieth that he was present uppon the beech with John Durdant his brother and did help save out of the shipp called the Golden Grape the goods expressed in the said John Durdant his deposicon And

87

that this deponent hath not nor had in his custody nor in the custody of any other to his use any more or other of the goods or provisions of or belonging to the said shipp.

John Pymer of Abbotsbury aforesaid fisherman deposed saieth that uppon the same day that the shipp called the Golden Grape was cast away uppon the beech he went thither where he tooke up and saved a barrell of raisins of the sunn, some smale quantity of loose fruit, two jarres of oyle, about thirty or forty lymons, an old bedsacke, and about a pound or two of wooll wich he hath in his custody and is and wilbe ready to deliver And that this deponent hath not nor had in his custody nor in the custody of any other to his use any more or other of the goods or provisions of or belonging to the said shipp.

Ralph Miller of Abbotsbury aforesaid husbandman deposed saieth that uppon the same day that the shipp called the Golden Grape was cast away uppon the beech he went thither where he tooke up and saved a barrell of raisins of the sunne, two jarres of oyle and some smale quantity of loose fruit wich he hath at home in his

87R

house and is and will be ready to deliver And that he hath not nor had in his custody nor in the custody of any other to his use any more or other of the goods or provisions of or belonging to the said shipp.

John Wallbridge of Abbotsbury aforesaid husbandman deposed saieth that upon the same day that the shipp the Golden Grape was cast away uppon the beech he went thither where he saved a barrell of raisins of the sunn wich he hath att home in his house and it is and wilbe ready to deliver And that he hath not nor had any more or other of the goods or provisions of that shipp.

William Hardey of Abbotsbury aforesaid husbandman deposed saieth that upon the same day that the shipp the Golden Grape was cast away uppon the beech he went thither where he tooke out of a barrell about an hundred pound weight of raisins of the sunne, and that there he tooke up alsoe a jarre of oyle, and about twelve or fowerteen lymons wich this deponents boy caryed home to his house And that this deponent hath not nor had any more or other of the goods or provisions of or belonging to the said shipp.

88

William Critchell of Abbotsbury aforesaid labourer deposed saieth that upon the next day after that the shipp the Golden Grape was cast away uppon the beech he went thither where he tooke and saved an hundred and seaventeen pounds of raisins of the sunn, wich he hath since delivered to Mr. John Senior of Waymouth, who thereuppon gave this deponent seaventeen pounds of the same fruit backe againe And this deponent saieth that he hath not nor had any more or other of the goods or provisions of or belonging to that shipp.

Angell Wood of Abbotsbury aforesaid husbandman deposed saieth that the next day after that the shipp called the Golden Grape was cast away uppon the beech he went thither where he saved a barrell of raisins of the sunn that had taken wett, wich he caryed home with him, and sold parte of that fruit for fowerteen shillinges, another parte thereof he hath spent, the remainder is in his house wich he is ready to deliver And that he hath not nor had any more or other of the goods or provisions of or belonging to the said shipp.

John Gibbons of Abbotsbury aforesaid fisherman deposed saieth that the

88R

next morning after the shipp called the Golden Grape was cast away uppon the beech he went thither where he tooke up and saved a certaine quantity of raisins of the sunn wich he caryed home and putt into three barrells, where they yett remaine, And that he then tooke up allsoe about twelve lymons And that he hath not nor had any more or other of the goods or provisions of or belonging to that shipp.

Hugh Boatson of Abbotsbury aforesaid fisherman deposed saieth that the same day that the shipp called the Golden Grape was cast away uppon the beech he went thither where he tooke up and saved three barrells of fruit, and certaine quantity of loose fruit, wich loose fruit he hath since spent, but the three barrells doe yett remaine whole in his custody wich he is and wilbe ready to deliver And that he hath not nor had any more or other of the goods or provisions of or belonging to the said shipp.

John Olliver of Abbotsbury aforesaid saylor deposed saieth that the same day that the shipp called the Golden Grape was cast away uppon the beech he went thither and soe aboard the said shipp from whence he took and saved two peices of silkes, wich he hath in his custody and is ready to deliver And that then he tooke up alsoe about forty seaven pounds of raisins of the sunn wich he hath allready deliver to Mr John

89

Senyor of Waymouth And that he hath not nor had in his custody nor in the custody of any other to his use any more or other of the goods or provisions of or belonging to the said shipp.

John Keat of Abbotsbury aforesaid fisherman deposed saieth that upon the same day that the shipp the Golden Grape was cast away uppon the beech he went thither and soe aboard the said shipp where he tooke up and saved about an hundred pound weight of fruit, a jarre of oile, and about thirty lymons, wich fruit he hath since sold for five shillings, and parte of the oyle he hath spent, the remainder is att home in his house in the said jarre And that he hath not nor had in his custody nor in the custody of any other to his use any more or other of the goods or provisions of or belonging to the said shipp.

Henry Bradford of Abbotsbury aforesaid husbandman deposed saieth that uppon the next day after the shipp the Golden Grape was cast away uppon the beech he went thither where he tooke upp and saved a certaine quantity of loose fruit wich he caried home with him and hath since spent And that he hath not nor had any more or other of the goods or provisions of or belonging to that shipp.

89R

Thomas Thistle of Abbotsbury aforesaid deposed saieth that the next day after the shipp called the Golden Grape was cast away uppon the beech he went thither where he tooke up and saved a barrell of raisins of the wich he caryed home, and (it being wett) emptyed the fruit out of the said barrell and sold the same for sixe and twenty shillings And that he hath not nor had any more or other of the goods or provisions of or belonging to the said shipp.

Stephin Hansford of Abbotsbury aforesaid husbandman deposed saieth that the next day after the shipp called the Golden Grape was cast away uppon the beech he went thither where he tooke up out of a barrell certaine raisins of the sunne wich he caryed home to his house, & hath since sold parte of thenm for fifteen shillings and fower pence, parte of the same (vizt) about halfe a bushell he hath spent in his house, and the remainder being about a pecke he hath yett in his custody And that he hath not nor had any more or other of the goods or provisions of or belonging to that shipp.

William Mallett of Abbotsbury aforesaid fisherman deposed saieth that the same day that the shipp called the Golden Grape was cast away uppon the beech he went thither where he tooke up and saved a certaine quantity of loose fruit, and a jarre of oile, wich oile this deponent sold to one whose name he knoweth not for

90

six shillinges, and parte of the said fruit to severall persons att the rate of two pence the pound for wich he received five shillings the residew thereof he hath spent And that he hath not nor had any more or other of the goods or provisions of or belonging to the said shipp.

Roger Ford of Abbotsbury aforesaid sailor deposed saieth that the Monday next after that the shipp called the Golden Grape was cast away uppon the beech he went thither where this deponent tooke up noething at all, but saieth that his sonne being then there did take up and save one barrell of raisins of the sunn, wich was taken from him by the country people, and about an hundred and halfe of loose fruit wich doe yet remaine in this deponents house And that this deponent hath not nor had any more or other of the goods or provisions of or belonging to the said shipp.

Peter Miller of Abbotsbury aforesaid fisherman deposed saieth that the next day after the shipp called the Golden Grape was cast away uppon the beech his sonn John Miller went thither where he tooke up and saved fower broken barrells of raisins of the sunn and a jarre of oyle wich he brought home to this deponents house, where his said sonn gave one of the said barrells unto three

90R

poore women wich helped him to save the same, the other three together with the said jarre of oile are att this deponents house wich he is and will be ready to deliver And that this deponent hath not nor had any more or other of the goods or provisions of or belonging to the said shipp.

Deposicons taken at Melcomb Regis aforesaid the eighteenth day of February in the year before named before us whose names are subscribed by virtue of the commissioners before expressed Francis Cape notary public being then also present.

William Burges of Abbotsbury aforesaid husbandman deposed saieth that the same day that the shipp called the Golden Grape was cast away uppon the beech he went thither with William Purchas of Abbottsbury aforesaid baker where they did save two barrells of raisins of the sunn wich they divided between them And this deponent did then alsoe save fower jarres of oile, one of wich was broken, another he hath since spent, the other two he hath att his house, and two peices of smale ropes, an iron bolt, about twenty lymons and oringes & a smale quantity of loose fruit wich he caryed home in his pocquetts And that this

91

deponent hath not nor had in his custody nor in the custody of any other to his use any more or other of the goods or provisions of or belonging to the said shipp.

Henry May servant unto Mr. Weare of Portesham aforesaid deposed saieth that uppon the next day after that the shipp called the Golden Grape was cast away uppon the beech he together with John White his fellow servant went with two horses to the Fleet side neer the said beech where Nicholas Hall and John Gardiner of Abbotsbury brought over to them two barrells of raisins of the sunn, wich they there broke open and emptied the fruit into his bagges, and desired this deponent and his fellow servant to cary the same to Abbotsbury for them, wich they accordingly did, for wich the said Hall and Gardiner gave this deponent and the said White about a pecke of raysins apeice; and that this deponent gave away his parte of the same. And that he hath not nor had any more or other of the goods or provisions of or belonging to the said shipp.

John Whyte beforenamed deposed saieth that what is conteyned in the deposicon of the said Henry

91R

May his fellow servant is troue And that this deponent hath not nor had any more or other of the goods or provisions of or belonging to the said shipp.

Henry Mills of Portesham aforesaid sailor deposed saieth that the Munday next after that the shipp called the Golden Grape was cast away uppon the beech he went thither where he tooke up about a bushell and halfe of loose raisins of the sunn wich he putt into a bagg and caried home with him And that he hath not nor had any more or other of the goods or provisions of or belonging to the said shipp.

Thomas Puckett of Abbotsbury aforesaid sailor deposed saieth that the same day that the shipp called the Golden Grape was cast away uppon the beech he went thither where he tooke out of a broken barrell about halfe a bushell of wett raysins of the sunn wich he putt into a bagg and caryed home with him And that att the same time Thomas Evans of Abbotsbury aforesaid being on shippboard did there take up some money in a smale linine bagge, wich he putt into his capp, and gave this deponent two peices of the same wich are testons, and gave the like number to Thomas Pitt, Robert Angell, and another

92

man of Wike Regis whose name this deponent knoweth not, and that the said men of Wike Regis not therewith contented did there take away from the said Evans his capp and the rest of the said money, but how money there was this deponent knoweth not And this deponent further saieth that on the Monday following he went thither againe in the company of his father where they did take up about a bushell of wett fruit wich they putt into a bagg and caryed home with them And that this deponent hath not nor had any more or other of the goods or provisions of or belonging to the said shipp.

Thomas Selley of Portsham aforesaid husbandman deposed saieth that the next day after that the shipp called the Golden Grape was cast away uppon the beech he went thither, where he did take out of a barrell about halfe a pecke of raisins of the sunn wich he caryed home with him And that he hath not nor had any other or more of the goods or provisions of or belonging to the said shipp.

92R

John Wood of Portsham aforesaid labourer deposed saieth that the next day after that the shipp called the Golden Grape was cast away uppon the beech he went thither where he saved three barrells of raisins of the sunn, two of wich were taken from him by somemen of Waymouth whose names this deponent knoweth not, the other he sold there uppon the beech unto Mr. Sandford and Robert Phillipps of Portsham aforesaid for two shillings. And this deponent saieth that he being aboard the said ship did there take up a peice of silver wich (as he is told) is the quarter parte of a peice of eight, wich he hath in his custody and is ready to deliver And that he hath not nor had in his custody nor in the custody of any other to his use any more or other of the goods or provisions of or belonging to the said shipp.

John Thresher of Abbotsbury aforesaid husbandman deposed saieth that the same day at night that the shipp called the Golden Grape was cast away uppon the beech he went thither where he tooke out of a barrell wich was there delivered unto him by a stranger whose name he knoweth not about two hundred pound weight of raisins of the sunn wich this deponent putt into a sacke and caryed home with him wich he is ready to deliver or to make satisfaction

93

for the same And that this deponent hath not nor had in his custody nor in the custody of any other to his use any more or other of the goods or provisions of or belonging to the said shipp.

John Watercombe of Abbotsbury aforesaid husbandman deposed saieth that the same day that the shipp called the Golden Grape was cast away uppon the beech he went thither where he did help save sundry parcells of goods wich were then delivered unto John Pope of Waymouth, And this deponent did then also save about threescore pounds of loose fruit twenty pounds of wich he sold for eleven grotes and a penny, the rest he hath spent, and two jarres of oile wich he hath since sold for six shillinges, And one whole barrell of raisins of the sunne wich he caryed home and hath yett in his custody And lastly this deponent saieth that he hath not nor had in his custody nor in the custody of any other to his use any more or other of the goods or provisions of or belonging to the said shipp.

93R

Deposicons taken at Melcomb Regis aforesaid the twenty second day of February in the year before named before us whose names are subscribed by virtue of the commissioners before expressed Francis Cape notary public being then also present.

John Hasslewood of Langton Hering in the county of Dorset clerk examined saieth that for his owne particular he was not uppon the beech at all after the shipp the Golden Grape was cast away neither hath he nor had any of the goods or provisions belonging to that shipp; onely he saieth that Thomas Moregen his servant (as he hath been told) was there where he did help to save severall barrells of raisins of the sunn, but what became of them he knoweth not; from whence he did bring a smale quantity of loose fruit wich was wett, And further he saieth that his wife did buy of John Benvile of Langton aforesaid one barrell of raisins of the sunn for wich she payed him twelve shillings And that William Charles of that parish did shew unto him one peice of eight wich he said he found uppon the beech, and that the said Charles then said that he had one, two or three peices more.

94

Peter Ford of Abbotsbury aforesaid husbandman deposed saieth that the next day in the morning after that the shipp called the Golden Grape was cast away he went uppon the beech where he did helpe to save seaventeen barrells of raisins of the sunne, seaven of wich were delivered to Symon More of Waymouth, one was stollen away uppon the beech, all the rest are in the custody of this deponent, save onely one barrell, wich being very wett hath been opened and most parte of the fruit as he believeth spent About the saving of wich goods and carying the same to Abbotsbury this deponent hath expended the sume of forty eight shillings and eight pence, wich he doth desire may be allowed unto him, as alsoe for his paines in salving the same, and then he shall and will be ready to deliver all that he hath And lastly this deponent saieth that he hath not nor had in his custody nor in the custody of any other to his use any more or other of the goods or provisions of or belonging to the said shipp.

John Pitt of Abbotsbury aforesaid husbandman deposed sayeth

94R

that he was present upon the beech with Peter Ford att the saving of the severall goods out of the shipp called the Golden Grape menconed and expressed in the deposicon of the said Peter Ford And that this deponent hath not nor had any more or other of the goods or provisions of or belonging to that shipp.

John Michell of Chickerell in the county of Dorsett aforesaid husbandman deposed saieth that the same day that the shipp called the Golden Grape was cast away upon the beech he went thither where he together with Thomas Bryer of Chickerell aforesaid did save three barrells of raisins of the sunne, and fowre jarres of oile, two of wich barrells were taken and caryed away by John Buntin, William Buntin and John Goddard of the said parish of Chickerell, the other barrell and the oyle he hath yett in his custody and is ready to deliver the same And further this deponent saieth that he did then alsoe save another barrell of raisins wich having longe layen in the sea had taken wett and were little worth, wich he hath since disposed of and given away And that this deponent hath not nor had in his custody nor in the custody of any other to his use any more or other of the goods or provisions of that shipp.

95

Thomas Bryer of Chickerell aforesaid husbandman deposed saieth that he was upon the beech with John Michell att the saving of the severall goods out of the shipp called the Golden Grape menconed and expressed in the deposicon of the said Michell And that this deponent did then alsoe take up about twenty pounds of wett fruit wich he caried home with him, And that he hath not nor had any more or other of the goods or provisions of that shipp save only one barrell of raisins, that was brought into this deponents house and there left by one John Ferice of Upway.

William Bussell of Chickerell aforesaid husbandman deposed saieth that upon the next day after that the shipp called the Golden Grape was cast away upon the beech he went thither where he did take out of some broken barrells about halfe a pecke of raisins of the sunne, wich is all that he hath or had of the goods or provisions of or belonging to the said shipp; save only that he hath in his custody three barrells of raisins of the sunn wich were brought into his house and there left but by whome this deponent knoweth not.

95R

Nicholas Bussell of Chickerell aforesaid husbandman deposed saieth that uppon the same day that the shipp called the Golden Grape was cast away uppon the beech he went thither where he together with William Newman, Gedeon Marshalsea, Mathias Way and Edward Marshalsea did save two barrells of raisins of the sunne, wich they caryed to the house of Thomas Newman of Chickerell aforesaid there to be kept And this deponent further saieth that he being aboard the said shipp did there take up and save one bagg of Spanish coine, in wich he doth conceive there are about two hundred peices of eight wich he hath in his custody and is ready to deliver And that this deponent did helpe save another bagg of money wich is by his uncle Thomas Bussell allready delivered unto the Viceadmirall And this deponent further saieth that John Stevens of Chickerell aforesaid did then give unto this deponent a pound or more of wooll wich was saved out of the said shipp for wich this deponent did give unto the said Stevens three peices of silver out of the bage that this deponent saved. And lastly this deponent saieth that he hath not nor had in his custody nor in the custody of any other to his use any more or other of the goods or provisions of or belonging to the said shipp.

96

Edward Marshalsea of Chickerell aforesaid husbandman deposed saieth that he was presente with Nicholas Bussell and the rest menconed in his deposicon at the saving of the two barrells of raisins of the sunn out of the shipp called the Golden Grape wich are in the custody the said Thomas Newman And that this deponent did alsoe there save about halfe a pound of wooll and a paper book conteyning about three quire of paper And that he hath not nor had any more or other of the goods or provisions of or belonging to the said shipp.

John Buckland of Chickerell aforesaid husbandman deposed saieth that the next day after the shipp called the Golden Grape was cast away uppon the beech he went thither where he tooke up about a pecke of raisins and that Mary Curters his servant did then alsoe take up about halfe a pecke of loose raisins wich they caried to this deponents house And that he hath not nor had any more or other of the goods or provisions of that shipp.

William Bunting of Chickerell aforesaid husbandman deposed saieth that the same day att night

96R

that the shipp called the Golden Grape was cast away uppon the beech he went thither, where he with the helpe of Gedeon Marshalsea did save one barrell of raisins of the sunn, wich is in the custody of Mr. William Marshalsea of Chickerell aforesaid And that this deponent hath not nor had any other or more of the goods or provisions of that shipp.

John Bunting of Chickerell aforesaid husbandman deposed saieth that the same day att night that the shipp called the Golden Grape was cast away uppon the beech he went thither, where he with the helpe of Nicholas Dyker of Chickerell aforesaid did save nine barrells of raisins of the sunn, fowr of wich they delivered to William Lovell of Fleet, and fower more Walter Bond of Waymouth tooke from them, and left this deponent and the said Dyker but one barrell wich they divided between them And that this deponent hath not nor had any more or other of the goods or provisions of that shipp.

John Davye of Chickerell aforesaid husbandman deposed saieth that the next day after the shipp called the Golden Grape was cast away uppon the beech he went thither where he tooke up and saved about a peck of loose raisins of the sunn And that

97

he hath not nor had any more or other of the goods or provisions of or belonging to that shipp.

Gedeon Marshallsey of Chickerell aforesaid husbandman deposed saieth that he was uppon the beech the same day that the shipp called the Golden Grape was cast away where he with Nicholas Bussell and others did save two barrells of raisins which were caryed and left at the house of Thomas Newman, And that he did helpe save one other barrell of raisins with William Bunting wich are in the custody of this deponents father, And this deponent did then alsoe save about a quarter of a pound of wooll wich he hath in his custody And that he hath not nor had any more or other of the goods or provisions of or belonging to that shipp.

Henry Nosciter of Langton Herring aforesaid fisherman deposed saieth that the next day after that the shipp called the Golden Grape was cast away uppon the beech he went thither where he did helpe save six barrells of raisins fower of wich were

97R

delivered unto Mr John Allin of Waymouth, the other two barrells the said Mr Allin gave unto this deponent and Thomas Comage of Langton for saving the rest And that this deponent did alsoe there take up a peice of a barrell in wich were about thirty six pounds of raisons, wich together with the other barrell that he had he sold for about seaven shillings And this deponent further saieth that he bought of a woman of Steepleton (whose name he now remembreth not) one barrell and halfe of raisins for wich he payed her fower and twenty shillinges, and sold the same againe to John White of Sherbourne for forty shillings And this deponent allsoe saieth that he did likewise there helpe save about eight or nine barrells of raisins more and three or fower and thirty jarres of oyle wich were left in the keeping of Robert Hunt of Wike Regis And that this deponent hath not nor had any more or other of the goods or provisions of or belonging to that shipp.

Angell Whyte of Langton aforesaid husbandman deposed saieth that uppon Saturday being the day that the shipp called the Golden Grape was cast away uppon the beech he went thither where he continued untill Monday night following during wich time he saved twenty barrells of raisins, whereof William Lovell of Fleet

98

had tenn, Walter Bond of Waymouth and his company five, John Philips of Abbotsbury one, Trivetts of the same place one, and all the rest were taken from him but by whome he knoweth not, And that he hath not nor had any more or other of the goods or provisions of or belonging to that shipp.

Thomas Comage of Langton aforesaid deposed saieth that the same day the shipp the Golden Grape was cast away uppon the beech he went thither where he saved neer a barrell of raisins part of wich he hath since spent, the rest he sold for fifteen shillinges And that he hath not nor had any more or other of the goods or provisions of or belonging to that shipp.

Edward Huxford of Langton aforesaid fisherman deposed sayeth that uppon the next day after the shipp called the Golden Grape was cast away uppon the beech he went thither where he saved one barrell of raisins of the sunn wich he caryed home and hath in his custody And that he hath not nor had any more or other of the goods or provisions of or belonging to that shipp.

98R

William Dream of Langton aforesaid husbandman deposed saieth that the same day the shipp the Golden Grape was cast away uppon the beech he went thither where he saved one barrell of raisins of the sunn wich he hath in his custody & is and will be ready to deliver And that he hath not nor had any more or other of the goods or provisions of or belonging to that shipp.

Deposicons taken at Melcomb Regis aforesaid the twenty fourth day of February in the year before named before us whose names are subscribed by virtue of the commissioners before expressed Francis Cape notary public being then also present.

Richard Buttler of Upway in the county of Dorsett aforesaid husbandman deposed saieth that since the shipp the Golden Grape was cast away he bought severall parcells of goods that came out of that shipp That is to say one barrell of raisins of the sunne of William Lovell of Fleet for

99

twenty shillinges, one barrell of raisins of John Allin of Fleet for twenty shillings, of wich sumes this deponent payed them but halfe in hand, one barrel of raisins of John Williams of Fleet for tenn shillings, and one other barrell of Richard Damer of Little Waddon for wich this deponent payed him five shillinges in money and caried home to his house another barrell for him wich was worth five shillinges more And this deponent further saieth that Thomas Masterman of Upway did buy att Fleet six barrells of raisins of the sunne, wich he sold and sent unto Sturminster Newton but to whome this deponent doth not know, And that Mr. Benjamin Bale of Upway bought one barrell William Oldish of Upway one barrel Eugenius Vincent two barrells, Owen Hendey and Giles Hendey three barrells, and Walter Paty one barrell. And that this deponent hath not nor had any more or other of the goods or provisions of that shipp.

John Goddard of Chickerell aforesaid husbandman deposed saieth that the same day the shipp called the Golden Grape was cast away uppon the beech he went thither where he with

99R

Robert Damer and Edward Kerley did save seaven barrells of raisins of the sunne and fower jarres of oile, wich they caryed to Chickerell aforesaid and there left the same in the custody of Mr Tristram Knapton clerk And this deponent further saieth that he was present with Thomas Bussell of Chickerell aforesaid att saving the bagg of money by him in his deposicon confessed and wich he hath delivered to the Viceadmirall And that this deponent hath not nor had in his custody nor in the custody of any other to his use any more or other of the goods or provisions of or belonging to that shipp.

John Burdett alias Stevens of Chickerell aforesaid husbandman deposed saieth that the same day at night that the shipp called the Golden Grape was cast away uppon the beech he went thither where he saved a barrell of raisins of the sunne, about the quantity of apound of wooll and a jarre of oile, and a barrell of ollives, and that the raisins are in the custody of Mr. Knapton, the ollives John Senyor of Waymouth hath, the rest are in this deponents hands And he further saieth that being aboard the said shipp he found and tooke upp one peice of eight & that Nicholas Bussell of Chickerell aforesaid did then give unto him three pieces

100

of eight And that this deponent hath not nor had in his custody nor in the custody of any other to his use any more or other of the goods or provisions of or belonging to that shipp.

William Purchas of Abbotsbury aforesaid baker deposed saieth that the same day that the shipp called the Golden Grape was cast away uppon the beech he went thither where he saved two barrells of raisins wich he emptied into fower potts and soe caryed the same home, of wich he sold an hundred and a quarter to a widow of Cerne for two pence halfe penny the pound, by wich meanes he made fifty shillinges of the same besides all his chardges. And he further saieth that he then alsoe saved two bolts of peices of silks one of wich being wrapt in a cape John Pope of Waymouth tooke from this deponent warning himselfe Mr. Viceadmiralls man, the other this deponent sold part to one of Taunton for sixe pounds and one shilling, and part thereof (vizt) twelve yards to Captain Strangwayes for eighteen shillinges And this deponent then allsoe saved fowre jarres of oyle, five peices of brasse and and old

100R

paire of breeches with a knife in them all wich he hath in his custody and is ready to deliver And this deponent further saieth that John Pymer of Abbotsbury did then allsoe save eleven jarres of oyle, two barrells of raisins of the sunne and as much wooll as a man might well graspe in both his arms, and the said Pymer told this deponent that Roger Gibbs of Abbotsbury did then save a bagge of wooll. And lastly this deponent saieth that he this deponent hath not nor had in his custody nor in the custody of any other to his use any more or other of the goods or provisions of or belonging to the said shipp.

John Gardiner of Abbotsbury aforesaid deposed saieth that the next day after that the shipp called the Golden Grape was cast away uppon the beech he went thither where he tooke up about a pecke of raisins of the sunne wich he caryed home with him, & that he hath not nor had any more or other of the goods or provisions of or belonging to that shipp.

John Angell of Abbotsbury aforesaid deposed saieth that he was uppon the beech the Monday morning after that the

101

shipp called the Golden Grape was cast away where he bought three barrells of raisins of the sunne wich cost him eleaven shillinges, parte whereof he sold and made neer about forty shillinges of the same, wich money he is and will be ready to repay, the residew he hath spent And that he hath not nor had any more or other of the goods or provisions of or belonging to that shipp.

John Wattson of Abbotsbury aforesaid fisherman deposed saieth that the same day the shipp called the Golden Grape was cast away uppon the beech he went thither, but he did not save or take up any of the goods belonging to the same, But saieth that uppon the Monday following this deponents sonn John went thither where he did save and send home to this deponents house neer about the quantity of a barrell of raisins of the sunne parte of which this deponent sold and made of the same about fower or five shillinges the remainder he hath spent And that this deponent hath not nor had any more or other of the goods or provisions of or belonging to that shipp.

Joseph Miller alias Robinson of Abbotsbury aforesaid fisherman deposed saieth that the same day after the shipp called the Golden Grape was cast away upon the beech he went thither where he saved fower barrells of raisins, one of wich was stollen from him another he shared with two women that did help him, the rest he hath in his custody wich he is ready to deliver And he did then alsoe save there one jarre of oyle wich he alsoe hath in his custody And that he hath not nor had any more or other of the goods or provisions of or belonging to that shipp.

Robert Damer of Chickerell aforesaid husbandman deposed saieth that the same day att night that the shipp called the Golden Grape was cast away upon the beech he went thither where he saved five jarres of oyle, one of wich was broken, the other fower he hath in his custody And he further saieth that he with Edward Kerley, and others did allsoe save eight barrells of raisins of the sunn five of wich they caryed to the house of Mr. Knapton the Minister, the other three to the house of William Bussell where they doe yet remaine for ought this deponent doth know to the contrary, And this deponent alsoe saieth that he did then save about an

ounce of wooll, wich he now delivereth, and that he and Nicholas did save between them another barrell of raisins wich being wett they opened and shared the fruit between And that this deponent hath not nor had any more or other of the goods or provisions of that shipp.

Edward Kerlye of Chickerell aforesaid husbandman deposed saieth that upon the same day att night that the shipp called the Golden Grape was cast away upon the beech he went thither where he did helpe save eight barrells of raisins of the sunn five of wich were caryed to the house of Mr. Kapton, the other three to the house of William Bussell, and fower jarres of oyle wich are in the custody of the said William Bussell, And that he was alsoe present with Thomas Bussell att the saving of one bagg of money wich the said Bussell hath delivered to Mr. Viceadmirall And that this deponent hath not nor had any more or other of the goods or provisions of or belonging to that shipp.

Michael Langford of Chickerell aforesaid yeoman deposed saieth

that uppon the Monday after that the shipp called the Golden Grape was cast away uppon the beech he went thither where he bought of John Carter of Fleet one barrell of raisins of the sunne for wich he payed him fower shillinges And that this deponent hath not nor had any more or other of the goods or provisions of or belonging to that shipp.

Nicholas Burdett alias Stevens of Chickerell aforesaid husbandman deposed saieth that the same day that the shipp called the Golden Grape was cast away uppon the beech he went thither where he saved a barrell of raisins of the sunne and a jarre of oyle wich he caryed to the house of Mr. Knapton, where it yett remaines And that he had then upon the beech given him by a Welshman that lives in the Isle of Portland about a pound of wooll wich this deponent hath since given to Thomas Daniell of Waymouth And that this deponent hath not nor had any more or other of the goods or provisions of or belonging to that shipp.

William Way of Chickerell aforesaid husbandman deposed saieth that John Mills this deponents servant being uppon the beech did save out of the shipp called the Golden Grape three barrells of raisins

103

of the sunne wich he brought to this deponents house where they doe yett remaine And that this deponent hath not nor had any more or other of the goods or provisions of or belonging to that shipp.

William Newman of Chickerell aforesaid husbandman deposed saieth that the same day that the shipp the Golden Grape was cast away uppon the beech he went thither where he did help save two barrells of raisins of the sunn, about two or three ounces of wooll, and a smale firkine of ollives wich olives he sold to Mr. Hurding for two shillinges, the raisins and the wooll he hath att home in his house And that he hath not nor had any more or other of the goods or provisions of that shipp.

Nicholas Dyker of Chickerell aforesaid husbandman deposed sayeth that the next day after the shipp the Golden Grape was cast away uppon the beech he went thither where he together with John Bunting did save nine barrells of raisins of the sunne

103R

fower of wich Walter Bond of Waymouth had from them, and William Lovell of Fleet hath fower more, the other this deponent and the said Bunting shared between them And that this deponent hath not nor had any more or other of the goods or provisions of or belonging to that shipp.

Henry Way of Chickerell aforesaid husbandman deposed saieth that he was twice uppon the beech after that the shipp called the Golden Grape was there cast away where he did save two barrells of raisins of the sunn, a jarre of oyle, and a locke of wooll, and that he delivered the oyle unto Thomas Bryer of Chickerell aforesaid, but the raisins and the locke of wooll he hath in his owne custody And that he was present with Thomas Bussell att the saving of the bagg of money wich the said Bussell hath delivered to the Viceadmirall And that this deponent hath not nor had any more or other of the goods or provisions of the said shipp.

William Stickland of Chickerell aforesaid husbandman deposed saieth that he was present uppon the beech with Robert Damer, John Goddard and others

104

and did with them help save out of the shipp the Golden Grape two barrells of raisins of the sunne, and fower jarres of oile wich were caryed and left att the house of William Bussell in Chickerell aforesaid And that this deponent hath not nor had any more or other of the goods or provisions of that shipp.

Mathias Way of Chickerell aforesaid husbandman deposed sayeth that he was present uppon the beech with William Newman, Nicholas Bussell, and others and did help save out of the shipp the Golden Grape two barrells of raisins of the sonne wich were caryed and left att the house of Thomas Newman in Chickerell aforesaid And that this deponent hath not nor had any more or other of the goods or provisions of that shipp.

William Benvile of Langton aforesaid husbandman deposed saieth that the next day after that the shipp the Golden Grape was cast away uppon the beech he went thither where he tooke out of a barrell about halfe a bushell of raisins of the sunn wich he putt into

104R

a bagge and caried home with him And that he hath not nor had any more or other of the goods or provisions of or belonging to that shipp.

William Charles of Fleet in the said County of Dorsett husbandman deposed saieth that he being uppon the beech the next day after the shipp the Golden Grape was cast away did there take out of a barrell about a bushell of raisins of the sunne wich he putt into a bagg and caried home with him And that he hath not nor had any more or other of the goods or provisions of or belonging to that shipp.

John Godding of Fleet aforesaid deposed saieth that the same day the shipp the Golden Grape was cast away he went uppon the beech where he saved out of the said shipp one bundle of plate weighing about thirty or forty pounds wich he delivered to Mr. Mohun being fast mayled, And that he did then alsoe help to save fower barrells of raisins of the sunne wich were likewise delivered to the said Mr. Mohun And that this deponent hath not nor had any more or other of the goods or provisions of or belonging to the said shipp.

Robert Murrey of Fleet aforesaid fisherman deposed saieth that his daughter Constance Murrey being uppon the beech after the shipp the Golden Grape was there cast away did bring home to this deponents house about three pecks of raisins of the sunne And that this deponent hath not nor had any more or other of the goods or provisions of or belonging to that shipp.

Thomas Carter of Fleet aforesaid sailor deposed saieth that he went uppon the beech the same day that the shipp the Golden Grape was cast away where he together with Thomas Allen did save fower barrells of raisins of the sunn wich are in the custody of the said Thomas Allen And that this deponent hath not nor had any more or other of the goods or provisions of or belonging to that shipp.

John Allen of Fleet aforesaid husbandman deposed saieth that the same day the shipp called the Golden Grape was cast away uppon the beech he went thither in the company of William Lovell, Robert Tooledge, and Robert Bryer where they did save three barrells of raisins of the sunn wich are in the custody of the said William Lovell And further this deponent saieth that he together with the said Robert Tooledge, William Lovell, Robert

105R

Bryer, John Williams, and John Allen this deponents sonne did save twelve barrells of raisins of the sunne more sixe of wich they delivered uppon the beech to one that named himselfe the Viceadmiralls man the other sixe they kept to themselves (vizt) to each of them one, And that this deponent sold the barrell that he had unto one Richard Buttler for twenty shillings, tenn shillings whereof he payed to this deponent the residew he doth yett owe unto him And lastly this deponent sayeth that he hath not nor had in his custody nor in the custody of any other to his use any more or other of the goods or provisions of or belonging to the said shipp.

John Butcher of Fleet aforesaid fisherman deposed saieth that he went uppon the beech the same day that the shipp called the Golden Grape was cast away where he did helpe save ten barrells of raisins of fruit but came of them he knoweth not, and that he allsoe tooke up there about halfe a bushel of wett fruit wich he putt into a cape and caryed home with him And this deponent alsoe saieth that he saw in Mr. Mohun's house six barrells of raisins of the sunne And that this deponent hath not nor had any more or other of the goods or provisions of or belonging to the said shipp.

106

Robert Tooledge of Fleet aforesaid husbandman deposed saieth that he was uppon the beech the same day that the shipp the Golden Grape was cast away where he did helpe save three barrells of raisins of the sunn wich are in the custody of William Lovell, And that the said Lovell & this deponent with fower others menconed in the deposicon of John Allen did save twelve barrells of raisins of the sunne more, sixe of wich they delivered to one that named himselfe Drake servant to Mr. Viceadmirall the other sixe they divided between them (vizt) to each man one, whereof this deponent hath one And this deponent did allsoe take up there one smale peice of silver, and together with the said William Lovell and Robert Bryer did save one muskett wich he hath in his custody And that he hath not nor had any more or other of the goods or provisions of or belonging to that shipp.

Christopher Lovell of Fleet aforesaid fisherman deposed saieth that he was upon the beech the same day that the shipp the Golden Grape was cast away uppon the beech where he did save

106R

two barrells of raisins of the sunne one of wich he delivered to William Lovell for the Viceadmirall, the other he sold for eight shillings And that he hath not nor had any more or other of the goods or provisions of that shipp.

John Williams of Fleet aforesaid fisherman deposed saieth that he was upon the beech the same day that the shipp called the Golden Grape was there cast away where he did help save divers barrells of raisins of the sunn of wich he had one barrell to himselfe wich he caryed home and sold to one Richard Buttler for eight or nine shillinges And that this deponent hath not nor had any more or other of the goods or provisions of or belonging to the said shipp.

Robert Bryer of Fleet aforesaid fisherman deposed saieth that he was upon the beech the same day att night that the shipp called the Golden Grape was cast away where he did save and had a barrell of raisins wich he caried home where he kept them by the space of a week, about wich time (they being very wett) he opened the said barrell and sold parte of the said fruit for about two or three shillinges, and hath since spent the rest And that he hath not nor had any more

107

more or other of the goods or provisions of or belonging to that shipp.

Anthony Carter of Fleet aforesaid saylor deposed saieth that he was upon the beech the same night that the shipp the Golden Grape was cast away where he tooke up a bandolier and some fruit out of a barrell wich he caryed home in his coat, he alsoe saieth that Thomas Perkins servant to Mr. Mohun did then shew him one peice of silver wich came out of the said shipp And this deponent further sayeth that the next day he together with Joseph Keat and Robert Allen did save eight barrells of raisins of the sunn wich Walter Bond of Waymouth tooke from them and gave them noe satisfaction at all for saving the same And that he hath not nor had any more or other of the goods or provisions of or belonging to that shipp.

John Boyte of Langton aforesaid fisherman deposed saieth that he was upon the beech the next day after the shipp the Golden Grape was cast away where he tooke out of a barrell and uppon the deck of the said shipp about a pecke of raisins wich he caried home with him

107R

And that he hath not nor had any more or other of the goods or provisions of or belonging to the said shipp.

Richard Boyte of Langton aforesaid fisherman deposed saieth that he was upon the beech the next day after the shipp the Golden Grape was cast away where he did take up a smale quantity of raisins wich he caried home in his pocketts And that he hath not nor had any more or other of the goods or provisions of that shipp.

Edward Bridge of Langton aforesaid fisherman deposed saieth that the next day after the shipp the Golden Grape was cast away he was upon the beech where he tooke up about a pecke of loose fruit wich he hath since spent And that he hath not nor had any more or other of the goods or provisions of or belonging to that shipp.

Adam Gawden of Langton aforesaid husbandman deposed saieth that the next day after the shipp the Golden Grape was cast away upon the beech he went thither where he saved a barrell of raisins wich he caryed home with him And that he hath not nor had any more or other of the goods or provisions of that shipp.

108

John Genge of Langton aforesaid husbandman deposed saieth that the same day at night that the shipp the Golden Grape was cast away upon the beech he went thither where he tooke out of a barrell about three pecks of raisins wich he caryed home with him And that afterwards he saved halfe a barrell more of raisins a jarre of oyle, a paire of iron tonges, an old knife and an earthen cupp wich he alsoe caryed to his house And that he hath not nor had any more or other of the goods or provisions of that shipp.

John Benvile of Langton aforesaid fisherman deposed saieth that he went uppon the beech the same day att night that the shipp the Golden Grape was cast away where he saved one barrell of raisins wich he caryed home and hath since sold to Mr. Hasslewood for twelve shillings but this deponent is not yett payed for the same And that he hath not nor had any more or other of the goods or provisions of or belonging to that shipp.

John Haywell of Langton aforesaid fisherman deposed saieth

108R

that he was uppon the beech the next day after the shipp the Golden Grape was cast away where he saved one barrell of raisins wich he hath in his custody And that he hath not nor had any more or other of the goods or provisions of that shipp.

Robert Lovell of Langton aforesaid fisherman deposed saieth that he was uppon the beach the Monday next after the shipp the Golden Grape was cast away where he saved two barrells of raisins one of wich he delivered to John Allen of Waymouth, the other this deponent caried home and sold for fower shillings And that he hath not nor had any more or other of the goods or provisions of that shipp.

William Dyke of Langton aforesaid husbandman deposed saieth that he was uppon the beach the same day att night that the shipp called the Golden Grape was cast away where he did take up and save a smale firkin of raisins conteyning about three pecke wich he hath att home in his custody And that he hath not nor had any more or other of the goods or provisions of that shipp.

109

Thomas Boyte of Langton aforesaid fisherman deposed saieth that he was uppon the beach the next day after the shipp the Golden Grape was cast away where he did take out of a barrell about a pecke of raisins wich he caried home with him And that he hath not nor had any more or other of the goods or provisions of that shipp.

Thomas Mitchell of Langton aforesaid fisherman deposed saieth that he was uppon the beach the next day after the shipp the Golden Grape was cast away where he saved two peices of barrells of raisins in both wich were about five peck in all wich this deponent caryed home and sold to one John White for thirteen shillings And that this deponent hath not nor had any more or other of the goods or provisions of that shipp.

John Hendey the younger of Langton aforesaid deposed saieth that he was uppon the beech the same day that the shipp the Golden Grape was cast away where he saved two bolts or peices of silkes wich he delivered to Mr. Mohun's

109R

sonne And that this deponent hath not nor had any more or other of the goods or provisions of or belonging to that shipp.

William Murrey of Langton aforesaid fisherman deposed saieth that he was twice uppon the beach after the shipp the Golden Grape was cast away att wich times he did save about halfe a bushell of raysins in all And that he hath not nor had any more or other of the goods or provisions of that shipp.

John Kippen of Langton aforesaid fisherman deposed sayeth that he was uppon the beech the same day att night that the shipp the Golden Grape was cast away where he did save halfe a barrell of raisins parte of wich he sold for five shillings the remainder he hath yett att home And that he hath not nor had any more or other of the goods or provisions of that shipp.

William Charles of Langton aforesaid husbandman deposed saieth that he was uppon the beech the same day that the shipp the Golden Grape was cast away where he tooke up about halfe a bushell of raisins, thirty limons and two peices of eight And that he hath not nor had any more or other of the goods or provisions of that shipp.

110

Jasper Charles of Langton aforesaid husbandman deposed saieth that he was uppon the beech the same day att night that the shipp the Golden Grape was cast away where he tooke up about a pecke of raisins wich he caried home with him in a bagg, and about a pecke of lymons wich John Pope of Waymouth tooke from him And that this deponent hath not nor had any more or other of the goods or provisions of that shipp.

Thomas Battin of Langton aforesaid fisherman deposed saieth that uppon the Monday after the shipp the Golden Grape was cast away uppon the beech he went thither where he tooke out of a barrell about halfe a pecke of raisins wich he caryed home with him and hath since spent And that he hath not nor had any more or other of the goods or provisions of or belonging to that shipp.

110R

Deposicons taken at Melcomb Regis aforesaid the twenty eighth day of February in the year before named before us whose names are subscribed by virtue of the commissioners before expressed Francis Cape notary public being then also present.

William Hipsley of Corton in the County of Dorsett aforesaid husbandman deposed saieth that uppon the next day after that the shipp called the Golden Grape was cast away uppon the beech he went thither in the company of Richard Halston, Mr. Stocker his baylive where they and some other company saved thirteen barrells of raisins whereof they left three there; the rest the said Halston and the rest of the company divided between them And that this deponent hath not nor had to his owne use any part of the goods or provisions of that shipp.

Richard Hardey of Corton aforesaid husbandman deposed saieth that uppon the next day after that the shipp called the Golden Grape was cast away uppon the beech he went thither where Richard Halston, Mr.

111

Stocker his baylive did take up and cary home in a cart to his owne use two barrells of raisins and three sacks full of raisins, And two barrells of raisins for Richard Royle of Waddon, and one barrell for Robert Battin & one barrell for Richard Sampson of Shilvinghampton, wich was all the goods that the said Halston caryed thence to this deponents knowledge And that he this deponent hath not nor had any of the goods or provisions of or belonging to that shipp att all, save onely about seaven or eight pounds of raisins wich the said Halston gave this deponent after they came back to Corton.

Leonard German of Abbotsbury aforesaid husbandman deposed saieth that the same day that the shipp the Golden Grape was cast away upon the beech he went thither where he saved two barrells of raysins one empty barrell, and some loose fruit wich he caried home in his pocketts All wich he hath in his custody and is and will be ready to deliver And that

111R

he hath not nor had any more or other of the goods or provisions of or belonging to that shipp.

Henry Haywell of Abbotsbury aforesaid fisherman deposed saieth that the next day after the shipp the Golden Grape was cast away upon the beech he being hyred by Mr. Nicholas Strangwayes did goe with his boat in the company of Christopher Doby, Edward his sonn and Richard the sonn of this deponent downe the Fleat neer that place where Peter Ford did put aboard the said boat nine barrells of raisins wich this deponent and his said company caryed to Abbotsbury and delivered att the house of the said Mr. Strangwayes. And that this deponent did then take up upon the beech about halfe a bushell of raisins wich he putt into a bagg and caryed home with him And that he hath not nor had any more or other of the goods or provisions of or belonging to that shipp.

Roger Motyer of Abbotsbury aforesaid fisherman deposed saieth that the next day after that the shipp the Golden Grape was cast away upon the beech he went thither where he saved a barrell of raisins and about three pecke of loose

112

raisins wich barrell Walter Bond of Waymouth tooke from him, the other raisins this deponent caryed home in his coat And that he hath not nor had any more or other of the goods or provisions of that shipp.

Walter Haywell of Abbotsbury aforesaid sailor deposed sayeth that upon the Sunday after the shipp the Golden Grape was cast away he went upon the beech on horseback, where his wife and his daughter did take up about forty pounds of loose fruit wich this deponents caryed home And that he hath not nor had any more or other of the goods or provisions of that shipp But saieth that his sonn Arthur Haywell had a barrell of raisins given unto him by Walter Bond of Waymouth wich he sold to William Clerk of Abbotsbury for two shillinges and six pence.

Maximilian Mohun of Fleet aforesaid Esquire saieth that a stranger brought unto him being upon the beech a boxe taken out of the shipp the Golden Grape with letters in it and a book of accompt of Thomas Redwood Master of

112R

that shipp, wich he now delivereth to the Commissioners And the said Mr. Mohun alsoe saieth that he hath in his custody a blacke peice of taffata sarcenett, wich he hath caused to be dryed, about seaven or eight barrells of raisins, two of wich are broken open, a chest belonging to one of the company of the said shipp in wich is an hansaw a chessle, and some other smale trifles and a jarre of oile, which are all the goods (as he remembreth) that he hath in his custody belonging to that shipp the said Mr. Mohun saieth moreover that he caused eight and twenty peices of silke and two parcels of plate to be putt together upon the beech and preserved wich were afterwards taken and caried away by some of the inhabitants of Portland.

John Battin of Gerards Waddon husbandman deposed saieth that he was uppon the beech the next day that the shipp the Golden Grape was cast away where he tooke up about three peckes of raisins of the sunn wich he putt into a bagg and caryed home with him And that he hath not nor had any more or other of the goods or provisions of that shipp.

113

Thomas Hayward of Abbotsbury aforesaid fisherman deposed saieth that the Monday after the shipp the Golden Grape was cast away uppon the beech he went thither where he tooke up about three peckes of raisins wich he caried home with him in a paire of fishpotts on horseback And that he hath not nor had any more or other of the goods or provisions of that shipp.

John Browne of Abbotsbury aforesaid fisherman deposed saieth that he was uppon the beech the next day after the shipp the Golden Grape was cast away where he together with John Clerke of Abbotsbury aforesaid did save three barrells of raisins of the sunne, one of wich they sold to Thomas Daniell of Waymouth, and the other two to severall other persons whose names this deponent doth not now remember And that he hath not nor had any more or other of the goods or provisions of that shipp.

John Clerk of Abbotsbury aforesaid fisherman deposed saieth that he was present with the said

113R

John Browne upon the beech att the savinge of the three barrells of raisins of the sunne out of the shipp the Golden Grape menconed & expressed in the deposicon of the said Browne one of wich they sold to the said Thomas Daniell for five shillinges and the other two to severall other persons unknown to this deponent, And this deponent did then alsoe take up fower oringes out of the said shipp And that he hath not nor had any more or other of the goods or provisions of that shipp.

John Philips of Abbotsbury aforesaid fisherman deposed saieth that he was uppon the beech the next day in the afternoon after that the shipp the Golden Grape was cast away where he tooke up certaine loose fruit wich he caried home in his linine drawers And that he hath not nor had any more or other of the goods or provisions of that shipp. And this deponent further saieth that about three or fowre dayes after one George Paine of Abbotsbury did shew unto this deponent certaine peices of eight amounting to fowerteen shilling sterl: wich he said was the moity of certaine peices of eight by him taken up uppon the beech within the liberty of Sir John Strangwayes, for wich he had been soe much troubled by the said Sir John's servants, & that he delivered the other moity to Mr. Osbourne the Minister of Abbotsbury

114

Richard Paine of Abbotsbury aforesaid fisherman deposed saieth that the next day after that the shipp called the Golden Grape was cast away uppon the beech this deponent followed two of his daughters to that place whither they were gonn before, whome he then found to have taken up about a peck and halfe of wett raisins wich they putt into a bagg and caryed home with them, And that is all the goods wich he or they have or had of or belonging to that shipp.

William Lovell of Fleet aforesaid husbandman deposed saieth that the same day that the shipp the Golden Grape was cast away uppon the beech he went thither where he with Robert Tooledge, John Allin and Robert Bryer did save three barrells of raisins wich they caryed to this deponents house together with one of the company of the said shipp who was very sicke (where this deponent kept the said sicke man seaven or eight dayes, and then he was removed to Mr. Mohun's house where he remained untill he dyed;) And then having refreshed the said sick man and himselfe he went uppon the beech againe where he and his company did take out of the said shipp and twelve barrells more of raisins of the

114R

sunne six of wich one, that named himselfe William Drake and Mr. Viceadmiralls servant, tooke from them, and left the other six with them for salvage, of wich this deponent had one And this deponent further saieth that when he was aboard the said shipp he tooke up a bagge of money wich was fast sealed, but since this deponent hath opened the same, and telling the money found there to be two hundred peices of eight, of wich this deponent hath six score, the other fower score he delivered to John Pollard of Fleet who was present with this deponent at taking the same up. And this deponent alsoe saieth that he and his company did then alsoe save the maine bonnett saile of the said shipp, wich afterwards they delivered to John Pope of Waymouth who demanded the same from them in the name of the Master of the said shipp And moreover this deponent saieth that Christopher Lovell of Fleet hath in his custody the fore yard of the said wich this deponent did helpe to save And lastly this deponent saieth that he hath not in his custody nor in the custody of any other to his use any more or other of the goods or provisions of or belonging to that shipp.

115

Deposicons taken at Melcomb Regis aforesaid the first day of March in the year before named before us whose names are subscribed by virtue of the commissioners before expressed Francis Cape notary public being then also present.

Daniell Andrews of Wyke Regis aforesaid fisherman deposed sayth that he being uppon the beech the same day the shipp the Golden Grape was cast away did see Thomas Carter of Fleet to have in his hand under his capp a bagg of money with wich the said Carter went away thence but how much was in the same this deponent knoweth not.

Tristram Knapton of Chickerell aforesaid clerk saieth that he hath in his house seaven whole barrells of fruit, a peice of a barrell of olives, a jarre of oyle, and a smale quantity wich goods were brought thither by Nicholas Stevens, Henry Way, John Stevens, John Godard, Robert Damer and

115R

Edward Kerley wich they had fetched from the beech neer the place where the shipp called the Golden Grape was cast away.

John Pollard of Fleet aforesaid husbandman deposed saieth that he was uppon the beech the same day that the shipp the Golden Grape was cast away and thence went aboard the said shipp where he did take out of a barrell about halfe a bushell of raisins wich he putt into a bagg and caryed home And this deponent further saieth that whilest he was aboard the said shipp he saw William Lovell of Fleet take up a bagg of money there, wich he caryed a shore, whome this deponent presently followed, and demanded parte thereof as being present with him when he tooke the same, whereuppon the said Lovell with his knife did cutt open the said bagg, and told the money therein, of wich he delivered fower score peices great and smale to this deponent, and kept six score to himselfe wich was all that was in the said bagge And lastly this deponent saieth that he hath not nor had any more or other of the goods or provisions of that shipp.

116

Deposicons taken at Melcomb Regis aforesaid the fourth day of March in the year before named before us whose names are subscribed by virtue of the commissioners before expressed Francis Cape notary public being then also present.

Thomas Carter of Fleet aforesaid sailor sworne and reexamined saieth that what is conteyned in his former deposicon is true And that he hath not nor had in his custody nor in the custody of any other to his use any more or other of the goods money wares or provisions that are or were in or belonging to the said shipp then what he hath in his former deposicon expressed.

John Wills of Chickerell aforesaid husbandman deposed saieth that the next day after the shipp the Golden Grape was cast away uppon the beech he went aboard the said shipp where he saved three barrells of raisins of the sunn wich are in

116R

the house of William Way of Chickerell, and about halfe a pecke of wett raisins wich this deponent hath since eaten And that he found in the feilds of Chickerell a peice of a rope belonging to the said shipp wich is allsoe in the said William Way's house And that this deponent hath not nor had any more or other of the goods or provisions of or belonging to that shipp.

Giles Hendey of Upway in the County of Dorsett aforesaid thatcher deposed saieth that the Wednesday next after that the shipp called the Golden Grape was cast away uppon the beech he went to Fleet where he bought of Richard Bryer of Fleet a broken barrell of raysins of the sunn out of wich parte of the fruit had been taken for wich this deponent payed the said Bryer twelve shillinges And that this deponent hath not nor had any more or other of the goods or provisions of that shipp.

Francis Sandford of Upway aforesaid husbandman deposed saieth that uppon the Tuesday next after the

117

shipp the Golden Grape was cast away he this deponent and one George Girdler of Upway aforesaid did buy between them a certaine quantity of raisins of the sunne of one Edward Baily servant to Samuel Tackle of Waymouth for wich this deponent payed five shillinges, and the said Girdler was to pay five shillings more And that this deponent hath not nor had any more or other of the goods or provisions of that shipp.

Deposicons taken at Melcomb Regis aforesaid twenty eighth day of March in the year of our Lord 1642 before us whose names are subscribed by virtue of the commissioners before expressed Francis Cape notary public being then also present.

Thomas Masterman of Upway aforesaid yeoman deposed saieth that about two or three days

117R

after that the shipp the Golden Grape was cast away he went to Fleet neer the sea side where he bought of Robert Tooledge two barrells of raisins of the sunn for wich this deponent payed him two and thirty shillinges one other barrell of raisins of Richard Bryer of Fleet for fowerteen shillinges, and two other barrells of raisins of another man of Fleet whose name he now remembreth not for thirty shillinges; many of wich raisins (for that they were wett) he threw away, others he gave away, and some he sold, but made not of them in all above thirty shillings And that he hath not nor had any more or other of the goods or provisions of that shipp.

John Ellis

John Arthur

1642

Oia ipsa p? veritata arta fuerunt perut superimo expressedest in puntia mier?

Francis Cape Notary publicque 1642

118

HCA Inquiry People Index

Haywell, John 108R

Haywell, Walter 112R

Hazard als Wallis, John 61R

Hellyer, William 83R

Hemmings, Morgan 44R

Hendey (younger), John 109R

Hendey, Giles 117

Hendey, Percivall 72

Hendey, William 66R

Hillary, William 84R

Hipsley, William 111

Holmes, Agnes 41R

Housely, William 75

Hunt, Ann 26R

Hunt, Robert 25R

Hunt, Thomas 26

Huxford, Edward 98R

Hynde, Joett 79R

James, Robert 74R

Jennings, William 82

Jolliff, Marc 84

Keat, John 89R

Keat, Joseph 35

Kellway, Henry 59R

Kerlye, Edward 102R

Kippen, John 110

Knapton, Tristram 115R

Langar, Catherine 35R

Langford, Michael 102R

Lano, Owen 76R

Laverock, John 85R

Limbrey, Ralph 37

Lock, Ralph 48R

Lovell, Christopher 106R

Lovell, Robert 109

Lovell, William 114R

Lyne, Henry 30

Lyne, John 23

Mallett, William 90

Marshallsey, Gedeon 97R

Marshalsea, Edward 96R

Martin, Edward 38

Masterman, Thomas 117R

Mathews, Alice 82

Maunders, Joseph 38

May, Henry 91R

Meech, Henry 26

Meech, John 61R

Meech, Thomas 59

Michell, Margery 60R

Miller als Robinson, Joseph 102

Miller, Peter 90R

Miller, Ralph 87R

Milles, John 50R

Mills, Andrew 27

Mills, Henry 92

Mines, Thomas 42

Mitchell, John 95

Mitchell, Thomas 109R

Mitchell, Thomas 31

Mohun, Maximilian 112R

More, Symon 36R

Motyer, Roger 112

Munday, Robert 49

Murrey, John 15

Murrey, Robert 105

Murrey, William 110

Newcome, Robert 79R

Newman, William 103R

Newman, William 86

Nosciter, Henry 97R

Olliver, John 89

Owfley, Philip 80R

Paine, Bartholomew 33

Paine, Mary 33

Paine, Richard 114R

Painter, Samuel 78R

Peck, Thomas 16

Peirce, Daniel 31

Peirce, John 73

Peirce, Richard 75

Peirce, Robert 72R

Philips, John 114

Philips, William 37R

Phillis, William 10

Pierce, Edward 81

Williams, Henry 69R
Williams, John 107
Williams, Nicholas 55R
Wills, John 116R
Wills, Thomas 65R
Winter, Anthony 14
Winter, John 63
Winter, William 53R
Wood, Angell 88R
Wood, John 93
Woodcocke, Roger 43
Wykes, William 38R

People mentioned

, AUSTINE 27 & 50R
, one 100R
, welshman 103
, widow 100R
, woman 98
ALLEN the ELDER, JOHN 48
ALLEN, JOHN 105R
ALLEN, JOHN 105R
ALLEN, MATTHEW 27
ALLEN, ROBERT 107R
ALLENN, JOHN 82R
ALLIN, JOHN 98
ALLIN, MAGDALEN 64 & 67
ALLIN, MATHEW 50R
ARTHUR, Mr 56 & 85
ARTHUR, Unknown 54R
BALE, BENJAMIN 99R
BASTIN, GEORGE 44R
BATTIN, AGNES 67
BELLETT, HENRY 63R
BELLETT, WILLIAM 63R
BELLETT?, 63R
BENVILE, ANNE 75
BERRY, HENRY 63
BOND, JAMES 44
BOND, JOANE 32R
boy, a 68
BROWNE, AGNES 65
BUNNE, RALPH 39R

BUTTLER, 65
BYET, ROBERT 81R
CADE, BERNARD 15R
CADE, JOHN 15R
CADE, WILLIAM 15R
CAKE, 53R
CARTER, JOHN 103
CHERITY, Mr 15
CHIPP, JOANE 68R
CHIPP, ROGER 68R
COLES, ELIZABETH 82R
COXE, HENRY 53R
CREWS, BARTHOLOMEW 70
CURTERS, MARY 96R
DAMON, THOMAS 43
DANIELL, THOMAS 34 & 103 & 113R
DOBY, CHRISTOPHER 112
DOBY, EDWARD 112
DOBY, Unknown 56
DOBYE, JOHN 18
DOWE, Mr 85R
DRAKE, WILLIAM 115 &106R
DUTCHMAN, a 7R
DUTCHMAN, a 7R
DUTCHMAN, a 7R
DUTCHMAN, a 7R
DYKER, ROGER 35
EVANS, GEORGE 53
FEAVER, 12R
FERICE, JOHN 95R
FILDEW, JOHN 35R
FORTUNE, Unknown 79
FOWLER, GILES 45
GALPING, Mrs 57R
GARLAND, HENRY 84
GAWDEN, ROBERT 57R
GEALE, ROBERT 17
GIBBS, ROGER 101
GIBSON, Mr 9R
GILBERT, RICHARD 18 & 72
GREY, BENEDICT 50R
HALL, NICHOLAS 91R

SINGER, JEFFERY 83
SMART, NICHOLAS 14
SMITH, ROBERT 50R
STEVENS, JOHN 115R
STEVENS, JOHN 96
STEVENS, NICHOLAS 115R
STOCKER, Mr 110R
STOCKER, Mr 67
STRANGWAYES, Captain 100R
STRANGWAYES, Sir JOHN 114
STRANGWAYS, NICHOLAS 112R
STRODE, Mr 5R
STRODE, Mrs 75
THISTLE, JEFFRY 85
THRESHER, HENRY 60R
THRESHER, HENRY 62
THRESHER, WILLIAM 69
TOOLEDGE, GEORGE 57R
TOOLEDGE, JOHN 64
unknown, ABRAHAM 70
Unknown, Unknown 22R
Unknown, Unknown 53
Unknown, Unknown 53
Unknown, Unknown 59
Unknown, Unknown 59
Unknown, Unknown 65
unknown, unknown 70
Unknown, Unknown 82R
VINCENT, EUGENIUS 99R
WAKE, JOHN 66
WATSON, JOHN 101R
WATSON, JOHN 101R
WAYMAN, GEORGE 50R
WEARE, Mr 91R
WHITE, JOHN 109R
WHITE, JOHN 98
WHITE, MARTIN 43R
WHITTLE, ALICE 36
WIGGOTT, WILLIAM 75
WILKINS, RICHARD 61
WILLIAMS, RICHARD 26R
WILLIAMS, ROBERT 29R
WILLIAMS, SARAH 55R

WILLIAMS, WILLIAM 68
WILLS, JOHN 66 & 70
WINTER, 27R
WINTER, WALTER 50R
WOODE, JOHN 56R
WOODFORD, Unknown 56R
YARDLEY, RICHARD 67

Appendix 1 Protestation Returns 1641

Because of the turmoil between the King and Parliament in 1641 prior to the Civil War, Parliament passed an anti Popery law in July 1641 decreeing that everybody over the age of 18 would swear an oath of allegiance to King Charles and the Church of England but in practice this applied only to males over the age of 18. Each parish incumbent was to read the oath to their parishioners and witness their signature and note any who would not sign as recusants (see Roddipoll-Radipole) or make note of anybody away at the time. The oaths seem to have been taken between 23 and 28 February 1641(2) so is as near a comparable contemporary account of the male over 18 population with regard to the wreck of the *Golden Grape* on 11 December 1641 and the witnesses at the Court of Admiralty Inquiry held between the 10 January 1641(2) and 28 March 1642, the new year being on 25 March.

The following list is an extract for the towns and villages relevant to those who attended or benefited from the wreck of the *Golden Grape*. The Protestation Returns for Dorset were published in 1912 and edited by E.A. & G.S Fry. I have recognised several instances of v being taken as a u but have left it as originally transcribed so an open mind to variations in names is essential. There are gaps where the original documents were damaged but some good guesses can be made especially where partial names have minimus, maximus, senior or junior and can be matched.

Witnesses to the oaths were the rector, clerke or vicar plus overseers and churchwardens and even constables. Those that could not sign as witnesses made their mark and an x next to the name denotes this.

ABBOTSBURY

[About ten names missing]
.... ..adford
..... Forde
.... Clarke
.... ate senr
(there is a John Keate junr)
.... sher senr
(there is a John Thresher junr)
..... Toolarge
..... Trauers
..... Jacob
[about fifteen names missing]
..... Farre
.... diner
.... berts
.. .... mways
.... y Slade
... liam Hardy senr
.. oore Joliffe
.. hn Miller
Richard Labour
Stephen Hallett
Samuel Ford
.... lett
[about four names missing]
..... Dammon
Richard Boatswayne
Robert White
Richard Coward
Sampson Labour
John Charity
Henry Bayly
William Purchas
Richard Bythewood
John Angell
Christopher Jay
Hugh Newman junr
Robert Puckett
Robert Hayward
Joseph Roberts
John Matchill
Hugh Boatswayne junr

Richard Keate
Thomas Bristow
John Durdant
Ralph Miller
Roger Boatswayne
Richard Thystle
Walter Bayly senr
William Meer....
Henry Reade
Thomas Ham
Richard Russell
Henry Hutchins
Phillip Mollett
John Blanchard
Mark Bythewood senr
Henry Lake
Henry Harris
Richard Bridle
William Doby senr
Richard Hawkins
William Dennys
John Watson senr
Christopher Doby
John Thystle
William Vye
John Payne
George Payne
Henry Lovell
Richard Payne
John Swateridge
John Miller
John Cooper
Angel Wood
Osmund Farre
Roger Bayly
William Ober
Richard Bayly
William Critchell
Richard Flory
John Keate junr
George Fever
William Mitchell
Henry Thystle
William Mollet
John Critchell
Robert Mullyns

John Mollet senr
Henry Fever
John Hawkins
Thomas Evans senr
Silvester Wallis
Walter Bayly junr
John Thresher junr
John Watercombe
Richard Hawkins junr
John Samways
Thomas Carter
Richard Haywell
Richard Toolarge
Henry Hall
Peter Purchas
Richard Gybbes
John Thresher minimus
John Ober
Thomas Scammell
George Ferman
John Turner
Christopher Bartlett
Christopher Sherin
John Pound
Stephen Edmunds
Thomas Bro .. shall
John Mollet junr
Walter Moore
Robert Downton
George Taylour
Richard Derry
George Genge
William Rose
Nicholas Hall
Leonard Ferman
Henry Hardy
Henry Bythewood
Richard Rose senr
John .....
Henry Harris senr
William Bryer
Henry Elli...
John Bayly
Richard Porter
John Labour
William Helyar

William Durdant
William Doby junr
John Harvy
Robert Spence
Ralph Martyn
John Bayly junr
Walter Haywell
John Oliver senr
Henry Bradford
Thomas .....
Richard Churchill
Roger Harris
Henry Miller
Matthew Henvill
William Perkins
Robert Sweet
Richard Wallis
Thomas Evans junr
John Haywell
Thomas Thystle
[about ten names missing]
John Tryvett
John Hawkins minimus
Robert Fill
Thomas Puckett junr
Peter .....
John Harris
Thomas Puckett minimus
Henry B . . . .
John Payne
Thomas Pidd.....
Edward Doby
Richard By.....
John Bryer
John Gybbons
James P.....
Stephen Hansford
William Flory
Arthur Hay.....
Thomas Watercombe
Richard Henvill
Roger Vi.....
Roger Motyer
Edward Henvill
Edward Ly.....
William Pyttman

John Jenkins
William .....
Thomas Miller
John Bonger
Thomas .....
Henry Groves
Matthew Bonger
Henry .....
Raynold Farre
William Burges
[a few more names missing]
Thomas Mitchell junr
James Hill
Nicholas Samwayes
John Motyer
[about five names missing]
John Browne

Witnesses herof are
Edw. Osborne, Vicar
Henrie Garland,
Churchwarden
Will' Hawkens,
Churchwarden
John Hardye, overseer
William Hardye, overseer
X his marke
John Pollard, Constable

CHICKERELL

. . . Marshalshay
Mighaell Langford
Henry Marshalsay
Thomas Newman
Nicholaus Avrill
William Buntyn
John Davye
Thomas Bryar
Nicholaus Dickar
. . atthias Weys
Richard Bryne
Edward Marshallsay
Thomas Bryne
Fidiah Marshallsay

Henry Wey
Wm Marshalsay
William Bussell, sen.
John Stickland
John Stevens
Nicholaus Stevens
John Goddard
Richard Keate
William Bryar
John Buntyn
Roger Dickar
William Newman
William Stickland
Robin Dammin
Nicholaus Bussell
George Tillar
William Avrill
Christopher Baylie

Tristram Knapton, clerke
Willam Bussell) overseer
x William Wey) overseer
x Thomas Stevens) churchwarden
x Thomas Bussell) churchwarden

FLEET

Max Mohun, esq.
Max Mohun, gent.
Henry Hassard, marchant
Robert Murrey
Thomas Allin
Robert Tullage
Christofer Lovell
Stephen Godwyn
William Lovell
Fruncis Bennett
Thomas Parkins
Morgan Hustes
Robert Lovell
Samuell Lovell
John Allin
John Butcher

John Williams
John Curtise
John Carter
Thomas Carter
John Murrey
John Godwyn
Robert Allin
Christofer Pollet
John Pollet
Richard Briar
Robert Briar
William Carter
Anthony Carter
Henry Gardiner
William Chaules

Ferdinando Talour, vicar
Robert Murrey) church-
John Godwyn) wardens

LANGTON HERRING

Jesp. Stone
John Genge
Willm. Dunne ?
Edw. Huxford
Richard Haywell
Edward Bridge
Adam Gaudin
John Boyt
Richard Boyt
John Gullifer
Richard Hurding
Willm. Charles
Willm. Winter
George Charles
Henry Benfeild
Nicolas Puckett
Thomas Nossiter
John Heywell
John Keepin ?
Thomas Batten
Robert Louell
Henry Nossiter

Aldry Charles
John Hendy
Jesp. Charles
Willm. Tarry
Willm. Murren
Daniel Curtes
Thomas Cumidge
Willm. Nossiter
John Benfeild
Thomas Michell
Willm. Benfeild
Willm. Dike
Willm. Hendy
Tho. Boyt
John Hendy

Jo. Haslewoode, rect. *ibm.*
x Willm. Dike) church-
x Willm. Hendy) wardens
x Thomas Boyt) ou-
x John Hendy)seers

MELCOMBE REGIS

Fabyan Hodder
Henry Michell
Thomas Wallis
Thomas Giear
Jno Cade
George Churches
Ilger Craford
Charles Lawrence
John Witte
Andrew Richards
Jon Hodges
Thomas Louelaces
Jno Semor
John Swettman
Phillip Kind
Nathanell Allen
Roger (blank)
Justinan Bagge
Jereme Bagge
John Lattimor
Will. Randelle

Thomas Farr
Richard Billes
John Puller
John Callaway
Will. Baylly
Thomas Baylly
Christoffer Baylly
Edward Punches
Edward Hownsley
Daniel Winser
Robert Poncknold
Frances Harris
Henry Sanders
Robart Sanders
Will. Hollard
Robert Baylly
Richard Sammon
Simon Strette
John Tantton
Thomas Holla . . .
John Sande . . .
Petter Green
John Curtise
Jeremy Geruase
John Darby
William Archer
William Ironse
William Shaddocke
Michaell White
Jonathan Leddor
Watter Odey
Robart Pitte
David Hellard
James Hardy
John Kinge
Robart Hardy
Nicollas Cooper
Roger Ossard
Joyce Flower
John Hardinge
Richard Smith
William Reade
Andrew Ebarne

John Gilberd
Josiah Darby
Edward Allen
John Anar
Andrew Pitte
Raphe Presty
Thomas George
Frances Sanders
Christoffer Lattimor
Thomas Lnooden (sic)
William Gillett
. . . Chapman
. . . Hingson
. . . Meech
. . . Stone
. . . . . . Aylwin
. . . Wattes
. . . Hodders
Richard Harrison
Richard Odey
Arther Hollman
Onen Hollman
Henry Hollman
William Gardner
Jereme Banidge
John Cadde junor
John Gardner
Henry Rosse
John Arthur
George Florey
Richard Torner
Joseph Pitt
Robart Wisse
William Bolt
Henry Backmay
Griffen Wortley
George Allen
Marten Whitte
Thomas Joanes
Raphe Treuit
John Lake
Roger Woodcoke
Morgen Quilliams

Edward Bond
William Hardy
William Coxe
Bartholomew Hayne
John Nottley
Edward Lake
Roger Biled
Robart Sanders
William Gillett
Robart Whitte
Thomas Maye
Nicollas Gilbert
John Serrell
John Mihills
Henry Russell
Nathaniell Hunte
John Chamers
John Fildewe
Morgaine Quiliames
Gregory Banidge
Henry Knight
Giles Newmane
Thomas Comes
Thomas Vivens
Richard Baily
Briant Snodden
Robert Hillerd
Henry Tanton
Thomas Samways
George Gillet
Lambert Cornelius
Thomas Wintter
Lennord Hillard
John Longe
John Hingston
Edmund Smith
Henry Caue
Justinen Hingston
Lennord Moticer
Thomas Wellmane
George Weaman
John Hodder

Richard Dammen
Thomas Hingston
William Motier
Simone Browen
William Andrews
I . . . s Vey
John Mintoren
Nickles Miner
Will. Vernell
John Geale
William Wills
. . . hn Paine
Henry Walrond
Lindel Gille
. . . regory Hunte
William Ebber
Richard Bolte
. . . es Edwards
John Stagge
John Elles
. . . regory Bakeway (?)
Joseph Watts
Frances Gape
. . . illiam Mintoren
Edward Courtney
Thomas Waltham
John Beare
Edward Linsy
John Samways
Henry Baily
James Napper
John Williams
Thomas Dandey
Roger Moulin
Richard Bolte
Henry Whitell
Roger Comes
Andrew Price
Roger Gille
Robert Gauden
Phillip Dyer

Thomas Gauden
John Chille
Adam Foxe
Morgen Pittman
Nathaniell Hunte
John Sanders
Henry Gipson
Marke Passons
Thomas Knight
James Newe

Ita testamr
Richard Marwell, rect.
John Arthur, churchwarden
George Churchey, ouseere
Edward Hodder, ouseer
James Cornish, constable

PORTISHAM

Batten
Tawbutt
P . . sley
Meeche, sen.
Sandford, sen.
Rose
Bartram, sen.
Bartram, ju.
.... rd Bartram
John Batten
William Harvy
Edward Joy
Robert Wylls
Charles Wood
George Stone
John Hendy
Thomas Selly
William Rawlins, sen
Williams Rawlins, jun
Robert Rawlins
Lawrence Culliford
John Rawlins
   Bayly
. . .   arvy
. . . .

. . . .
Jeffery Samwaies
Thomas Sandford, sen.
Thomas Sandford, ju.
John Meeche
John Deeringe
John Sandford, ju.
Thomas Deeringe
John Wood
Thomas Wylls
Walter Riccard
John Riccard
George Toolarge
Hugh Mychell
Henry Thresher
George Moore
Walter Sandford
William Bellett
Henry Bellett
Richard Samwayes
Samuel Samwayes
Seraphin Mowlam
Henry May
William Wyttle
Robert Kelsey
John Hancocke
Thomas Amizer
Robert Amizer
Robert Douch
John Spicer
William Symonds
Henry Urry
Andrew . . .
. . . . . .
. . . . . .
. . . . . .
. . . . . .
... yes
.. . . yter
.. . . wylls, sen.
. . . mas Plowman, sen
Thomas Plowman, jun.
Jesper Stone
William Hawkins

Samuel Samwayes
Hugh Browne
Thomas Hazard
John Peeters
Bartholomew Crue
Robert Meeche
William Wallis
Anthony Hardy
John Hardy
Joseph Hardy
Richard Wallis
. . . Perrett
. . . Michell
. . . Raskelly
. . . Addames
. . . Addames
Thomas Wylls
Robert Cheyney
Thomas Hardinge
Humphry Puckett
Thomas Plowman
Richard Wilkins
Thomas Samwayes
Robert Jones
William Thresher
Henry Smith
Mathew Stroud
Henry Williams
Thomas Stroud
John Squibb
William Hendy
Richard Sumsey
Richard Holston
Thomas Samond
William Ispley
Richard Hardinge
Richard Hardy
Walter Harris
George Wynter
Thomas Chipp
Robert Addames
Robert Bugg
Joseph Harvy

Robert Chipp
Richard Daminge
Ralfe Wallis
Richard Rowden
Henry Russell
Robert George
John Sweete
Humphry Sanders
John Selly
John Whyte
Robert Gawden

There are wantinge from
home wch have not
taken the Protestacon
vizt.
Laurence Culliford, absent
ever since wee receyued it

John Galping, mynister
Willim Weare) war-
Robert Symonds) dens
William Farre (ou-
John Wynter) seers

PORTLAND

Robert Pitt
Morgan Boyle
Ralph Bunn, sen.
. . . rd Prince
. . . xander Atwool
. . . . . Byatt
. . . Knight
. . . Owesley
. . . ert Lano
. . . anyell Pearce
. . . ward Tobie
William Knap
John Nowell
Thomas Mynes
Thomas Mitchell
Andrew Atwooll
William Atwooll
Thomas Stoodleigh, sen.

Bartholomew Mitchell
John Pearce
Angell Stoodleigh
John Hinde
Thomas Stoodleigh, jun.
Phillip Boyte
William Elliott
John Flew, sen.
John Elliott, med.
Phillip Peerce
William Wiggatt
William Beaton
Thomas Dowe
Robert Atwooll, med.
John Stone
Christopher Willes
Sydracke Stone
Thomas Paynter
James Bendfild
Phillip Bendfeild
Robert Atwooll, sen.
Stephen Dryer
John Elliott, jun.
Richard Bendfield
Ralph Bunn, jun.
William Bendfield
Henry Pitt
Leonard Haywell
Simon Durrant
Bartholomew Cumbean
John Cumbean
William Hinde
Geoffrey Byatt
Joell Hinde
Andrew Gardner
Samuell Paynter
Owen Elliott
William Ouesley
Robert Newcombe
Edward Pearce
Robert James
William Pitt, jun
William Pearce, jun
Phillip Owesley
Giles Pearce
Robert Bendfield

Frauncis Sweete
Robert Follett
Ralph Elliott
William Sweett, sen
William Cumbean, jun.
Richard Smyth
Andrew Cumbean, jun.
Robert Peerce
William Sweett, jun.
William Gibbs
Edmond White
Zacheus Jenninges
Andrew Cumbean, sen.
Zacheus Spurlinge
Owen Atwooll
Lyonell Knight, jun
Will. Peerce, sen.
George Atwooll
Richard Atwooll, jun.
Gasper Gaytch
John Angell
John Prince
Emmanuell Hendy
William Wesley, jun.
Markes Hardy
Luke Knapp
Jonathan Nowell
Richard Pitt
William Pitt
Simon Barrett
Edward Tobie
John Tobie
William Spurlinge
Robert Nowell
Lancellot Atwooll
Charles Gaytch
William Prancker
Richard Peerce
Henry Dally
John Elliott, sen.
John Flew, jun.
. . . . . n Peerce
Beniamin Peerce
William Jennings
. . . Portland
. . . Newrnan

.. . . ence Atwool
.. . . mas Geale
Nicholas Beadfild
Zachary Peerce
. . . Stoodleigh
. . . Cumbean, (?) sen.
…..es
. . . Mitchell
.. . .Hodges
Percival Hendy
Richard Clarke
Richard Gilbert
Lionell Knight, sen.
Richard Elliott
Edward Atwooll
……….
(torn) . . . Wiggats?
George Benfeild
Alexander Gorben
John Haynes
Ralph Prouse
Richard Stradlinge

Of the Castle

WilliamStrode, lieuetenaunt
John Louerocke ?
Robert Hone
Christopher Gibbes
Richard Martine
Henry Hardy
Robert Bunn
Richard Meadway
Aaron Hamblinge

Thomas Bragg, curate of Portland
Robert Wiggett) ch-
Robert Flew) wardens
Thomas Ellet, constable
Owen Lano) over-
x Robert Byatt) seers

RODDIPOLL

. . . Williams, gent
. . . bte Knight
Willm. Rose

John Florrence
George Golding
James Buddage
Peter Avary
James King
Geffery Gibbs
Martinn Penny, sen
Ellis Gulliford
Thomas Disket
John Batten
Willm. Twinney
James Bennet
Thomas Dibben
Nicholas Bryght
Richard Ames
John King
Martinn Penny, jun.
Thomas Hill
John Keate
Jethro Daber
Richard Bishopp
Willm. Bishopp

Richard Marwell, rector
Nicholas   Hopkins   x
churchwarden
Rychard Beale) x
Henry Pitman) ouseers
Alexander Kayns & Peter Durant) being recusants do refuse the protestation

WEYMOUTH

Mr Edward Cuttance, maior
Mr Mathew Allin
Mr Henry Cuttance
Mr John Thornton
Mr James Gyar
Mr William Charity
Christover Hall
George Backalar
Richard Pitt
Richard Coxe
William Harrison
Joseph Maunders
John Ellett

Samwell Cribb
William Kneeler
Beniamin Bryar
Robert Symmes
James Coomes
John Samwayes
Edward Samwayes
William Stownt
John Dry, ju
Thomas Ridle
Ralphe Locke
Henry Spicer
Edward Allin
Richard Keate
William Davies
William Winter
John Hoble
Thomas Parmiter
Nicholas Marriner
Maximinian Loder
John Loder
Thomas Loder
John Chippe
John Fowler
Robert Bendle
John Locke
James Spicer
Robert Smith
Nicholas Cuttance
James Dowridge
William Williams
Faithfull Angell
Nicholas Zangar
John Parmiter
John Elburne
Thomas Gill
Tangy Craze
John Tackle
Roger Rose
John Addams
Reboam Mynor
William Symond
Gregory Coxe
Henry Hinctly
John Harvy
Stephen Coven

Thomas Lyne
John Mills
Edward Thistle
Edward Redditt
Richard Wilson
Mathew Cawsen
Michaell Flanne
Roger Harte
Richard Mattocke
Robert Clittery
William Long
William Urvin
John Payne
John Wall, junr
Richard White
John Ellett, ju.
John White, ju.
William Dry
Nicholas Hebbert
Roger Read
George Pitt
Bryant Spicer
John Jumpe
Davy Barker
James Bull
William Cotten
John Cotten
John Dry, min.
William Cate
Stephen White
Martin Hammell
Thomas Barber
Michaell Currier
Bryant Tyler
William Baker
Robert Stunfford
Clement Cawly
William Wice
William Snelling
Richard Codde
Richard Browne
William Hare
Andrew Cotten
John Churchill
Ralphe Limbry
Stephen Jessopp

.----- ('torn')
Joh . . .
Mat. . . .
Ca . . .
Ed ...
Walter . . .
William Champe
Cornelius Ellis
William Motier
Thomas Bowden
William White
John Rashly
William Weeks
Martin Bond
Henry Sparrow
Thomas Parmiter, junr
John Allen, senr
James Peach
William Phillips
Thomas Allexander
Walter Piddall
Richard Heale
Robert Sympson
John Hammell
Thomas Barnes
William Barnes
William Alford
Richard Brooke
Peter Harte
John Cole
Richard Dawly
John Berry
Nathaniell Abbott
Richard Sturton
Anthony Batter
Davy Traddy
George Dashwood
Henry Stocker
Robert Derby
Peter Cornelius
John Kanaway
Andrew Pitt
George Basten
George Browne
John Wall, min.
William Wall

Clement Clarke
Thomas Danyell
John Pope
Samwell Tackle
Nicholas Preston
James Leddoze
....
. . . Holmes
. . . Druer
. . . Cuttance
. . . Gardiner
. . . Motier
Edward Chappell
Thomas George
Roger Chipp
William Cade, sen.
William Cade, junr
William Williams junr
William Averill
Peter Aplby
Richard Harvy
James Cornish

Edward Couttanes, mayor
Ferdinando Talour, curat
John Wall, churchwarden

WYKE REGIS

.... Speccott, esq
.... Martin, gent.
..... Nopp
..... Smart
..... Smart
. . . ony Clapcott
William Davie
Anthony Winter
James Bond
Thomas Hunt
William Waram
Daniel Andrews
Leonard Sanford
John Hodgins
Thomas Gray
John Geale
Walter Winter
Thomas Wade

Richard Stickland
Robert Winter
William Cumbin
Robert Bishop
Thomas Peeke
George Cumbin
John Lyne
Robert Geale
John Spracland
John Allin
Thomas Motier
Peter Waram
Richard Mills
.. . . n Gray
…. ew Pitt
….. lliam Cade
John Andrews
Andrew Mills
Sander Lee
Nicholas Jeffris
Bennet Gray
Joseph Nowell
John Boyt
Brian Feaver
John Churchill
John Pitt
Salomon Barrett
William Bishop
Walter Legge
Francis Spratt
William Bishop, jun.
Nicholas Feaver
John Whyte
Owen Gibbens
Richard Batty
Henry Meech
William Stone
John Murrey
Phillip Salter
Nicholas Pitt
John Baylie
William Standeigh
Augustine True
Thomas Baylie

Thomas Rainolds
William Boyt
Thomas Angell
George Pitt
Arthur Gray
Nicholas Bundall
Nicholas Williams
Nicholas Charles
Phillip Pitt
David Pitt
Thomas Pitt
Sander Geale
Robert Angell
William Boyt
Thomas Bryne
John Bayle
Bartholomew Williams
Thomas Curtise
William Way
John Curtise
Nicholas Chappell
Nicholas Addm

Ferdinando Talour, curat
John Jeffris, churchwarden
Henry Harnest) ouseers
Andrew Pitt)
Robert Hunte, const.

Appendix 2 Weymouth & Melcombe Ships

Ships are repeated to show range of years, or change of ownership or Captain

Name	Tons	No. of men	No. of Guns	Owner(s) or ship type	Captain	Age in years	Date & Source
Abigail	120			Henry Michell	John Michell & W. Collins		SDP 1626
Abigail	100			Joseph Lysley and others	J.L.		SDP 1630
Abigall	100		10	Henry Michell		20	MW 1628 At Home
Aid	u			John Mitchell	John Mitchell		EP 1598
Amity	60			Nicholas Jones	Nicholas Wright		EP 1591
Anne Huddy				William Huddy and John Reynolds	Hugh Preston		EP 1589
Anne Huddy					Henry Thin		EP 1590
Archangel							sent Weymth 1584
Ark	50		2	Thomas Ledoze & Henry Cuttance		8	MW 1628 At Home
Bark Bond	56			John Bond, William Pitt, Richard Pitt, William Holman	David Geyer		EP 1589
Bark Bond					Edward Bond		EP 1590
Bark Bond					Roger Geyer		EP 1591
Bark Brave					Oliver Hillyard		
Bark Brooke				John Brooke, Thomas Bagg, William Hodder and John Willis	Thomas Bagg		EP 1590

Name	Tons	No. of men	No. of Guns	Owner(s) or ship type	Captain	Age in years	Date & Source
Bark Brooke					Thomas Bagg		EP 1591
Bark Randall	60			John Randall, Sir George Carey, Sir Walter Raleigh & others	Thoms Lowther		EP 1590
Bark Sutton	70	40		Hugh Perasons			Armada 1588
Bark Way or Bark Sutton	70			Brooke	Mark Bury		EP 1589
Black Dogg				Fabian Hodder			House of Commons 1642
Blessinge				W. Martell & T Chappell			1631
Caramouchy	25		2	David Gyre		10	MW 1628 At Home
Carouse	30			Roger Page	Oliver Knott		EP 1589
Carouse				John Pitt			
Catherine or Little Catherine	35			Robert White	Robert White		EP 1590
Catherine or Little Catherine	35						EP 1591
Catherine White (or Great Katherine)	u			Robert White	Giles Baynard		EP 1598
Catherine White (or Great Katherine)	u			Robert White	Giles Baynard		EP 1598

Name	Tons	No. of men	No. of Guns	Owner(s) or ship type	Captain	Age in years	Date & Source
Christian	40			John Reynolds and others	J.R.		SDP 1630
Christian	80			?			T H Cert. May 1630
Content	40		5	Henry Russell & John Gardner		10	MW 1628 At Home
Content	50		6	John Blackforde & Capt. Pettifitz		8	MW 1628 At Sea
Content	40			Henry Russell	Henry Hinckley		SDP 1627
Content	60			Stephen Reynolds and others	S. Reynolds		SDP 1628
Content	60			Rich. Russell	Henry Hinckley		SDP 1628
Corymuch	30			pinnace to King David	N. Corney		SDP 1629
Damosell	20			pinnace to Sarah & Katherine			SDP 1627
Daniel			7	Richard Gregory			1577
Desire	30			William Davis & Elizabeth Drier		10	MW 1628 At Sea
Desire	50			pinnace to Dolphin	Robt. Damon		SDP 1629
Diamond				John Reynolds			1600
Dolphin	100			Edward Linze and others	Gabriel Cornish		SDP 1629
Dragon	80			Thos. Powlett & others	John Lockyer		SDP 1626
Dragon	80			Edward Roy			SDP 1627
Dragon	140			John Lockyer	John Lockyer		SDP 1628

Name	Tons	No. of men	No. of Guns	Owner(s) or ship type	Captain	Age in years	Date & Source
Dragone	80			John Lockier	Gyles Bond and Francis Saunders		SDP 1625
Eleanor	30		4	Henry Waltham & William Charytie		8	MW 1628 At Sea
Eleanor	45			Wm. Simpson	Wm. Simpson		SDP 1628
Eleinor					Laurence Prowse		1587
Elenor of Weymouth					Amyas Preston		1586
Elizabeth	90		5	William Waltham & Thomas Gyre		30	MW 1628 At Home
Elizabeth	100			Wm Waltham & Thos. Geyer	Wm. Collins		SDP 1627
Elizabeth	50			Rich. Champion and others	R.C.		SDP 1628
Ellinor	60			Thos. Waltham and others	R. Champion		SDP 1630
Endeavour	35			Henry Rogers	Ephraim Reynolds		EP 1591
Expedition	70	50					Armada 1588
Fellowship	40		3 but capable of 5	Richard Berry		20	MW 1628 At Home

Name	Tons	No. of men	No. of Guns	Owner(s) or ship type	Captain	Age in years	Date & Source
Flower	40			Henry Cuttance			1625-30 Let. of m.
Flower	40			Henry Maior	Henry Maior & Portland Bunne		SDP 1626
Flower	40			pinnace to Gift of God	Portland Bunne		SDP 1627
Flying Drake	40			John Haynes and others	J.H.		SDP 1628
Flying Harte							1633
Fortune	50		4	John Wall & Richard Wall		8	MW 1628 At Sea
Francis	u			Henry Drake	Henry Drake		EP 1598
Francis				William Walton			
Francis, of Weymouth			57				MW MDS 1597
Friendship	40						SDP 1627
Friendship	60			Thos. Chaplin and others	T.C.		SDP 1629
Galleon of Weymouth	100	50			Richard Miller		Armada 1588
Gallion of Weymouth					Jas. Whittinge		1586
George Gregory				Richard Gregory			1577
Gift	140			Robert Bassett	Robert Bassett		SDP 1626
Gift of God	120			Henry Cuttance			1625-30 Let. of m.

Name	Tons	No. of men	No. of Guns	Owner(s) or ship type	Captain	Age in years	Date & Source
Gift of God	120			Henry Cuttance	Edward Cuttance		SDP 1627
Godfreede				W. Pitte	W. Goste		1582
Golden Hind or White Lion	120			Edward Lewes	Richard Lewes		EP 1591
Golden Rial or Ryall	120	50		Thomas Middelton			Armada 1588
Grace	u			John Randall	Edward Baynard		EP 1598
Great Katherine	80		8	Robert White & John Blackford		20	MW 1628 At Home
Great Katherine	100			Robert White and others	R. W.		SDP 1628
Greyhound	35			pinnace to Christian			SDP 1630
Guift	140			Robt. Bassett	R. B.		SDP 1626
Harry and John	140			John Gardner and others	Henry Russell		SDP 1630
Heart's Desire				John Randall & Walter Raleigh			1596
Heathen	60	30					Armada 1588
Hope	70			Robert Maior and others	R. Maior		SDP 1627
Hopewell	25			John Gallott & Henry Cuttance		9	MW 1628 At Home
Hopewell	30		4	John Blackfood & William Collins		20	MW 1628 At Sea

Name	Tons	No. of men	No. of Guns	Owner(s) or ship type	Captain	Age in years	Date & Source
Hopewell	40		4	John James & John Blackford		10	MW 1628 At Sea
Hopewell	40		capable of 4	John Damon		5	MW 1628 At Sea
Hopewell	25			pinnace to Truelove 1626	Clement White		SDP 1626
Hopewell	30			pinnace to Dragon	Robt. Roy		SDP 1626
Hopewell	36			pinnace to Phoenix	Thos. Prowse		SDP 1626
Hopewell	36				T. Prowse		SDP 1626
Hopewell	60			pinnace to Stephen			SDP 1627
Hopewell	60			Arnold Bassett	Arnold Bassett		SDP 1628
Hopewell	60			Henry Mayor and others	H.M.		SDP 1629
Jane Bonaventure	20			Roger Geyer	Roger Geyer		EP 1590
Jesus				John Bond			
Joane	30			pinnace to Ellinor			SDP 1630
John Gregory				Richard Gregory			1577
Judith	40		6	Jonas Dennis & Peter Salenesne		16	MW 1628 At Sea
Judith	70			Jonas Dennys	Jonas Dennys		SDP 1627
Judith	80			John Sacheverell	J.S.		SDP 1629

Name	Tons	No. of men	No. of Guns	Owner(s) or ship type	Captain	Age in years	Date & Source
Jupiter				Bound to La Rochelle with salt			Blown ashore N coast Spain February 1556
Katherine	66	30					Armada 1588
King David				Captain John Arthur			Civil War 1643
King David	60			David Guyer and others	John Lockier		SDP 1629
Laurence							1590?
Leopard	240			John Freake. Esq	Nich. Strangways, capt		SDP 1626
Leopard	240			John Feake			T H Cert. May 1626
Leopard of Poole	240			Nicholas Audney of Weymouth and others	Nicholas Audney		SDP 1627
Lion				Richard, William & Henry Pitt			
Little John or Gift of God	20			John Peters	Richard Skinner		EP 1591
Long John	140			Henry Waltham	Francis Saunders		SDP 1630
Margaret	60		6	Thomas Polhill & Nich. Cornew		12	MW 1628 At Sea
Margaret	60			pinnace to Leopard	Nich. Audney		SDP 1626

Name	Tons	No. of men	No. of Guns	Owner(s) or ship type	Captain	Age in years	Date & Source
Margaret	60				Nich Audney, master		SDP 1626
Margaret	100			Gabriel Cornish and others	Gabriel Cornish		SDP 1628
Margaret	100			Robt. Salter	R.S.		SDP 1629
Marigold				Raufe Horsey and others	R. H.		SDP 1629
Mary				Fabian Hodder			Civil War 1648
Mary	50			pinnace to Pilgrim			SDP 1629
Marygold	60			Jonathan Downs	Jonathan Downs		SDP 1628
Marygold	140			Henry Cuttance	Edward Cuttance		SDP 1629
Matthew				Richard, William & Henry Pitt			
Mayflower				John Pitt			1593
Mermaid	40			pinnace to Sarah Bonadventure			SDP 1627
Mermaid				pinnace to Sarah Bonadventure			SDP 1628
Michael Gregory				Richard Gregory			1577
Niger	90			Jonathan Downes			SDP 1630
Palacra	80	6		Stephen Dennis			SDP 1626
Pearl	u			William Walton	William Hall		EP 1598

Name	Tons	No. of men	No. of Guns	Owner(s) or ship type	Captain	Age in years	Date & Source
Peter	50		capable of 4	John Wall & Richard Wall		20	MW 1628 At Sea
Phoenix	35		4	John Gardner & John Lockier		10	MW 1628 At Home
Phoenix	40			John Lockyer	John Lockyer		SDP 1626
Phoenix	40			pinnace to Gift			SDP 1626
Phoenix	40			John Lockier, merchant	J.L.		SDP 1626
Phoenix	40			pinnace to Dragon			SDP 1627
Phoenix	40			pinnace to Dragon			SDP 1628
Phoenix	50				Alex. Clattery		SDP 1630
Pilgrim	100		6	John Gallott & William Holmes		16	MW 1628 At Sea
Pilgrim	140			John Moncke and others	J.M.		SDP 1628
Pilgrim	160			John Blachford and David Guyer	Capt. Holmes		SDP 1629
Pilgrim, of Weymouth	200			John Hill, of Dorchester			SDP 1627
Prudence							1621
Prudence				William Walton			
Riall	160			Thomas Myddelton & Erasmus Harby	William Myddelton		EP 1590

Name	Tons	No. of men	No. of Guns	Owner(s) or ship type	Captain	Age in years	Date & Source
Robert and John	40			pinnace to Elizabeth			SDP 1627
Rose					Francis Sanders		1617
Saloman							sent Weymth 1584
Samuel	50		capable of 4	Henry Russell. James James		8	MW 1628 At Home
Samuel or Golden Hind	60			Philip Boyte of Portland			1580
Samuel or Golden Hinde				Philip Boyte			1580
Samuel or Golden Hinde				Luca Guido alias Warde			1581
Sara	90		8	David Gyre & William Holmes		7	MW 1628 At Sea
Sarah	100			Robt. Guyer and others	R.G.		SDP 1629
Sarah and Katherine	50			John Hill	Thos. Chaplin		SDP 1627
Sarah Bonadventure	100			Henry Waltham & David. Geyer			SDP 1627
Sarah Bonadventure	100			John Davis and others	John Davis and John Randoll		SDP 1628
Scout	60			pinnace to Leopard	Wm. Lovell		SDP 1627
Seadragon				Henry Rogers			1590s

Name	Tons	No. of men	No. of Guns	Owner(s) or ship type	Captain	Age in years	Date & Source
Seahorse	80		4	Henry Michell		12	MW 1628 At Home
Sealove				pinnace to Dragone 1625	John Reeves		SDP 1625
Seraphim				John Bond & John Pitt			
Shuttle	40		4	Richard Wright & Henry Russell		4	MW 1628 At Home
Shuttle	30			George Cornish			1625-30 Let. of m.
Shuttle	30			Rich. Champion	Rich. Champion		SDP 1626
Shuttle	30			Rich. Wright & others	Gabriel Cornish		SDP 1627
Shuttle	50						SDP 1630
Speedwell	25			pinnace to Dragon			SDP 1627
St Nicholas	90			Peter Salleneuve	Peter Salleneuve		SDP 1626
Stephen	100			Stephen Pettifiz and others	Stephen Pettifiz		SDP 1627
Sunday					Henry Duffield		EP 1589
Swift			10	Henry Cuttance & Thomas Ledoze		10	MW 1628 At Home
Swiftsure	40						SDP 1630
Thomasine	120			Jonas Dennys and others	J.D.		SDP 1629
Tobacco Pipe	u			John Reynolds	Ephraim Reynolds		EP 1598

Name	Tons	No. of men	No. of Guns	Owner(s) or ship type	Captain	Age in years	Date & Source
Truelove	60		7	Peter Salenesne & Henry Cuttance		12	MW 1628 At Sea
Truelove	100			Edward Roy & others	Edward Roy		SDP 1626
Truelove	80			Peter Salleneuve	Peter Salleneuve		SDP 1628
Truelove				Thos. Gaynour	T.G. and Walter Davies master; Benj. Denny Lieut.		SDP 1633
unnamed	30			pinnace to Judith			SDP 1627
unnamed				pinnace to Marygold			SDP 1629
unnamed	40			pinnace to Thomasine			SDP 1629
Willing Mind	80			Rich. Wright and Gregory Bavidge	R. White		SDP 1630

1625-30 Let. of m.　　1625-30 Letters of marque

EP　　Kenneth R. Andrews Elizabethan Privateering

SDP　　Some Dorset Privateers

T H Cert. May 1626　　Trinity House Certificate

Appendix 3 Hodder's letter to Weld

LETTER FROM FABYAN HODDER TO HUMPHRIE WELD 1676

To the Honourable Humphrie Weld
Att Weld House in Weld Street
London

Post pd 3d

Portland Castle the 22 May 1676

Honourable Sir
Be pleased to know that I have received your [letter] of the 13th current wherein
you write of you coming downe shortly. John Peeters left his porters place
in the Castle this day 3 weekes and is gone to his owne new house to live
butt useth to come heither sometimes as the rest doe, for that ther is no
porter to give answer to any gentleman or others which come a[nd] try oftentimes
to see the Castle. I have used my best endeavour to procure another that may be fitt
to have that place and hope I shall prevayle if your honour think it fitt and
give your answere per next: little attendance of soldiers except att night and
then nott many: all being weary of the place and calling for pay, without which
and a certayne establishment of it I believe they will leave of: and for your sute
of Sir Edward Sydenham his executors for the profits of Portland I know nott
the worth of a penny ever since my coming heither, butt only a horse leaft in
the common the sommer, which they usually lett out at 13lb 4 s per anno which
they have endeavoured to take away these 2 last yeares butt I have prevailed
with them and doe yet keep itt: Nott els att present to trouble your honour doe
commit you to God and remayne

Your honourable humble servant
Fabyan Hodder

Appendix 4 Portland Castle Wages

The Establishment of Port-Island.

Captaine att 24lb a yeare or 1 shilling and 3¾ d per diem
Lieutenant att 12d per diem
Eleaven souldiers and gunners whereof two att 8d per diem a peece and the rest att
8d per diem a peece.
[The total per day figure for all eleven is given as 5shillings and 10 pence which
means the daily rate for the rest of the soldiers was 6d per day.]
The Captaine Lieutent. Souldiers and gunners are to be payd out of his Majesties
revenue of Dorsetshire & Devonshire and halfe yeares pay of one county & the
succeeding halfe yeares pay out of the other.
13th 9br 1661
Extract
William Clark

Portland Castle – wages for 2 years, 1677 to 1679

The Names of the Captaine Lieutenant Gunners Souldiers & Porter that are at
Portland Castle, who are all paid from the 10th of April 77 to the 25th March 1679

	L	s	d
1) Fabyan Hodder, Lieutenant att 12d per diem	36	10	00
Comes to the 2 yeares			
2) Henry Norvell Gunner 8d the day comes to	24	05	04
3) Robert Bartlett Porter at 8d the day	24	05	04
4) John Peeters Souldiers	18	05	00
5) Percival Hendey	18	05	00
6) Thomas Combine	18	05	00
7) John Flann	18	05	00
8) Thomas Garnett	18	05	00

176   05   08

Deduct out of which from the 25th of March, to the 10th of
April from the Capt beeng 16 days

L	s	d						
Gunners & Porter	1	01	4		3	17	4	
5 souldiers	2	10	0		172	8	4	
	3	17	4					

L	s	d					
172	8	4 Deduct Pendage which is			008	12	00
Dedeuct 4d debenter @ marke a peece					002	13	04
					11	05	04
					161	03	00

	L	s	d				
Capt Hodder for 2 yeares	36	10	00	Cap: 35	02	7.5
Gunner	24	05	04	22	02	1.5
Porter	24	05	04	22	02	1.5
John Peeters	18	05	00	16	03	1.5
Thomas Combyne	18	05	00	16	03	1.5
Percivall Hendey	18	05	00	16	03	1.5
John Flann	18	05	00	16	03	1.5
Thomas Garnett	18	05	00	16	03	1.5
	176	05	08	160	04	02

172 8 4	Deduct		15	02	08
			161	03	00

Take out 1s 9d out of every pound
for pendage & the deduction from the 25th
of March to the 10th of Aprill & the
furthest cullume shoes what cleere
moneys is due to each.

Additional note: -
Soldier John Peters was the Customs Officer for Portland until 1681 when it was
discovered he was in with the local smuggling gangs.

Appendix 5 W & MR Mayors

Weymouth & Melcombe Regis

1571-72	Bernard Maior
1572-73	Thomas Samways
1573-74	
1574-75	Robert Gregory
1575-76	Owen Ranolds (Reynolds)
1576-77	Monsell
1577-78	William Pytt (Pitt)
1578-79	W. Pytt
1579-80	Richard Pitt
1580-81	Thomas Howarde (Hayward)
1581-82	Thomas Hayward
1582-83	John Allyn (Sept 82 to May 83)
1582-83	J. Mounsell (May to Sept 83)
1583-84	Bartholomew Allyn
1584-85	Hugh Randall
1585-86	J. Mockett
1586-87	W.Pytt
1587-88	Richard Pitt
1588-89	
1589-90	William Dottrell
1590-91	J. Bond
1591-92	John Brook
1592-93	V. Barefoot
1593-94	Thomas Barefoot
1594-95	W. Dotterell
1595-96	
1596-97	William Waltham
1597-98	J. Mockett
1598-99	John Bond
1599-00	John Bond
1600-01	
1601-02	Matthew Allen
1602-03	William Holman
1603-04	Thomas Barfoot
1604-05	
1605-06	William Waltham
1606-07	J. Pitt
1607-08	John Mockett
1608-09	John Bond
1609-10	John Pitt
1610-11	John Bond
1611-12	Robert Knight
1612-13	George Pley
1613-14	Henry Micheil
1614-15	Roger Fry
1615-16	John Roy
1616-17	William Waltham
1617-18	John Pitt jnr.
1618-19	Thomas Giear
1619-20	Matthew Pitt
1620-21	John Bond
1621-22	Edward Roye
1622-23	Henry Waltham
1623-24	Matthew Allan
1624-25	Henry Michell
1625-26	Henry Russell
1626-27	Edward Linzee
1627-28	Thomas Lockier
1628-29	David Gyer
1629-30	Jacob James
1630-31	Thomas Giear
1631-32	John Thornton
1632-33	Henry Cuttance
1633-34	Thomas Wallis
1634-35	John Lockier
1635-36	John Cade
1636-37	Thomas Ledoze
1637-38	Henry Michell
1638-39	Edward Linzee
1639-40	George Churchey
1640-41	James Giear
1641-42	Edward Cuttance

1642-43	Matthew Allan
1643-44	J. Thornton
1644-45	Thomas Wallis
1645-46	Thomas Waltham
1646-47	James Giear
1647-48	Thomas Ledoze
1648-49	William Holmes
1649-50	John Brown
1650-51	John Arthur
1651-52	George Pley
1652-53	John Swetnam
1653-54	Robert Wall
1654-55	Robert Giear
1655-56	Thomas Waltham
1656-57	James Giear
1657-58	Henry Waltham
1658-59	Captain Roger Cuttance
1659-60	Captain George Pley
1660-61	Henry Rose
1661-62	Alexander Clatworthy
1662-63	Thomas Hide
1663-64	Richard Yardley
1664-65	Theophilus Byett
1665-66	Benjamin Gage (Gach, Gaitch)
1666-67	George Pley, the younger
1667-68	Sir Henry Cuttance
1668-69	Arnold Sellanova (De Sellanova)
1669-70	Richard Piercey
1670-71	George Pley
1671-72	J. Woder
1672-73	Arnold Sellanova
1673-74	Richard Biles
1674-75	Tobias Bury
1675-76	Lambert Cornellius
1676-77	Thomas Hide
1677-78	Richard Yardley
1678-79	Richard Biles
1679-80	Benjamin Gaitch

Bibliography

History of Weymouth and Melcombe Regis
The Borough of Weymouth and Portland – A Mayoral History by *Maureen Attwooll.*
Dorset Protestation Returns preserved in the House of Lords 1641-1642 ed. *E.A. & G.S. Fry*
The History and Antiquities of the County of Dorset – *John Hutchins.*
Descriptive Catalogue of the Charters, Minute Books and other Documents of the Borough of Weymouth and Melcombe Regis, A.D.1252 To 1800, With Extracts and Some Notes by *H.J. Moule.*
The Illustrated Armada Handbook – *David A. Thomas*
Studies In Dorset - *Maureen Weinstock*
More Dorset Studies – *Maureen Weinstock*

Spanish Trade
The Spanish Treasure Fleets – *Timothy R. Walton*
Spain's Men of the Sea – *Pablo E. Perez-Mallaina*
The Spanish Seaborne Empire – *J.H. Parry*
Seventeenth Century Europe – *L.W. Cowrie*
Trade, plunder and settlement – *Kenneth R. Andrews*

Armaments
The Armouries of the Tower of London, I Ordnance – *Howard L. Blackmore*

Dutch Trade
Foreign NGOs in the Dutch Navy 1642-97 paper given at 43rd Exeter Maritime History Conference, 2009 - *Andrew Little*
The Dutch Seaborne Empire – *C.R. Boxer*
Seventeenth Century Europe – *L.W. Cowrie*
The Perspective of the World, Volume 3 – *Fernand Braudel*

Civil War
The Crabchurch Conspiracy – *Mark Vine*
Great Civil War in Dorset – *A.C. Bayley*
Dorset in the Civil War – *Tim Goodwin*

Roads
Packhorse Waggon and Post – *J.Crofts*

Piracy & Privateering.
Elizabethan Privateering – *Kenneth R. Andrews*
Trade, plunder and settlement – *Kenneth R. Andrews*
Captives – *Linda Colley*
Pirates Worldwide Illustrated History, Buccaneer Explorers – *David Cordingly*
A True Relation of the Lives and Deaths of the two most Famous English Pyrats,
Purser, and Clinton; who lived in the Reigne of Queene Elizabeth – *Thomas
Heywood* 1639
The Pirates of Purbeck (Article in DNHAS 1949) – *C. L'Estrange Ewen*
Dorset Elizabethans at Home and Abroad – *Rachel Lloyd*
Piracy and Privateering in the Golden Age Netherlands – *Virginia W. Lunsford*
On the Spanish Main – *John Masefield*
Descriptive Catalogue of the Charters, Minute Books and other Documents of the
Borough of Weymouth and Melcombe Regis, A.D.1252 To 1800, With Extracts and
Some Notes by *H.J. Moule*
The Safeguard of the Sea – *N.A.M Rodger*
Some Dorset Privateers – *Henry Symonds* – 1909
The Sea Dogs – *Neville Williams*

The Golden Grape
Researcher Dr Sylvia England for locating the High Court of the Admiralty
document in the National Archives (PRO) for me.
The History of the Ship – *Richard Woodman*
Mariners Mirror – Volume 97:1 2011 pp103-126 The Whipstaff - *John Harland*

Recommendation

I read Mark Vine's book "The Crabchurch Conspiracy" about the Civil War with growing fascination about the events and history of Weymouth and Dorset in those turbulent times and recognised the main conspirator Fabian Hodder as being the organiser of the salvage of the *Golden Grape*. Mark is a very gregarious and talented, yet modest, individual and I subsequently met him at various Civil War re-enactments in Weymouth. When he knew I was writing a book about a shipwreck from the same period, he was enthusiastic and always willing to answer questions or review further research I had found.

In 2009 The Dolmen, a local Celtic Folk Rock band lead by the charismatic and very skilful songwriter Taloch (aka Tony Jameson), produced a themed album called "The Crabchurch Conspiracy" with most of the lyrics written by Mark, based on his book of the same name. You expect any band's album to have one or two mediocre tracks or ones that don't suit your taste but every song, plus the sound effects of battle and the narration was evocative, inspiring and a pleasure to hear, certainly worthy of turning into a full blown musical in the future.

Fittingly in February 2010 I went along to the Old Town Hall opposite the Boot Inn in Weymouth to hear The Dolmen perform it live, in celebration of the Conspiracy in February 1645. What better location, where so much Weymouth history and infamy took place, than in that Tudor grade 2 listed building, near to the old West Gate of Weymouth.

Equally talented local artist Semi Vine, Mark's wife, did the illustrations for the album cover and I commissioned Semi to paint her characteristically iconic picture of the *Golden Grape* in rough seas, together with a couple of sketches to illustrate the story of the salvage.

Early in 2011 The Dolmen launched their Pirate double CD album "Spirits of the Sea" telling the stories of various pirates. Again Mark was a major contributor to the lyrics together with Taloch and band member Josh Elliott. The appeal and success of the pirate themed album led to bookings for them in Holland and Germany throughout the summer, inspiring further albums from the band.

Guardians of the Old Town Hall (GOTH) was formed in 2009 to take on the lease of the Grade II Listed Building and renovate it in accordance with the conditions laid down by Weymouth and Portland Borough Council, the owner. Once completed, the object is to create a heritage centre focusing on the local history, particularly the English Civil War and the Battle of Weymouth of 1645 now known as the Crabchurch Conspiracy. It is envisaged that the downstairs hall will be used primarily for arts and performance, while both halls can be used as a community space.

Obviously Mark's book and connection with the English Civil War Society were profound influences.

If you have the chance I exalt you to read Mark's book, listen to The Dolmen's album and visit and support the Old Town Hall and celebrate the history of the area.

Selwyn Williams, December 2011

The Future

I started diving in February 1966 at the age of 15 and was soon taken on local wrecks but I had always wondered what lay beneath the sea off Chesil Beach. I researched the known ships and aircraft that were wrecked there. In the early 1970s I teamed up with Les and Julie Kent and we discovered and identified several, and subsequently bought the rights to five 18th century shipwrecks and one 19th century shipwreck. For some unknown reason we were called pirates in our local diving club but in a book published in 2003 we had risen? to "Sea Dogs of the Twentieth Century". Atkinson was a real Pirate and Drake was a real Sea Dog.

Early in 2011, at the age of 60, I teamed up with local pioneering deep-wreck diver and dive charter boat skipper & owner Grahame Knott, to share our knowledge and further investigate Deadman's Bay. Not only did his sidescan surveys turn up many targets to do with the shipwrecks that I part own, but also the many other shipwrecks off Chesil Beach.

As leader of "The Shipwreck Project", Grahame has brought together a team of highly skilled underwater photographers, experienced divers and wreck historians with the intention of locating, filming and surveying pre-20th century wrecks. Like me he wants to find and share the history and stories of these local inshore wrecks.

I think the challenge and appeal of wreck research and wreck diving could be summed up by the then United States Secretary of Defence Donald Rumsfeld, at a Press Conference at NATO Headquarters, Brussels, Belgium, June 6, 2002

"…there are no "knowns." There are things we know that we know. There are known unknowns. That is to say there are things that we now know we don't know. But there are also unknown unknowns. There are things we do not know we don't know".

Either the words of a perspicacious genius or perhaps a diver who decompressed too quickly but the common outcome is the search for greater knowledge, that is the fascination and the real treasure.

So to find out the latest developments go to
http://www.deadmansbay.co.uk

or to Grahame's website: -
http:///www.theshipwreckproject.blogspot.com/

Index